Political Analysis

POLITICAL ANALYSIS

An Introduction   second edition

M. Margaret Conway
University of Maryland

Frank B. Feigert
*State University of New York,
Brockport*

ALLYN AND BACON INC.
Boston   London   Sydney   Toronto

Library of Congress Cataloging in Publication Data

Conway, Mary Margaret, date
  Political analysis.

  Includes bibliographical references and index.
  1. Political science. I. Feigert, Frank B.,
joint author. II. Title.
JA66.C58 1976   320   76-10686

ISBN 0-205-05512-5

Contents

List of Figures   *ix*

Preface   *xi*

PART I   INTRODUCTION   1

Chapter 1   Approaches to Political Analysis   3

What Is Politics? *4*   Theory in Political Science *4*   Benefits of the
Scientific Approach *6*   Relationship of Political Science to Other
Disciplines *8*   Methodology *8*   Emphasis of Political Science
Research *9*   Intellectual and Institutional Origins of New
Approaches *11*   Assumptions Underlying Empirical Theories of
Politics *14*   Notes and References *15*   Study Questions *17*

Chapter 2   Political Science as Science   19

The Nature of Science *19*   The Language of Science *20*
Scientific Method *22*   Scientific Theories and Laws *29*
Values in the Study of Politics *34*   Scientific Revolutions *38*
Notes and References *40*   Study Questions *42*

Chapter 3   Research Methods   43

Research Design *43*   Review of the Literature *49*   Data
Collection Methods *52*   Data Management *71*   Using Statistics to
Test Hypotheses *80*   Summary *92*   Notes and References *93*
Study Questions *97*

PART II   APPLICATIONS   99

Chapter 4   Personality   101

Approaches to Personality *101*   Effects of Individual
Psychological Variables on Political Behavior *103*   Typologies of
Political Personalities *112*   The Analysis of Individual Political
Actors *119*   Notes and References *123*   Study Questions *128*

Contents

Chapter 5 **Attitudes, Beliefs, Opinions, and Values** **129**

Definition of the Concepts *129* Dimensions of Attitudes and
Attitude Objects *132* Saliency and Perception *134*
Determinants of Attitudes *136* Attitude Change *137* The Study
of Values *147* Summary and Critique *149* Notes and
References *151* Study Questions *155*

Chapter 6 **Political Socialization** **157**

Definitions of Political Socialization *158* Theoretical Models of
Political Socialization *159* Discontinuities in Political
Socialization *164* Agents of Political Socialization *165*
Children's Political Orientations *171* Adult Socialization *173*
Problems in Researching Political Socialization *174* Notes
and References *182* Study Questions *187*

Chapter 7 **Role** **189**

Definitions of the Role Concept *189* Role Systems *191* Role
Conflict *193* Role Socialization *196* Power and Role Behavior
198 Uses of the Role Concept in Theory Building *199* Notes
and References *206* Study Questions *208*

Chapter 8 **Group-Level Analysis** **211**

Influences of Groups on Individuals *212* Group Influences on
Politics *216* Pressure Techniques of Groups *218* Groups and
Political Conflict *221* Critique of Group Analysis *226* Notes
and References *229* Study Questions *232*

Chapter 9 **Decision Making** **235**

Rational Decision Making *239* The Community Power Context
251 Critique of Decision-Making Approaches *263* The Problem
of Integrating Approaches *265* Notes and References *267*
Study Questions *270*

Chapter 10 **Systems Analysis** **273**

Eastonian Analysis *274* Parsonian Structural-Functionalism
281 Almond's Systemic Structural-Functionalism *287* Stability
and Change *290* Critique of Approaches Based on Systems
Analysis *292* Notes and References *297* Study Questions *300*

Chapter 11 Communications Analysis   **301**

Definition of Concepts *301*   Low-Level Analysis: Interpersonal
Communication *305*   Middle-Level Analysis: The Mass Media
308   Upper-Level Analysis: Communications and the Political
System *313*   Integrating the Levels of Analysis *315*   Critique of
Communications Analysis *317*   Notes and References *322*
Study Questions *325*

Chapter 12 Theory and Politics   **327**

Applying Approaches to Research Problems *331*   Political
Analysis and Practical Politics *346*   Notes and References
352   Study Questions *356*

Glossary   *357*

Index   *361*

List of Figures

Figure 2–1. *Levels of Theory and Observation 21*
Figure 2–2. *Steps in the Scientific Method 25*
Figure 2–3. *Relationship of Theory, Law, and Hypothesis 30*
Figure 3–1. *Hypothetical Interactions of City Council Members: A Sociogram 61*
Figure 3–2. *Categories of Individual Behavior in Groups 62*
Figure 3–3. *Sample Coding According to Codebook 75*
Figure 5–1. *Balance Theory of Attitude Consistency 140*
Figure 5–2. *Shifts in Attitude Change 141*
Figure 9–1. *Marginal Costs and Marginal Utility in Gaining Information 242*
Figure 9–2. *Hypothetical Decision Possibilities 245*
Figure 9–3. *Likelihood of Receiving Benefits According to Hypothetical Decision Possibilities 246*
Figure 9–4. *Types of Power Structures 263*
Figure 10–1. *Boundary Relationships between Congressional and Presidential Systems 275*
Figure 10–2. *Basic Eastonian System 279*
Figure 10–3. *Parsonian Scheme for a Total System 283*
Figure 10–4. *Relationship of Parsonian Functions with Environment 284*
Figure 10–5. *Parsonian Functions in the Political System 285*
Figure 10–6. *Parsonian Functions in the Legislative Subsystem 285*
Figure 11–1. *Hypothetical Cause-and-Effect Relationships of Communications 319*
Figure 12–1. *The Development of Public Policy 332*
Figure 12–2. *Party Competition and Social Welfare Policies 334*
Figure 12–3. *A Simple Systems Policy Model 334*

Preface

In preparing this work for its second edition, our primary purpose of examining and critiquing current approaches to theory in political science remained unchanged. We examine the underlying assumptions and the logic of the methods used to develop explanatory theory. We also explore the basic concepts employed by selected approaches, and present some of the generalizations about politics that each approach sets forth. After laying the groundwork for a scientific approach to politics, specific theories are presented. Micro-level theories of individual and small-group behavior are discussed first, and we then progress to macro approaches to the behavior of groups, nations, and the international system.

There are several features that distinguish this edition from its predecessor. At the suggestion of numerous readers, we have added a chapter that introduces the student to research methods—to how political scientists collect and analyze data. Research design, primary and secondary sources, field-collection devices used by political scientists, and basic statistical concepts are considered. This chapter is not a "how-to-do-it" manual; rather, it gives the student an appreciation of the strengths and weaknesses of various theories and findings discussed in later chapters. An introduction to rational decision-making theory, an increasingly popular approach of many political scientists, is presented in the chapter on decision-making theory in order to make the student aware of the pitfalls of applying a theory to both macro and micro levels. Rational decision-making theory works well in analysis of micro-level problems, but it is difficult to successfully apply at the macro level.

In this edition, we have also tried to present a more readable work, one that can continue to be used by readers at introductory, as well as advanced, levels. Names and references to scholars and researchers appear as endnotes for those who wish to follow-up on the sources discussed. Study questions appear at the end of each chapter, and a glossary of basic concepts and terms is provided. We trust that these changes will help the student to comprehend some of the major questions and interim answers of current political science.

A special debt is owed to those who have commented so ably in helping us to prepare this edition. Included are C. Anthony Broh, Kenneth Deutsch, Milton L. Boykin, Karl L. Krueckenberg, David R. Williams, and James L. Danielson. We have followed their suggestions as closely as possible, and absolve them of any errors of fact or interpretation. Research assistance was provided by Mikel Wyckoff, and the typing chores were cheerfully performed by Jean Amberg and Adele Catlin. Robert J. Patterson continues to be a cheerful and understanding editor, and we are happy to continue our relationship with him and with Allyn and Bacon. Copy-editing chores were skillfully handled by Cynthia Hartnett. Fran Feigert once again prepared the index, and Ben and Danny continued to cooperate.

M.M.C.
F.B.F.

Political Analysis

PART
I

INTRODUCTION

The first section of this book focuses on questions basic to an understanding of the nature of modern political science: What is scientific method? Can political science use scientific method? What are scientific theories and laws? Is it possible for political science to develop scientific theories and laws? Can political science be value free, or is all political science research biased by the values of those who do the research?

Chapter 1 discusses the nature of laws and theories that might be developed to explain the political behavior of individuals and of political collectivities, such as legislatures, states, and nations. Before we consider which theoretical approaches can be used to analyze a political problem, we must know what is meant by terms such as law and theory. The application of scientific method to political science research involves certain problems. The nature of these problems and their solutions are discussed in chapters 2 and 3. In Chapter 2 we also consider how the values of the researcher might influence the selection of research problems and their analysis. Related to this is a consideration of ethical problems in social science research. Techniques of research are considered in Chapter 3. How do political scientists collect the data necessary for research? How do we manage large amounts of data? How do we analyze and interpret data?

CHAPTER

1

Approaches to Political Analysis

A president elected by the largest popular margin in the history of the United States resigns in disgrace. An unpopular war drags on, destroying the land where it is fought, the lives of 50,000 young men, and the political spirit and economic balance of this nation. Oil-exporting nations seize control of their own resources from foreign-based corporations, drastically altering international political and economic relations. Yet the momentous significance of these changes is not recognized by most citizens, nor, it sometimes appears, by many politicians. The explanation and interpretation of political changes and events such as these are the tasks of political scientists.

Examining presidential selection and resignation, political scientists might ask such questions as: How can we explain the voting behavior of American citizens? How do politicians seek to manipulate public opinion? What determines the degree of success of attempts at manipulation? What factors explain patterns of presidential behavior? How do values affect political behavior?

The Vietnam War prompts examination of the factors that influence foreign policy and a nation's commitment to its foreign policy. This war raised further questions: What is the role of public opinion in foreign policymaking, as opposed to its role in domestic policymaking? What causes political leaders to misperceive foreign or domestic situations? The energy crisis provokes such questions as: How does control of a scarce and vital resource affect international power relationships? What are the implications for domestic politics of a change in control over a scarce and vital resource?

Many political scientists, along with other social scientists, focus attention and research efforts on finding answers to questions such as these.

WHAT IS POLITICS?

There are many ways to define *politics,* but we will define it here as the activities within and related to the political system. The *political system* includes the government, i.e., the formal institutions and processes that make, execute, and enforce laws of a society; the political system also extends to the activities of many individuals, groups, and extra-governmental institutions that relate to or affect the government in a significant way.

This definition of politics includes ideas about the government, such as its beliefs, ideologies and philosophies, and actions. In our time, all institutions at some time and in some way are affected by and tend to become involved with government. Labor unions, businesses, families, private universities, colleges, and schools are all affected in some way by government decision making. They also seek to affect government decision making, thereby becoming active elements in the political system.[1]

THEORY IN POLITICAL SCIENCE

Political scientists study domestic violence, patterns of revolution, political modernization, and the relationship of domestic violence to international conflict, as well as the more traditional subjects usually associated with political science, such as constitutional law and history, political parties, legislatures, and political philosophy.

Types of Theory

The term *theory* has several meanings. Commonly but incorrectly it is used to mean an hypothesis or conjecture. More appropriately, it refers to analysis of the interrelationships between ideas or concepts. The types of theory used by political scientists in part determine the central focus of their research and the kind of subject studied.

Speculative theory examines different relationships and aspects of a subject without sufficient evidence to support the conclusions advanced. *Non-speculative* is based on verifiable evidence. *Empirical theory* is derived from a careful consideration of experience and observation of recurring events. *Normative theory* is concerned with moral imperatives of behavior, values, or goals prescribed for an individual, group, or society.

Is normative theory non-speculative? Probably not, because by its very nature it deals with questions by making value judgments. Is empirical theory speculative? Technically, no. Generally, we can say that the current theoretical concerns of political scientists are with speculative–normative theory and non-speculative–empirical theory.

This text will present the research methods and theoretical approaches used to develop empirical theories, which are non-speculative. These theoretical approaches, which make possible description and explanation of political and social problems, are one basis for developing solutions to domestic and foreign policy problems. In order to understand policy problems and to critically evaluate solutions proposed for them, knowledge of the methods used to derive explanations of the causes and consequences is essential. Equally essential is an understanding of the theoretical approaches on which analyses are based. The development of empirical theories results in accurate and extensive description of political and social behavior, explains that behavior, and makes possible an understanding of what conditions cause a particular political problem.

The boundaries of the subject matter of political science are rather all-encompassing. Social problems lead to demands for political action and public policy. If air is polluted or inflation is rampant, pressure for government action arises. Groups and interests in society demand government intervention in their conflicts. Government is viewed as the solver of problems and the resolver of conflicts, and political science takes as its boundaries the study of the activities of government and its related political processes.

This broad focus naturally leads to an increased interrelationship between political science and other social science disciplines such as sociology, psychology, and economics. We study human behavior in politically relevant situations or activities. Therefore, theories that generally describe and explain human behavior are also useful in understanding human behavior in a political context.

Controversy over Theory and Methods

Early in the 1950s, advocates of the development of rigorous empirical theory became the protagonists in a controversy about the appropriate subject matter and research methods for political science. According to many, the focus of political science should be "to discover the extent and nature of uniformities in the actual behavior of men and groups of men in the political process." This approach came to be labeled "the behavioral approach."[2] Commenting on the behavioral approach, Dahl stated it somewhat differently, although his thrust was the same:

> . . . the behavioral approach is an attempt to improve our understanding of politics by seeking to explain the empirical aspects of political life by means of methods, theories, and criteria of proof that are acceptable according to the canons, conventions, and assumptions of modern empirical science.[3]

The behavioral wing was skeptical about the prior accomplishments of political science. Among the behavioral advocates there was a strong bias for scientific methods of research, which they felt would create a more soundly based knowledge of political processes. They wanted to make political science more scientific in its empirical content and to provide an orientation "which aims at stating all the phenomena of government in terms of the observed and observable behavior of men."[4] Advocates of the scientific approach, which grew out of the behavioral movement, believe that scientific methods can be applied to all areas of political science research.

BENEFITS OF THE SCIENTIFIC APPROACH

The minimum goal of political science is to develop "a body of systematic and orderly thinking about a determinate subject matter."[5] Systematic empirical theories of politics make it possible to explain and to predict human behavior in the political arena. In order to develop empirical theories, emphasis must be placed on adapting new methods of observation derived from other academic disciplines.

General agreement exists on the need for new ways of thinking about politics because the concepts used previously were not conducive to the development of rigorous theories.[6] Variations in individual political motivation, performance in political roles, or attitudes associated with different forms of political participation cannot be adequately evaluated with the language used to discuss legal processes or government institutions. Furthermore, whatever terms we use in political analysis should be useful in discussing political behavior anywhere it occurs—in Africa and Asia, as well as in America and Europe.

Traditionally, the study of politics employed such concepts as executive, federalism, law, representation, sovereignty, and institution. The new approaches to the study of politics employ concepts that permit us to go beyond institutional structures and processes. They amplify political study to include social patterns that occur within traditionally studied institutions and outside those institutions. They recognize that politics is not confined by institutional boundaries. These conceptual schemes provide us with new units of analysis for the study of politics.

Thus the focus of the latter chapters of this book is on attitudes, beliefs, and values of persons involved in politics; on political roles and orientations; on the influence of personality in political behavior; and on the processes by which individuals, groups, and communities make decisions. Many of these concerns are not new to the study of politics, but the way in which they are studied (i.e., the methods used) and the language used in studying them is different from that traditionally employed in political analysis. New approaches to the study of politics facilitate the development of descriptions and explanations of political events that can be applied to any country and across time.

For example, what are the similarities between the political revolutions in the American colonies in 1776, in France in 1789, in Mexico in 1911, in Russia in 1918, and those occurring in Latin American and African nations today? How can we explain the patterns of domestic political violence in politically developed and politically modernizing societies? How does domestic violence relate to patterns of international conflict? The development of theories of politics requires that we work with language that can be used to evaluate similar patterns of behavior or events occurring in different

7

cultures and in different historical periods. Only then can we develop political theories of significant scope. In other words, we search for the commonalities of what may otherwise be considered unique events, situations, or processes.

RELATIONSHIP OF POLITICAL SCIENCE
TO OTHER DISCIPLINES

Together with psychology, anthropology, sociology, and economics, political science focuses on the behavior of people in social settings.[7] The boundaries between these academic disciplines have been drawn by distinctions between their different roles: economics focuses on behavior relevant to the production of goods and services, while sociology examines men and women in a number of different social roles, such as a member of a family, a religious unit, or other social group. The distinctions are based on abstracting certain elements of an individual's behavior from other elements. However, we cannot deny that these elements coexist and exert mutual influence. For example, in the process of exercising authority over their children, parents create expectations about the behavior of wielders of power that may influence their children's later reactions to political authorities.[8]

Each of the social science disciplines can contribute to a better understanding of politics through the application of its theories of human behavior to political science. A general theory of motivation developed by psychologists can help us understand patterns of motivation for types of political participation, such as party organization work versus candidacy for public office. The study of politics in a sense has become interdisciplinary because it uses concepts and theories of other behavioral sciences to understand social, psychological, and cultural influences on behavior in the political realm.

METHODOLOGY

Much emphasis has been placed by recent political science research on problems related to how we study politics, i.e., on methodological problems.[9] If political science is to develop empirical theories, it will require more precise methods of making observations, of categorizing what is observed, and of measuring variables.

Some critics mistakenly perceive this concern with better tools of observation, categorization, and measurement to be the sole aim of many innovative researchers. The need for better methods of measurement and observation, such as content analysis[10] and attitude scaling,[11] has led political scientists to learn to apply these observational techniques developed in other academic disciplines. Many political scientists have also sought to develop their knowledge of statistics and mathematics in order to describe more systematically and to draw inferences more accurately from the phenomena they observe.[12] The ultimate aim of concerns with conceptual language, better tools of observation, measurement, categorization, and interdisciplinary knowledge is the development of empirical political theory.

EMPHASIS OF POLITICAL SCIENCE RESEARCH

Historical Emphases

Among the dominant characteristics of political science as it existed in the pre-World War II period were the following:

1. An emphasis on the study of institutions to the exclusion of political processes
2. The neglect of the study of non-American political systems, the focus being largely on Western European systems
3. A very strong tendency toward description of existing institutions, rather than analysis and development of systematic generalizations about political behavior that would account adequately for similarities, differences, and changes in political processes
4. A fascination with institutions or political patterns perceived by the researchers as unique, and consequently a failure to consider adequately the premise of uniqueness; also, a failure to develop generalizations, which cannot, of course, be derived from the study of phenomena conceived of as unique
5. A tendency to take the characteristics of the political system for granted, thereby ignoring changes in the political system or differences in rates of change over time within one system or between different political systems

6. A view of science as raw empiricism, rather than as the development of systematic theories through the thoughtful gathering and analysis of data in order to test specific hypotheses
7. A strong reformist tendency, with emphasis on value judgments specifying what *ought* to be the nature of political structures and institutions, occasionally accompanied by polemics for the adoption of the political scientist's preferred reforms of the political system
8. A neglect of the findings of other social science disciplines that would contribute to the understanding of political behavior[13]

Political scientists from the 1880s to the 1930s generally held a common set of beliefs about the problems and the research methods appropriate to the discipline. The features of this predominant consensus were:

1. A lack of concern with political systems as such, including the American system, which amounted in most cases to taking properties and requirements of political systems for granted
2. An unexamined and mostly implicit conception of political change that was blandly optimistic and unreflectively reformist
3. An almost total neglect of theory in any meaningful sense of the term
4. An enthusiasm for a conception of science that rarely went beyond raw empiricism
5. A strongly parochial preoccupation with things American that stunted the development of an effective comparative method
6. A confining commitment to concrete description[14]

The New Consensus

A new consensus about the nature of the discipline evolved in the mid-1960s. Among the factors contributing to the development of this consensus was a concern with the political system as such. The consensus focused on examining relationships that recurred in a pattern; this focus resulted in a convergence of the theoretical interests operating in discrete areas within the discipline.[15] We would expect to find greater congruence than in the past between theoretical developments in the study of political participation in the United States and in the study of political participation in other countries.

10

Also evolving was a revival of interest in political theory and a concern with the relationship between empirical theory and empirical investigation.[16] Theory guides research by indicating what concepts are relevant and therefore what facts are pertinent. A third contributor to the evolution of a new consensus about the scope of political science was a recommitment to the goal of science.[17]

The new consensus anticipated in the mid-1960s has not evolved. The debate continues in political science about what problems or topics we should study and how we should study them. This period of debate about the subject matter and methodology of political science has been called the "post behavioral era."[18]

INTELLECTUAL AND INSTITUTIONAL ORIGINS OF NEW APPROACHES

Intellectual Origins

Some American scholars involved in politics as journalists or politicians saw the need for an alternative method of studying the traditional subject matter of political science. One sociologist and journalist, writing in 1908, argued that political science should focus on human behavior in political situations, emphasizing group relationships and activities in the political process.[19] Another advocated greater attention to psychological factors in political behavior. [20] One scholar used ideas drawn from psychology in his research and greatly influenced the use of variables and analytic techniques in political science research.[21]

The writings and later the teaching in American universities of a number of European scholars influenced the direction of political science. For example, an Englishman advocated attention to psychological factors that affect individual political behavior in a book first published in 1908.[22] A Swede published in 1937 an analysis of European political behavior that received considerable attention in this country.[23] The crisis in Europe during the 1930s brought to this country a number of scholars strongly influenced in their approach to political analysis by European sociologists. The writings of a number of European social theorists received wider exposure through the teaching and research of the refugee scholars.[24]

Institutional Origins

During the Second World War, political scientists descended from the ivory towers to assume a variety of responsibilities in the federal government.[25] Some who were assigned to administrative functions realized that an emphasis on legal processes and institutions resulted in ignorance of much of the political process and concluded that the answers to important questions could not be provided by such an approach. Many political scientists were assigned interdisciplinary research responsibilities that brought them into contact with the terminology, findings, and research methods of sociology, economics, and psychology.

Other institutional factors, perhaps peculiar to the American environment, have exerted influence and provided support for changes in the study of politics. In 1945 the Social Science Research Council established a Committee on Political Behavior, which, by sponsoring conferences and granting research support, stimulated the growth of the behavioral movement within political science.[26] Another committee of the Social Science Research Council, the Committee on Comparative Politics, introduced new theoretical and methodological approaches to the study of comparative political systems.

Philanthropic organizations, such as the Ford, Carnegie, and Rockefeller foundations, made large contributions to frequently very expensive research projects. By their selection of research proposals to finance, they have had a significant effect on the direction of the discipline, both in terms of subjects studied and research methods used. A number of agencies of the federal government have financed research aimed at the description of political processes, the development of empirical political theories, and the development of new methods of research. For example, research on patterns of international conflict and alliances, nation-building, and conditions conducive to the outbreak of domestic violence has been financed by Department of Defense agencies. The National Science Foundation has also contributed to the development of empirical theory and research methodology and the training of political scientists in research techniques.

The emphasis on development of empirical theory has been institutionalized within the discipline in a number of ways. Data archives and research methodology training programs have been developed by many universities on a cooperative basis. The most prominent example is the Inter-University Consortium for Political Research. The Consortium is a cooperative arrangement between the Center for Political Studies at the University of Michigan and political science departments in approximately 225 American and foreign universities, colleges, and research institutions. It collects and disseminates to member departments political science data, such as election results from the United States and other countries, congressional roll-call data, and data obtained from survey research on significant aspects of political behavior. The Consortium also operates summer training programs for faculty and students from member departments. Through Consortium efforts, greater sophistication in research techniques is promoted and data are made more readily available. A number of individual universities have also developed data archives specializing in particular regions of the world or in a particular aspect of political science.[27]

Other indications of the institutionalization of empirical theory are found in the advent of specialized journals, which focus either on specific types of political problems or on interdisciplinary research. These include periodicals such as *The Journal of Conflict Resolution, Administrative Science Quarterly, Comparative Political Studies, Comparative Politics, Urban Affairs Quarterly, Public Choice, Behavioral Science,* and *American Behavioral Scientist.*

The widespread acceptance of the changes in political science is shown by the predominance of articles based on empirical research in political science journals. Commercial textbook and monograph publishers also appear to have received a favorable response to new approaches within the discipline, as indicated by their publication lists. Undergraduate and graduate courses for political science majors require an introduction to empirical theory and to sophisticated research methodology. Since World War II, political science has experienced extensive changes in the types of subjects studied, research methods used, and its stated goals.

The emphasis on the development of non-speculative—empirical theory led to a counter-movement within American political science in the late 1960s and 1970s. This movement advocated a more direct concern with policy outcomes. To some "post-behavioralists" this implied selecting research problems because of their immediate policy relevance, advocating a particular solution of the policy problem within the context of one's research, and involving

13

national and regional organizations of political scientists in advocating particular public policies.

ASSUMPTIONS UNDERLYING
EMPIRICAL THEORIES OF POLITICS

A number of assumptions are made in developing empirical theories of politics.[28] We first assume that there are discoverable uniformities in political behavior. This means we believe that behavior is not random, but rather that men and women behave in a regularized fashion when engaging in political acts, such as voting in a presidential election, enacting legislation, or deciding on the constitutionality of laws.

Can we accept the assumption of uniformities of behavior? Although the people who cast their votes at the ballot box, in the legislature, or in the courtroom change over time, the act is the same kind of act. Problems, issues, and demands change, but patterns of behavior can be abstracted over time. For example, legislators are subjected to pressures from different clienteles, such as interest groups, party organizations, and officials in the executive branch. The nature of the pressures and the characteristics of the clienteles can be analyzed and studied at different points in time and in different political systems. The relationship between voting behavior of individual legislators and significant cue givers inside the legislative chamber such as committee chairpersons, caucus chairpersons, or party floor leaders can be examined to find patterns of relationship. We are not assuming that the same problem or issue is present or that the same person remains in office, but that human behavior in political situations is not random, but patterned, and that these patterns can be observed.

We further assume that regularities of behavior can be expressed by generalizations that approximate the universality of a scientific law or theory in the natural sciences. However, the universality of regularities in political behavior is not assumed arbitrarily; it is established through the procedures of scientific investigation that emphasize careful observation of behavior. If we are to observe behavior carefully, then we must pay attention to the development of criteria and of techniques for the observation and measurement of behavior.

One can study political events and arrive at generalizations unbiased by the observer's personal values. A political scientist can assert value judgments and present empirical explanations, but it is possible and necessary to keep the two distinct and separate. We can study values and assert value judgments, but we cannot assert the validity of the value judgments through use of scientific methods.

Research must be guided by theoretical concerns to adequately contribute to the development of knowledge about the political activities of people. Conversely, theories that adequately explain politics must be developed through empirical research.

NOTES AND REFERENCES

1. Other definitions of the subject matter of political science cite the study of legal governments. For this and discussion of the possible scope of political science, *see* Charles S. Hyneman, *The Study of Politics* (Urbana: University of Illinois Press, 1959). The authoritative allocation of values in a society is discussed in David Easton, *The Political System* (New York: Alfred A. Knopf, 1959), pp. 129–31; *idem, A Framework for Political Analysis* (Englewood Cliffs, N.J.: Prentice-Hall, 1965), p. 50; and *idem, A Systems Analysis of Political Life* (New York: John Wiley and Sons, 1965), pp. 21–22. For the study of power, authority, or rule, *see* Robert A. Dahl, *Modern Political Analysis* (Englewood Cliffs, N.J.: Prentice-Hall, 1963), p. 7.

2. Samuel J. Eldersveld, Alexander Heard, Samuel P. Huntington, Morris Janowitz, Avery Leiserson, Dayton D. MacKean, and David B. Truman, "Research in Political Behavior," in S. Sidney Ulmer (ed.), *Introductory Readings in Political Behavior* (Chicago: Rand McNally and Company, 1961), p. 8.

3. Robert Dahl, "The Behavioral Approach in Political Science: Epitaph for a Monument to a Successful Protest," *American Political Science Review* 55 (December 1961): 767.

4. *Ibid.*, p. 766.

5. David B. Truman, *Items* (New York: Social Science Research Council, 1951).

6. Heinz Eulau, *The Behavioral Persuasion* (New York: Random House, 1963), pp. 14–19; Eldersveld, *et al.,* in Ulmer (ed.), *Introductory Readings in Political Behavior,* p. 8; Karl Deutsch, *The Nerves of Government* (New York: The Free Press, 1963), pp. 22–50.

7. *See* Dahl, "The Behavioral Approach," p. 769.

8. For discussion of the evidence for this, *see* Robert Hess and Judith Torney, *The Development of Political Attitudes in Children* (Chicago: Aldine Publishing Company, 1967), pp. 99–101; Fred I. Greenstein, *Children and Politics* (New Haven: Yale University Press, 1965), pp. 50–51; Dean Jaros, "Children's Attitudes toward the President," *Journal of Politics* 29 (May 1967): 368–87.

9. Albert Somit and Joseph Tannenhaus, *The Development of Political Science* (Boston: Allyn and Bacon, 1967), p. 179; Dahl, "The Behavioral Approach."

10. Robert C. North, Ole Holsti, M. George Zaninovich, and Dina Zinnes, *Content Analysis* (Evanston, Ill.: Northwestern University Press, 1963).

11. Basic works on attitude scaling include William S. Torgeson, *Theory and Method of Scaling* (New York: John Wiley and Sons, 1958); Allen L. Edwards, *Techniques of Attitude Scale Construction* (New York: Appleton-Century-Crofts, 1957). For examples of attitude measures, *see* John P. Robinson, Jerrold G. Rusk, and Kendra Head, *Measures of Political Attitudes* (Ann Arbor: Institute for Social Research, 1968).

12. Several works have been published focusing on statistical measures valuable to political scientists. They include the following: V. O. Key, Jr., *Statistics for Political Scientists* (New York: Thomas Y. Crowell Company, 1954); Hubert M. Blalock, Jr., *Social Statistics,* 2nd ed. (New York: McGraw-Hill, 1972); Linton C. Freeman, *Elementary Applied Statistics for Students in Behavioral Science* (New York: John Wiley and Sons, 1965); Sidney Siegel, *Nonparametric Statistics for the Behavioral Sciences* (New York: McGraw-Hill, 1956); Celeste McCullough and Loche Van Atta, *Statistical Concepts: A Program for Self-Instruction* (New York: McGraw-Hill, 1963); William Hays, *Statistics for Psychologists* (New York: Holt, Rinehart and Winston, 1963).

13. For critiques of political science theory and methodology, *see* Roy Macridis, *The Study of Comparative Government* (New York: Random House, 1955), pp. 7–22; Richard Snyder, "A Decision-Making Approach to the Study of Political Phenomena," in Roland Young (ed.), *Approaches to the Study of Politics* (Evanston, Ill.: Northwestern University Press, 1958), pp. 3–15; David Easton, *The Political System.*

14. David B. Truman, "Disillusion and Regeneration: The Quest for a Discipline," *American Political Science Review* 59 (December 1965): 866.

15. *Ibid.,* p. 869.

16. *Ibid.,* p. 870.

17. *Ibid.,* p. 871.

18. *See,* for example, George J. Graham, Jr., and George W. Carey, *The Post Behavioral Era: Perspectives on Political Science* (New York: David McKay Company, 1972).

19. Arthur F. Bentley, *The Process of Government* (Evanston, Ill.: Principia Press, 1939). First published in 1908.

20. Charles Merriam, *New Aspects of Politics* (Chicago: University of Chicago Press, 1925), p. 11.

21. Harold Lasswell, *Psychopathology and Politics* (New York: The Viking Press, 1960). First published in 1930.

22. Graham Wallas, *Human Nature in Politics* (Lincoln: University of Nebraska Press, 1962). First published in 1908.

23. Herbert Tingsten, *Political Behavior: Studies in Election Statistics* (London: P. S. Kind and Son, Ltd., 1937).

24. The writings of these social theorists include Max Weber, *Theory of Economic and Social Organizations,* trans. Talcott Parsons (New York: Free Press, 1947); Vilfredo Pareto, *Selections,* Joseph Lopreato, ed. (New York: Thomas Y. Crowell, 1965); Gaetano Mosca, *The Ruling Class,* trans. Hannah Kahn (New York: McGraw-Hill, 1939).

25. For a discussion of this influence, *see* Robert A. Dahl, "The Behavioral Approach."

26. *Ibid.*

27. *See SS Data,* published quarterly by the Laboratory for Political Research, University of Iowa, for a listing of various data archives and data sets available.

28. For further discussions of the assumptions made in social science research and their validity, *see* John Kemeny, *A Philosopher Looks at Science* (Princeton, N.J.: Van Nostrand and Company, 1959), chap. 15; Ernest Nagel, *The Structure of Science* (London: Routledge and Kegan Paul, 1961), chaps. 13 and 14.

STUDY QUESTIONS

1. Define the following:
   politics
   government
   political system
2. What is the difference between normative and empirical theory?
3. What assumptions underlie efforts to develop empirical political theories?
4. What was the set of intellectual, institutional, and financial factors that caused American scholars to orient themselves to the development of empirical political theories?

CHAPTER
2

Political Science as Science

By applying the scientific method developed and employed in the natural and behavioral sciences, political scientists increase our understanding of political processes. Scientists observe and manipulate variables in order to examine what happens under different conditions.[1] The function of science is generally perceived as the establishment of general laws or theories that explain the behavior with which a particular discipline is concerned.[2] For political scientists, the subject is political behavior as it is manifested by individuals, institutions, and nations. If we can develop empirical theories, we can understand the common characteristics of events and predict the nature and probability of occurrence of certain political behaviors.

THE NATURE OF SCIENCE

Any science has two major objectives: the description of phenomena—in this case political behavior—and the establishment of general principles by which these phenomena can be explained and predicted.[3] Three qualities denote the nature of science. First, descriptions and explanations are based on empirical, or observable, evidence. Second, concern with the facts is unaffected by the scientist's definition of what is good or what would be the preferable condition. In other words, science is value free. Objectivity prevails because the nature of scientific inquiry should permit basing statements on empirical evidence.[4]

There are two views of scientific activity. One sees science as an essentially static activity that systemizes information about the world; people who engage in scientific enterprises discover new facts and seek to explain them. The dynamic view regards scientific activity as the development of theories and of conceptual frameworks to promote the discovery of facts and relationships.[5] The basic purpose of *political* science is dynamic: to form theories that will explain the facts of the political universe.

For a good scientific explanation, we must have well established general theories, and we must be in possession of facts known independently of the phenomena to be explained. The phenomena to be explained must be capable of being logically deduced from the general theories and known facts.[6] We could say therefore that the aim of science is to discover "what the facts truly are"[7] and to explain their existence through theories and laws.

THE LANGUAGE OF SCIENCE

What do the terms *fact* and *theory* mean?

A *fact* is an empirically verifiable observation about the nature of reality on which agreement can be achieved, at least in principle.[8]

A *theory* is a set of interrelated concepts, definitions, and propositions that presents a systematic view of phenomena by specifying relationships among variables, with the purpose of explaining and predicting the phenomena.[9]

As such, a theory is a universal statement which we can never know to be entirely true. Let us compare a fact and a theoretical statement about political behavior. To say that Joe, the labor union shop steward, always votes for the Democratic candidate for president is a statement of fact. To say that membership in labor unions is associated with voting for the Democratic candidate is a theoretical statement.

Propositions or *generalizations,* referred to in the definition of theory, are statements of the relationships of concepts.

A *concept* is an abstraction formed by inference from particulars.[10]

20

Examples of concepts used in political science are justice, equality, political stability, domestic violence, international conflict, group membership, and alienation. Another example of a generalization relating two concepts is "the higher the level of domestic violence within a nation, the greater the level of international conflict in which that nation is involved." (*See* Figure 2–1.)

Science operates at levels of both theory and observation. Because theory deals with concepts—which are abstractions—and the relationships between concepts, theories cannot be directly tested. We must work with observable phenomena that can be used as indicators of concepts. Indicators are called variables.

> A *variable* is a property to which numbers can be assigned and which can stand for a concept in a theory. Variables can be observed and in some fashion measured.

Figure 2–1 represents the relationship between domestic conflict and involvement in international conflict. The concept of domestic violence is translated from an abstraction into a variable labeled "the index of violent domestic acts," which is measured by counting the number of murders, riots, violent demonstrations, and strikes per 100,000 population per year (*see* Table 2–1). The international conflict concept is translated into a variable called "the international aggression index," which is measured by recording the number of threats, mobilizations of troops, economic sanctions,

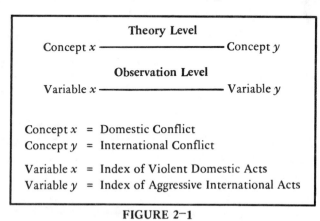

FIGURE 2–1

Levels of Theory and Observation

TABLE 2–1. *Translation of Concept into Variable into Measurement*

Concept	Variable	Measurement
Domestic Violence	Index of Violent Domestic Acts	Sum of the number of murders, riots, violent demonstrations, and strikes per 100,000 population per year.
International Conflict	International Aggression Index	Sum of the number of threats, troop mobilizations, economic sanctions, and military uses of force in which a nation engages in a year.

expulsions of diplomats, and military uses of force in which a nation engages per year.

At the level of theory, the relationship between concepts is a generalization. At the level of observation, the possible relationship between variables is called an *hypothesis.*

An *hypothesis*, then, is simply the suggested relationship between variables.

In Figure 2–1, the hypothesis is that if the index of violent domestic acts in a nation is high, the level of aggressive international acts by that nation will also be high.

SCIENTIFIC METHOD

A scientist, political or otherwise, begins with an awareness of an unexplained phenomenon that can be stated as a problem for investigation. Types of problems that might be of concern to political scientists are:

1. Why do some countries have several major political parties, some have two major political parties, and others have only one?
2. The development of political parties is a relatively recent phenomenon. Why did they develop?

3. Do all political parties perform the same functions in governing a nation?
4. Some countries created after the Second World War have had relatively stable government systems, while others have been relatively unstable. Why has this occurred? What contributes to government instability?
5. Why do some legislators consistently support liberal domestic programs, others consistently oppose them, and still others vary in their support of these programs?
6. Does the nature of the constituency, the personality of the legislator, his position in various power systems in the legislature, his role orientations, or his personal values influence his voting behavior?
7. Why are some countries more likely to engage in acts of international conflict than others? Is their international behavior related to their level of domestic violence?

All of these problems can be analyzed by the scientific method, a cycle or a process in which we start with facts and end up with facts. The set of facts for which we wish to account also forms a statement of the problem: certain countries have stable governments; other have very unstable ones; or some legislators support liberal domestic programs, while others oppose these programs. If we want to develop generalizations about the facts, we must concern ourselves with a class of objects sharing specified characteristics. To designate this class of objects, we use a concept. The concepts used in the previous examples are "stable government," "liberal domestic program," "domestic violence," and "international conflict."

The Inductive Stage. The first stage in scientific method is the inductive stage, when hypotheses are formed to fit the observed facts that are to be explained. We move from particular facts or observed phenomena to an hypothesis—a conjectural, tentative statement about the relationship between two or more observed phenomena. For any set of phenomena, there are probably several hypotheses that could be formulated to express the relationship between phenomena, although only one is selected to be tested. Hypotheses are formulated on the basis of one's previous knowledge of the subject; hence, the basic requirement for scientific research is an encyclopedic knowledge of previous research and findings in the field. Hypotheses can also be generated on the basis of knowledge of subject matter of a similar nature. With knowledge of physics and biology, one can develop hypotheses about communication patterns within formal and informal organizations.

Hypotheses are general statements, suggestions of the connections between variables. How does one determine which of several possible hypotheses to select for testing? One rule is to select the hypothesis that is simplest in its formulation of the connections between the variables. A second is to select that which appears most probable. A necessary requirement is that the hypothesis will make possible the explanation of all the known facts.

The Deductive Stage. The second step in scientific method involves deductive methods. We deduce the logical consequences of the hypothesis by observing facts. More specifically, we deduce what particular facts would be present if our hypothesis about the relationship between the variables stated in the hypothesis is valid.

Hypothesis Testing. The third step of scientific method is to check to see if the facts we deduced from our hypothesis are present. If they are, we have failed to reject the hypothesis. What we verify is not the hypothesis itself, but the logical, or observable, consequences of the hypothesis. We test the relationship expressed by the hypothesis by examining to see if other facts, which would be expected to occur if the hypothesis were not invalid, actually do occur. Sometimes the third step is referred to as the "falsification" step, because we are trying to reject the hypothesis. *See* Figure 2–2.

Testing the Hypothesis: Examples

Let us return to the relationship between domestic violence and international conflict. The hypothesis is that the index of violent domestic acts is related to the index of international aggression. This implies that the two indices will vary together in a sample of nations. If they do, then countries ranking high on the index of violent domestic acts would also rank high on the index of international aggression, and countries ranking low on one index would rank low on the other index. If the hypothesis is rejected, it is because the relationship between the index of violent domestic acts and the index of international aggression could easily have occurred by

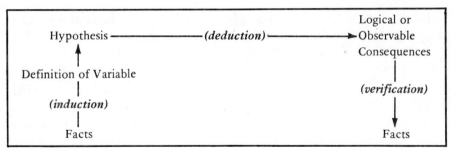

FIGURE 2-2

Steps in the Scientific Method (Modified and elaborated from John Kemeny, *A Philosopher Looks at Science* [New York: D. Van Nostrand, 1959], chap. 9.)

chance. We can never completely test an hypothesis; all possible occurrences of the hypothetical relationship cannot be tested because of obvious limits on time and observation. Not only can we not test for all possible occurrences of predicted relationships, but our observations or measurements are at best only approximations. We can reject an hypothesis, however, if the hypothesized relationships are not found.

Scientific research actually tests the obverse of the specified hypothesis, that is, the hypothesis of no relationship. This hypothesis, called the *null hypothesis,* states that no relationship exists between the variables. We reject the null hypothesis—but do not reject the positive hypothesis—only if the relationships found were very unlikely to have occurred by chance. For example, it is common practice to reject the null hypothesis and accept the research hypothesis only if the relationship is likely to occur by chance five times out of one hundred times. This is why the third step is referred to as a falsification step. In effect, we can never completely verify an hypothesis, but we can reject it. Using our research example, null and research hypotheses can be stated in this way:

Null Hypothesis (H_o): Index of violent domestic acts is not related to the international aggression index.
Research Hypothesis (H_a): Index of violent domestic acts is related to the international aggression index.

Let us consider a problem in political analysis. We observe that a person who considers himself to have little influence on

25

political events rarely votes, while another perceives himself to be politically effective and always votes in elections. From this set of facts we establish an hypothesis: "Individuals who believe themselves to be politically effective are more likely to vote than individuals who do not believe themselves to be politically effective." The logical consequences of this hypothesis are that those who are politically effective will vote and those who do not perceive themselves to be politically effective will not vote in a particular election. We then can interview a sample of the eligible electorate after an election has been held, ask questions designed to measure the presence and perhaps the degree of political effectiveness, and find out whether or not the individuals voted. On the basis of our observations we can either reject (falsify) our hypothesis or not reject it.

The actual outcome of previous research on this question is that there is a tendency for those who feel more politically efficacious to vote with greater frequency, but there is not a perfect relationship between degree of political efficacy and voting turnout. Therefore we must modify our hypothesis to account for the discrepancies, perhaps by adding other influential variables, such as the individual's degree of interest in the election outcome, his belief that the outcome of the election will make a difference to him, his strength of commitment to a political party, his concern with campaign issues, and his reaction to the candidates in the election. The modified hypothesis, in turn, should then be tested.

Concepts

The building blocks of theories are concepts. Examples of concepts used in political science are: authority, power, class, influence, society, conflict, legitimacy, political system, and political efficacy. Generally, concepts must have two characteristics to be useful in any scientific study:

1. A concept must have a clear empirical referent, i.e., a basis in experience. When using ordinary language, we unconsciously accept this requirement. The process of learning a language is in part the process of associating the name for a class of objects with the

objects, such as the concept "tree" with the type of object to which that concept refers.

2. A concept must be conducive to the formulation of a theory.*

Defining Concepts Used in Research. A well-developed science requires a number of concepts for which a common set of definitions has been agreed on and accepted by those in the scientific discipline. A science still in its infancy, such as political science, must develop a set of commonly defined units of analysis. How can concepts be defined?

A basic distinction must be made between two methods of defining concepts. Philosophers seek *real definitions* of concepts, that is, their essential characteristics. A political philosopher, for example, would seek to identify the essential characteristics of the thing we call justice. His concern is with the analysis of meaning, with analytic definition, without recourse to empirical analysis.

The other type of definition—*nominal definition*—is the type used by scientists. Nominal definition provides meaning by stipulation; i.e., we name the set of characteristics that will constitute the concept. There are two ways of arriving at a nominal definition of a concept: (1) by a constitutive definition, which defines a concept in terms of other concepts, and (2) by an operational definition, which defines a concept either by how it is measured or by what experimental operations were used. When a concept is given a measured operational definition, we define the concept by describing the procedures used to measure it. If, for example, we want to study the existence of authoritarian attitudes among citizens of a country, a measured operational definition would be the set of attitude statements presented to a sample of citizens for their agreement or disagreement. A more familiar example would be the measurement of academic achievement. The academic achievement of a student can be measured by his or her gradepoint average, rank in class, or rank on an achievement test; all these are measured operational definitions of academic achievement.

---

*A distinction can be made between concepts and constructs. A *construct* is a concept deliberately created for use in scientific research and for theorizing. The term "party cohesion," used in studying the voting unity of a political party in a legislative body, is an example of a construct.[11]

An experimental operational definition presents the manipulations used by the researcher to activate the existence of the concept. Experimental definitions take the form of if/then statements. They specify the operation to be performed; if it is performed successfully, then the concept is present. This can be expressed in this way:

If ... operation ⟶ successful result ⟶ then ... concept
　　　(O)　　　　　　　　　　(R)　　　　　　　　(C)

For example, we say that if a substance is placed in water and the substance dissolves, then the substance is soluble. This is an experimental–operational definition of solubility because it provides a test for the presence or absence of the concept.

As yet political science lacks a set of concepts for which generally accepted definitions, constitutive or operational ones, have been developed. This handicaps any science. The inability of those working with the concept of power, for example, to agree on a common meaning for the concept has led some political scientists to suggest that the concept of power cannot be useful in building empirical political theories.

Types of Concepts. Concepts can be categorized by various characteristics. Some are merely classificatory, denoting the class of objects to which a thing belongs. In this sense they are a set of "either-or" labels to apply to an object. We can refer to voters as Republican, Democrat, or Independent, although these classifications may be too broad. We may wish to elaborate a set of concepts that take account of the degree to which a quality is present in the objects under study. We can do this by specifying concepts that indicate degrees of rank-order variation, or comparative degrees of a quality present in the objects. For example, we can establish categories of "Strong Democrat," "Weak Democrat," "Independent," "Strong Republican," and "Weak Republican." This set of concepts is comparative. A further refinement would be to specify quantitatively to what degree a quality is present in an object; for example, we could specify someone as 99.44 percent Democratic. In political science, concepts are usually classificatory or comparative.

The set of concepts that provide the political scientist with a conceptual scheme should be appropriate to the problem studied, exhaustive, and mutually exclusive. In a study of voters' self-perceived party affiliation, for example, we should have at a minimum categories of Republican, Democrat, Independent, and Other. If we leave any one of them out, the set of concepts would not be exhaustive. And, if we have a "Democrat–Republican" category, the set would not consist of mutually exclusive categories.

SCIENTIFIC THEORIES AND LAWS

The development of scientific knowledge follows from the development or creation of theories. We must examine more closely the nature of scientific theories and the process by which they are formed.

We have defined a theory as a "set of interrelated concepts, definitions, and propositions that presents a systematic view of phenomena by specifying relationships among variables, with the purpose of explaining and predicting the phenomena."[12] Another way of thinking about theory is as a group of laws, usually rather few, from which other laws, usually a larger number, have been deduced and from which one expects to deduce still more laws. The laws that serve as the premises of deductions are called the axioms of the theory; those that appear as conclusions are called its theorems.[13] Propositions, or generalizations, would be considered laws in this definition of theory. The distinction between scientific laws and theories is this:

> Statements of individual fact are explained by laws; laws are explained by theories.[14]

How do theories and laws relate to hypotheses? A theory is composed of laws (or generalizations); a law suggests to a scientist how puzzling events can be explained. The suggested explanation takes the form of an hypothesis. The concepts contained in the theory are transformed into variables, and the means of measuring the variables is specified. These relationships are shown in Figure 2–3. It should not be assumed that scientists and philosophers of science agree on what a theory represents. There are varying ideas of what a theory does—or should—represent. One could say that theory is conceived of in realist, instrumentalist, and descriptive roles. [15]

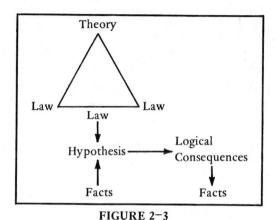

FIGURE 2–3

Relationship of Theory, Law, and Hypothesis

According to the realist interpretation, a theory is either true or false. One evaluates a theory in terms of the success of efforts to falsify it, or more accurately, to falsify deductions from the theory. Scientific theories, like hypotheses, cannot be directly verified. The logical consequences deduced from a theory can be tested by observation; if the conclusions are rejected, then the theory itself is not accepted. However, even if theories are not rejected by falsifying the consequences through repeated testing, they are accepted only tentatively because we cannot test all possible occurrences of the consequences. According to the realist interpretation, no theory contains within itself the test or proof of its own axioms; however, by formalizing a theory (converting its verbal or descriptive statements into mathematical statements), one can test the logical correctness of the deductions made within the theory.[16]

The instrumentalist view of theory is that it cannot be considered as an accurate description of reality. A theory is only a means of organizing one's perceptions of reality. As such, it provides rules for organizing and drawing inferences and is considered useful if it performs these functions. A third interpretation views theory as descriptive; theories are not true or false, but describe aspects of reality in a simplified form. According to this interpretation, theories also do not explain.

To summarize, because theories are not tested directly, they always involve some degree of uncertainty. A scientist can test the validity of an hypothesis, which is derived from a theory, by observing to see if the facts, predicted as logical consequences of the hypothesis, do indeed occur. An hypothesis tested many times and not rejected is accorded the status of a scientific law, and laws are associated by theories.

Universal and Statistical Theories. Distinctions can be made between types of empirical theories and laws. Some philosophers of science make a distinction between universal and statistical laws, or universal and statistical theories. The distinctions refer to the degree of probability assigned to the generalization. In a statistical generalization, less than 100 percent probability in specifying the outcome of the designated conditions is obtained. For example, we say that if conditions A, B, and C occur, then the probability of X occurring is .85. In contrast, in a universal generalization, we can state that if conditions A, B, and C occur, the probability of X occurring is 1.00. The generally accepted goal for a science is to develop universal generalizations, and many social scientists work on the assumption that universal generalizations ultimately can be achieved in all of the social sciences.

Individualistic versus Holistic Theory. Individualistic theory uses concepts that refer to aspects of individual behavior. Supporters of this position argue that all behavior, including that of groups of any size or character, can be explained in terms of concepts that refer to individual behavior. The opposing view, referred to as holism, argues that a group, the AFL–CIO, the United States Senate, or the United States of America, is more than the total of the characteristics of the individuals who compose the group. In other words, the group characteristics cannot be reduced to the concepts appropriate for analyzing individual behavior, and different concepts and theories are necessary for adequate explanation.

Theory and Meta-Theory. Meta-theory is middle-range theory, which focuses on limited sets of data and is of limited scope. Middle-range theories "consolidate otherwise segregated hypotheses and empirical uniformities."[17] It is questionable whether the distinction between theory and meta-theory serves any useful analytical purpose.

Theory and Scientific Methods

Although a progression from hypothesis to law to theory is implied here, developments in science do not always follow such a progression. As Figure 2–3 indicates, we can deduce certain other relationships from a theory and test and confirm or reject those relationships. If we reject them, the theory must be modified so that it does not conflict with our observations.

Theories then guide the research process as well as result from that process. They indicate the nature of the data to be examined, and formulation of new or expanded theories indicates new relationships. These are capable of being tested indirectly, resulting in further extension or revision of the theory. In effect, a theory contains relevant criteria that indicate the nature of the data to be used to test the hypotheses deduced from the theory.

The basic aim of political science is to form theories to explain the facts of the political universe. Explanations in science require the following: (1) well established laws or theories; (2) facts known independently of the facts to be explained. Explanation occurs when the facts to be explained can be deduced as a logical consequence of the laws or theory and the other known facts.

An example of explanation of physical phenomena can illustrate the nature of scientific explanations. On a cold morning, we find that the water in a car radiator has frozen. Why did that happen? We can explain this occurrence by reference to a general theory and other known facts. The general theory specifies that substances change their form with certain changes in temperature. The freezing point for water is 32° F (an independently known fact). We also know that the temperature has fallen below 32° F. Combining the general theory of the freezing of substances with the knowledge that the temperature has dropped below 32° F, we can deduce why the water in the car radiator is frozen. We have explained the facts by relating them to a general theory. This is the nature of scientific explanation: an occurrence or set of facts is explained when it can be deduced from a law or theory.[18]

If our generalizations are only statistical, limits are placed on the development of theory because the theory does not allow deductions to be made. An event (set of facts) is explained when it can be deduced from a theory and other facts, known independently of the facts to be explained. If we have only statistical theories, explanation in this sense cannot occur.

What is the difference between an explanation and a prediction? An explanation accounts for the facts *after* they have occurred. A prediction, made on the basis of a general law and other known facts, accounts for facts *before* they have occurred.

Scientific Laws

Much confusion in science arises from the use of the term "law." Law is understood by many people to imply a moral imperative, an "ought" of behavior. It also has a deterministic connotation, in the sense that if an aspect of individual behavior is described by a scientific law, individuals will behave in the manner described; i.e., they do not have a free will to determine their own behavior.

This confusion can be eliminated by clarifying several points. First, a scientific law serves as a description of the connection between facts: it does not determine anything. Scientific laws merely serve to describe what has been observed to exist within the limits of probability or chance. But if theories that relate laws by deduction can be used to predict events, is not the notion of free will then abrogated? What is necessary for perfect predictability? We would have to have a complete set of theories covering every possible form and type of human behavior, knowledge of all the relevant facts, sufficient mental capabilities to evaluate the facts and laws, and adequate time in which to do computations. These requirements demonstrate that perfect predictability, while logically possible, actually is highly improbable because individuals have a choice or free will. All we can say is that individuals exercise choice in predictable, regular patterns.

If we accept theory as a set of empirically tested generalizations—not a set of deductively structured generalizations—then we have valid theories for political science.

Evaluating Theories

By what criteria can we evaluate theories? Theories can be evaluated in terms of their capability to account for things we wish to explain.

This is a functional criterion for evaluating the usefulness of a theory. If one theory is better able to explain a set of events, it will be accepted more readily.

A second criterion is the logical consistency of the theory, which can only be achieved when the theory is in the form of universal generalizations.

A third criterion is the ability of the theory to suggest other generalizations that can be deduced from it. These generalizations can then be tested and contribute to the further elaboration of the theory.

Another criterion in evaluating theory is the ease with which concepts can be operationalized. This is not to say that all concepts in a theory must be capable of being defined operationally; some concepts are defined constitutively.

Another criterion is the extent to which the generalizations of the theory have been tested and the quality of the data upon which they are based. Extensive and rigorous testing of hypotheses, using sound sets of carefully collected data, is a more reassuring reason for accepting a theory.

In science, argument is also made for parsimony. If one has a choice between two theories that are equally satisfactory as explanations, preference is generally given to the simpler and less complicated of the two.

VALUES IN THE STUDY OF POLITICS

Some accuse political scientists of treating all subjects as being of equal merit, or value. This would mean, for example, that a communist or fascist political system is equal in value to a democratic system.

The charge that researchers consider all things as of equal value is unfounded. No value in itself can be proven superior by means of scientific method. One can use scientific method in means-ends analysis, where the end has been selected on the basis of other than scientific criteria. But scientific method is also used to evaluate the alternative means available for the achievement of that end. Much government decision-making research is of this type. For example, once the Congress declared it to be the policy of the United States to promote through public resources and laws full employment of all persons desiring to work, social scientists using scientific method could indicate to government officials alternative means of achieving that goal and their various possible effects. However, the decision to promote full employment, expressed in the Full Employment Act of 1946, is a value judgment, grounded in ethical and moral considerations, not in scientific method.

Some argue that *value-free* political science is impossible, but *value-laden* does not necessarily mean *biased.* Bias is an "instance where an investigator's values have, in fact, led to misperceptions in descriptions, or to attributing unwarranted validity to generalizations."[19] Value judgments are defined as "statements which assert that something is good or desirable."[20]

Philosophers of science generally agree that the researcher's values may enter into research in several different ways, such as in the selection of a research subject or problem. This, however, does not necessarily result in biased research results. One selects a problem, such as the nature of prejudice, the relationship between domestic instability and international conflict and violence, or the process of political modernization in developing countries and its relationship to economic development, because in some way one's personal values are related to or affected by the problem. The research can be conducted without biasing the conclusions with one's values, if one follows the prescribed, generally accepted methods of research and makes clear the processes by which conclusions are reached. In that manner, others can check and criticize the appropriateness of the conclusions drawn from the evidence.

The selection of the facts to be studied also is susceptible to value judgments. For example, if a researcher studying the treatment of citizens by the police ignored the use of derogatory and disrespectful language by police in minority group interactions, he would be neglecting to study what minority group members regard as police brutality. His values would be acting as a perceptual screen, leading him to disregard this as an aspect of police mistreatment of citizens.

Values may also lead one to biased conclusions through the incorrect assessment of the facts or evidence relating to an hypothesis. For example, if one were studying police brutality, what level of physical or verbal mistreatment of citizens by police would constitute a high incidence of police mistreatment? Would 5 instances out of 1000, 25 out of 1000, or 75 out of 1000 be the lower limit for a "high incidence of police brutality"?

While a definition indicates the relevant characteristics of a concept, an element of value may be attached to the concept in the statement of those characteristics, if care is not taken in their specification. Much criticism has been directed at some aspects of structural–functional analysis for this reason. In this kind of analysis, we ask what institutional structures perform what political functions. We would consider, for example, how interests of various groups in society are aggregated in the political system and communicated to political decision makers. A major concern is with how articulation and aggregation processes work to maintain the political system. It is argued that such a focus on system stability or on system maintenance represents a bias against change or reform by the researchers. The concept we wish to study would have to be defined and operationally measured in such a way as to preclude introduction of bias.

Underlying the problem of defining the concept without introducing a value is the problem of values within the theory on which the research is based and which the research is designed to test or elaborate. Because we lack well-developed theories in political science, values are more likely to create problems. Donald Searing points out that:

> When axioms are introduced in social research as unstated or poorly formulated assumptions, they are easily shaped by the investigator's values and can become untenable characterizations of individual or social systems.[21]

Searing says that values also can enter into the research process in the interpretation of data. The extreme position is that all objects and situations are selectively perceived and selectively interpreted, making value-free research impossible. But a scientific discipline develops agreed-upon patterns of perceiving and interpreting data. In other words, the theories and methods of a scientific discipline create and impose generally accepted patterns of observing and interpreting phenomena. Some of these problems can be illustrated by examining the controversies growing out of studies of community decision making and the distribution of power in local communities. (These topics are examined in much greater detail in Chapter 9.) Sociologists who study community power start from a different theoretical basis than political scientists, working as they do with stratification, or social-class, theories. Political scientists have attacked this as an inadequate theoretical perspective that ignores characteristics of political processes and groups in the political process. Some have argued for research more directly based on decision theory.

Early sociological studies tended to ask general questions, such as "Who makes decisions in this community?" or "Who has power?" This type of orientation was criticized for lack of focus. Political scientists argue that one can test for the existence of a power elite only if one examines a representative sample of key decisions and evaluates patterns found in that representative sample of key decisions.[22] Two crucial problems in concept formation are also at the center of the controversy: (1) How should "decision" be defined? (2) How should "power" be defined? Because researchers have defined these concepts differently, they have reached different conclusions about how power is distributed and who influences decisions.

Indices of power in community studies have included: "(1) who participates in decision making and (2) who prevails in decision making."[23] According to Polsby, power can be assessed by the capability of an individual to change the relative probability of an outcome through his or her influencing others in the situation.[24] Distinctions can also be made among power, influence, authority, and manipulation, which could contribute to a clarification of the nature of community power and decision making.

Definitions of "decision" also vary among researchers. Dahl defines a decision as "a set of actions related to and including the choice of one alternative rather than another."[25] A second definition is a "policy involving severe sanctions (deprivations),"[26] which implies that decisions exist only when sanctions have been or could be involved.

The way in which lines of conflict are drawn in a society, as well as political structures and processes, limits the possible political outcomes. This situation, in effect, is a bias within a political system, which operates systematically to favor some and not others. It is sustained by non-decision making, i.e., "a decision that results in suppression or thwarting of a latent or manifest challenge to the values or interests of the decision-maker."[27] Demands for allocative changes, or redistribution of power, are prevented from being made, and access to the decision-making process is denied.[28] Critics argue that sociologists and political scientists who have studied community power have ignored non-decisions. According to the critics, this is a function of bias created by the researchers' values that has affected the theoretical base, definition of concepts, data selection, and data interpretation of the studies.

Values can enter into research in the process through which one selects the decisions to be studied. The procedures for ensuring the representativeness of decisions and nondecisions are very important. Also, if one says that only certain kinds of issues are those in which key decisions are made, by specifiying those issues, one's values enter into the research.

Problems of bias can also arise when a researcher is evaluating the influence of individuals' values on their political behavior. The nature and intensity of relevant values must be accurately measured so that their influence on political behavior can be correctly inferred. Advances in research techniques in political science and in other disciplines have increased the ease with which this can be done.

SCIENTIFIC REVOLUTIONS

In any discipline, certain assumptions are made that limit and direct the nature of theorizing and research. These include beliefs about the basic units of the subject matter, the patterns of possible interrelationships between them, and the research techniques and procedures by which they may be investigated. As Kuhn states, "Normal science, the activity in which most scientists inevitably spend almost all their time, is predicated on the assumption that the scientific community knows what the world is like."[29] Landmarks in the development of a discipline, which Kuhn calls scientific revolutions, are accompanied by the rejection of one scientific theory in favor of another. Discussing scientific revolution, Kuhn says:

> Each produced a consequent shift in the problems available for scientific scrutiny and in the standards by which the profession determined what should count as an admissible problem or as a legitimate problem-solution.

And each transformed the scientific imagination in ways that we shall ultimately need to describe as a transformation of the world within which scientific work was done. Such changes, together with the controversies which always accompany them, are the defining characteristics of scientific revolutions.[30]

The replacement of an old theory by a new one requires reconstruction of prior knowledge.

The collection of group commitments shared by members of a scientific community can be labeled its *disciplinary matrix*. This disciplinary matrix has four components: a set of symbolic generalizations; a belief in the appropriateness of particular models that supply members of the community with preferred analogies and metaphors; a set of shared values; and a set of exemplars, learned through participation in the discipline, which provide a pattern of problem formulations and problem solutions generally accepted in the scientific community. The central element is the last, which Kuhn asserts can be labeled a paradigm. A paradigm functions as a device for selective perception, structuring the perception of a problem and the relationships among concepts and providing the basis for perceiving similarities among problems that permit their solution to be achieved through a single theory.

In a scientific revolution, some of the similarities of relationships that were previously accepted are discarded. A pattern of selective perception is no longer shared by all in the scientific community; adherents of the old disciplinary matrix and the new look at the world differently. Some of the scientific terms which previously had a meaning commonly understood by all now mean different things to various members of the scientific community. In effect, different language groups are created, and the groups perceive scientific problems and relationships among concepts differently. A scientific revolution occurs when one disciplinary matrix replaces another; perhaps the key element of this shift is the basic paradigm underlying the scientific community's work. A basic characteristic of a mature science is the existence of a paradigm that guides and shapes research.

Kuhn argues that paradigms are significant because they are most capable of resolving the set of problems with which scientists are most concerned at a certain time. The aims of science are to describe the facts, match facts with theory, and elaborate existing theory; scientific endeavor does not usually work to develop a new theory with a new focus and different conceptual framework. A new paradigm usually meets with considerable opposition from adherents of the old paradigm. However, as anomalies become apparent in the existing paradigm, a crisis occurs, and eventually a new paradigm is generated, largely as a creative act. A new conceptual structure is produced to replace the older; the battle line is drawn between adherents of the old and the new, and the outcome is largely influenced by the relative capabilities of the two paradigms to focus on significant questions, explain anomalies, and serve as vehicle for the conduct of what Kuhn calls normal science. As Kuhn points out,

> . . . paradigms differ in more than substance, for they are directed not only to nature but also back upon the science that produced them. They are the sources of the methods, problem-field, and standards of solution accepted by any mature scientific community at any given time.[31]

Political science is now in a pre-paradigm stage of development. Several candidates for a paradigm exist, all in various stages of development and elaboration. Each of these rivals differs in the concepts it employs, in its conceptual elaboration, and in its focus on problems.

NOTES AND REFERENCES

1. Gustav Bergmann, *Philosophy of Science* (Madison: University of Wisconsin Press, 1957), p. 3.

2. R. B. Braithwaite, *Scientific Explanation* (New York: Harper Torchbooks, 1960), p. 1.

3. Carl G. Hempel, *Fundamentals of Concept Formation in Empirical Science, International Encyclopedia of Unified Science,* vol. II (Chicago: University of Chicago Press, 1952), p. 1.

4. Quentin Gibson, *The Logic of Social Inquiry* (London: Routledge and Kegan Paul, 1960), p. 3.

5. Fred N. Kerlinger, *Foundations of Behavioral Research* (New York: Holt, Rinehart and Winston, 1965), p. 9.

6. John Kemeny, *A Philosopher Looks at Science* (Princeton, N.J.: D. Van Nostrand, 1959), chap. 9.

7. Morris Cohen and Ernest Nagel, *An Introduction to Logic and Scientific Method* (London: Routledge and Kegan Paul, 1934), p. 391.

8. *See* William J. Goode and Paul K. Hatt, *Methods in Social Research* (New York: McGraw-Hill, 1952), p. 8; and Vernon Van Dyke, *Political Science: A Philosophical Analysis* (Stanford, Calif.: Stanford University Press, 1960), p. 56.

9. Fred N. Kerlinger, *Foundations of Behavioral Research,* 2nd ed. (New York: Holt, Rinehart and Winston, 1973), p. 9.

10. *Ibid.,* p. 29.

11. Hempel, *Concept Formation in Empirical Science,* p. 39.

12. Kerlinger, *Foundations of Empirical Research,* p. 9.

13. Bergmann, *Philosophy of Science,* pp. 31–32.

14. *Ibid.,* p. 17.

15. *See* Ernest Nagel, *The Structure of Science* (London: Routledge and Kegan Paul, 1961), chap. 6, *passim.*

16. Abraham Kaplan, *The Conduct of Inquiry* (San Francisco: Chandler Publications, 1964), pp. 295–98.

17. Robert K. Merton, *Social Theory and Social Structure,* rev. ed. (Glencoe, Ill.: The Free Press, 1957), p. 280.

18. For more extensive discussions of explanations in science, *see* Kemeny, *A Philosopher Looks at Science,* chap. 9; Kaplan, *Conduct of Inquiry,* pp. 327–69; Bergmann, *Philosophy of Science,* pp. 75–84; Van Dyke, *Political Science,* chap. 3; Eugene J. Meehan, *The Theory and Method of Political Anlaysis* (Homewood, Ill.: Dorsey Press, 1965), chaps. 4 and 5.

19. Donald Searing, "Values in Empirical Research: A Behaviorist Response," *Midwest Journal of Political Science* 14 (February 1970), p. 74.

20. *Ibid.,* p. 75.

21. *Ibid.,* p. 95.

22. Robert A. Dahl, "A Critique of the Ruling Elite Model," *American Political Science Review* 52 (June 1958): 463–69.

23. Nelson Polsby, *Community Power and Political Theory* (New Haven, Conn.: Yale University Press, 1963), p. 4.

24. *Ibid.,* p. 5.

25. Robert A. Dahl, "The Analysis of Influence in Local Communities," in Charles Adrian (ed.), *Social Science and Community Action* (East Lansing: Michigan State University Press, 1960), p. 26.

26. Harold D. Lasswell and Abraham Kaplan, *Power and Society* (New Haven: Yale University Press, 1950), p. 74.

27. Peter Bachrach and Morton S. Baratz, *Power and Poverty* (New York: Oxford University Press, 1970), p. 44.

28. *Ibid.*

29. Thomas Kuhn, *The Structure of Scientific Revolutions,* 2nd ed. (Chicago: University of Chicago Press, 1970), p. 6.

30. *Ibid.*

31. Kuhn, *Structure of Scientific Revolutions,* p. 102.

STUDY QUESTIONS

1. Define the following:

   fact   generalization
   theory   variable
   concept   paradigm
   hypothesis   law
   null hypothesis

2. What are the objectives of science?

3. What is necessary for scientific explanation?

4. How are the following related: hypothesis and variable? variable and concept? hypothesis, law, and theory?

5. What is scientific method? How does it contribute to the development of scientific explanations? What is the role of theory in scientific explanation?

6. What are the ways in which concepts can be defined?

7. How do values affect scientific research? Can scientific research be unbiased?

8. What criteria can we use to evaluate scientific theories?

9. How does development of a new paradigm affect scientific research?

CHAPTER
3

Research Methods

The principles of scientific method require a rigor and precision of thought to define the problem, to formulate and test the hypothesis, and to avoid intrusion of the researcher's values in the research process. In a sense, we are dealing with the epistemological basis of empirical political science, that is, *how we know something and what we know.*

This chapter provides an overview of how we operationalize the scientific method. In no sense can the discussion here be construed as a nitty-gritty, how-to-do-it course for the would-be researcher. Rather, we have provided examples of research and bibliographical references in order to guide those who wish to pursue the topics more closely. Some of the considerations that guide the work of political scientists engaged in empirical research are presented in the following sections.

RESEARCH DESIGN

To conduct any research, empirical or normative, the researcher must carefully follow several steps. Starting with a broad idea of what will be studied, the researcher must narrow and sharpen his or her focus to the point where there is an explicit problem that can be investigated, i.e., he or she *formulates the problem.*

Let us take as an example some research by one of the authors.[1] Starting with a general interest in presidential–congressional relations in the Nixon years, we had many possible research options. Should our research concentrate on foreign policy? Domestic policy? Or both? Should we explore specific aspects of either one? On an intuitive basis, it was apparent that there was a high degree of tension between the two branches long before the impeachment and resignation crisis of 1974. Was there a way to measure this tension? Could measuring legislative–executive tensions be placed in the framework of a larger theoretical context that would guide the research?

Preliminaries

Step 1: Formulating the Problem. A decision was made to analyze congressional response to presidential vetoes in the Nixon years. This was only one of several possibilities that could have been explored; it was chosen because in the researchers' opinion it provided the strongest possible test of legislative–executive tensions. However, it must be conceded that this is in itself a personal judgment that might not be defensible. Having chosen the extreme situation, where the issues are drawn and the president has thrown down the gauntlet to the Congress, generalizations about congressional–presidential relations would have to be carefully drawn. Only congressional response to presidential vetoes were to be examined, vetoes made by a Republican president facing a Democratic Congress. The problem was formally stated in this way:

> Given the normal tensions that exist between the legislative and executive branches of national government, how does Congress behave in reaction to presidential vetoes? Do some congressmen act to support the presidential veto more than others? Do some congressmen show a bias for congressional prerogatives? If there is a range of congressional response to presidential vetoes, how can we show that range, and what are its correlates?

Step 2: Determining Whether the Problem Can Be Studied. The next step is to show that the problem is amenable to study, i.e., to demonstrate that it can be observed and measured. We could have easily answered the research question in normative terms, suggesting that the president was right or wrong on certain issues and that the Congress did or did not have the wisdom and votes to sustain or override vetoes. For the problem to be researched empirically, however, one must anticipate later steps in the process: searching the literature and available data resources.

Step 3: Reading the Literature. The first requirement for empirical research is a thorough knowledge of the subject gained through a careful reading of all available sources, such as journals and indices that provide information on what research has been done, by whom, and with what methods and results (*see* pp. 49–52). A careful reading of the literature may further refine the problem, as well as suggest methods for collecting data.

The researcher probably has a fair idea of how to go about collecting data. Data collection in part may be limited by the availability of time, money, and personnel. For example, we might have interviewed congressmen and senators to determine why they supported or opposed the president on each bill he had vetoed or if they had advance knowledge from the White House that a veto was forthcoming before the Congress voted on it. However, conducting extended interviews was beyond our resources of time and money. We were thus forced to rely upon the documentary record of congressional roll-calls in the *Congressional Record,* a readily available source in most college and university libraries.

Step 4: Developing a Research Design. At this stage, it is essential to develop an outline or plan for the research. Although some may prefer to do this in a fairly informal manner, it is probably best to write an explicit design in specific outline form.[2] Although many would probably like to avoid this step, the design should be a guide to the research, showing the carefully thought out steps that must be followed. Written steps and procedures also serve as a checklist to which the researcher can refer constantly. The design should also provide for all or most contingencies.

Step 5: Determining Significance of the Problem. One must also show that the problem has some significance and is worth studying. Presidential–congressional relations became increasingly tense in the Nixon years. At the time our study was initiated, it was apparent that the House Judiciary Committee would conduct hearings on Nixon's impeachment. Were there clues beforehand that Congress was becoming more independent of the President on legislative matters—to the extent that the president lacked leadership over the congressional wing of his own party? Was Nixon receiving support from Democrats during this period? Obviously, there was an inherent interest in the subject, making the problem highly significant. We also felt that the problem was significant because presidential vetoes have been largely ignored by political scientists. The researchers believed that this constituted what is known as a "gap in the literature," or an area in which scholars have not previously delved.*

Step 6: Placing the Research in a Theoretical Context. From a careful reading of the literature (Step 3), it should become apparent to the researcher how his study builds upon and departs from previous work. In other words, the proposed problem is placed within a context. To determine the context of his problems, the researcher asks the following questions: Is there a body of empirical theory to which this problem relates? Or does this problem test a normative body of theory? Does it have implications for normative theory and / or empirical theory? In a sense, this step also should demonstrate the significance of the problem.

In our veto study, we placed our research within the context of a major work that contended that Congress was ineffectual because each chamber was divided not only on party lines, but on the basis of prevailing loyalties to the legislative or to the executive branch. Thus it was posited by earlier research that within the House and Senate one could find *Presidential Democrats, Presidential Republicans, Congressional Democrats,* and *Congressional Republicans.* The author of this long-accepted study described this situation as "four-party politics."[3] From his intuitive observations, the theory appeared to be solid, but it remained to be tested. This was the task which we set for ourselves.

There were normative theory implications for this study as well. Democratic theory posits a link between the electorate and the government. Although it is generally conceded that this link—if it exists—is imperfect at best,[4] what are the implications for democracy in America if the four-party theory is valid?

---

*At this stage, researchers must always contend with the influence of their ego on their research. In this case, the researchers plunged ahead, convinced that they had an opportunity "to make a new contribution to the literature." Some might contend that the only significance of their research was its reporting in this text, a point with which we shall not argue!

Step 7: Formulation of Hypotheses. In Chapter 2 we outlined the scientific method and discussed the inductive process of proceeding from particular to general statements. In a sense, we have been using inductive reasoning up to this stage of the research design. We started with known facts (presidential vetoes, congressional votes) and an interest in their relationships. The relationships were summarized in terms of a concept: an orientation to the executive or to the legislative branch of government.

We hypothesized that "The dimension of presidential–congressional support is independent of party, seniority, or ideological position." This is a *null hypothesis* because no relationship between variables was hypothesized. Our secondary, or corollary, hypothesis was that "The House tends more toward congressional support and the Senate more toward presidential support." *The hypotheses were stated for testing purposes—not to support the researchers' intuitions.* Without having examined the data, we had no reason to necessarily believe that the hypotheses would be supported or denied. Our intent was to test the hypotheses and let the chips—and data—fall where they may. Further, we explicitly stated the hypotheses in a written research design to inhibit a conscious or unconscious tendency to alter the hypotheses once the results were known. The relationships of variables (or absence of them) are more important than proving the researchers to be "right" or "wrong."

Step 8: Establishing Formal and Operational Definitions. There are several concepts in our null hypothesis that need formal and operational definitions. Science is concerned with nominal definitions, which name the characteristics that constitute the concept. The conceptual scheme, based on the concepts, must be appropriate, exhaustive, and mutually exclusive.

We easily defined *party* as Democrat and Republican, since these were the only parties organized in the Congress in the Nixon years. If congressmen were elected as Independents or on a third-party label, we defined their party as the established party that includes them for seniority purposes. *Seniority* was also readily definable: the number of years of continuous service in a particular chamber. For the purpose of the research design, ideological position of congressmen was considered as the score assigned to each congressman by a pressure group, the Americans for Democratic Action. We selected this pressure group because their scale is deliberately devised to represent positions on a conservative–liberal continuum. At one end of the scale (0) were "strong conservatives" and at the other end (100) were "strong liberals."

Each definition of a concept involved in the statement of our problem meets the test of a conceptual scheme, because they are appropriate, exhaustive, and exclusive. Because the concepts are testable and measurable, they can therefore be considered operational definitions. We later employed a common statistical test to ascertain whether these concepts are associated with or independent of the major variable in the hypothesis.

"The dimension of presidential–congressional support," which was the major concept, was defined in terms of how strongly a congressman was oriented toward the executive or legislative branch of government. If *Presidential Democrats* and *Presidential Republicans* did exist, they might be revealed by determining who votes to sustain and who votes to deny the president's prerogative of the veto. Bearing in mind that our data-collection method (recording congressional roll calls published in the *Congressional Record*) had already been specified, we had several possible means of operationalizing the dimension. We could have simply tabulated congressional votes on bills vetoed by the president and then devised a score for each vote. For example, a score of 1 would equal a vote to pass the bill over the veto, i.e., an expression of support of congressional prerogatives; a score of 0 would equal a vote to sustain the veto, i.e., support of the presidential prerogative. These scores could be totalled, providing a continuum for each session of Congress. If nine bills were vetoed and voted on again, the "dimension of presidential–congressional support" would range from 0–9, if it had been operationally defined this way.*

In establishing operational definitions, it is also necessary to specify how they will be measured quantitatively, in order to allow appropriate statistical measures to be employed. The researcher must be prepared to specify exactly which relationships will be examined and how. Will they be measured by using simple tables? What measures of association and correlation will be used? The researcher

---

*Although it was not defined this way, the option was briefly contemplated before it was rejected in favor of a more complicated scoring system based on congressional votes before and after the veto. Some political scientists never do things the easy way. However, for the sake of simplicity, in our example we shall assume that the data were scored and categorized as described in this paragraph.

must seriously consider exactly how the hypothesis will be tested. Before we turn to hypothesis testing, we shall explain in greater detail the sources used by political scientists.

REVIEW OF THE LITERATURE

The first requirement for empirical research is a comprehensive knowledge of the literature on the subject in question. By *literature,* we mean journal articles and books that relate in any way to the subject. Many beginning students define their topics too narrowly and look only for articles that deal directly with their hypothesis. For instance, a researcher seeking to examine the presence of ideology in the electorate in the 1972 American presidential election might confine himself to articles that deal solely with that election or only to articles dealing with ideology in that election. This limits what the literature might show the researcher. The relative presence or absence of ideology in an election is not a new topic for political scientists; it has been widely researched in many elections, at the national and local levels in the U.S., as well as in other countries.

For that matter, one could be developing a research design based on a future event and conclude that, since it has not occurred, there could be nothing at all of value in searching the literature. Construing a topic too narrowly or conceiving of it in a given time perspective only suggest that there is something unique about the topic. This presumption cannot be made without testing and without comparison with previous events of a similar nature.

The nature of the literature to be examined is obviously dependent upon the topic under consideration. We commonly distinguish between primary and secondary sources. A *primary source* contains the raw information from which analyses can be made and is the source in which that information initially was reported. *Secondary sources* repeat or analyze information that appeared elsewhere. There are finer distinctions between primary and secondary sources. Newspapers, for instance, are usually considered secondary sources for most purposes. But, if one were interested in the editorial slant of a given newspaper, editorials and letters-to-the-editor might be considered primary material because they provide the raw material from which the political scientist can make subsequent analyses.

In empirical research, we attempt to ground our work in evidence that is most often of a primary nature. Data collection methods (surveys, content analysis, observation) are considered primary sources, but they are not primary in the sense of the literature.

Most of the literature we use may therefore be considered secondary in nature, presenting analyses of data collected by or otherwise made available to other scholars. The search for such literature may be illuminating for the researcher, since he may discover that the topic was previously treated in the same way that it is now being considered. But one can generally expect that all relationships have not been thoroughly examined, given limitations of time, resources, money, and the training of previous researchers. A review of the literature might lead the researcher to consider placing greater emphasis on aspects of the general problem not previously considered in depth. It could also become apparent that a given problem has not been examined in depth for a considerable time and that changes in assumed relationships might have taken place. Finally, it may become apparent that previous work is invalid for one reason or another and is in need of serious re-examination. Major gaps in previous research may suggest themselves, since social and behavioral research is seldom a planned and methodical attack on a general problem. A search of the literature can reveal what has been done, what has not been done, and what remains to be done.

Indices and Periodicals. Although published indices and bibliographies are necessarily selective in nature and can become rapidly dated, they can be invaluable for focusing on a subject. The index most frequently used by political scientists is the *Social Sciences and Humanities Index,* [*] which lists journal articles according to broad classifications and subcategories. Again, the researcher must be careful not to construe his own topic in too narrow a manner in searching for appropriate titles. The *Public Affairs Information Service* also classifies articles that can be of value to the political scientist. Some journals provide very specialized indices. The Keyword-in-Context (KWIC) index is a convenient means of locating very specific subject matter in articles that have appeared in that journal. *International Political Science Abstracts,* found in many college and university libraries, is a valuable reference tool because it

---

[*]Formerly the *International Index to Periodicals.*

gives short abstracts of articles relating to the discipline. *ABC—Pol Sci* lists the table of contents of over 300 political science journals and provides author and subject indices to articles in those journals.

The journals we most often use include, but are not limited to, the following:

American Behavioral Scientist (bi-monthly)

American Journal of Political Science (quarterly—KWIC, 1957–1971, formerly the *Midwest Journal of Political Science*)

American Journal of Sociology (bi-monthly)

American Political Science Review (quarterly—KWIC, 1906–1968)

American Politics Quarterly

American Sociological Review (bi-monthly)

Annals of the American Academy of Political and Social Science (bi-monthly)

Current History (monthly)

Foreign Affairs (quarterly)

International Social Science Journal (quarterly)

Journal of Politics (quarterly)

Journal of Conflict Resolution (quarterly)

Political Science Quarterly

Polity (quarterly)

Public Opinion Quarterly

Review of Politics (quarterly)

Social Forces

Social Sciences Quarterly (formerly the *Southwestern Social Sciences Quarterly*)

Western Political Quarterly

World Politics (quarterly)

In addition to periodicals, there are books that deal directly or indirectly with the topic. Of course, not all books will be in possession of one library, but inter-library loan arrangements allow a researcher to obtain almost any desired text.

An invaluable source of primary and secondary information is material published by government agencies at local, state, national, and international levels. Local and state documents are not always accessible because they are seldom indexed comprehensively. At the national level, the researcher can first consult the *U.S. Government*

Documents Index. The range of information published by the federal government is astonishing, and what the researcher finds is often unpredictable. There may be information on trade unionism in African nations, speeches by important government officials, testimony before congressional committees, and enormous bodies of data, such as from the decennial census. Much of the information published by the U.S. Government Printing Office may seem to be of no conceivable value to the political science researcher, although some data are available nowhere else. In terms of its sheer quantity, government data can often serve as a major starting point for empirical research.

DATA COLLECTION METHODS

The Ethics Involved

In the conduct of empirical research on one's fellow human beings, the researcher must constantly maintain a decent respect for the personal rights and sensitivities of the people he investigates and describes. This holds true for racial, religious, or ethnic groups as much as it does for individual political officeholders or citizens.

One of the first premises of behavioral research is the *right of privacy.* If some do not wish to be the subject of research, they must not be forced into this situation. Further, confidentiality must be offered to the subject and maintained by the researcher if requested. The specific content of who said what, who feels what, and who behaves how must be respected and guarded. Many readers probably have been approached in the course of their college career by some surveyer or psychological tester. Would the reader feel at all comfortable with the knowledge that his or her responses to a survey could be made public and could be identified as his or her own? Even if the subject feels that he "has nothing to hide," the researcher must be respectful of the privacy of others. Great embarrassment can result when specific individuals are identified with remarks, attitudes, or behaviors of a personal nature.

Because of these problems and because personal interviews are not always appropriate or possible, there are other numerous devices for collecting data of which social scientists may avail themselves. We turn first to methods that involve little personal contact for the researcher, before considering those that may directly confront the ethics of the researcher.

Content Analysis

Any form of research requires careful analysis of the written word. The method of content analysis particularly lends itself to discerning underlying themes and patterns in written materials. This is a crucial task because written materials provide raw and systematized data from which the empirical researcher will attempt to draw inferences; ". . . in general terms *content analysis is the application of scientific methods to documentary evidence.*"[5]

Scientific method requires a rigorous application of objective methods of classification and description in all empirical approaches to data collection and analysis. Content analysis carefully, objectively, and precisely uncovers elements that are germane to the hypothesis and to its fundamental concepts.

Applying the Content Analysis Method. Assume that we were interested in the editorial stance of several newspapers on a presidential program. We hypothesize that *"editorial support of a president's program is related to the patterns of presidential election endorsement in newspaper editorials."* If a newspaper endorsed the president while he was running for office, we would expect that it would be more likely to approve of his specific and general programs.

We must provide an operational definition of each of these concepts. *Presidential endorsement* will be interpreted as meaning an endorsement—after the presidential nominating conventions but before the election—in which the paper specifically states that it is endorsing the candidate; or, in one or more of its pre-election editorials it urges its readers to vote for the candidate; or, in an editorial it states that the candidate is more qualified to hold office than his opponent. *Editorial support of or opposition to a president's program* may seem easy to define. However, we must first define what we mean by a *presidential program.* Several possibilities exist, but we will use one that states that the president has taken a position in favor of several specific bills, and we will determine his position by an impartial source, such as the *Congressional Quarterly.* It might be objected that executive approval of bills does not necessarily mean that the president has incorporated those bills into his program. Therefore, we shall impose an additional criterion: Not only must each bill receive presidential approval in advance of its passage, but it must have been favorably mentioned in his State of the Union address or have been the topic of a special message to Congress.

Editorial support or opposition could be expressed as an "approve/disapprove" dichotomy or as a continuum of *strong approval, weak approval, no position, weak disapproval, strong disapproval*. Let us opt for the continuum to determine support or opposition and assign numerical equivalents to each point on the continuum:

−2 = Strong disapproval
−1 = Weak disapproval
  0 = No position taken
  1 = Weak approval
  2 = Strong approval

The assigned numbers are abitrary and are not necessarily true values; that is, a score of 2 (strong approval) is not necessarily twice as strong as a score of 1 (weak approval). The numbers are assigned for statistical convenience only. This caveat applies to other data collection devices and will become clearer when we discuss statistics at the end of this chapter.

In order to achieve a degree of objectivity in our procedure, we draw up a set of rules, designed so any person reading an editorial should come to the same judgment. We select three persons to read and judge the editorials and train them in the use of the rules. For purposes of limiting our illustration, we decide to examine one newspaper that endorsed the president in his campaign for election and one that opposed him. According to explicit rules, our panel of readers judged whether or not a paper was considered a presidential supporter. Each newspaper was examined for a one-week period before the bill was voted on; *see* Table 3−1 for the judgments.

One need not be a statistician to draw the following conclusions about the data in Table 3−1. The judges showed a high degree of agreement on each editorial, suggesting that there is a degree of *reliability* to any of their judgments. *If* there were a bias in the way they judged the editorials, it was a uniform bias. Second, each "judge" was able to discriminate between editorials that approved

TABLE 3–1. *Initial Judgments of Editorial Positions (Based on Contrived Data)*

Day of Editorial	Newspaper A (endorsed president)			Judges	Newspaper B (opposed president)		
	X	Y	Z		X	Y	Z
Sunday	2	2	1		−1	−1	−2
Monday	0	0	0		−1	−1	−1
Tuesday	1	1	1		0	0	0
Wednesday	0	0	0		0	0	0
Thursday	1	2	2		0	0	0
Friday	0	0	0		−2	−2	−2
Saturday	2	1	2		−2	−1	−1
Totals	6	6	6		−6	−5	−6

and those that disapproved. Third, in the scoring process, none of the three "judges" revealed a systematic bias by always using the same categorization of approval or disapproval. They could use both strong and weak approval or strong and weak disapproval. The rules were apparently clear to each of the evaluators, and they were able to make judgments that were, by and large, consistent internally as well as with each other. Finally, and most important, it would appear that our hypothesis is validated (although we have yet to apply any statistical tests to the results).

Do we know that the results are indeed valid in their content, construct, and predictive aspects? (*See* pages 89–92 on this point.) Do the two newspapers represent an appropriate sample of all newspapers? Do the three evaluators represent a fair sample of potential judges? In other words, we must question whether the results can be generalized, a test to which all empirical research must be subjected, regardless of the nature of the data, how the data were collected, or by whom.

Other approaches to content analysis are not covered here. The uses to which content analysis can be put are many and varied, and, if properly applied, can provide information without personal risk to the subjects of the research paper. Content analysis has been used to determine the authorship of several of the Federalist Papers;[6] the policy focus of campaign debates;[7] and a broad variety of other factors, including individual personality variables.[8]

Carefully used, content analysis can provide us with valuable information along the broad spectrum of concerns to which the political researcher may turn. As the analysis of the Federalist Papers shows, content analysis can enhance the historical perspective of an argument and provide necessary background, as well as establishing a baseline for noting the development of long-term trends.

Aggregate Data Analysis

For a considerable time, political scientists have relied on the collection and analysis of aggregate data, i.e., data that describe persons or events collectively. The basic unit of analysis is not the individual or an event, but either of these considered with others of a similar nature. Data can be aggregated at a number of levels, including political ones (state or nation).

By definition, aggregate data do not describe attitudes or behaviors of individuals. To do so would be to commit what has been called the "ecological fallacy," or inferring individual characteristics from aggregate ones or from the environments in which individuals may be found.[9] For example, if a study of election returns showed that members of an ethnic group were unusually supportive of a particular candidate, one could not draw the conclusion that all members of that group supported the candidate. An even more grievous error would be to impute motivations or attitudes from such data. Even if the data were to show that 100 percent of the voting population of an ethnic group supported a candidate, it would be impossible to state with any degree of certainty *why* they supported the candidate.

Nonetheless, aggregate data analysis is a time-honored practice in political science, and not without good reason. For the researcher who does not have extensive resources of time and money, it is not too difficult to obtain access to large bodies of data, aggregated at various levels. The U.S. Census, for instance, is a treasury of information that may be fruitfully exploited by the analyst who has carefully worked out a research design. Data are reported in the census from the lowest unit of aggregation (the census tract, or area which can be covered by a single census enumerator) and then are aggregated to higher-level units, such as towns, cities, counties, states, and the nation as a whole. The census provides raw information on population, age, ethnicity, income, sex, and occupation. Combined with other data sources, such as electoral information found in official reports of government units or in the *America Votes* series,[10] the information can be highly useful to the analyst seeking to make generalizations at a particular level.

Determining the level of analysis is a major difficulty of using aggregate data.[11] Since the data represent an accumulation of information derived from individuals or units of government, at what level should we examine them? The higher the level of aggregation, the less we can comprehend the range of individual variations. If we were using the state as the basic unit of analysis, for example, a great deal of variation at the county or city level might be obscured by discussing data aggregated at this higher level. Or suppose we were examining the degree of party competition in the United States. If we measured party competition at the state level, we might be ignoring substantial intrastate variation, since there could be widespread differences in competition between the counties of each of the states. Further, if we were to measure at the county level, a unit for which we can obtain data rather readily, we would have to deal with not fifty cases but more than 3,000, which would greatly complicate our task. But it could be argued that there can be wide variation in competition levels even within a county, within some cities, towns, and even precincts. The lower the level of aggregation, the greater the task of data collection. The analyst must make a decision as to what level will give the most information for the least cost. This is a decision that crops up constantly in all empirical analysis when the research design is being drawn up.

A great advantage of aggregate data is that they can be used to analyze trends. The perspective gained from *longitudinal analysis*—the examination of a problem over time—is a most valuable one, especially for the development of empirical theories that explain and predict. We have just begun to develop a body of survey data at the national level that provides electoral information covering the last 20 years.[12] Since many sets of aggregate data can be found for geographic or government units that go considerably beyond the national unit, we can provide a historical perspective that otherwise might be impossible. For that matter, aggregate data may be the only means by which we can arrive at judgments of past political behavior that is not conducive to the study by interview or survey techniques.

The study of elections in this and other countries long depended on aggregate data, which continues to be a major means by which we can study changes over time. Suppose we were interested in the major party realignments that have occurred in American electoral history. It is patently impossible to go back and interview individuals long dead, but data for constant units—counties and states—are available to measure changes in how people within those units vote. Thus we can ascertain where and when changes have taken place and under what conditions, and attempt to draw inferences as to why people changed their voting behavior.[13]

Although aggregate data may be readily available, their validity and reliability are always questionable. In census information, for instance, we have a wide body of richly detailed information that goes back to 1790. To accept these data uncritically might be to commit a major error. Census information has been gathered from people (who may have faulty information or who may intentionally or unintentionally withhold information), processed by people, placed in tabular form by people and printed by people—all of whom are quite susceptible to error. The means by which census information is initially gathered is generally considered excellent, but even the Bureau of the Census candidly admits to its own limitations, and so informs the user in its own reports. Other aggregate data, such as election returns, may incorporate deliberate misrepresentation constituting electoral fraud.[14] Censuses and similar information sources from developing or totalitarian countries are also quite suspect, since officials often try to make the most favorable case for themselves and their governments.[15]

Finally, the use of aggregate data is simply not possible in certain types of studies. Analyses of individual personalities, motivations, attitudes, and values cannot be carried out with aggregate data. Studies of political socialization, for example, are not amenable to aggregate data analysis.

Despite these limitations, aggregate data analysis has been with us for some time and is likely to continue to be a major source of information for political scientists. Used alone or in combination with other data collection methods, it can be a rich source of information for political scientists in many specialized areas. Like all techniques, it must be used carefully, with full awareness of its potential and its limitations.

Observational Approaches

Observation of behavior is a common means of collecting data. This can be done in several ways. The researcher can be a participant or nonparticipant in the behavioral situation, and the fact that the research is being conducted can be known or unknown to the subjects. To illustrate this, imagine a study in which the researcher is attempting to determine the presence or absence of certain legislative roles in a city council. (For definitions of the role concept, *see* pages 189–191.) (Let us ignore for the moment exactly how this could be determined.) The conduct of the observation has important consequences for the outcome. If the observer were to simply sit in the audience during formal proceedings, the subjects of the research may or may not know that they are being observed. If they are aware of being observed, one or more members of the city council might consciously or unconsciously alter their normal behavior patterns, thus affecting the possible outcomes. The point of the research may be to determine what their characteristic behavior is, in which case one would not want betray the presence of the observer. The observer in this case would have to be unobstrusive in his behavior. However, the researcher might also want to determine what city council members felt were the ideal roles for their positions. City council members might adopt an entirely different posture (considered their ideal role) if they knew they were being observed. Since the researcher is seeking to observe both the real and desired roles, both options would have to be employed. In the first instance, where the fact of the research is not known, a norm can be established. At a later time, the fact that the research is being conducted and its professed purpose—determining role behavior—can be communicated to the council members. The observer can then note role changes that have taken place, if any, and come to conclusions about the influence of observers (the public or a researcher) on role behavior in a public setting.

A researcher can also be a participant in the proceedings. If the researcher were a member of the city council, an entirely different outcome might take place. His fellow members might react to him in his researcher role and in whatever legislative roles he might assume. Unless the participant–observer were to announce at the very outset his intention to conduct a study, one could consider the researcher's methods as morally obnoxious since he would be seen as manipulating his peers.[16]

This charge does not have to necessarily apply, however. In 1974 Richard Fenno accompanied and observed incumbent congressmen in their home districts, seeking to determine who is contacted by the representatives and the functions performed by constituent–representative interactions.[17] In order to conduct the observations, Fenno obviously required the consent of the congressmen, whom he also apprised of the nature and purpose of the research. He found himself pressed into service from time to time, distributing campaign literature, driving a congressman from place to place, and handling sundry other duties. Discussion also took place with congressmen, although it could not be neatly classified as in-depth interviews. Fenno refers to his procedure as one of "soak and poke"; he immerses himself in a problem and tries to intuitively arrive at meaningful and valid conclusions. This procedure does not lend itself readily to scientific measurement because another observer, with the same or different congressmen, might arrive at different conclusions. However, it is difficult to see how a charge of manipulation is necessarily applicable in this or other cases of data collection by participant–observers.

In order to avoid problems of influencing the reactions of those being observed, the researcher, as a non-participant observer, should not allow the fact of the research to be known. There are several means by which one can conduct such observations. A researcher observing social interactions within a group could determine the relative existence of cliques or subgroups in a larger context. *Sociometric diagramming* of interactions, based upon observed instances of individuals conversing with each other, is one way of portraying what has been observed. In our hypothetical five-member city council, the pattern indicated in Figure 3–1 might prevail on certain types of issues.

In Figure 3–1, **A** emerges as the discussion leader because **A** had contact with more members than any other individual. **E** is an isolate, communicating only with **A**, the apparent leader. If this were a fairly consistent pattern of interaction between council mem-

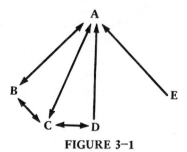

FIGURE 3–1

Hypothetical Interactions of City Council Members: A Sociogram

bers on most issues, and **E** was the only member of his part on the council, or a member of an ethnic minority in the city and on the council, it might be possible to draw inferences about the effect of those variables. Sociometric diagramming is obviously most easily accomplished in the analysis of small groups.[18]

Bales' Interaction Process Analysis is a major means of observing individuals in group situations.[19] This approach is based upon the need of any group with a common purpose to solve common problems. These problems are *orientation,* or a definition of the problem to be solved; *evaluation,* the finding of common values so that different task solutions may be evaluated; *control,* or the problem of interpersonal influence within the group; *decision-making,* which is the underlying purpose of the group itself; *tension-management,* in order to facilitate the group's purpose; and *integration* of the various group members in the effort. Figure 3–2 illustrates the types of behavior that can be noted for each individual in a small-group situation according to Bales' analysis. Scores can be entered by the researcher for each member of the group under study; the scores establish the empirical norms of that group.

The two major types of observational systems of data collection, sociometric diagramming and interaction process analysis, are susceptible to certain types of error in their application. This is also true of other observational techniques not mentioned here. At least seven types of errors have been described.[20] For example, if individual observers are susceptible to error, it is also possible and likely that two or more observers might not agree in their descriptions or ratings of behavior. Observational techniques, then, often entail the problem of the observer's reliability.

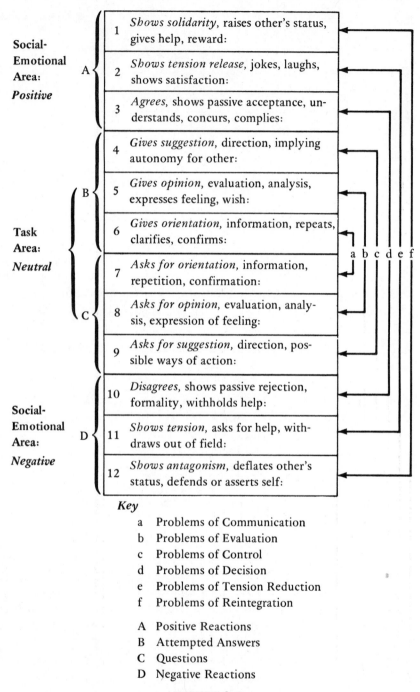

Social-
Emotional
Area:
Positive

A

1	*Shows solidarity,* raises other's status, gives help, reward:
2	*Shows tension release,* jokes, laughs, shows satisfaction:
3	*Agrees,* shows passive acceptance, understands, concurs, complies:

Task
Area:
Neutral

B

4	*Gives suggestion,* direction, implying autonomy for other:
5	*Gives opinion,* evaluation, analysis, expresses feeling, wish:
6	*Gives orientation,* information, repeats, clarifies, confirms:

C

7	*Asks for orientation,* information, repetition, confirmation:
8	*Asks for opinion,* evaluation, analysis, expression of feeling:
9	*Asks for suggestion,* direction, possible ways of action:

Social-
Emotional
Area:
Negative

D

10	*Disagrees,* shows passive rejection, formality, withholds help:
11	*Shows tension,* asks for help, withdraws out of field:
12	*Shows antagonism,* deflates other's status, defends or asserts self:

a b c d e f

Key

a   Problems of Communication
b   Problems of Evaluation
c   Problems of Control
d   Problems of Decision
e   Problems of Tension Reduction
f   Problems of Reintegration

A   Positive Reactions
B   Attempted Answers
C   Questions
D   Negative Reactions

FIGURE 3–2

Categories of Individual Behavior in Groups (Robert F. Bales, *Interaction Process Analysis: A Method for the Study of Small Groups* [Reading, Mass.: Addison-Wesley, 1950], p. 9. Reprinted by permission.)

More fundamental a problem is how the researcher classifies behavior, i.e., how he structures the possible behaviors of individuals under study. This of course is related to the entire premise on which the study has been based. There is no quick and ready solution to these problems.

Survey Research

Survey research is now the major data collection device used by political scientists and their colleagues in the allied social sciences. We distinguish this type of research from in-depth interviews primarily in terms of the nature of the sample selected; that is, *survey research* is characterized by large samples that can be taken as representative of even larger populations.

We again warn that our comments on data collection cannot serve to qualify the reader to use the techniques we are describing. [21] For several reasons, this is especially true of the sample surveys described here. Any type of research that elicits personal information and attitudes from a respondent must be conducted with the greatest of care. These few pages could not begin to describe the various means by which we can seek to elicit and protect information of a personal nature. Further, properly conducted sample surveys involve a highly complex technology that is susceptible to error at every stage. The student or teacher who feels that a survey is a quick or easy or even a fun way to gather information is poorly advised.

Some idea of the complexities involved can be gained by consulting Table 3–2. Each of the steps represented in the table is an abbreviation of a very detailed procedure. Let us assume, for instance, we have formulated an hypothesis. It should represent something more sophisticated than a "fishing expedition" which merely seeks to find out "how people feel about things." Even if "people" were specified as to the nature of the population, and "feel" were made explicit in terms of direction, intensity, and cognitive basis of attitudes, and "things" were clearly defined in terms of events, situations, persons, or values, we would still be left wondering why the researcher is contemplating undertaking such a very complex task.

Surveys are among the most criticized and least understood research tools available in the social sciences. Few persons, including many political scientists, have been rigorously trained to understand the complexities involved. There is often a mystique about surveys

TABLE 3–2. *Steps in Survey Research*

1. Hypothesizing	Deciding what it is you want to study
2. Designing	Establishing the procedures and methods to use
3. Planning	Figuring materials and personnel needed
4. Financing	Arranging support for the survey
5. Sampling	Choosing people to be interviewed
6. Drafting	Framing the questions for use in the field
7. Constructing	Planning the format of the questionnaire
8. Pre-Testing	Determining whether the questions elicit the data desired
9. Training	Teaching interviewers how to gather information correctly
10. Briefing	Showing interviewers how to use the questionnaire
11. Interviewing	Securing data from respondents
12. Controlling	Seeing that the interviewing gets done
13. Verifying	Assuring that the collected data are accurate
14. Coding	Preparing the data for analysis
15. Processing	Organizing data mechanically or electronically
16. Analyzing	Interpreting the data
17. Reporting	Sharing the new knowledge

Source: Charles H. Backstrom and Gerald D. Hursh, *Survey Research* (Evanston, Ill.: Northwestern University Press, 1963), p. 19. Reprinted with permission.

that both attracts and repels. Some cite survey findings as if they were definitive, without any awareness of the probabilistic basis of this device or the hazards it involves. The attractiveness of supposedly "learning by doing" is used by many undergraduates and their instructors to justify survey research. While there *may* be no substitute for practical experience, that experience should be grounded in a thorough knowledge of the technique, acquired *before* the research is undertaken. Indeed, if training and knowledge have been gained, *the researcher who wants valid results, achievable within resources of time, money, and personnel, may benefit by selecting a data collection device more appropriate to the problem under investigation than survey research.*

There is a large and useful literature on survey research, and one would be well-advised to consult the basic works in the field. [22] *Public Opinion Quarterly* updates knowledge of survey research techniques; those planning to use this tool could profit from the experience of others reported in this journal.

There are research problems for which only survey research would be appropriate. When a researcher wants to generalize about attitudes, behaviors, and relationships of large populations, survey research is his primary tool. However, the population (in survey research sometimes referred to as the *universe*) may be so large that obtaining an adequate sample is beyond the researcher's resources and capabilities. For this reason, and because large bodies of data exist which have not been fully exploited, there is always the possibility of *secondary analysis,* or a re-examination of data acquired (usually by others) at some earlier time.

Because surveys require the willing cooperation of the population, the increased use of survey research could affect its future use. Maximum utilization of previously acquired data can at least slow the possibility of wearing out our welcome as researchers in the social sciences.[23] Those surveyed by fellow students might appreciate how local populations in college towns feel when a group of students led by an enthusiastic faculty member swoops down upon the streets with clipboards and questionnaires in hand.

Empirical researchers share their data and results with others in order that others can examine or more fully exploit the data. There are several institutionalized arrangements for sharing data. [24] *SS Data,* a quarterly issued by the Laboratory for Political Research at the University of Iowa, provides current information on data sets made available to them through various archives. Concentration of data in sources like this facilitates the research process by minimizing costs of time and money.

If secondary analysis is not appropriate and the information is not obtainable by means other than through survey research, then a formidable series of steps must take place. Assume we have finished Step 1 ("hypothesizing" in Table 3–2) of a sample survey. Let us now conveniently "wish away" the next two steps of designing and planning. The next step, financing, can be the ultimate stumbling block, depending upon how the interviewer is approached. If the interviews are *personally conducted,* it is not unusual to spend $30 to $40 for *each interview,* and this amount often only covers the fee of the interviewer alone. If the survey is conducted by telephone, the costs are considerably reduced, but there are attendant risks as well, such as greater misunderstanding, lower response rates, and the fact that some individuals may not have phones or may have phones with unlisted numbers. The final sample of a survey by phone may not be representative. *Questionnaires* sent by mail are by far the cheapest way to interview, but obtaining a high response rate is difficult, and the costs can still approach $1 per potential respondent. If large samples are required, the costs of any approach can be well beyond the means of many researchers.

Once financial problems are solved, *sampling* begins. Samples are taken in order to achieve representativeness when it is not possible to interview the entire population under study. In order to generalize from the sample population to the universal population described by the researcher (e.g., college-age students), the sample must be as representative as possible. In order to achieve respresentativeness, *probability samples* are used; these allow us to estimate the probability of any one person in the universe being included in the sample. Many newspaper polls or "straw polls" do not and cannot meet this assumption, and their validity is therefore highly questionable. They are referred to as *non-probability samples* and are commonly rejected in respectable empirical research.

We can distinguish between three types of probability samples: the simple random, the stratified, and the area, or cluster, sample. All three basically operate on the principle of randomness, and we shall not attempt to describe them here.[25] Suffice it to say that if the principles of randomness and known probability are not met through one of these three sample types, the research conducted is highly susceptible to charges of being invalid and unreliable. We may not be able to generalize our findings from such samples back to the universe, or population, being described.

In drawing a sample, *sample size* is a critical factor. To the uninitiated or uninformed, it may seem that samples of 1,500 or so, commonly used by national survey organizations such as Gallup and Harris, are insufficient to generalize to large populations, such as voting-age adults in the United States. As evidence of this, some point to the famous *Literary Digest* poll in 1936, which received more than two million returns and inaccurately predicted that Governor Alf Landon of Kansas would beat President Roosevelt by some 20 percentage points—exactly the reverse of the actual outcome. The *Literary Digest* poll was completely non-random, whereas Gallup, Harris, and most currently respectable survey organizations utilize probability samples, commonly of the area type. Area samples assure, within limits of probability, that a representative sample can be taken in a large geographic area. Smaller sample sizes can be used, depending upon factors such as the level of error that the researcher wishes to tolerate, available financing, homogeneity of the population under study, type of probability sample used, and how the data are to be utilized.[26] A researcher with limited financial resources wishing to use a random sample, for instance, can limit his sample to 196 respondents, with a margin of error of 7%, and a confidence level of 95%. By this we mean that he can be 95% certain of the results, ± 7%. For instance, if he were to find that his sample showed that 60% favored mandatory price controls, he could be 95% confident that 53% to 67% of the population from which the sample was drawn held this opinion.

Questionnaire construction is a formidable problem (Step 7 in Table 3–2). The information desired for the survey is dependent upon the hypotheses under investigation, and each question must have a rationale in the research design. The phrasing of questions is critical, as is the order in which they are posed. Questions should be worded in such a way that there is no suggestion of a "right" or "wrong" or "desired" response. The researcher may opt for two basic types of questions: the "open-ended," which allows the respondent to answer in his or her own words; or the "close-ended," which provides answers from which the respondent may choose. The order of questions is also highly important. A quick way to assure a low response rate is to start with questions perceived by the respondent as of a very personal nature, such as income. Since the reliability of the survey is dependent upon achieving a maximum response from those sampled, the researcher must make every effort not to alienate the respondents. Further, if related questions are placed in a sequence, the respondent might develop a so-called "response set," in which he provides answers that he perceives to be consistent, rather than answering spontaneously.[27]

We need not go through the rest of the steps involved in survey research to emphasize the numerous sources of error. Studies can be properly conducted, with reliable and valid results, if the researcher is extremely careful in handling the seemingly infinite details. The reader of empirically oriented political science literature should be cognizant of the problems involved and not be overly willing to dismiss these problems or to accept the reported results uncritically. On the other hand, to dismiss the results of survey research on the basis of the method itself is to dismiss worthwhile knowledge.[28]

In-Depth Interviews

In certain instances, research cannot take advantage of very large survey samples, records of individual or group behavior, formal documents, or observations of behavior, or it cannot rely completely on these sources. In such cases, it may be possible or desirable to conduct in-depth interviews with a limited number of respondents.[29]

The purpose of the research guides the means by which respondents are selected. In some research, interviews should to some extent represent a large population, in which case normal sampling procedures can be applied. In other research, one cannot determine representativeness beforehand for various reasons, for example, a study that seeks to develop hypotheses that are subject to replication later. Such a procedure would actually be a version of a *case study*, where the researcher in the initial phases attempts to determine the existence of an event, situation, or process. A study of political ideology attempting to explore what people believe about politics and suggesting why they believe what they do, was conducted with a sample of fifteen persons.[30] This exploration can by no means be declared definitive, but it is highly suggestive and has been the source of numerous testable hypotheses explored in other works. Another study drew on interviews with ten men, involving roughly fifteen sessions of two hours each. Included were various types of written questionnaires as well as personal in-depth interviews.[31] Again, there is no claim made about the representativeness of the ten persons interviewed, but the results have suggested hypotheses for social scientists in several disciplines.

In other research, the very uniqueness of the person or persons selected for interviewing may be the crucial factor. Given the opportunity, a political scientist would scarcely reject the opportunity to spend some time conducting an in-depth interview with the president or chief justice of the United States Supreme Court simply because such a person does not meet the specifications for "representativeness." Although this is an extreme example, there is a distinct set of possibilities open to the researcher who concentrates on interviewing elites. One would be remiss to reject a chance to record the attitudes of such persons if they are at all germane to the research project. Journalists and those oriented toward the behavioral sciences have long used the in-depth interview to gather information from elites that was otherwise unobtainable, and we should not exclude information gained from this procedure.

Structured Interview. The *structured interview* consists of a set of detailed questions on specific topics. Questions are phrased so that they are open-ended or closed-ended, as they are in normal survey research. Closed-ended questions may be particularly useful for obtaining information of a demographic character and for providing data on social characteristics of the respondent. Open-ended questions can be used to gain some of this information as well. Both types of questions may be used, where appropriate, to elicit attitudes and to find the cognitive base of the values and opinions held by the respondent. In interviewing elites, it is often especially important to probe for the reasons a respondent holds certain opinions.

Unstructured Interview. Although by no means restricted to elite studies, *unstructured interviews* primarily employ open-ended questions and allow the interviewer to cover broader areas and to follow up responses that promise to be especially fruitful. For instance, an interview with a major government official in an oil-producing country of the Middle East could be conducted with the specific aim of attempting to discern future oil-pricing policies. The unstructured interview is not aimless, but quite purposive in nature. The researcher can follow up responses in a more complete manner than the structured situation would normally allow. If the official being interviewed indicates that future prices would be contingent upon actions by the United States, the interviewer might follow this response by probing further: Is the official referring to U.S. policy toward Israel? What policies might be perceived by the Arab countries as friendly or hostile to their cause? Is the official referring to possible import taxes the U.S. might levy, or to a maximum price level the U.S. might establish? How would the Arabs regard options currently contemplated in Washington? The more flexible nature of an unstructured interview can provide information in depth, of a variety not possible with the structured interview. The two types are not necessarily exclusive, and the researcher should make provision, where necessary, for using either or both types in preparing for the interview.

Conducting the Interview. There are several difficulties associated with structured and unstructured interviews. Both types require a comfortable interview situation to ensure that the respondent provides valid responses. A hostile or uncomfortable situation could cause the respondent to abruptly terminate the interview or to give artificial responses. It can also be quite difficult to attempt to replicate the results, especially with an unstructured interview. Interviewees are not selected on the basis of their representativeness of a wider population. Entirely different results may be achieved by a different interviewer, especially if he interviews at a different time, even if the same persons were interviewed.

Before the interview begins, the researcher plans how to record responses. These plans are subject to change, according to the wishes of the respondent. Tape recording ensures that responses are noted in entirety, but some respondents may feel uncomfortable in the presence of a tape recorder, perhaps because they believe that strict confidentiality cannot be maintained under those conditions. They may ask the interviewer not to record their answers by this method, or they may respond with careful answers, contrived to be publicly acceptable. In the conduct of a structured interview, especially one using closed-ended questions, the interviewer can easily write down all responses as the subject chooses from among the options provided. For open-ended questions, however, the problem of recording lengthy responses by hand can cause the interviewer to fall behind and to miss important points. The respondent may also feel less comfortable in this situation. Finally, the interviewer could conduct an unstructured interview without taking notes at all and rely on memory to reconstruct the interview in note form as soon as it ends. The necessity for this may occasionally arise, and some researchers actually prefer this method, but questions of validity are bound to arise since an extra variable—the reseacher's memory—has been introduced into the process.

Managing and interpreting interview data is difficult. In interviewing small numbers of people or even one person, some of the problems of large-scale survey research do not arise. With small interview samples, it should not be necessary to devise schemes to codify the data in order to process them on a computer. Bias in several forms can enter into the analysis of the information reported on small samples. If the interview situation were warm and congenial, the researcher might unconsciously accept the opinions and information in a less-than-critical manner. Or, if the researcher sensed a hostile attitude on the part of an interviewee, he may reject the information out of hand.

Even if the researcher's feelings could be set aside, the problem of whether or not to accept the respondent's replies at face value still remains. Consciously or unconsciously, the interviewee may distort replies in several ways. In other words,

> How much help any given report of an informant will be in reconstructing "objective reality" depends on how much distortion has been introduced into the report and how much we can correct for this distortion.[32]

The means to correct this problem are essentially intuitive. Basically, they all involve checking the plausibility of the respondent's account. The reliability of the respondent is open to question if, after checking with other sources, his information cannot be verified. Any information that cannot be corroborated, by other interviewees or by reference to other sources, would be suspect and probably dismissed.[33] However, the fact that a respondent misleads the interviewer can be revealing and can open up other avenues for the researcher. This is especially true in elite interviewing.

The in-depth interview, then, can be a highly useful device to elicit information from a broad range of subjects. However, given the limited number of subjects who can conceivably be interviewed, it is best to supplement this technique with other data collection devices when feasible.

DATA MANAGEMENT

Once the data are acquired, using one or more techniques of collection, the researcher must decide how to analyze the data. If he has gathered data from one or several in-depth interviews, the amount of data can be easily sorted out. However, when analyzing observer data, aggregate data, or survey research data, the task of data management becomes more complex as the researcher tries to put his data into meaningful form.

The rapid development of computer technology has facilitated the analysis of large bodies of data and may even account in part for the rapid adoption of the empirical approach in the social sciences. When the researcher is aware that he can now analyze surveys of thousands of persons or combine census and election records covering many years, he is more willing to use data-based techniques of analysis. In this section we shall highlight some of the considerations facing the empirical researcher in managing his or her data and suggest how such techniques can raise further problems.

Coding

When we took surveys in high school, with a few hundred students comprising our sample, it was easy to spend an afternoon with a friend sorting through the questionnaires. All those who liked the cafeteria lunches in this pile, those who disliked the lunches in another pile. Count the results, perhaps calculate a percentage to impress the principal, then recombine the piles and start sorting out the next question. As primitive as this technique may be, it is basically how computers operate. The political scientist must first set up a classification system for handling large bodies of data, and the computer then sorts the data according to the categories created by the researcher. The classification system is referred to as the coding scheme, and it has its own governing principles, which are quite simple and easy to understand.

We start with a simple Hollerith card.* The card has 80 columns which can be used singly or in combination with others to provide the structure for the coding scheme. We shall return to our earlier example of congressional response to presidential vetoes to explain how a computer punchcard is coded. In any recent Congress there will be 435 representatives and 100 senators; data on each

---

*So called after the sociologist, Herman Hollerith, who devised the punchcard for use in the 1890 census.

legislator will occupy a single punchcard. Additional cards can be used as needed. *The same data (or variables) for each person or case are to appear in the same columns throughout.* Since there are always problems associated with data, the first step in the congressional study was to assign a unique identification number to each individual; this number appeared in the same columns on each card.

Each column on the Hollerith card is numbered from 0 to 9, allowing us to have as many as ten different values. It would be sufficient to use a single column if we only had ten congressmen. However, we have 535, a three-digit number. We then select the first three columns of the Hollerith card to serve as identification numbers for our congressmen in the study. We use three columns because taken together they offer us the ability to enter three-digit numbers from 000 to 999. Our first congressman might receive the number 001, the second 002, and third 003, and so forth, through 535. At this stage, we begin to establish a codebook for the study (*see* Table 3–3).

TABLE 3–3. *Sample Codebook*

Card Column	Item
1–3	Identification Number
	001 = Congressman Jones
	002 = Congressman Smith
	003 = Congressman Brown
	.
	.
	.
	535 = Senator Green
4	Chamber
	1 = House
	2 = Senate
5	Party
	1 = Democrat
	2 = Republican
6	First Roll-Call Vote after Presidential Veto
	1 = Yes
	0 = No
	9 = Not Voting

On a sheet of lined paper, we enter the identification number for each congressman in columns 1, 2, and 3. No other congressman has that identification number. In column 4, we enter a 1 if the person is a representative and a 2 if he is a senator. A 1 is recorded in column 5 if the person is a Democrat, and a 2 if a Republican. If the congressman voted *no* on the first roll call, he is recorded with a score of 2 in column 6, and so forth. For a sample instance of coding based on this codebook, *see* Figure 3–3.

Information occupies every column on the Hollerith card. It is not necessary to use every column, but many researchers find it useful to fully code the card, i.e., to have something in every column for which there is a variable. If we were to code only five roll calls, this would take us through column 10. If a congressman did not vote on a particular bill, a 9 would be recorded to indicate missing data; therefore, there would be data in every column (1–10) for every congressman. The remaining 70 columns of the 80-column card would then be blank.

In some instances, coding schemes suggest themselves. In other instances, we cannot assume a scheme. In survey research, for example, a close-ended question, to which the respondent might give a "yes" or "no" reply, is easily coded. For open-ended questions, however, there is substantial room for error in the way in which the information is coded. There may also be an unconscious bias in the coding scheme. Finally, the range of potential responses does not represent a particular problem since there is ample room on a Hollerith card for coding a wide range of responses.[*]

It is necessary to establish a coding scheme that classifies responses into useful categories but does not lose the impact of an extended verbal response. In establishing categories, the researcher may be guided by previous work, but he must also be prepared to make exceptions.[34]

Once the coding scheme has been established, the method of sorting responses into categories while coding begins. Let us assume that we already have a range of broad categories to cover why someone approves or disapproves of a candidacy. We have set up categories, such as domestic policy preference, foreign policy prefer-

---

[*]If a single column allows 10 responses to be coded (0–9) and two columns allow 100 responses to be coded (00–99), three columns will allow 1,000 responses to be coded, and so on.

Column						Interpretation
1	2	3	4	5	6	
0	0	1	1	1	1	Jones, House, Democrat, *Yes*
0	0	2	1	2	1	Smith, House, Republican, *Yes*
5	3	5	2	1	2	Green, Senate, Democrat, *No*

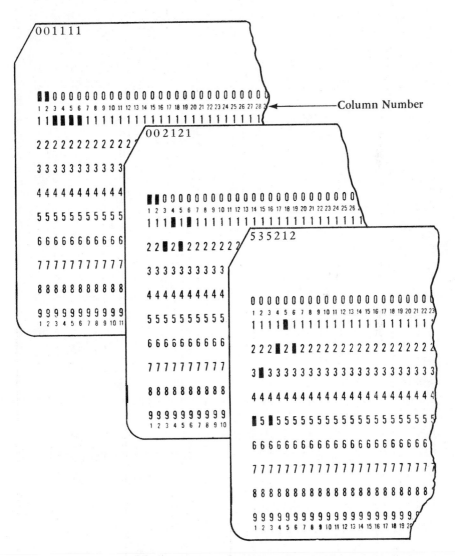

FIGURE 3–3
Sample Coding According to Codebook

ence, and the candidate's party affiliation. How are we to deal with a response such as "I don't know," or "I just like him." Have we provided for this possibility? Further, will two or more coders agree on the way to code a response? Has the reliability of each coder been established? A series of decision rules are necessary to guide those who code responses to questions; these must be clear and explicit so that all coders would do the same thing if confronted with the same situation. One could devise procedures to check and double-check coders, but this implies greater costs of time and personnel. A researcher can also resort to statistical tests of reliability of coders.

Obviously, much time and effort is expended on the coding process. It is a source of potential error, and the researcher must use every means and facility at his command to minimize errors and to reduce them as much as possible, lest the validity of the study be undone by sloppy work at this stage. It would be exasperating indeed if one were to go to great effort to assemble various data sources and then to imprecisely prepare the material for computer-assisted analysis.

Processing

Once the materials have been coded, they must be put in what is known as "machine-readable form"; that is, raw numbers have to be put into a form which a computer can "read." The coding process is merely an interim step in this procedure, reducing a range of variables to numerical categories. In this section we shall discuss the several means by which data are put into a form comprehensible to a computer, as well as how the materials are processed by computers.

Punching. There are two major means by which the coded data can be converted to punches or holes or a Hollerith card: optical scanner sheets and keypunches. The *optical scanner* is a device that converts pencil marks on a sheet of paper to punches on a card. Those who have taken multiple-choice examinations in large groups are familiar with this procedure. If you took the Scholastic Aptitude Examinations or their equivalent in high school, you recorded your responses on a sheet of paper, carefully marking your response as a letter or as a number. This is a self-coding process, and the possibility or coder error is reduced somewhat. The optical scanner converts the pencil marks to punches on cards, and the cards are then "read" by a computer and thereby computed.

Probably the more common way of processing a card is by keypunching. The *keypunch* is a device with a keyboard much like a typewriter keyboard. There is no lower case for letters, since all information is recorded in upper case or capitals, except for numbers. The operator of a keypunch sits in front of the machine and carefully reads the coding sheet on which you have entered information, such as that in Table 3–3, and "types" or "punches" the information onto Hollerith cards, in the precise columns indicated.

There is substantial room for error in this process and in the use of optical scanners, so it is often necessary to engage in a verification procedure. A device very closely resembling the keypunch and called a *verifier* is used to check the keypunching. Someone other than the keypuncher takes the punched cards, puts them into the *verifier*, and repunches the data. The verifier does not actually punch the data, but indicates that an error has been made when the hole in the card does not physically match what the verifier has just entered. For instance, if a Hollerith card has been punched with a "5" in column 37, and the verifier operator punches a "6" in that column, one of the two is wrong. A correction can be made if necessary. The other procedure, "sight verification," is immensely more time-consuming, but may be necessary in certain circumstances. In this procedure, the punchcards are conveniently "listed" on a *printer*, which provides a computer printout of all the punched cards. This printout accurately reproduces all the information that has been punched into the 80 columns of the Hollerith card. By comparing—card by card and column by column—the information on the printout with the original coding, it may be possible to locate errors in the punching process. For extensive sets this can be very time-consuming and tedious; it may also explain why so many political scientists wear glasses and mutter under their breaths.

Unit record equipment. The keypunch and the verifier are forms of "hardware," as it is known in machine processing, which are useful in preparing material for the computer. We refer to these items as unit record equipment. Other hardware which a well-equipped computer or data center may have might be a *card-sorter*. This is a machine into which one places the punched cards to get accurate counts, by column, of the codes that have been entered; they may be useful in verifying the data as well. The card-sorter operates at high speed, usually faster than 500 cards per minute, to sort the cards into bins, each bin representing a hole punched in that card. In our sample coding in Figure 3–3, if the punching is correct, when we "sort on" column 6 for the three cards represented, there should be two cards in the bin representing the number 1, and one card in the bin representing the number 0. If any number from 2 to 8 should appear, we would know that there is an error either in coding or in punching, since our codebook (Table 3–3) allows only the numbers 1, 0, and 9 for column 6. We could then locate and correct the card quickly.

Collators, another type of unit record equipment, sort cards together, commonly by the identification number. For instance, if we had had more than one card per case, we could have the collator merge the cards on the identification number, placing the first card before the second card for each case, and so forth.

Reproducers are machines that allow us to reproduce the punched cards so that we have duplicate decks of cards, an essential precaution in most data-processing applications. Decks can be easily destroyed, or folded, spindled, and mutilated beyond recognition, so it is generally advisable to have a spare deck of cards. This machine also facilitates a common practice among empirical political scientists of providing duplicate data decks for other individuals wishing to engage in secondary analysis using the data. In a matter of a few minutes the original data deck can be easily reproduced to send to others who have requested the opportunity to analyze the data.

An *interpreter* is also a useful device, since it can print at the top of the cards the information that has been punched in the respective columns. If printed information from the cards is missing on the reproduced deck, the interpreter can be used to print the information, column by column, at the top of the cards.

This description is not exhaustive and only serves as an introduction to the student. There are other kinds of unit record equipment in computer centers, and the student may profit from an informal visit to his or her local installation. Most personnel associated with academic computer centers are more than willing to give of their time and energy to help others in the most simple and the most complex tasks. An informal tour of the machine room can probably overcome "computeritis," and can offer ideas on how computer hardware can be used to facilitate research.

Computers. While there is a wide variety of computers, ranging from the very small and uncomplicated to the extremely large and complex, most share certain common characteristics. They all receive information from an input device, process it, and deliver it through an output device.

There are several input devices. The most common is the card reader, a machine that "reads" the data, according to the dictates of the program. The program itself is a set of instructions to the computer in a "language" which the computer can "understand." For instance, using our previous example of a coding scheme, a program can be inserted in the card reader before the data deck that instructs the computer to read only the columns dealing with party and the first roll-call vote. The card reader then reads only columns 5 and 6. Other input devices include paper tape readers and teletypes (typewriters linked to the computer). Any input device can only operate on instructions contained in a program.

The program itself may perform a number of operations. Whatever input device is used (cards, paper tape, magnetic tape, etc.), the program will instruct the computer to perform an operation or series of operations, such as constructing a table with columns and rows neatly labeled or calculating percentages and statistics.

At this point we should emphasize that computers are not "smart." They can only perform the simplest of tasks. Their virtue lies in their ability to do repetitive tasks of varying simplicity or complexity at extremely high speeds. In simple arithmetic terms, they can only add, subtract, multiply, and divide. They do not "know" how to do these tasks, but can only do so by the instructions provided in the program. If the program is in error, then the computations will be in error. If the data the computer reads are not precisely where it has been told to find the data (e.g., columns 5 and 6 in our example), it cannot find the data and correct the problem. If it has been programmed to calculate a percentage incorrectly, it will do so, precisely as programmed, and never "know" the error. An old acronym in computer processing and programming is GI = GO, or "Garbage In = Garbage Out."

For many processing applications, it may not even be necessary for the researcher to write his or her own program. Most computers are supplied with a series of programs to perform the most common tasks. The researcher need only consult the program library at his computer installation, secure a description of the program and how to use it, and follow instructions *precisely.* In addition to these package programs, the computer center may avail itself of certain large programs which are of special use to those in the social sciences. Some programs have become standard in computer installations around the world.[35]

Obviously, we do not bother to use the computer for all applications. However, when using large data sets, and when a repetitive task in which a high degree of accuracy is desired must be accomplished, computers are generally more efficient than sorting things out on the living room rug with some friends, as we did in high school.

After the information has been read and processed according to instructions, it proceeds to an output device. This may be a high-speed printer operating in excess of several hundred lines per minute, a card puncher in the event we need cards containing interim results for later processing, or magnetic tape. Again, the machine can only do what is instructed, within its own physical limits. If the computer does not have a magnetic tape capacity, it cannot react to an instruction that tells it to store the information on magnetic tape. If it has been told how to properly calculate a percentage, but the program does not use the word "percentage," but rather the word "elephant," the computer will print the word "elephant" next to the percentage. While it is often considered desirable for researchers to learn how to program a computer and thereby achieve a greater degree of flexibility, it is common for many political scientists to use only package programs, following instructions to the letter, secure in the knowledge that they have a series of instructions that the computer can use.

USING STATISTICS TO TEST HYPOTHESES

Knowledge in a discipline accumulates through careful and repeated testing of hypotheses, ultimately leading to the development of theories. How does one test an hypothesis?

Two types of statistical evaluation are found with some frequency in political analysis. The first of these is the degree to which two or more variables are associated, i.e., *association* or *correla-*

*tion.** The second procedure is to determine the extent to which a pattern of observations (such as the association or correlation of variables), occurs by chance. We refer to this as a *test of significance.*

To determine association, we ask to what extent two variables vary together. We shall continue to use our research problem of congressional response to presidential vetoes. Part of our hypothesis was that "the dimension of presidential–congressional support is independent of party . . ." We provided an operational definition of the concept "dimension of presidential–congressional support" by coding *yes* votes as "1" and *no* votes as "0" for nine roll calls. *Yes* votes were votes to pass the bills over presidential vetoes, exercises of a congressional prerogative. *No* votes were votes to sustain the president's veto. Our dimension ranged from 0 to 9, with 0 representing the strongest position in favor of the president and 9 representing the strongest position against the president. For purposes of simplicity, we instructed the computer to recode the information so that scores of 0 to 4 represent a presidential position and scores of 5 to 9 represent a congressional position. It is obvious that we are "wasting" a certain amount of data by subsuming the fine differences into only two categories, rather than ten, and perhaps risking oversimplification by reducing the number of categories. The results are shown in Table 3–4.

Statistical significance is measured by the chi-square test in this example. The measure of association was Contingency Coefficient C, adjusted for its highest possible value; hence, the notation C_{adj}.[36] In our four examples in Table 3–4, we find the following:

Table 3–4A, C_{adj} = .000, no association

    3–4B, C_{adj} = .068, virtually no association

    3–4C, C_{adj} = .275, weak association

    3–4D, C_{adj} = .411, moderate association

Thus, the degree of association between party, chamber of Congress, and presidential–congressional support varies considerably, depending on the ways in which we have structured the problem.

---

*Association and correlation do not necessarily have the same meaning, but for purposes of illustration, we shall consider them synonymous.

TABLE 3–4. *Scores on Presidential–Congressional Dimension, by Party and Chamber (Hypothetical Data)*

Table 3–4A

	Party	
	Democrats	Republicans
Congressional (5–9)	60%	60%
Presidential (0–4)	40%	40%
Total	100%	100%
N	321	214

$$\chi^2 = 0, p = 0, C = 0$$

Table 3–4B

	House Only	
	Democrats	Republicans
Congressional (5–9)	69%	64%
Presidential (0–4)	31%	36%
Total	100%	100%
N	261	174

$$\chi^2 = 1.0, .50 > p > .30, C_{adj} = .068$$

In Table 3–4A, it is fairly obvious, even without the statistics computed below, that there are no differences between the parties. On the surface, it seems that we have validated the first part of our hypothesis "that the dimension of presidential–congressional support is independent of party . . ." Within the House, although we notice a 5% difference between Democrats and Republicans, the statistic calculated below Table 3–4B data shows that the observed differences between the ways in which the two variables are associated is

Table 3-4C

Senate Only

	Democrats	Republicans
Congressional (5–9)	22%	40%
Presidential (0–4)	78%	60%
Total	100%	100%
N	60	40

$\chi^2 = 3.918, p < .05, C_{adj} = .275$

Table 3-4D

	House	Senate
Congressional (5–9)	67%	29%
Presidential (0–4)	33%	71%
Total	100%	100%
N	435	100

$\chi^2 = 49.246, p < .001, C_{adj} = .411$

Note: As a correlation coefficient approaches 0, it shows a weak relationship between variables. As it approaches 1.0, it shows a strong relationship between variables.

quite likely due to chance (between 30 and 50 times out of 100) and that the correlation is quite weak.* In the Senate (*see* Table 3-4C), the differences between the two parties are stronger and are associated by chance roughly 5 times in 100.† Further, the correlation coefficient in the Senate is stronger than it is in the House. When we

---

*For those skilled in statistical usage, the authors are aware of the problems of using C as a correlation coefficient. We have chosen it for illustration purposes only.

†In the behavioral sciences, .05 is generally considered the threshold of statistical significance, thus, any value of p equal to or less than .05 is "statistically significant." We discuss this in more depth later in this chapter.

ignore party entirely and compare the House and Senate (Table 3–4D), the differences are dramatic. Statistically, the observed differences of association between the House and Senate and the classification as presidential or congressional supporters are likely to have occurred by chance less than 1 time in 1000 times. We have substantiated the second part of our hypothesis—"the House tends more toward congressional support and the Senate more toward presidential support."

However, we must modify our findings for the first part of our hypothesis. Although Table 3–4A showed that there were no differences between the two parties on the dimension of support, Table 3–4C shows that there were real differences. Thus, we may say that for the House our original hypothesis suggesting independence from party is valid. For the Senate, however, this is not the case, because our data showed significant differences between the two parties.

Types of Data

Whatever the source of data, it can be classified for purposes of analysis.

The first level of measurement is described as *nominal-scale,* which is analogous to the classificatory concept. Numbers can be used to describe persons, events, or other categories of analysis in a classificatory sense. Thus, people may be Democrats or Republicans and voters or nonvoters. Similarly, they may have a range of occupations, such as doctor, craftsman, or clerk. Nominal-scale data have no underlying continuum, and these classifications are mutually exclusive.

Ordinal-scale data are classified on a comparative basis and suggest an underlying and continuous distribution of some quality. For example, a person may describe himself as a Strong Democrat or Republican, a Weak Democrat or Republican, or an Independent Democrat or Republican. (The examples chosen here are used by the Center for Political Studies at the University of Michigan to augment the traditional self-classification of individuals as Democrat, Republican, or Other.) The classification of voters then follows a continuum, such as Strong Democrat, Weak Democrat, Independent Democrat,

Independent, Independent Republican, Weak Republican, and Strong Republican. An ordinal scale for categories of low, medium, and higher education operationally defines these terms by specifying the number of grades completed, such as 0–8, 9–12, and education beyond high school.

Interval-scale data carry the classification process a step further and correspond roughly to the quantitative concept, although numbers can be used to implement the lower-level nominal and ordinal scales. Like the ordinal scale, interval-scale data assumes an underlying continuum or order, but this type of data also has equal intervals between the classifications and an assigned zero point. The example of educational level used for ordinal classification above would be modified in the following way to meet interval-scale requirements. We might set up a scale based upon an equal interval of four years of education, such as 1st to 4th grades, 5th to 8th, 9th to 12th, and completion of college. Income can be classified as $0 to $2,999, $3,000 to $5,999, $6,000 to $8,999, and so on. An equal interval is built into each categorization of education and income in these examples. Given these qualities, it is possible to assign numbers "with the positions of the objects on an interval scale so that the operations of arithmetic may be meaningfully performed on the *differences* between these numbers."[37] This type of data is rarely used in behavioral political science because it is difficult to establish a "common and constant unit of measurement."[38] A fourth way of structuring data is to establish a *ratio-scale.* A ratio-scale has a true zero point and the ratio between any two intervals on the scale is constant and independent of the measurement unit.

The differences between these types of data are stressed because proper statistical usage proceeds from this point; i.e., the appropriateness of every statistical test is determined in part by the level, or scale, of the data. When a researcher wishes to examine the data through the use of statistics, a proper determination of the level of the data used must be made. The choice of statistical test, whether of association and correlation or of statistical significance, is determined in part by the nature of the data. In the research example we are using, the party classification (Democrat or Republican) is clearly of a dichotomous nominal scale. The presidential–congressional support variable might also appear to be nominal, but some would argue that there is an underlying continuum (0 to 9) and that the data scale is therefore ordinal. Statisticians often disagree among themselves on these points, as do empirical political scientists.

One can also test hypotheses by drawing probabilistic inferences about the population studied, based on observations from a sample of the universe population. One can draw two types of inferences. The first, generally called *estimation,* involves estimating the true value of a population characteristic (called a *parameter*) from the estimate based on the sample data. For example, we take a random sample of 3,000 members of the voting-age population. From the responses of individuals to the question of which party candidate each will support in the next election, we estimate the population characteristic's value from observations based on a random or probability sample.

The second type of inference statistics involves *hypothesis testing.* For example, a research hypothesis is stated, indicating that association exists between two concepts in the population about which we wish to generalize. A null hypothesis is then stated, which posits that no relationship exists between the variables in the population we want to study. A statistical test appropriate to the type of data is selected, and the size of the sample population is determined. Generally, the larger the sample size, the lower the error, or the more accurate the results. A level of significance is set generally at .05. This means that if the distribution of our observations is so improbable as to have occurred in only 5 out of every 100 samples, then we must reject the null hypothesis.

Of course, in order to apply such a test, the sampling distribution of results associated with the particular statistic must be known. A sampling distribution would indicate the probability of obtaining each of the possible outcomes; for example, we could develop a sampling distribution for obtaining from 10 heads and 0 tails to 0 heads and 10 tails on the flip of a coin. Tests of significance are characterized in the following manner:

First and foremost, a test of significance is a formal procedure for making a decision between two hypotheses about some characteristic of a population (parameter) on the basis of knowledge obtained from a sample (sample statistic) of that population. Typically, one of these hypotheses, the hypothesis tested, is termed the "null hypothesis," and the other is termed the alternative.

Testing for significance involves a comparison of the differences between the sample statistic and the parameter specified by the null hypothesis with a theoretically determined sampling distribution. This comparison allows estimation of how often such a difference would occur if the difference were due to random errors in the sample selection process (sample error). The significance level that results from the comparison gives the relative frequency (probability) with which a sample statistic of the obtained size or more extreme size would be expected to occur over repeated trials (samples) utilizing the same probability sampling method on the same population if the hypothesized value for the population parameter (null hypothesis) were true.[39]

The null hypothesis is rejected if the probability of obtaining a statistic of that size by chance is sufficiently low. At what level of probability should the rejection of the null hypothesis be set? That is a function of the risks involved in making a wrong decision. Can one afford to reject an hypothesis of no association when it is in fact correct 10 times out of 100, or 5 times out of 100, or 1 time out of 100? That is a function of the subject under consideration and the hypothesis being tested, and it is up to the judgment of the researcher. This is one point in the research where the investigator's values may enter. It is important that the level of probability (.10, .05, .01) be selected before the test is made; this avoids introducing the unacceptable bias of adjusting the standard to the situation—rather than testing the hypothesis by a fixed criterion of significance.

We have essentially stated the hypothesis of congressional response to presidential vetoes in null (H_0) form by positing that congressional response was independent of party. In more precise statistical terms, we would state the hypothesis as: "there is no significant difference between the parties and scores on the presidential–congressional dimension." We may now apply a test to measure the statistical significance of the observed distribution.

The chi square (χ^2) is frequently used in political science research. In Table 3–4A, we accept the null hypothesis that "there is no significant difference between the parties on their scores on the presidential–congressional dimension." For the House (Table 3–4B), we must also accept the null hypothesis, but for the Senate we must reject the hypothesis, since we found statistically significant differences by showing that the likelihood of obtaining that distribution was approximately 5 in 100. The null hypothesis (H_0) for Table 3–4D data would state that "there are no significant differences between House and Senate on scores of the presidential–congressional dimension. However, we find that there are significant differences, and that the likelihood of obtaining those differences by chance is less than 1 in 1,000.

By rejecting the null hypothesis (H_0) we run the risk of rejecting it when it is valid. On the other hand, we may also commit the opposite error of accepting the null hypothesis when it is invalid. Since statistics only reflect chance and probability, we must accept these risks. However, we can now state with some degree of confidence and precision that the distribution is statistically significant. We provided a commonly accepted basis for examining distribution by employing a test appropriate to that end, rather than indulging in unsubstantiated guesses about the significance of the distribution.

Analytical significance is different from statistical significance, a point which commonly eludes novices in empirical research. Although data in tables 3–4C and 3–4D are statistically significant according to an established criterion (such as .05), they may or may not be analytically significant to the political scientist. Suppose, for instance, that Table 3–4D distinguishes between the House and the Senate on a question of no relevance to our hypothesis. A researcher might be hypothesizing a relationship between regional background and committee assignments. Even if the regional distribution of committee assignments in the House and Senate showed statistical significance, it would be of no immediate analytical significance to our hypothesis, which did not directly take this into account. Now assume that the question is relevant to the hypothesis, although the distribution lacks statistical significance. The nonsignificance should not deter the researcher from examining the meaning behind it. If the relationship is normally found by others to significantly differentiate House and Senate, it would be incumbent upon the researcher to explore the reasons behind the lack of significance he found in his research. The researcher is guided by a number of considerations, and statistical significance is merely one of his guides, not his tyrant.

The use of inferential statistics has certain requirements. For example, the sample must be drawn from the population randomly or by a known probability; otherwise, the sample results cannot be generalized to the universal population with any assurance of validity. To obtain a simple random sample, each individual in the universe under study must have an equal and known probability of being included in the sample, and each must have an independent chance of being included in the sample.

Reliability and Validity

Reliability. Reliability refers to the extent to which a measuring instrument produces consistent, precise, and accurate results. For example, if a student were to take the same exam five times and his responses to a set of multiple choice questions on the exams were to vary greatly each time, the questions would be said to be unreliable as a measure of knowledge of the subject matter. Other synonyms for reliability of a measurement instrument are *dependability, predictability,* and *stability.*

There are several methods of evaluating reliability, distinguished by their focus on its different aspects. The example in the preceding paragraph is *test—retest evaluation of reliability.* One could also develop two forms of the same test (or measuring instrument) and examine the extent to which scores on the equivalent forms are associated. Reliability could also be judged by dividing the test into equal parts and correlating the responses on the two parts. This method examines the internal consistency of the measuring instrument.

Validity. Four kinds of validity can be distinguished: predictive, concurrent, content, and construct. *Content validity* refers to the representativeness or sampling accuracy of the measuring instrument. For example, do the statements in an attitude scale measuring economic conservatism adequately sample the concept's possible range of content? Researchers generally agree that evaluation of content validity is largely based on the judgment of the researcher, although others may be requested to assist in the evaluation.

As an example of an evaluation of content validity, let us look at the most commonly used measure of the concept "sense of political efficacy." The researchers who first used this concept defined it as "the feeling that individual political action does have, or can have, an impact upon the political process, i.e., that it is worth while to perform one's civic duties."[40] Political efficacy is measured by an attitude scale constructed on the basis of agreement or disagreement with the following statements:

1. "I don't think public officials care much what people like me think."
2. "Voting is the only way people like me can have any say about how the government runs things."
3. "People like me don't have any say about what the government does."
4. "Sometimes politics and government seems so complicated that a person like me can't really understand what's going on."[41]

Do the four statements in the political efficacy scale adequately sample the content of the attitude, as defined by the researchers? For example, do individuals who block trains at embarkation terminals to prevent shipment of war materials feel politically inefficacious? If they thought their actions would not have an impact on the political process, would most of them still demonstrate? Such individuals could respond to all four statements in such a way as to indicate no political efficacy as measured by the scale, but still feel highly efficacious as that term is defined by the researchers. In other words, the content validity of the scale in this example is questionable because the statements do not adequately sample the wide range of political methods used in our political system to influence decision making.

When students sack the ROTC building on campus or demonstrate against government policies in a peaceful fashion, do they feel that this can affect political processes? If they do, but do not respond with the efficacious answers to the above statements, should they be classified as having a low sense of political efficacy? Were the demonstrators in the Chicago streets at the 1968 Democratic National Convention totally devoid of a sense of political effectiveness? Or did they believe that through their protests they could have an impact on political outcomes? The researchers' definition of political efficacy was appropriate at the time of their first election studies, but in a time of political instability, of questioning of the established political processes and institutions, and of the use of confrontation politics, their measure of political efficacy may well be lacking content validity.

External criteria are often used to evaluate research instruments. In this approach to validity, the researcher checks by comparing characteristics of the outcome to results obtained by other means; this is referred to as *concurrent validity.*

Predictive validity is obtained by evaluating the measuring instrument on the basis of outcomes obtained after the measurement was made. For example, a university evaluates the probable academic success of potential students on the basis of College Board scores and high school grades. The measure has predictive validity if, after students have been admitted, it proves to be a good measure of their academic success.

Construct validity evaluates the meanings of the concepts (constructs) involved in the hypothesis, law, or theory being considered. Construct validity is thus concerned with theory and theoretical concepts and empirical evaluation of hypothesized relationships. "One must try to validate the theory behind the test . . . there are three parts to construct validation: suggesting what constructs possibly account for test performance, deriving hypotheses from the theory involving the construct, and testing the hypotheses empirically."[42]

Let us consider a problem of construct validity in political science. Members of the United States House of Representatives have before them a bill to change the system of aiding persons of low income. The bill would abolish existing aid programs and replace them with income supplements that would bring incomes up to a minimum level specified by law. Under this system, the head of a household must accept work or training for work if he or she is physically able to do so. Let us focus on the problem of construct validity as it refers to the interpretation of the congressman's vote on this issue. What is the meaning of the vote in terms of what theories can explain it? One could argue that the vote reflects the congressman's attitude toward social welfare. Therefore, a vote for the bill would reflect support for aid to more impoverished members of our society. However, a congressman might view people on welfare as "do-nothing loafers," but support the bill because it would require able-bodied persons to work in order to receive income supplements. A third congressman might not have any clear understanding of the detailed and complex contents of the bill; he votes for the bill because the committee chairman argued it was a good bill. This congressman takes his voting cues from the relevant committee chairman. A fourth congressman may support the legislation because the president requested it, and as a member of the president's political party, his party loyalty guides his voting decisions. A fifth congressman may vote for the bill because an influential constituent asked him to support the legislation. A sixth congressman may support it because an interest group in his district urged his support of the bill. We have listed six different reasons for the pro-income supplement vote, reflecting attitudes toward six different objects and/or situations. The validity of using the roll-call vote as a measure of attitudinal support for income supplements *per se* is thus very dubious. Specifically, the construct validity of the roll-call measure is highly questionable.

The dependent variable (the variable to be explained) in the example above is the vote cast by each congressman. What theory and what concepts related to that theory can be used to analyze the dependent variable of the congressman's vote? Congressmen have a number of voting decisions to make on very detailed and complex legislation. Since each can have knowledge in depth of only a few legislative proposals, each must seek voting cues from respected sources who know more about a particular legislative proposal. Over a period of time, congressmen develop a pattern of cue-seeking and cue-receiving. One can examine the general pattern of cue-seeking and evaluate each congressman's vote on income supplements legislation to see if it follows or deviates from the congressman's general pattern of cue-receiving. In other words, the vote also can be explained in terms of decision-making theory. Other theoretical approaches can and have been used; for example, the vote could reflect a congressman's attitudes toward the party's stand on issues; attitudes of presidential support or opposition; or role orientations toward constituencies. In each case, the vote is conceptualized in terms of a particular theory, and the research attempts to validate the theory behind the concepts.

SUMMARY

In reading empirically based work, the student should pose a number of questions, including:

1. Does the research problem have substantive and theoretical significance, or is it trivial?
2. Is the hypothesis clearly stated?

3. Are concepts isolated and defined operationally?
4. Is the methodology explicitly stated? Is it appropriate to the ends of the research? Are other methods more appropriate?
5. Does the research reflect an underlying theory and design? Or does the design and execution of the research possibly serve to buttress the author's values?
6. Is the work consistent? Does it address itself to the stated problem, or does the author attempt to validate other unrelated hypotheses? Are the concepts consistently operationalized or do different value-laden interpretations skew the final work so that the author may only appear to have validated his hypothesis?

Although this list of questions is not exhaustive, it is a reminder of the precision with which empirical work must be conducted.

NOTES AND REFERENCES

1. Frank B. Feigert and Robert S. Getz, "Congress and the Nixon Vetoes: A Test of Burns' Four-Party Thesis" (Paper prepared for delivery at the annual meeting of the American Political Science Association, San Francisco, September 2–5, 1975.)

2. There are many available versions of what a research design should accomplish and do. One of the most useful is in Delbert C. Miller, *Handbook of Research Design and Social Measurement,* 2nd ed. (New York: David McKay Company, 1970), pp. 3–6.

3. James MacGregor Burns, *The Deadlock of Democracy: Four-Party Politics in America* (Englewood Cliffs, N.J.: Prentice-Hall, 1963).

4. Warren E. Miller and Donald E. Stokes, "Constituency Influence in Congress," *American Political Science Review* 57 (March 1963): 45–56.

5. Ole R. Holsti, *Content Analysis for the Social Sciences and Humanities* (Reading, Mass.: Addison-Wesley Publishing Company, 1969), p. 5. Emphasis added. Two good introductions to the subject are in Robert C. North, Ole R. Holsti, M. George Zaninovich, and Dina Zinnes, *Content Analysis: A Handbook With Applications for the Study of International Crisis* (Evanston, Ill.: Northwestern University Press, 1963), and Holsti, *Content Analysis.*

6. Frederick Mosteller and David L. Wallace, *Inference and Disputed Authorship: The Federalist* (Reading, Mass.: Addison-Wesley Publishing Company, 1964).

7. John W. Ellsworth, "Rationality and Campaigning: A Content Anal-

ysis of the 1960 Presidential Campaign Debates," *Western Political Quarterly* 18 (December 1965): 794–802.

   8. Phillip J. Stone, Dexter C. Dunphy, Marshall S. Smith, and Daniel M. Ogilvie, *The General Inquirer: A Computer Approach to Content Analysis in the Behavioral Sciences* (Cambridge: M.I.T. Press, 1966), *passim.*

   9. W. S. Robinson, "Ecological Correlations and the Behavior of Individuals," *American Sociological Review* 15 (June 1950): 351–57; Hayward S. Alker, Jr., "A Typology of Ecological Fallacies," in Mattei Dogan and Stein Rokkan (eds.), *Quantitative Analysis in the Social Sciences* (Cambridge: M.I.T. Press, 1969), pp. 69–86.

   10. (Washington D.C.: Congressional Quarterly, 1975).

   11. For a critical analysis of this problem, demonstrating how different results may be obtained by the use of varying levels, *see* Douglas D. Rose, "National and Local Forces in State Politics: The Implications of Multi-Level Policy Analysis," *American Political Science Review* 67 (December 1973): 1162–73.

   12. Austin Ranney, "The Utility and Limitations of Aggregate Data in the Study of Electoral Behavior," in Ranney (ed.), *Essays on the Behavioral Study of Politics* (Urbana: University of Illinois Press, 1962), p. 100.

   13. *See* Walter Dean Burnham, *Critical Elections and the Mainsprings of American Politics* (New York: W.W. Norton and Company, 1970).

   14. Samuel J. Eldersveld's and Albert A. Applegate's *Michigan's Recounts for Governor: 1950 and 1952* (Ann Arbor: Bureau of Government, University of Michigan, 1954) presents data showing a persistent 2%–3% error in favor of the dominant party, where there was minimal competition between parties.

   15. Compare, for example: K.W.J. Post, *The Nigerian Federal Election of 1959* (London: Oxford University Press, 1963), chap. VI; Richard L. Sklar, "Nigerian Politics: The Ordeal of Chief Awolowo, 1960–65," in Gwendolyn M. Carter (ed.), *Politics in Africa* (New York: Harcourt, Brace and World, 1966), pp. 151–52; and Federation of Nigeria, *Review of the Federal Elections, 1959* (n.d.).

   16. Edward A. Shils, "Social Inquiry and the Autonomy of the Individual," in Daniel Lerner (ed.), *The Human Meaning of the Social Sciences* (Cleveland: Meridian Books, 1959).

   17. Richard Fenno, "Congressmen in Their Constituencies: An Exploration" (Paper delivered at the annual meeting of the American Political Science Association, San Francisco, Sept. 2–5, 1975.)

   18. *See* Thomas W. Madron, *Small Group Methods and the Study of Politics* (Evanston; Ill.: Northwestern University Press, 1969), pp. 25–26. Sociometric diagramming, it should be noted, can be accomplished by using survey research data as well. In this case, the researcher is not necessarily driven to distraction recording the interactions of many individuals simultaneously. For an

example, *see* Samuel C. Patterson, "Patterns of Interpersonal Relations in a State Legislative Group: The Wisconsin Assembly," *Public Opinion Quarterly* 23 (Spring 1959): 101–09.

19. Robert F. Bales, *Interaction Process Analysis: A Method for the Study of Small Groups* (Reading, Mass.: Addison-Wesley, 1950).

20. *See* especially G.C. Helmstadter, *Principles of Psychological Measurement* (New York: Appleton-Century-Crofts, 1964), pp. 191–93.

21. There are several good sources that cover the fundamentals of data collection. One of the most comprehensive is Mildred Parten, *Surveys, Polls, and Samples: Practical Procedures* (New York: Harper & Brothers, 1950; re-issued by Cooper Square Publishers, 1966). Other useful sources include Herbert H. Hyman, *Survey Design and Analysis* (Glencoe, Ill.: The Free Press, 1955); Morris Rosenberg, *The Logic of Survey Analysis* (New York: Basic Books, 1968); Charles H. Backstrom and Gerald D. Hursh, *Survey Research* (Evanston. Ill.: Northwestern University Press, 1963).

22. *See* note 21, above.

23. Herbert H. Hyman, *Secondary Analysis of Sample Surveys: Principles, Procedures, and Potentialities* (New York: John Wiley and Sons, 1972), p. 9. Response rates to surveys seem to be dropping rapidly at this writing. Over a 20-year period, one major commercial poll noted a drop of roughly 25% responding. *See* "Public Resenting Polling," *The New York Times,* October 26, 1975, p. 58.

24. *See* Hyman, *Secondary Analysis,* pp. 330–33 for a listing of 17 social science data archives operative as of 1970. The Inter-University Consortium for Political Research is probably best known, with more than 225 colleges and universities as dues-paying members, receiving data for their own students and faculty. Philip E. Converse, "The Availability and Quality of Sample Survey Data Archives within the United States," in Richard L. Merritt and Stein Rokkan (eds.), *Comparing Nations: The Uses of Quantitative Data in Cross-National Research* (New Haven: Yale University Press, 1966), pp. 419–40, provides necessary comments for those who engage in secondary analysis; his discussion is based upon the Inter-University Consortium's data bank.

25. *See* Parten, *Surveys, Polls, and Samples,* chapters vii and viii for a clear discussion of sample types and how they are drawn.

26. *See* Parten, chap ix.

27. Herbert McClosky, *Political Inquiry: The Nature and Uses of Survey Research* (New York: The Macmillan Company, 1969), p. 125, provides an example of one variety of response—the "acquiescence" response—or the tendency to simply provide positive answers to questions.

28. *See* McClosky, *Political Inquiry,* especially pp. 18–69, for a review and critique of the contributions made by survey researchers and suggestions as to where and how the technique might be further employed.

29. An excellent guide to this approach is Lewis Anthony Dexter, *Elite and Specialized Interviewing: Handbooks for Research in Political Behavior* (Evanston, Ill.: Northwestern University Press, 1970).

30. Robert F. Lane, *Political Ideology: Why the American Common Man Believes What He Does* (New York: The Free Press, 1962).

31. M. Brewster Smith, Jerome S. Bruner, and Robert W. White, *Opinions and Personality* (New York: John Wiley & Sons, 1956), pp. 48–60.

32. John P. Dean and William Foote Whyte, "How Do You Know if the Informant is Telling the Truth?" in Dexter, *Elite and Specialized Interviewing*, p. 126.

33. *Ibid.*, pp. 126–28.

34. *See*, for example, the codebooks used by the Center for Political Studies at the University of Michigan in their biennial national surveys.

35. Some computer programs are quite well known, such as SPSS (Statistical Package for the Social Sciences), BMD (biomedical statistical programs developed at UCLA), and OSIRIS (developed by the Inter-University Consortium for Political Research).

36. For those who wish to pursue this matter, C is calculated by taking the value of the chi-square in the following manner: Where N = the number of cases in the problem,

$$C = \sqrt{\frac{\chi^2}{N + \chi^2}}$$

The maximum value of C (C_{max}) in a square table is calculated as $C_{max} = (k-1)/k$, where k is the number of arrays, either rows or columns. Thus, for a 2 X 2 table, the maximum upper limit for C is $\sqrt{\frac{1}{2}} = .707 \ldots$" And thus, $C_{adj} = C/C_{max}$. George A. Ferguson, *Statistical Analysis in Psychology and Education*, 2nd ed. (New York: McGraw-Hill, 1966), p. 235.

37. Sidney Siegel, *Nonparametric Statistics for the Behavioral Sciences* (New York: McGraw-Hill, 1956), p. 26.

38. *Ibid.*, p. 28.

39. Denton E. Morrison and Ramon E. Henkel, "Significance Tests Reconsidered," *The American Sociologist* 4 (May 1969): 132–33.

40. Angus Campbell, Gerald Gurin, and Warren E. Miller, *The Voter Decides* (Evanston, Ill.: Row, Peterson, 1954), p. 87.

41. Lester Milbrath, *Political Participation* (Chicago: Rand McNally, 1965), pp. 156–67.

42. Fred N. Kerlinger, *Foundations of Behavioral Research* (New York: Holt, Rinehart, and Winston, 1964), p. 449.

STUDY QUESTIONS

1. What is the rationale for a research design? What are the principal steps in constructing a research design?
2. Why are operational definitions of concepts essential to empirical testing and analysis?
3. Explain the differences between primary and secondary sources.
4. Discuss the principal strengths and weaknesses of:
   content analysis
   aggregate data analysis
   observational approaches to analysis
   survey research
   in-depth interviews
5. How do the principles of data management relate to the principles of empirical research?
6. How does one test an hypothesis?
7. Define and illustrate the several "levels of data." Why are their differences important in statistical usage?
8. What is meant by:
   reliability?
   validity?

PART
II

APPLICATIONS

The remainder of this book focuses on specific approaches to political analysis and examines a number of approaches to political theory. What do we mean by approach? An approach "consists of criteria of selection—criteria to be employed in selecting the problems or questions to consider and in selecting the data to bring to bear on it; it consists of standards governing the inclusion and exclusion of questions and data."*

Approach can be contrasted to epistemology, method, and technique. Epistemology *generally refers to theories of knowledge, and especially to the grounds for knowledge, including its validity and its limitations.* Method *refers to the means used to acquire and manipulate data. Statistical analysis, for example, is a method used to draw inferences in testing hypotheses.* Technique *generally refers to a specific data-gathering device, such as survey research, or to a statistical measurement, such as a correlation measure of variables.*

Empirical theory that focuses on the behavior of individuals is micro theory. Chapters 4, 5, 6, and 7 present four broad approaches to the development of micro theories of politics. None of these approaches is new. They are present in the writings of many classical political philosophers, but their current use in political science has been expanded and enhanced

---

*Vernon Van Dyke, *Political Science: A Philosophical Analysis* (Stanford: Stanford University Press, 1960), p. 114.

by drawing on contemporary psychology, sociology, social psychology, and anthropology.

Systematically arranged, micro theories contribute to macro theory, the study of larger units. Chapters 8 through 11 consider group theory, decision making, systems, and communication. Each of these approaches must consider the findings of micro theory to develop a valid macro theory, i.e., a theory that explains and predicts behavior. Micro and macro theories are not mutually exclusive. In considering groups, we must be aware that individuals affect group behavior.

The task of operationalizing the variables upon which empirical theories rest is difficult and demanding. Each of the macro theories we consider suffers in this regard to some extent, but this criticism does not necessarily mean that they are invalid. One of the tasks of theory being to guide research, we can say that the nascent macro theories have generally fulfilled that purpose. The development of a paradigm for political science is still necessary, but only by organizing our research around such broad categories as we now do can we ultimately hope to have a valid empirical theory.

CHAPTER
4

Personality

Personality can be defined as "the dynamics of organization within the individual of those psychological systems that determine his unique adjustments to his environment."[1]

APPROACHES TO PERSONALITY

A personality theorist emphasizes motivation as the key element of personality and elaborates a set of motives viewed as guiding human behavior.[2] Other theorists conceive of personality as a complex of attributes or qualities called behavioral dispositions. Personality can be examined in terms of consistency, development of structure, potential for change, integration and motivation and control.[3] The consistency of personality characteristics can be evaluated in terms of the individual style of acting, thinking, and perceiving. Some psychologists emphasize the early stage at which an individual's personality structure is established.[4] Other psychologists believe that changes in personality can occur after the basic structure has been developed.[5]

Personality actually amounts to a set of inferences we make which are described in terms of concepts. Personality characteristics are inferred by a number of methods, such as observing an individual's expressive movements, determining his ideas about his behavior, through structured questionnaires, or by ascertaining his goal-oriented behavior. The operational concepts used to infer personality do not completely account for the theoretical notion of personality. Operational concepts, such as motive, drive, habit, trait, and need, are more restricted in scope.

Why study the relationship between political behavior and personality? Behavior is a function of the environment or situation in which an individual is located and of the psychological predispositions which that individual brings to the situation. If we want to explain political behavior, we need to understand aspects of personality that contribute to psychological dispositions that precede political behavior. Behavior, of course, reflects personality.

There are several approaches to the study of personality. One approach focuses on the traits that individuals may possess, such as sociability, dominance, tolerance, and self-control. As such, it emphasizes the individual's characteristic pattern of response to certain situations or stimuli.[6] Related to this approach is the classification of types of personality: individuals sharing a trait or set of traits are characterized as authoritarian, dogmatic, introverted, inner-directed, or other-directed.[7]

Another approach is based on a stimulus-response theory of learned behavior. The processes by which an individual develops his characteristic patterns of response to various stimuli are the central objects of such studies. This approach focuses on the drive that initiates a response and the response that satisfies the drive. Satisfaction reinforces the connection between stimulus and response. Learning the appropriate response is promoted by establishing the association between cues to the appropriate response and the initial drive.[8] In political research we might explore how some persons learn to satisfy certain needs and drives through political activity.

A third approach, based on Gestalt psychology, emphasizes the perception of phenomena as a whole and the perceiver's drive toward ordering his perceptual field in the simplest and most orderly fashion.[9]

Psychoanalytic theory is used to a limited extent in political science. The difficulties of using psychoanalytic propositions and operationalizing psychoanalytic concepts are acknowledged by political scientists.

Theoretical approaches to the study of personality are diverse because one approach alone cannot predict behavior. Psychologists continue to try various approaches in an effort to develop predictive capabilities. Studies of the psychology of political behavior are one of three types: the study of individual political actors; the development of typologies of political personalities; and the analysis of aggregative effects of individual personality characteristics on the political system.[10]

EFFECTS OF INDIVIDUAL PSYCHOLOGICAL VARIABLES ON POLITICAL BEHAVIOR

Motivation and control are concepts of most psychological theories.[11] Motivation particularly is extensively used by political scientists in the analysis of individual behavior.

Motivation

Some approaches to the study of motivation emphasize biological factors; behavior is viewed as a response to innate drives, such as hunger, sex, and thirst. Other approaches focus on sociological derivations of motivation, where motives are considered to be formed through social processes. Approaches emphasizing drive imply that men and women are compelled to behave in certain ways. Goals, incentives, and rewards, which focus on the end to be attained by behavior, are emphasized by other approaches. In general, concepts of motivation basically view motivation as the process of energizing, regulating, and/or directing behavior. The construct of motivation was elaborated by psychologists to account for human behavior because other constructs were deemed inadequate for explaining behavior.

Aristotle and Thucydides incorporated theories of motivation into their political analyses. They said that the drives that impel men to political action are needs for honor or prestige, desire for profit or material gain, and fear of disgrace or of loss of valued things.[12] Plato's thought contains a theory of motivation in which he views man as being motivated to compete. According to Plato, competitive drives are controlled by the rational part of man's being.[13]

Maslow's Hierarchy of Needs

Abraham Maslow suggests a hierarchy of five basic needs that stimulate human behavior: physical (food, water, sex); security; affection, love, and belongingness; self-esteem; and *self-actualization*. [14] Let us consider the implications of this set of needs for political behavior.

Thomas Hobbes argued in *The Leviathan* that the absence of security in the natural order of human relations leads men and women to form governments, and regulation by government authority bestows security upon society. Governments that cannot guarantee personal security of their citizens are more likely to lack support for their incumbents and probably also for their institutional structures and rules of political conflict.[15] Maslow perceives the need for security developing only after basic physical needs have been satisfied.[16] A starving man will take greater risks and will not be as concerned about his personal safety as a man who is adequately fed. Men who fear for their physical safety will not be concerned with the need for affection.

Reports from the Soviet Union about the famines of 1918 to 1922 and the purges of the 1930s and from Nazi Germany provide support for these assertions. Concentration camp internees focused on their basic physical needs and needs for security, ignoring or denouncing others in order to obtain satisfaction of these basic needs.[17] The lack of satisfaction of physical and safety needs—or even the threat of inability to satisfy these needs—can contribute to riots and civil disorders. The Catholic–Protestant conflict in Northern Ireland, urban riots in the United States in the 1960s, and the draft riots in New York in the 1860s can be partially ascribed to a lack of fulfillment of the needs for physical and emotional security. Studies suggest that unemployment results in desocialization, political apathy, and political alienation of the unemployed.[18] People employed in occupations that provide insecure incomes may be more likely to have high rates of voting for left or radical-left authoritarian political parties. One-crop farmers, miners, fishermen, and lumbermen are included in this group.[19]

The need to be loved and to belong to a group ranks third in Maslow's hierarchy of needs. To what extent can this need be related to political behavior? Several studies indicate that persons relatively isolated from society are more likely to support radical political movements, of the right or of the left. The politics of extremism has greater appeal to the socially isolated and to those alienated from social institutions.[20]

The fourth-ranked need suggested by Maslow is the need for self-esteem or self-respect. Some writers indicate that this may be a significant motive for political activity, particularly among those who seek elective political office.[21] The drive for a sense of equality can be considered an aspect of the need for self-esteem.[22] The political manifestations of such a need were evidenced in the woman's suffrage movement at the beginning of the twentieth century, in the Catholics' demands for civil rights in Northern Ireland in the 1960s and 1970s, and in the blacks' demands for equality in the United States since the Second World War. Evidence shows that political instability and civil violence are associated with the unequal distribution of resources, opportunities, and values within political systems.[23]

Although the need for self-esteem may be a motivating factor for political participation, it appears that persons with very high and very low self-esteem are less likely to participate.* Persons who score high in efficacy have been found to be more likely to vote and to take part in spectator activities (e.g., talking to others in support of a candidate) than to participate in gladiator activities, such as attending rallies or working in a political campaign.[25] A sense of political efficacy is highly associated with an individual's sense of personal effectiveness.[26] Generally the more highly educated tend to have a higher sense of political effectiveness and a higher sense of political efficacy.[27] However, the association of political participation with personal effectiveness varies with educational level, the association being stronger among people with less education.[28]

Some would argue that those who participate in politics do so because a minimum level of need for belongingness has been met and because initially they have a strong drive to satisfy social needs.[29] Studies show that political activists originally motivated to participate politically for other than social reasons are likely to report current satisfactions as being of a social nature and to report a

---

*We previously discussed the narrow scope of the political efficacy scale and the consequent problem of the content validity of the scale (pp. 89–90). The narrow operationalization of the concept of political efficacy has been found to more readily identify particular forms of political participation, such as voting and political discussion. A scale that more broadly encompasses facets of the given definition of political efficacy also would tend to produce high correlations to other forms of political participation, such as protest marches, demonstrations, and other confrontation politics.[24]

decrease in other types of rewards derived from their continued political activity.[30]

The fifth-ranked need specified by Maslow is the need for self-actualization; i.e., the need to develop one's capabilities and to pursue one's interests. Government activities perceived as inhibiting or preventing self-actualization stimulate opposition to government policy. The pursuit of happiness was declared by the Declaration of Independence to be an unalienable right and a justification for a colonial revolution. Those who perceive their unalienable right to the pursuit of happiness to be hindered by the social system or the government are likely to oppose the policies, institutions, or processes they perceive as limiting their self-actualization. Opposition to the Vietnam War, which drained $30 billion a year in resources from desired domestic programs and expended considerable human resources, is one example of this phenomenon. Others include demands for community control of local schools, arguments for segregation or desegregation of schools, movements to preserve undeveloped land in national parks and to develop local cultural centers and training programs in the arts.

Political elites may be primarily motivated by the need for self-actualization.[31] Perhaps studies of recruitment of political leaders should include as a relevant variable the existence of alternative opportunities for self-actualization. In certain environments or social situations, politics may be perceived as the most efficacious way to attain self-actualization. In the United States, immigrant groups historically have obtained upward mobility through the political system.

Maslow's motivational hierarchy suggests explanations for certain aspects of political behavior. However, evidence for the validity of his hierarchy of needs is far from conclusive. Maslow's orientation is toward the formulation of propositions, not the careful testing of propositions through empirical research. His work lacks careful operationalization of concepts, and there is insufficient experimental research by others to permit appropriate assessment of the worth of his theoretical propositions.[32]

Other Interpretations of Psychological Needs

Conscious and unconscious needs are satisfied by political participation. Consciously pursued needs include economic gain, social adjustment, and meaning and understanding. Unconscious needs include needs to release psychic tensions, to dominate or to defer, and to gain self-esteem.[33]

It has been argued that individuals with high levels of tension withdraw from politics. Tension release, however, can be achieved through some form of activity, of which political activity is one alternative.[34] Similarly, aggression can be externalized by participation in a political movement, such as the Nazi movement, the Students for a Democratic Society, the Ku Klux Klan, or in a radical political party, such as the Communist Party.

McClelland posits three dominant needs: achievement, power, and affiliation.[35] National economic development is associated with an emphasis on need for achievement.[36] Others have studied the relationship between the distribution of McClelland's needs and patterns of national political stability.[37] McClelland's primary needs approach has also been used in the study of recruitment of politicians and their behavior in office. Individuals with high achievement and power needs and low affiliative needs may be more likely to become organizational activists. Interviews with political and nonpolitical organizational elites indicate that half the political activists come from politically active families, but none of the nonpolitical organizational elite have such backgrounds. Family activity in politics is thus important in teaching individuals with certain needs that those needs can be satisfied through political participation.[38]

Differences in patterns of needs may be related to differences in patterns of behavior in political office. For example, individuals with high affiliative needs tend to be recruited for office by others, having no motivating desire to hold office.[39] Additional support for this proposition is provided by one study of motivation, recruitment, and performance of freshmen legislators in a session of the Connecticut legislature.[40]

Political activists ranking high in need for power and low in other needs may have little interest in influencing policy, focusing mainly on control and maintenance of the organization. Individuals high in need for achievement and low in affiliative and power needs may tend to focus on policy matters rather than organizational control, but are not likely to persist in efforts to influence policy. Those oriented toward influencing policy, who persist in this interest and activity, have been found to rank high in need for power and need for achievement. These activists are also interested in organizational maintenance and control.[41] The research on which these generalizations are based relied on a limited amount of survey data; essentially, it measured responses from two groups of twenty-three political activists and eighteen nonpoliticians. Although the research is stimulating because it suggests other hypotheses, considerably more research is required before an adequate test of the hypotheses is made.

Research indicates that need for achievement has several dimensions, which are independent of each other: a sense of mastery over the environment, trust in people, independence of family ties, and a desire for occupational accomplishment.[42] Those ranking high in optimism strive for excellence in all assigned tasks, but those ranking high in achievement needs work hard only at tasks that are perceived as a challenge. This may distinguish managers from those who seek to build a financial empire;[43] or it may provide a distinction between those who become active in appointive or party office and those who seek elective office. High need for achievement appears to be promoted by a warm and nurturing relationship with one's parents, accompanied by demands for excellence, expressed in a nonauthoritarian manner.[44]

Working with McClelland's three primary needs, other scholars researched the following questions: How do nations differ in their patterns of motivational drives? How has this varied over time? How, if at all, are variations in patterns of needs within nations related to political behavior within and between nations?[45] Examining plays and ballads popular in England over a 400-year period, McClelland found that achievement motivation and economic production were closely related. According to these popular expressions, production rose about fifty years after an increase in achievement motivation. The ballads correlated with production twenty-five years later. The ballads were interpreted as reflecting working-class values and the plays as reflecting middle-class values.

The relationship between the types of motives and values emphasized in 1925 and production in 1950 in nations located in temperate climates were also studied. The indicators of motives were the stories in children's schoolbooks. The predicted relationship between emphasis on achievement in 1925 and higher economic production in 1950 existed.[46]

What is the association between motivational patterns and variations in political behavior? Countries in which the need for power is emphasized and the need for affiliation is much lower in importance tend to have authoritarian governments.[47] The rise in emphasis on need for power in the United States has been accompanied by an expansionist foreign policy. Does the combination of high need for power and high need for achievement in a society result in psychological stress that has unpleasant consequences? One study examined the relationship of motivational patterns in seventeen westernized nations in 1925 to deaths in 1950 from psychogenic causes. Psychogenic illnesses are divided into two types: those related to inhibition and repression (causing ulcers and high blood pressure) and those due to aggressiveness and acting out of impulses. The high need for achievement prevalent in Western cultures in 1925 was found to be related to a high incidence of deaths of psychogenic origins, especially inhibitive and repressive origins. High need for power was related to a higher death rate from causes related to aggressiveness and acting out of impulses. Anglo-Saxon countries tended to rank high in deaths from conditions related to inhibition, Germanic cultures scored high in deaths related to aggressiveness, and Americans in deaths associated with both aggression and inhibition.[48]

Motivations in developed Western nations may follow a particular pattern. Once a high need for achievement is present in a society, the desire to achieve—without suffering inhibition, repression, and resulting frustration—grows. Incentive for power is then generated, and manipulation and exploitation of others follows. The unpleasantness in such a society would result in an increasing need for affiliation, love, and a sense of belonging. In the United States, needs for achievement and power were emphasized from 1840 to 1910. The need for affiliation began to be emphasized in the 1920s in the literature of the country, continuing through the 1930s. The New Deal's rhetoric and policies were an expression of this need for affiliation. The shift to a need for power then occurred, evidencing itself clearly by 1950.[49] An examination of popular songs, movies, television entertainment, and literature of the late 1960s and 1970s would probably indicate an emphasis on the need for affiliation and an accompanying orientation away from an internationalist and expansionist foreign policy.

Several questions remain unanswered. Why does achievement motivation come to be the dominant need in a society? Does the same cycle exist in societies at various stages of modernization and in various types of non-Western cultures? What causes a decrease in need for affiliation and the predominance of some other need such as need for achievement or need for power? Does the introduction or increase in rate of use of electronic communications media affect the rate of change in the cycle of needs or does it induce a change in the pattern of needs?

Several criticisms have been made of McClelland's work using motivational theories. The definition of motive used by McClelland is "a reintegration by a cue of change in an affective situation." [50] The affective base for motivation suggested by this definition has been criticized as lacking a logical and an empirical basis. Criticisms have also been made of the methods used to develop indices of key concepts in the hypotheses. For example, a number of measures of economic development are possible, such as gross national product, production of electrical power, production of coal, miles of railroad track, or number of telephones. Different measures of key variables may result in different conclusions. The original aim of the researchers was to develop a measure of need for achievement in any area of endeavor. The actual content of their measures, however, places a heavy emphasis on economic achievement; hence, the content validity as a general measure of achievement motivation is questionable. As the research was conducted, a reconceptualization of the basic concept of need achievement occurred.

McClelland and other researchers using his conceptualization of achievement motivation have generally focused on describing the patterns of motivation in a society and correlating the described pattern of individual motivations with selected measures of economic development at a later point in time. This involves many problems of making inferences. Can one assume that analysis of plays, ballads, stories, or school texts provides an adequate measure of the distribution of motivation in society? What kind of indicator would one use to study the current process of transmitting values in the United States? Could one infer the motivational patterns of a representative sample of the general citizenry or of the economic elite from an evaluation of popular records, best-selling novels, or the most frequently watched television programs? Assuming the cultural indicators are valid and representative, do they reflect the dominant motivation or distribution of motivations among individuals and groups in society who influence the rate of economic growth and the level of economic development? The selection of cultural forms to be studied for the way in which they transmit values, and the selection of the sample of items within the forms, can produce an unrepresentative sample. The leap from predominant themes in selected cultural artifacts to inferences about predominant motivations for society is a very large one, and highly subject to criticism.

Using content analysis to determine the relationship of needs to political behavior also presents problems in research. Sufficient reliability in scoring must be developed so that several individuals can analyze the same material and assign the same score to it. A scoring manual has been developed for investigators using content analysis techniques to measure achievement motivation in an attempt to resolve this problem. Objectivity in analysis is judged to exist if a set of investigators apply a common set of evaluative standards with a high degree of uniformity. The predictive validity of the measure of achievement motivation has been demonstrated through the measure's high—or at least statistically significant—correlation with a number of other measures of achievement, based on accomplishment in normal activities or on achievement in experimental situations.

McClelland assumes that the general level of achievement motivation in a society at one time is directly reflected in economic decision making at a later time. A better explanation might be achieved if it could be ascertained that certain kinds of training promote higher levels of achievement motivation and develop characteristics that orient individuals toward entrepreneurial activities. Those with higher levels of this set of characteristics, of which achievement motivation is just one, are more likely to be recruited into entrepreneurial activities, with higher levels of economic development following from that. A society may be structured so that those ranking higher in achievement motivation are more likely to be recruited into some other social roles in the dominant elite groups, such as the military, the church hierarchy, the bureaucracy, or the official party. Further research is needed to examine the concomitant elements of the entrepreneurial role and the extent to which individuals with higher levels of achievement motivation and the full set of entrepreneurial characteristics are recruited into economic decision-making roles. McClelland and those who use his approach are still faced with unresolved conceptual and operational problems, which must be resolved before valid inference from the individual to the social level can be made.

Other approaches to aggregative effects analysis are found in the survey studies of national political behavior that seek to explain levels of participation, direction of the vote, party image or party identification differences, and variations in political ideology.[51] Several studies have examined the relationship of sense of personal competence, sense of political competence, and political participation. Persons in the study who scored high in personal competence were more likely to have a higher sense of political efficacy, to perceive the government as responsive to the public's preferences and interests, and to indicate higher levels of trust in government than individuals low in personal competence.[52] In a study of five developed nations, the relationship between competence and efficacy varied. However, individuals high in political competence generally tended to perceive the bureaucracy and the police as more likely to treat them fairly and to be responsive to the individual.[53] Situational differences in the five nations in part account for the variations found. Also related to the sense of personal competence and trust in others is political trust, with the more alienated ranking lower in competence and trust in others.[54]

Personal control has been examined for its relationship to political attitudes. Some individuals may be overcontrolled (restrained in personal relationships) and others undercontrolled (unrestrained). One study found both overcontrolled whites and blacks to be more politically conservative than undercontrolled whites and blacks. Both overcontrolled blacks and whites were lower in political efficacy than undercontrolled blacks and whites. Among whites, personal control was related to attitudes on civil rights; undercontrolled persons were more supportive of pro-civil rights positions. The study's authors concluded that personality control was related to aspects of the political belief system, even when variables of race and social status remained the same.[55] This study is not sufficient to confirm propositions about the relationship between control and political attitudes because it is based on a sample of 538 individuals in one southern city at one point in time, but it indicates the nature of the relationships that might exist, and promises further research in this area. Of course, the content validity of the political efficacy scale needs to be considered in any future research.

TYPOLOGIES OF POLITICAL PERSONALITIES

A typological approach to personality and politics, advocated by Harold Lasswell, analyzed the development patterns of certain politi-

112

cal types in order to understand what experiences contributed to the development of types of traits.[56] Typologies of political personalities did not originate with Lasswell. The traditional terms "reformer," "martyr," "anarchist," and "liberal" imply styles of thought and action related to personality differences.

Lasswell's developmental approach is expressed by the formula, $p \} d \} r = P$, in which p stands for private motives of the individual as they are structured by his relationship with his parental family; d represents displacement of private motives from the family to public objects; r equals the rationalization of the displacement in terms of serving public interests; and P equals political man. The symbol $\}$ means "transformed into."[57]

Lasswell characterized "agitator" and "administrator" as two types of political personality. The agitator stresses the emotional response of the public. He tends to characterize all opponents as all bad, he is undisciplined, and he tends to emphasize the principles behind an issue.[58] Administrators are distinguished by their displacement of affective (liking or disliking) orientations on more immediate objects, rather than on remote, abstract principles. According to Lasswell, the developmental processes through which individuals come to exhibit the administrator personality may be quite different.*

Presidential Types

Barber has more recently developed a typology to analyze patterns of presidential behavior.[60] According to Barber, a president's style, world view, and character establish a pattern of personality, which interacts with the power situation and expectations about presidential behavior. The relationships between the president's personality

---

*More recently Lasswell suggested another classification of personality types: The nuclear type denotes a person who devotes total interest and energies to a particular objective, such as gaining an elective office. Co-relational types are associated with a particular role and its pattern of behavior; for example, politicians may be typically aggressive, dominating, and gregarious. Lasswell's developmental type demonstrates not only the personal qualities associated with a role but also shows how those qualities are developed. Lasswell argues that politicians are primarily motivated to seek power and to seek it through a specialized pattern of behavior. Developmental types can be established by analyzing the values, indulgences, and deprivations experienced in youth, the behavior that reflects these experiences, and the psychological mechanisms used to adapt to these.[59]

and the two other variables—the power situation and the expectations of others—determine the nature of a specific presidency.[61]

Style is a president's usual way of performing his political role. Style has three components: rhetoric, or communication patterns; personal relations with others; and preparation for decision making and management of policymaking. Or, to use Barber's words, style is "a collection of habitual action patterns in meeting role demands. Viewed from outside, a man's style is the observed quality and character of his performance. Viewed from inside, it is his bundle of strategies for adapting, for protecting and enhancing self-esteem."[62]

A president's world view consists of his politically relevant beliefs. Particularly important are his views of the nature and causes of social structures and processes, of human nature and social conflict, and morality and value conflict.[63] Barber defines character as the way in which a president orients himself to life.[64] The most important element in character is the individual's sense of self-esteem. Understanding of these variables is facilitated by examining the development of character, world view, and life style. Barber asserts that character is mainly developed in childhood, world view during adolescence, and style during early adulthood.

Five concepts—style, world view, character, the power situation, and the expectations of others—cluster into four presidential types. Aspects of character include activity or passivity, which reflects the energy with which one performs a task. A president can be highly active, such as Lyndon Johnson or John Kennedy, or highly passive, such as Calvin Coolidge. The second dimension is positive-negative affect, which refers to a president's attitude toward his activity. Some presidents, such as the two Roosevelts, received great enjoyment from their activities as president, but to others the presidency has been a great burden.[65] These two dimensions result in four presidential types; the four types seek different goals through political activity and perform in different ways.

Barber characterizes George Washington as a passive–negative type, who accepted presidential office out of a sense of duty. Passive–negative types of personality are usually too inflexible to perform well in presidential office. They tend to withdraw from the conflict and to find refuge in procedural rules and moral principles. John Adams is classified as an active–negative president, who invested great effort in his role but derived little pleasure from it.

Thomas Jefferson is cited by Barber as an example of an active–positive type, who enjoyed the presidential role and devoted considerable energy to it. The fourth president of the United States, James Madison, is considered a passive–positive type; as president he was given to compromise and indecision.[66]

Former president Richard M. Nixon has been classified as an active–negative president.[67] A basic characteristic of an active–negative president is his drive for power.[68] Certainly the Nixon administration is noteworthy for the centralization of executive power in a few members of the president's White House staff. Barber sees the character of Richard Nixon reflected in his presidential rhetoric; Nixon's speech announcing the invasion of Cambodia stressed themes of power, control, self-concern, and fear of defeat.[69]

Barber views presidential styles as deriving from initial political success. If a person has engaged in a successful political act, he or she will generally continue to be involved in political activity. The situation in which a style is initially used is accompanied by development of new confidence, different patterns of adaptation to groups, and increased public acclaim and attention.[70] The researcher can evaluate the condition surrounding the initial political involvement in terms of the future president's motives, the resources a person has, and the opportunities available to him.[71]

Another example of typological analysis is Barber's typology of freshman legislators, based on level of legislative activity and willingness to serve for at least three or more additional sessions of the legislature. Besides motivation, the legislators' self-perceptions and strategies of adjustment to others and to the situation were observed. Characteristics of submission, aggression, displacement, and projection were also used to distinguish legislators.[72] The research applied psychoanalytic theory, in-depth interviews, and content analysis to aspects of political behavior. The limited number of cases on which the conclusions are based require additional testing of the hypotheses before the findings can be accepted. Studying freshman legislators in one legislative session or a selected set of elected leaders in one country is not an adequate sample with which to test a theory.

One typological approach frequently used in political analysis derives from the study of the authoritarian personality.[73] The genesis of the study was an attempt to isolate psychological correlates and antecedents of ethnic prejudice, stimulated by the rise of Hitler and the Nazi extermination of Jews. The study argues that extensive co-variation (two or more variables varying together) exists between anti-Semitic attitudes, other ethnic prejudices, political conservatism, and certain psychological needs and characteristics. Authoritarianism has been explained as the result of childhood experience within the family, particularly of rigid discipline, resulting in anxieties about status. Repression of these anxieties is accompanied by aggression toward figures of authority, which is displaced onto socially outcast groups, such as racial and ethnic minorities.[74] The researchers examined nine aspects in the F (fascism) Scale. The authoritarian personality was said to have the following characteristics: conformist and conventional values; submissiveness to authority; concern with power, toughness, and identifying with a strong leader; generalized hostility; projecting unconscious emotional impulses; tending to condemn and punish individuals who violate or reject conventional values; rigid belief system; unsubjective and unimaginative; exaggerated concern with sex; punitive attitude toward those who violate or advocate violating sexual norms.[75]

A number of studies have examined the political correlates of the F Scale developed by this research. Party identification is not related to the F Scale score; however, authoritarianism was positively associated with preferences for more conservative candidates and a conservative ideology. Differences in authoritarianism were related to variations in motivation for voting, but not to differences in rate of voting. Nonauthoritarians in one study rated higher in political efficacy than authoritarians. The differences within parties were significant; nonauthoritarian Republicans were considerably more supportive of federal social welfare programs than authoritarian Republicans were.[76]

Another study of a sample of the national electorate using a conservatism scale and short versions of the F Scale concluded that authoritarianism was not related to attitudes on specific issues. A negative correlation also existed between original and reversed items on the F Scale.* The results of this research discouraged the use of

---

*The standard authoritarianism scale contains agree–disagree items for which the agree position is the authoritarianism position. Because some people have a tendency to agree with any statement (this is called an acquiescent response set), half the items on the authoritarianism scale used in the election study were worded so that the disagree position was the authoritarianism position. If the scale items measured authoritarianism, there should be a strong positive correlation between the negatively and positively worded items. Instead, a negative correlation occurred.

the authoritarian personality scale in later national electorate studies.[77]

Evidence indicates that the emphasis by the original researchers of the authoritarian personality on ethnic prejudice and political and economic conservatism as component parts of the authoritarian's belief structure is unwarranted. The research has been extensively criticized from conceptual and methodological perspectives. The F Scale has been alleged to measure *potential* fascism, not authoritarianism.[78] The samples used to develop and to validate the scales were criticized as unrepresentative. Controls over relevant variables, such as the level of education or the sophistication of the individual, were not exercised. Also criticized were the statistical analyses made of the data and the failure to test alternative hypotheses.[79]

Can inferences about psychological characteristics be drawn from attitude questions? The way in which a question is phrased may force a response that is not one the individual would normally give. One cannot easily ascertain the significance to the individual of the content of the statement or of the response.[80] The role of other situational characteristics impeding or promoting the expression of prejudice has generally been ignored. Findings that less educated, less intelligent, and lower socioeconomic status individuals are much more likely to score high in authoritarianism suggest that the scale measures sophistication rather than authoritarianism. A counter-argument is that F Scale items correlate with authoritarianism because less educated, lower socioeconomic status parents tend to be more authoritarian and pass on those attitudes to their children.[81]

The lack of consistent relationship between scores on the authoritarian personality scale and specific beliefs and attitudes has been subjected to further analysis. The authoritarian may be distinctive in how he holds beliefs, but not in the specific content of those beliefs.[82] Peer-group opinions can strongly influence the authoritarian personality's expression of his views.

The concern with personality types has led to research on the nature of belief systems and their effect on political behavior. A belief system consists of all beliefs and explanations that the individual accepts as true. The converse, the disbelief system, consists of all beliefs and explanations he accepts as false.[83] Three dimensions are present in the belief system: a belief–disbelief dimension; a central–peripheral dimension; and a time–perspective dimension. The central-peripheral dimension has three components: a central region, which encompasses basic beliefs about the nature of the physical world, the self, and others; an intermediate region, which contains beliefs about authority and persons exercising authority over the individual; and a peripheral region, representing beliefs about the rest of the world. The time perspective refers to beliefs about the past, present, and future. This dimension varies from narrow to broad; a narrow time perspective focuses on one time period and a broad perspective incorporates past, present, and future. There are varying degrees of similarity between beliefs that are accepted and beliefs that are rejected.[84]

Some belief–disbelief systems incorporate logically contradictory beliefs and judge objectively relevant facts to be irrelevant. The extent to which differences within the belief system are emphasized and similarities are minimized can be evaluated. This can be judged by the degree of knowledge an individual possesses about his beliefs and disbeliefs, and the degree of similarity between disbeliefs.[85] For example, what amount of knowledge underlies an individual's beliefs and disbeliefs about the Soviet Union and The People's Republic of China? Does he believe that communism in the Soviet Union involves the same ideology and practice as communism in China? A third measure of the belief–disbelief system is the number of disbeliefs within a person's total belief–disbelief system.

A measure of a general authoritarian belief system, labeled *dogmatism,* has been developed. The distinguishing characteristics of this style are intolerance of ambiguity, rigidity, and inflexibility. The basic distinction of a dogmatic authoritarian style is between open and closed belief systems. Open-mindedness and closed-mindedness are determined by evaluating the degree to which an individual relies on authority to restructure his belief system. Yielding to others, resisting the predominant culture, and relying on authority all have a common cognitive basis. That basis is the extent to which an individual distinguishes between the substance of the communication and the character of the source.[86]

Critics have argued that data do not support the assertion that there is a left-wing authoritarianism. Survey studies of samples of the American voting-age population do not provide this kind of evidence. The dogmatism scale and the F scale were applied to samples of English Communists and adherents of other English political parties. The Communists ranked lowest on the F Scale and higher on the dogmatism scale, but the differences on the dogmatism scale were not statistically significant.

It can be argued that the key to the character of an authoritarian is that he has a closed belief system and that he changes his beliefs only when authorities to whom he is highly responsive advocate policies or perceptions at variance with his own beliefs. Nonauthoritarians require a different kind of stimulus before they change their beliefs, which would make them aware of the logical inconsistency between their preferred values and professed beliefs.[87]

THE ANALYSIS OF INDIVIDUAL POLITICAL ACTORS

The analysis of individual political actors focusing on the psychological correlates of each actor's response to a political problem has been limited. The focus is usually on a major political figure who, through his personal judgments and actions, had a significant impact on the course of history. The best-known example is the analysis of Woodrow Wilson. Two students have suggested that Wilson's relations with his father caused him to develop such unsatisfied needs and patterns of perceptions that in certain kinds of situations he tended to make inappropriate decisions. Wilson was dominated, ridiculed, and humiliated by his father as a child, resulting in a low sense of self-esteem. As president of the United States, Wilson refused to compromise on particularly important issues, such as the Fourteen Points, other agreements of the Versailles Peace Conference of 1919, and the debate over ratification of the League of Nations Charter by the United States Senate.[88] Wilson's inability to compromise on issues central to his interests was a consequence of common defense mechanisms, especially repression and reaction formation.[89]

Defense mechanisms, which distort or deny reality, are means of adapting to extreme tension or stress. A number of defense mechanisms have been enumerated by psychologists. These include repression (refusing to perceive reality); fantasy (gratification through imaginary accomplishment); projection (attributing the source of anxiety to the external world rather than to one's own acts, impulses, or mental states); identification (compensating for one's feelings of inadequacy through associating oneself with an individual or institution regarded as superior); displacement (displacing feelings of hostility onto out groups or individuals regarded as unworthy or inferior); reaction formation (replacing an anxiety-producing feeling with its opposite, such as replacing hate with love); regression (withdrawing to an earlier and less mature level of development); emotional insulation (behaving passively); rationalization (convincing oneself that one's behavior is rational and therefore acceptable); and compensation (emphasizing admirable traits to compensate for other deficiencies or deprivations).[90]

A limited number of studies have used defense mechanisms to explain the behavior of political actors. Besides Woodrow Wilson, other subjects have been James Forrestal, the first secretary of defense of the United States, who ended his career by committing suicide, and Anton Cermak, a Great Depression-era mayor and political boss of Chicago. Cermak was the first and last foreign-born person to be elected mayor of Chicago, and some would argue he was the strongest political boss in the history of Chicago.[91] Some of these studies have been strongly criticized because of inadequacies in conceptualization and operationalization of concepts, and the way in which evidence was presented to support the propositions. The study of Woodrow Wilson, completed by Sigmund Freud and William C. Bullitt in 1938, sought to examine the psychological basis for his actions. Bullitt and Freud, who strenuously disagreed with some of Wilson's policies, have been accused of injecting their personal antipathies toward Wilson into the analysis. The researchers do admit that they had only limited access to facts. Historical material relevant to Wilson's personality is limited, so certainly the ability to describe his personality structure is also limited. Before one can accept the validity of the analysis, one must accept the theoretical structure created by Freud and used in this analysis. Because of the biases brought to the analysis by the authors, the use of psychoanalytic theory, and the paucity of data available, the study is highly suspect.

The study of James Forrestal, the U.S. secretary of defense who committed suicide shortly after his resignation from office in 1949, exemplifies the difficulties presented by the psychoanalytic approach. A precise statement of explanatory propositions, careful definitions of terms, and an exhaustive search for evidence to test the propositions is difficult to achieve. There are no explicit propositions in the Forrestal study, and data for testing the propositions are inappropriate. Transference and projection of Forrestal's own personality needs onto policy recommendations is alleged, but the presence of his needs and their relationship to policy recommendations is not convincingly established. It is necessary to show that policy recommendations would not have been made if the personality needs had not been present; in other words, that an objective basis for policy recommendations did not exist.

Criticism of many psychological studies stems from their reliance on Freudian psychoanalytic theory, which overemphasizes the impact of early childhood socialization experiences on later personality and behavior. The impact of socialization agents other than the family and post-childhood experiences is given inadequate attention by the psychoanalytic approach.

Of what use are such studies for political science? They can add to the description of historical events, but do they contribute to the expressed aim of political science—the development of explanatory theories? The analysis of single personalities cannot validate a theory of behavior, although it can be argued that an accumulation of case studies can lend support to a theory. The weight of evidence is based on the attempt to explain behavior of a political actor that deviates from what would normally be expected from an actor in that role and in that situation. The first problem, then, is to establish what normal behavior is. Statistical variance and the significance of that variance are difficult if not impossible to establish by analyzing one political actor.

The psychological analysis of individual political actors should not be limited to actors exhibiting pathological behavior patterns.[92] The psychoanalytic approach can be used to account for role performance characteristics, as in the analysis of presidential or legislative behavior. The correlation between expectations applied to a particular role by others, personality characteristics, and individual style can be examined. This is particularly useful in studying patterns of political leadership and the relative success of particular leaders in a political office.[93]

Critique of Single Case Studies

Because psychological variables have an immediate relationship to political behavior, they are valuable topics for study. For example, if we are interested in voting behavior in the next presidential election, the psychological state of the individual and the immediate situation in which the vote is cast are the variables that are most contingent to the event of voting. This justification has been used by researchers to make a social-psychological analysis of voting behavior in which major explanatory variables are perceptions and attitudes, rather than the social and economic characteristics of the voters, characteristics commonly used by other studies of voting behavior.[94]

One researcher says that social variables constitute the environment that influences the development of psychological predispositions. Personality processes and dispositions can be classified functionally, considering dispositions as attitudes. Attitudes function to perform object appraisal, to mediate relations with others, and to maintain ego-defensiveness. As such, the first two function in evaluating the relevance and consequences of political situations and actors' activities for the individual and govern his relations with political actors.[95] The externalization and ego-defense functions have been emphasized in Lasswell's political man formulation, the studies of individual political actors, such as Woodrow Wilson, "Boss" Cermak, and James Forrestal, and the analysis of authoritarianism and of dogmatism.

Using psychological variables to account for variations in political behavior among individuals and nations presents several problems for the researcher. Some problems are methodological. Can one adequately assess the nature of psychological variables, such as alienation, through the use of scales measured by a questionnaire? Psychological analysis of individuals first examines behavior patterns and then seeks to identify the psychological factors underlying the behavioral patterns. The development of psychological characteristics in childhood and later in life are stressed, but the validity of inferences about the nature of childhood experiences and implications for personality of such experiences are difficult to establish.

The nature of a situation may place constraints on how and the extent to which personality influences political behavior. In some situations personality is more a determining factor. When an individual's reference groups are in conflict, when appropriate behavior is unclear or undefined, or when current expectations about appropriate behavior appear to conflict with expectations that applied in the past, an individual's personality becomes more directly involved.

Expectations of how political officeholders ought to behave may limit the range of behavior in office. If expectations do produce specific behavior, personality differences then would seem to have little influence. But even if the range of behavior is limited, differences can exist within that range, for example, variations in presidential style. Also, the limitations on the behavior of an occupant of a political position can be minimal.

Some argue that personality types are randomly distributed in various political roles. However, other researchers have presented preliminary evidence that tends to refute this assertion. A study of the recruitment of political and nonpolitical organization leaders and a study of the characteristics of legislators[96] indicate that some psychological characteristics of political activists differ from those of control groups.

Several general criticisms can be made of research on the relationship between psychological characteristics of individuals and their political behavior. The samples used to test the hypotheses are often unrepresentative. Researchers tend to develop research measures and to test hypotheses on captive populations of college students who in many ways are not representative of the general population. This has negative implications for the content validity and the construct validity of their research. Research instruments that may be appropriate for measuring the presence or absence of a variable among college students could be inappropriate for the general population. College students differ from the adult non-college population not only in age and educational attainment but also often in their value systems, range of experiences, and attitudes.

Where results are compared with established norms for a particular research instrument, the researcher may be unaware that the norms may have been established through research on individuals who are not representative of the adult population. Establishment of norms through testing measures on activist members of middle-class organizations is still quite common. When a research instrument is developed through evaluation of results from nonrepresentative samples of the population or through use with other populations, the content validity is suspect. Use of measures lacking in content validity then contributes to the absence of construct validity.

NOTES AND REFERENCES

1. Gordon Allport, *Personality: A Psychological Interpretation* (New York: Holt, 1937), p. 48.

2. Henry A. Murray, *Explorations in Personality* (New York: Oxford University Press, 1938), pp. 152–226.

3. Richard S. Lazarus, *Personality and Adjustment* (Englewood Cliffs, N.J.: Prentice-Hall, 1963), pp. 37–40.

4. *See,* for example, Sigmund Freud, *The Interpretation of Dreams,* A. A. Brill, trans. (New York: Macmillan, 1933).

5. *See,* for example, C. G. Jung, *Analytical Psychology* (New York: Pantheon Press, 1968).

6. Gordon W. Allport, *Personality.*

7. David Riesman, Nathan Glazer, and Reuel Denney, *The Lonely Crowd* (Garden City, N.Y.: Doubleday and Company, 1953); Harold D. Lasswell, *Psychopathology and Politics* (New York: The Viking Press, 1960); James David Barber, *The Lawmakers* (New Haven: Yale University Press, 1965).

8. *See,* for example, Neal E. Miller and John Dollard, *Social Learning and Imitation* (New Haven: Yale University Press, 1941).

9. For Gestalt theory, *see* Wolfgang Kohler, *Gestalt Psychology* (New York: Liveright, 1929) and Kurt Koffka, *Principles of Gestalt Psychology* (New York: Harcourt, Brace, 1935). Gestalt psychology has influenced social psychologists whose work in turn has influenced political scientists in their studies of political behavior. For psychoanalytic theories, *see* Erik Erikson, *Childhood and Society* (New York: W. W. Norton, 1950); *The Basic Writings of Sigmund Freud,* A. A. Brill, ed. (New York: Random House, 1938); C. G. Jung, *The Integration of Personality* (New York: Farrar and Rinehart, 1939); Karen Horney, *The Neurotic Personality of Our Time* (New York: W. W. Norton, 1937).

10. Fred I. Greenstein, *Personality and Politics* (Chicago: Markham Publishing Company, 1969).

11. Richard Lazarus, *Personality and Adjustment.*

12. *The Politics of Aristotle,* Ernest Barker, trans. (London: Oxford University Press, 1958), Book V, chap. 11; *The Complete Writings of Thucydides,* John H. Finley, Jr., trans. (New York: The Modern Library, 1951).

13. *Timaeus,* in *The Dialogues of Plato,* B. Jowett, trans. (New York: Random House, 1937), vol. II, 69 ff.

14. Abraham Maslow, "A Theory of Human Motivation," *Psychological Review* 50 (1943): 370–96; *Motivation and Personality* (New York: Harper & Row, 1954).

15. Thomas Hobbes, *The Leviathan,* Michael Oakeshott, ed. (Oxford, Eng.: Basil Blackwell, 1960).

16. Maslow, *Motivation and Personality,* pp. 80–92.

17. Pitirim A. Sorokin, *Man and Society in Calamity* (New York: E. P. Dutton and Company, 1942); Eugenia S. Ginzburg, *Into the Whirlwind* (Harmondsworth, Middlesex, England: Penguin Books, 1968); Bruno Bettelheim, "Individual and Mass Behavior in Extreme Situations," *Journal of Abnormal and Social Psychology* 38 (1943): 417–52.

18. George C. Homans, *The Human Group* (New York: Harcourt, Brace, and World, 1950), pp. 334–51; Mira Komarovsky, *The Unemployed Man and His Family* (New York: Dryden Press, 1940), pp. 112–22; E. Wright Bakke, *Citizens Without Work* (New Haven: Yale University Press, 1940), pp. 46–70;

Michael Aiken, Louis A. Ferman, and Harold L. Sheppard, *Economic Failure, Alienation, and Extremism* (Ann Arbor: University of Michigan Press, 1968).

19. Seymour Martin Lipset, *Political Man* (Garden City, N.Y.: Doubleday and Company, 1960), p. 231.

20. *Ibid.*, p. 175.

21. Harold D. Lasswell, *Politics: Who Gets What, When, How* (New York: Meridian Press, 1958), p. 13; Barber, *The Lawmakers,* pp. 217–25.

22. James C. Davies, *Human Nature in Politics* (New York: John Wiley and Sons, 1963), pp. 45–63.

23. *See* Hayward R. Alker, Jr., *Mathematics and Politics* (New York: Macmillan, 1965), pp. 108–10.

24. For a discussion of the political efficacy scale, *see* Angus Campbell, Gerald E. Gurin, and Warren E. Miller, *The Voter Decides* (Evanston, Ill.: Row, Peterson, and Company, 1954), pp. 187–94; Lester Milbrath, *Political Participation* (Chicago: Rand McNally, 1965), pp. 156–57.

25. Milbrath, *Political Participation,* pp. 56–57.

26. *Ibid.*

27. *Ibid.*, p. 59.

28. *Ibid.*, p. 57.

29. *Ibid.*, p. 58.

30. Samuel J. Eldersveld, *Political Parties* (Chicago: Rand McNally, 1964), p. 287; M. Margaret Conway and Frank B. Feigert, "Motivation, Incentive Systems, and the Political Party Organization," *American Political Science Review* 62 (December 1968): 1170.

31. Davies, *Human Nature in Politics,* p. 61.

32. For an extended discussion of the application of Maslow's need hierarchy to political behavior analysis, *see* Jeanne Knutson, *The Human Basis of the Polity* (Chicago: Aldine-Atherton, 1972). *See also* Stanley Renshon, *Psychological Needs and Political Behavior* (New York: The Free Press, 1974).

33. Robert E. Lane, *Political Life* (Glencoe, Ill.: The Free Press, 1959), pp. 101–31. *See also* Graham Wallas, *Human Nature in Politics* (Lincoln: University of Nebraska Press, 1962), pp. 53–61; Harold D. Lasswell, *Politics,* pp. 1, 26–27.

34. Davies, *Human Nature in Politics,* chap. 3; John Dollard, Neal E. Miller, Leonard W. Doob, O. H. Mowrer, and Robert R. Sears, *Frustration and Aggression* (New Haven: Yale University Press, 1939), chap. 7; Lane, *Political Life,* pp. 115–24.

35. *See* David C. McClelland, *The Achieving Society* (New York: The Free Press, 1961), pp. 36–62, for a discussion of the concepts and measurement procedures.

36. *Ibid.*, pp. 89–97.

37. Stanley A. Rudin, "The Personal Price of National Glory," *Trans-Action* 2 (Sept.–Oct. 1965): 4–9.

38. Rufus Browning, "The Interaction of Personality and Political System in Decision to Run for Office: Some Data and a Simulation Technique," *Journal of Social Issues* 24 (July 1968): 98.

39. *Ibid.*, p. 103.

40. Barber, *The Lawmakers*, pp. 214–17.

41. Browning, "Interaction of Personality and Political System," p. 103.

42. *See* Bernard Berelson and Gary Steiner, *Human Behavior* (New York: Harcourt, Brace, and World, 1964), p. 260; Roger Brown, *Social Psychology* (New York: The Free Press, 1965), chap. 9.

43. McClelland, *Achieving Society*, pp. 227–28.

44. *See* the discussion on research on the subject in Edward Zigler and Irvin L. Childs, "Socialization," in *Handbook of Social Psychology*, Gardner Lindzey and Elliot Aronson, eds. (Reading, Mass.: Addison-Wesley, 1969), vol. III, pp. 543–54.

45. Rudin raises these questions and indicates the various approaches being used to provide answers in Rudin, "Personal Price of National Glory."

46. McClelland, *Achieving Society*, passim.

47. *See* Rudin, "Personal Price of National Glory," p. 6.

48. *Ibid.*, pp. 6–8.

49. *Ibid.*, p. 9.

50. D. C. McClelland, J. W. Atkinson, R. A. Clark, and E. L. Lowell, *The Achievement Motive* (New York: Appleton-Century, 1953), p. 28.

51. John P. Robinson, Jerrold G. Rusk, and Kendra B. Head, *Measures of Political Attitudes* (Ann Arbor: Center for Political Studies, Institute for Social Research, 1968), pp. 649–99.

52. *See* Milbrath, *Political Participation*, pp. 59–60, 80.

53. Gabriel Almond and Sidney Verba, *The Civic Culture* (Princeton, N.J.: Princeton University Press, 1963), pp. 214– 21.

54. Milbrath, *Political Participation*, p. 80; Almond and Verba, *Civic Culture*, p. 285.

55. James W. Dyson and Douglas St. Angelo, "Personality and Political Orientation," *Midwest Journal of Political Science* 12 (May, 1968): 202–23.

56. Harold D. Lasswell, *Psychopathology and Politics.*

57. *Ibid.*, pp. 74–75.

58. *Ibid.*, p. 78.

59. For a complete discussion of these types, *see* Harold D. Lasswell, "A Note on 'Types' of Political Personality: Nuclear, Co-relational, and Developmental," *The Journal of Social Issues* 24 (July 1968): 81–91.

60. James David Barber, *The Presidential Character* (Englewood Cliffs, N.J.: Prentice-Hall, 1972).

61. *Ibid.*, pp. 6–7.

62. *Ibid.*, p. 7.

63. James David Barber, "Classifying and Predicting Presidential Styles: Two Weak Presidents," *Journal of Social Issues* 24 (July 1968): 52.

64. Barber, *The Presidential Character*, p. 7–8.

65. *Ibid.*, p. 8.

66. *Ibid.*, pp. 11–13.

67. *Ibid.*, pp. 13–14.

68. *Ibid.*, p. 422.

69. *Ibid.*, p. 441. For other analyses of Richard M. Nixon, *see* Eli S. Cheesen, *President Nixon's Psychiatric Profile* (New York: Peter H. Wyden, Publisher, 1973), and Bruce Mazlish, *In Search of President Nixon* (New York: Basic Books, 1972).

70. Barber, "Classifying and Predicting Presidential Styles," p. 61.

71. *Ibid.*, p. 62.

72. *Ibid.*, passim.

73. T. W. Adorno, Else Frenkel-Brunswik, Daniel J. Levinson, and R. Nevitt Sanford, *The Authoritarian Personality* (New York: Science Editions, 1964), parts I and II.

74. *Ibid.*, chap. 10.

75. *Ibid.*, pp. 255–57.

76. Robert E. Lane, "Political Personality and Electoral Choice," in Nelson Polsby, Robert Dentler, and Paul A. Smith (eds.), *Politics and Social Life* (Boston: Houghton Mifflin, 1963), pp. 231–43.

77. Angus Campbell, Philip Converse, Warren Miller, and Donald Stokes, *The American Voter* (New York: John Wiley and Sons, 1960), pp. 512–15.

78. John P. Kirscht and Ronald C. Dillehay, *Dimensions of Authoritarianism* (Lexington: University of Kentucky Press, 1967), pp. 57–69.

79. *Ibid.*, p. 7–29; R. Christie and M. Jahoda, *Studies in the Scope and Method of the Authoritarian Personality* (Glencoe, Ill.: The Free Press, 1954).

80. Solomon E. Asch, *Social Psychology* (New York: Prentice-Hall, 1952), pp. 536–38.

81. Kirscht and Dillehay, *Dimensions,* pp. 37–39; Greenstein, *Personality and Politics,* pp. 108–10.

82. Milton Rokeach, *The Open and the Closed Mind* (New York: Basic Books, 1960).

83. *Ibid.*, p. 33.

84. *Ibid.*, p. 34.

85. *Ibid.*, pp. 36–39.

86. *Ibid.*, p. 60.

87. Roger Brown, *Social Psychology*, pp. 541–43.

88. Sigmund Freud and William C. Bullitt, *Thomas Woodrow Wilson, Twenty-Eighth President of the United States: A Psychological Study* (Boston: Houghton Mifflin, 1967); Alexander L. George and Juliette L. George, *Woodrow*

Wilson and Colonel House: A Personality Study (New York: Dover Publications, 1964).

89. George and George, *Woodrow Wilson and Colonel House*, pp. 11–12.

90. *See* Lazarus, *Personality and Adjustment*, pp. 20–23 for a discussion of these processes.

91. Arnold A. Rogow, *James Forrestal: A Study of Personality, Politics, and Policy* (New York: Macmillan, 1963); Alex Gottfried, "The Uses of Socio-Psychological Categories in a Study of Political Personality," in Heinz Eulau, Samuel J. Eldersveld, and Morris Janowitz (eds.), *Political Behavior* (Glencoe, Ill.: The Free Press, 1956), pp. 125–32.

92. For an extensive presentation of this argument, *see* Betty Glad, "Contributions of Psychobiography," in Jeanne N. Knutson (ed.), *Handbook of Political Psychology* (San Francisco: Jossey-Bass, 1973), pp. 299–321.

93. *See* Barber, *The Presidential Character.*

94. Campbell, *et al., The American Voter*, pp. 24–37.

95. M. Brewster Smith, "A Map for the Analysis of Personality and Politics," *The Journal of Social Issues* 24 (July 1968): 15–28.

96. John B. McConaughy, "Certain Personality Factors of State Legislators in South Carolina," *American Political Science Review* 44 (December 1950): 897–903.

STUDY QUESTIONS

1. Define the following:

personality	authoritarianism
Maslow's need hierarchy	dogmatism
need for achievement	defense mechanisms
personal control	belief system

2. How can the hierarchy of needs suggested by Abraham Maslow be used to explain political behavior of different social groups in the United States?

3. How might McClelland's motivational theory be used to explain differences between the foreign policies of nations?

4. Using Barber's typology of presidential behavior, characterize the presidency of Gerald Ford.

5. What problems exist in using personality concepts and theories to explain political behavior?

CHAPTER
5

Attitudes, Beliefs, Opinions, and Values

Does the public approve of the president's domestic policies? Does the public think he has been doing a good job as president? What is the attitude of white blue-collar workers toward a guaranteed annual wage, mandatory health insurance, equal opportunity employment laws, or increased property taxes to improve the public schools? Which do Americans value more highly—peace, freedom, equality, or prosperity? Do political beliefs of midwestern Republicans differ significantly from those of midwestern Democrats? Do political beliefs vary with the level of education or population of residential towns? These types of questions, which are asked by political scientists, politicians, and the interested public, probe political attitudes, values, beliefs, and opinions. In this chapter we shall examine how relationships among values, beliefs, attitudes, opinions, and political behavior are studied. First we must define these concepts.

DEFINITION OF THE CONCEPTS

Beliefs represent an individual's description of his or her environment. One can distinguish between a belief *in* something and beliefs *about* something.[1] A belief in God, which is a belief *in* something, is not a matter of fact but an act of faith and as such cannot be tested empirically. A belief *about* something can be tested empirically. The belief that government is no more corrupt than any other decision-making body in society and the belief that competition between conflicting interests is a satisfactory method of maintaining a distribution of power in society can be tested empirically.

An attitude is a predisposition, but of what kind is a subject of considerable debate. Is an attitude a predisposition to respond, to evaluate, to experience, to be motivated, or to act? *Attitude* is a relatively enduring organization of interrelated beliefs that describe, evaluate, and advocate action with respect to an object or situation; each belief has cognitive, affective, and behavioral aspects. Each attitude is a predisposition which, when suitably activated, results in some preferential response (a tendency to respond in a particular way).[2] Psychologists debate the basis on which a response is made.

Is a response based on cognition or evaluation or both? A preferential response may be directed toward a situation or object, to others who share one's preferential response, or to the maintenance of the attitude itself. Some psychologists point out that "an individual's attitude toward something is his predisposition to be motivated in relation to it."[3]

Psychologists distinguish attitude from motive in several ways. A motive is characterized by a drive state that appears, disappears, and reappears; an attitude does not have a drive state. An attitude refers to the likelihood that a drive state can be aroused. Attitudes are directed toward less specific objects than motives. When an object has been associated with reduction of a drive, behavior tends to be directed toward that object when the motive is aroused again. The concept of attitude emphasized here is "a state of readiness for motive arousal."[4] Within this framework, an attitude is distinguished from a motive by the presence of a cognitive as well as an affective component. Attitudes differ from beliefs in that they have an affective component.

Social psychologists do not agree on a definition of the term opinion. We will define *opinion* as a verbal expression of an attitude;[5] public opinion would then be the verbal expression of attitudes on public issues and events. Attitudes can be expressed by a variety of behavioral forms, such as facial expression, gesture, or action; an opinion is one of many ways of expressing an attitude. We shall define *public opinion* as "a view on political or politically relevant issues held by persons with an interest in those issues."

One or several functions may be performed for the individual by holding certain attitudes.[6] First, attitudes perform a cognitive function, enabling the individual to organize his environment. The individual does this by developing a pattern of response to a set of similar stimuli. Attitudes also serve an ego-defensive function, protecting the individual from threatening stimuli. Calling police "pigs" serves to protect some individuals from the threat they perceive the police present. Attitudes also express values, enabling the individual to indicate to others the nature of his character. Finally, attitudes serve a utilitarian function, enabling one to obtain things that one values. For example, a politician who holds a certain set of attitudes and acts on the basis of those attitudes, finds them utilitarian if they enable him to be elected to the office he desires.

A *value* can be defined as "an enduring belief that a specific mode of conduct or end-state of existence is personally or socially preferable to an opposite or converse mode of conduct or end-state of existence."[7] A *value system* is "an enduring organization of beliefs concerning preferable modes of conduct or end-states of existence along a continuum of relative importance."[8] Values can be categorized as instrumental or terminal. *Terminal values* are idealized end-states, such as peace, equality, freedom, and a comfortable life. *Instrumental values* refer to modes of conduct. Some are moral values, such as honesty and love, and others are values directed toward self-actualization or competence, such as intelligence, imagination, and independence.[9]

Values differ from attitudes in that they refer to a single belief, while an attitide is an enduring organization of several beliefs.[10] Attitudes refer to more specific objects or situations than values, which dictate general standards. While an individual may have thousands of attitudes, the number of his values may be far fewer. One researcher has identified eighteen terminal and eighteen instrumental values.[11] Values determine one's attitudes, and an attitude may be the product of several values.[12]

Several questions have concerned behavioral scientists who study opinions, beliefs, values, and attitudes. How do they develop? (One approach to this question is indicated in Chapter 6.) How do attitudes, beliefs, opinions, and values change? What kinds of people hold what values, opinions, beliefs, and attitudes? What are the consequences of the distribution of opinions, beliefs, values, and attitudes in different societies? According to the nature of what is studied and the method used to study it, we usually focus on verbal expressions and infer from them the nature of their underlying beliefs, values, and attitudes. Other methods can be and have been used to assess the nature of attitudes, beliefs, and values. These include an examination of forms of behavior rewarded or punished by agents in the social and political system. Social scientists study the values instilled in children by parents in a particular country by observing what kinds of behaviors are punished or rewarded. [13] Values and actions promoted by the political system are explained by observing the kinds of relationships to the local government encouraged or discouraged through treatment of individual citizens by the local bureaucracy or the police. [14]

Public opinion is frequently described in terms of its patterns of distribution among different ethnic and religious groups and among residents of geographical regions and social classes. Public opinion is also studied by measuring the degree of conflict and consensus on issues and its change over time; the variations between mass and elite opinion; the intensity of opinion on issues; the saliency of the issues to the public; and the formation of opinion through socialization experiences. [15] The link between public opinion and public policy is also of central concern to political science.

DIMENSIONS OF ATTITUDES AND ATTITUDE OBJECTS

Among the basic properties of an attitude are the direction of the attitude and the intensity of feeling toward its object. [16] Terms used to describe the direction are comparative, such as good–bad, agree–disagree, like–dislike, and fair–unfair. In studying attitudes and opinions, we are concerned not only with their direction and intensity but also with their stability over time and the extremity of the attitude in comparison to the mode or mean of a population group. [17] Attitudes and opinions also are latent; they become active after perception or recall of the appropriate stimulus, which may not occur even if the stimulus is presented to the individual. [18] We can also describe the organization of attitudes in terms of several other structural dimensions. [19] Among these are the differential (the extent to which various parts are articulated), the time perspective (past, present, or future orientation), and the range of phenomena represented by an attitude structure. Another aspect of attitude organization that can be studied is the values that form the frame of reference for an attitude.[20] Attitudes and opinions may be inconsistent as different objects come into focus. For example, an individual may express support for equal employment and desegregation of schools but be opposed to fair housing laws.[21]

The information on which an individual bases a set of beliefs, attitudes, and opinions can be examined. To find strong opinions associated with a lack of knowledge about the issues involved is not unusual. Frequently researchers find that an individual is unaware of the implications of his or her opinions. Another aspect that can be studied is the degree of integration or isolation of attitudes and opinions. An individual with strong ideological opinions has well-integrated and internally consistent political attitudes, with each related to the others.[22]

In order to understand the nature of attitudes it is also useful to characterize the perceived objects, which are the focus of the attitude. Researchers have focused on the dimensionality, inclusiveness, centrality to the individual, and social character of attitude objects.[23] Some objects involve a greater number of variety of elements than others; for example, studies have found that voting choice in France involves two dimensions: a clerical–anticlerical dimension and left–right dimension.[24] Researchers have only recently developed methods for more adequately treating multidimensional attitude objects.[25] The number of properties of an object, which are perceived in a cluster, determines the inclusiveness of an attitude. One can have a generalized attitude toward the federal government and distinct attitudes toward its particular aspects, such as the president, the Congress, a Supreme Court decision, and draft, defense, and welfare policies. An attitude toward the federal government is much more inclusive than an attitude toward a Supreme Court decision.

"Centrality of an attitude object" means the importance of the object to the individual or its persistence in his realm of awareness. An attitude toward military policies would probably be more central to a draft-eligible 20-year-old than to a 65-year-old congressman. An object need not be inclusive and also central to an individual; it can be inclusive but remotely related to the individual. For example, the average citizen's attitudes on foreign-aid policy, communism, or exploration of outer space are not concerned with objects that have an immediate bearing on his life.

There usually is not a one-to-one correspondence between an attitude and related behavior. A number of attitudes may be related to a particular behavior. For example, a citizen may vote for a particular presidential candidate whose issue stands he prefers, although he personally dislikes the candidate and also dislikes his political party. In this case, three attitudes are involved, focusing on three different objects, all of which are related to voting choice. The positive and strong attitude toward the issue outweighs the negative and weak attitude toward the other two components.

Other factors may result in a tenuous link between an object of an attitude and behavior directed toward that object. These factors include the situation in which the behavior occurs and motivation and attitudes toward the situation.[26] One study examined the acceptability of non-whites in public accomodations by writing letters to hotels and motels to inquire if non-whites were permitted to register. In this situation (written exchange of communications), more hotels indicated that they would not register minority group members than was actually the case when non-whites tried to register in person. The face-to-face situation resulted in different behavior.[27] An attitude also may remain latent until aroused by a particular motive, drive, or need.

SALIENCY AND PERCEPTION

The public policy implications of values, beliefs, attitudes, and opinions has been a subject of much interest but limited research. Generally it is agreed that the policy implications are in part a consequence of the salience—the importance or significance—of the value, belief, attitude, or opinion to the individual.[28] The connection of attitude with policy is also a function of the way in which public policy is expressed and how the policymakers perceive the public's attitude toward an issue. This aspect has been labeled "latency of opinion." On any issue there is an attentive public, which is concerned about the problem, and an inattentive public, which ignores the problem.[29]

Politicians may be aware of the direction and intensity of attitudes held by an inattentive segment of the public, attitudes which could be motivated to action by a pronouncement of public policy to which the inattentive public would be opposed. If more stringent air safety rules for private planes were being considered, policymakers would be aware that owners of private airplanes may be angered by such a policy pronouncement. The policymakers' actions may be inhibited without any activity by those who would oppose such a policy. In his discussion of policymaking, David Truman presented an analysis of the influence of interest groups in American politics.[30] Individuals who share a common attitude that may be activated by an event are referred to as a *potential interest group*. Latent attitudes mobilized by government inaction often result in political activity. This phenomenon was manifested in the 1963 March on Washington for civil rights, by political protest demonstrations during the 1968 nominating conventions, by organizations opposing the Vietnam War, and by defeat of open-housing referenda in local elections.

Mobilization of a latent attitude by a stimulus is not a simple stimulus–response mechanism. Perceptual screens, poor communication, and inadequate information impede the process. Studies of selective perception have resulted in a number of propositions about the activation of latent attitudes. Generally individuals perceive only a small and selective (non-random) sample of the stimuli presented to them. Stimuli that are selected to be perceived are a function of a previously learned response, from which an individual develops a set of expectations about possible stimuli. The motives governing an individual at the time a stimulus is presented also determine his response. The intensity with which a stimulus is presented also has a major influence on its perception or non-perception.[31] A newspaper account of a student riot presented on the obituary page will not gain much attention; however, if the story becomes a front-page feature, the stimulus achieves much greater intensity. If a political convention delegate reads about a riot at the convention site in the newspaper, the stimulus is probably received with minimal intensity. However, if he is tear-gassed, clubbed, or shoved through a plate glass window, the stimulus is presented with a stronger intensity.

People also tend to perceive what they need or want. The greater the motivation is, the greater is the tendency to ignore unrewarding cues. Hence, politicians under pressure to conclude a war with victory or an honorable peace and generals under pressure from politicians to bring about such a conclusion tend to perceive stimuli that indicate the desired outcome will occur and not to perceive contradictory or unfavorable events (stimuli). To the thirsty man in the desert, the mirage of an oasis appears; threatening stimuli such as hovering vultures tend not to be perceived.

Experimental studies of perception indicate that when stimuli can be organized in several different ways, the best organization is continuous, simple, closed, and symmetrical.[32] Selection and organization of stimuli are affected by our expectations and motivations; i.e., we tend to perceive that which we expect, need, and desire. This can account in part for a politician predicting a sure victory in an upcoming election when he is about to experience an overwhelming defeat. In politics and policymaking, as elsewhere, the more ambiguous the stimulus or the stronger the motivation, the more likely the stimulus will be interpreted as the individual desires.

DETERMINANTS OF ATTITUDES

A number of determinants of attitudes have been suggested by researchers in social psychology and political science; these include changes in physiological conditions, such as occur with maturation and aging; experience within a particular institution, such as child-rearing practices in the family; socialization activities within an economic institution (corporation) or social organization (college fraternity); non-verbal communication, such as facial expression or gestures; and verbal communications. Most studies of attitude change have focused on the effects of verbal communications.[33]

Formation of beliefs, attitudes, and values begins at an early age, with parents exerting the major influence on their formation. In later years education, personal experience, peer-group influence, and perhaps rebellion against parental attitudes, beliefs, and values result in a deviation from earlier learned patterns (see Chapter 6). However, children who rebel against their parents are more likely to carry that rebellion into politics if their parents are very interested in or active in politics.[34] This does not occur frequently in the United States because of the low salience politics has to most Americans. Research results indicate that individuals with more education differ in certain basic values and attitudes from those with less education, but we are not sure whether this is a consequence of education or of differences in family background and personal experience. The selection process determining who advances to higher levels of education may be the primary factor.[35] The suggestion that education results in a change or modification of attitudes, beliefs, and values learned in early life is based on several arguments. One is that education provides the information base that can cause an individual to doubt earlier learned patterns. Education can also suggest the variety of alternative attitudes. Awareness of the range of alternatives presumably results in increased tolerance of values and attitudes held by others.

ATTITUDE CHANGE

Considerable research on politically relevant attitudes has examined the effect of verbal communication on attitude change. One can structure analysis of the process of attitude change in a number of ways. Several different ways to explain attitude change have been developed by psychologists.

Component analysis examines components of the independent variable of communication. These components are the characteristics of the source of the communication, the structure and content of the message, the characteristics of the channel used to deliver the message, the nature of the person receiving the message, and the characteristics of the goal of the communication. A goal of a communication could be the long- or short-term effects of the issue or problem with which the communication is concerned, or the type of effect sought (e.g., change in attitude or behavior).[36]

Component analysis of the dependent variable of attitude change focuses on the importance of the communication, comprehension of its message, whether the suggestion for change contained in the message was yielded to, retention by the receiver of the attitude change, and action based on the changed attitude.[37]

Research has been directed toward examining the range of effects of communication on communication change. Experimental studies usually focus on the degree to which an individual changes in order to accept a new attitude. Much of our interest in political research is on the final result of the attitude change process—the action that results from the effort to persuade by communicating. A political campaign director is concerned with the effect that his candidate's television appearance has on building his support. Political research might be concerned with how voters adopt a new party affiliation or with the consequences of adopting a new party identification.

Undoubtedly there is considerable interaction among the five components of the independent variable of attitude change. The credibility of the source is probably affected by the structure of the message. One cannot adequately assess the impact of one aspect of the independent variable without taking into account the other four elements.[38] It may be that not all the possible components of attitude change are always present in an attitude-change situation. For example, if post-hypnotic suggestion is effective, no conscious yielding by the subject to the suggestion of the hypnotist would have occurred.[39]

The social judgment approach to attitude change argues that an individual evaluates communications in terms of how close the message is to his or her own position.[40] Attitude change is determined by the distance between the individual's current position and the position presented by the message. Attitude change will occur toward the position advocated in the message if the position is not too distant (within the "latitude of acceptance") from that already held by the individual. Assimilation is the process by which the attitude position advocated by the message is accepted into the receiver's attitude structure. If the message position is too distant from that held by the individual, it is rejected. It is argued by the social psychologists who developed social judgment theory that the individual tends to shift his or her attitude position away from that advocated by the message. This shift away from the position presented by the message is called the "contrast effect."

Research indicates that individuals who hold extreme attitude positions are much less likely to change their attitudes in the direction advocated by a message than are those who hold more moderate positions.

In social judgment theory, the crucial variables of attitude change are the saliency of the issue to an individual; his or her already existing attitude position; and the distance between the existing attitude position and the position advocated by the message. An individual who is very much concerned with the attitude object is more resistant to changing the attitude. A stronger message will result in greater attitude change, provided that the change advocated does not fall in the individual's zone of rejection.

Cognitive approaches have been used to examine attitude change. Underlying these cognitive approaches is the assumption that beliefs, attitudes, values, and behavior tend to be organized in meaningful, rational ways; i.e., attitudes are organized into structures which appear to be consistent to those that hold them. If inconsistency of a certain magnitude is perceived, pressure is generated for attitude change to bring about an acceptable level of consistency.

Balance theory, an early cognitive approach to attitude consistency, asserts that an individual's attitudes toward himself or herself (P), another person (O), and an object (X) are balanced or unbalanced.[41] A balanced state exists if the three attitudes held by a person are all positive, or if two are negative and one is positive (*see* Figure 5–1). An unbalanced state is presumed to generate tension, which results in an attitude change in the relationships among P, O, and X so as to create a balanced state. Extensions of balance theory have suggested that balance is a matter of degree, it is not simply existent or nonexistent.

In Figure 5–1, unbalanced political attitudes are represented by a voter who likes the candidate of Party A and favors increased military spending. The candidate, however, is against increased defense spending. According to balance theory, this imbalanced state should result in a change of one sign to a negative; the voter could change to a negative attitude toward the candidate or change to a negative position on increased military spending.

The drive toward consistency of political attitudes has been found in several studies. For example, a study of the American electorate found that approximately three-fourths of the individuals who in 1956 held issue attitudes inconsistent with their party identification by 1958 had shifted either their party identification or their issue stand so that the two were consistent.[42] This tendency toward consistency of policy preference with party identification varies with the strength of party identification, as well as with the particular issue.[43] Patterns of attitudinal consistency are also related to the time at which a voting decision is made and to patterns of political participation.[44]

The co-orientation approach to attitude change focuses on communications among individuals, rather than on an internal state within an individual. A perceived difference in salient attitudes that

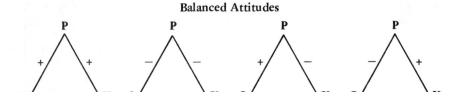

Balanced Attitudes

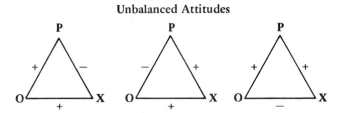

Unbalanced Attitudes

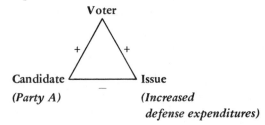

Example: Unbalanced Political Attitudes

Voter

Candidate   Issue
(Party A)   (Increased
                            defense expenditures)

FIGURE 5-1

*Balance Theory of Attitude Consistency (Positive and negative signs
refer to the relationship between the two variables represented by
points of the triangles.)*

results in intergroup communications influences patterns of communications between two or more individuals so that their attitudes
toward an object or another individual become congruent.[45]

The principle of congruity is the basis for another cognitive
consistency theory of attitude change, which focuses on an individual's attitude, his attitude toward others, and his attitude toward an
idea.[46] According to the principle of congruity, if an individual
favorably values another person, but does not value an idea that the
other person values, this individual will change both his attitude
toward the other person and his attitude toward the idea.

In Figure 5-2A, two attitudes are indicated on a continuum
ranging from −7 to +7. The individual has a positive attitude toward

a political party's presidential nominee which is scored at +5 on the continuum. He has a negative attitude on an issue position taken by the party's nominee, which is scored at −3. Since the more strongly held attitude is more resistant to change, we can predict that the degree of attitude change is inverse to its proportional share of attitude intensity. In other words, the issue attitude would shift to 5/7, or to a +3 position, and attitude toward the presidential nominee would shift to 2/7, or to a +3 position (see Figure 5–2B).

An attitude that is highly related to other attitudes will change in the degree and direction that minimizes the amount of total change among the related attitudes. The principle of congruity formulation permits quantification of concepts so that precise predictions of the direction and degree of attitude change are possible.

Research during the 1960 election examined attitude changes among individuals who held favorable attitudes toward the Democratic party and unfavorable attitudes toward a Catholic candidate for president or unfavorable attitudes toward John F. Kennedy; change in attitude from before the convention nominating Kennedy to after the convention was measured.[47] Individuals who favored the Democratic party most were most likely to change their attitudes toward Kennedy; the greatest degree of change also occurred among these individuals. Those who favored Kennedy but did not favor the party were most likely to change their attitude toward the party to a favorable one.

Cognitive dissonance theory, developed by Leon Festinger, predicts that inconsistency between cognitive elements will not be tolerated by the individual if the inconsistency is above a certain magnitude.[48] Festinger defines cognition as "any knowledge,

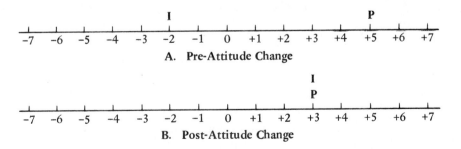

A. Pre-Attitude Change

B. Post-Attitude Change

FIGURE 5–2

Shifts in Attitude Change

141

opinion, or belief about the environment, about oneself, or about one's behavior.[49] Two elements are dissonant if, "considering these two [elements] alone, the obverse of one element would follow from the other."[50] For example, if one believes smoking cigarettes causes lung cancer and one smokes cigarettes, the two elements are dissonant. Cognitive dissonance can be caused by a number of sources, such as exposure to new information, cultural values, conflicting past experiences, the withdrawal of previously existing social support, or change in a related opinion.[51] The pressure to reduce dissonance is a function of the magnitude of the dissonance. Festinger suggests that dissonance can be reduced by changing behavior, by changing the situation to which a cognitive element belongs (which may contradict reality), or by adding new cognitive elements.[52] The smoker who views smoking as contributing to lung cancer can reduce his dissonance by giving up smoking cigarettes; he can start using a filter in the belief that this adequately reduces the inhalation of cancer-causing agents; or he can read and believe articles claiming that scientific research has not proven that smoking cigarettes causes cancer.

Reduction of dissonance may be inhibited by the resistance to change of behavioral or environmental cognitive elements. Festinger also suggests that the maximum dissonance that can exist is equal to the resistance to change of the least resistant element.[53] If two cognitive elements are highly resistant to change, a high level of dissonance exists. If one intensely dislikes a political candidate but has a strong attachment to the candidate's party and has always supported the nominees of that party, a high degree of dissonance is created by the existence of the candidate.

Cognitive dissonance theory suggests that an individual will seek to avoid information and situations that create dissonance, but only limited research evidence supports this proposition. Cognitive dissonance theory says that the greater the incentive provided to a person to perform an undesirable task, the less of an attitude change there will be. Research evidence has not always supported this hypothesis; attention to and retention of the stimuli and other rewards may also influence behavior and attitude change. Reduction of dissonance may occur only under free choice conditions—not under the forced choice conditions usually present in psychology experiments.

Other theoretical explanations have been offered for the behavior and attitude patterns for which cognitive dissonance theory seeks to account. Individuals may be inferring attitudes from behavior when the salience of their behavior is low (as in psychological experiment tasks), rather than changing their attitudes to match their behavior.[54]

Festinger's work has stimulated considerable research using his approach to attitude change, and he and others have conducted a number of studies that have contributed to the elaboration and refinement of his theory.[55] The propositions of his work can be tested using a variety of subject matter. For example, one variable considered in the theory of cognitive dissonance is the role social support plays in retaining or changing cognitive elements. The magnitude of dissonance created when someone expresses an opinion contrary to one's own is related to the number of other cognitive elements of the opinion that are consonant with one's own, and with the number of individuals with whom one shares opinions. The more of either element, the less the magnitude of dissonance will be. Other relevant variables include one's assessment of the relevance and the attractiveness of the individual or group expressing a contrary opinion, and the degree of dissonance between all cognitive elements of which the two dissonant elements are a part.[56]

Reduction in dissonance resulting from social disagreement can be brought about by changing one's own opinion, by influencing those expressing the contrary opinion, by reducing the magnitude of the disagreement, or by discrediting the person or group expressing the dissonant opinion. One can attribute another's conflicting opinion to motives, experiences, or other characteristics different from one's own; such a rationalization might lead to tolerance of an opinion.

The propositions about dissonance and change in cognitive elements as a consequence of social support variables provide a theoretical base for examining many aspects of political behavior. For example, one can test hypotheses about change in vote intention as a consequence of changes in perceptions of social support for a candidate. Or one could study voting behavior in the legislature as a function of consonance between significant cue givers and other legislators on policy issues or party affiliation. The theory of cognitive dissonance is formulated to lend itself to empirical research focusing on a number of different substantive questions. The concepts can easily be operationalized, and data can be collected for testing hypotheses using experimental and survey research methods.

Consistency theories of balance, co-orientation, congruity, and cognitive dissonance all assume that an individual experiences tension when cognitive elements are not in balance and that this tension leads to efforts to reduce it, which may result in a change of attitude. Consistency theories differ from each other in certain respects. Balance, congruity, and dissonance theories focus strictly on internal states. Congruity is concerned with interpersonal relations. The theories state that there are different methods of tension reduction; e.g., for attitude-change theory, it is mainly balance and congruity; for behavioral change, and also for attitude change theories it is co-orientation and dissonance. The abilities of the theories to precisely predict the degree of attitude change also varies. Elaborations of balance theory and congruity theory can predict the direction and degree of attitude change most accurately.

Psychologists have approached attitude change on the basis of what function it serves for the individual; thus, attitudes supposedly change when the needs of the individual change.[57] One study assessed the psychological functions that attitudes of Americans toward the Soviet Union served. The researchers of this study defined attitude as "a predisposition to experience, to be motivated by, and to act toward a class of objects in a predictable manner."[58] The characteristics of an object of an attitude are differentiation, saliency, time perspective, informational support, and object value. In this study, saliency was defined as "the extent to which a particular object or class of objects is central to the everyday concerns of a person."[59] The researchers declined to make a distinction between attitudes and opinions because both refer to the kind of predisposition with which they were concerned.[60]

This study was concerned with the adjustive functions served by an individual's holding a certain opinion toward the Soviet Union; the study hypothesized that the possible functions of holding an opinion were object appraisal, social adjustment, and externalization. Object appraisal means assistance in evaluating or assessing objects or situations as they relate to one's own interests. Social adjustment is facilitation (or disruption) of one's relations with others. Externalization occurs when analogies between external events and inner, personal problems are perceived, and the attitude

144

established is a reflection of the method which the individual has adopted for dealing with his inner difficulty. This works as a tension-reduction mechanism for the individual.[61] To evaluate the functions of attitudes, the researchers did an in-depth study of opinions toward Russia held by ten American men. From these case studies they drew a number of conclusions about the functions of attitudes or opinions. They found that the attitudes of the ten men had different contents, were differently structured, and had differing valences. The orientations toward the Soviet Union could be characterized as approach, avoidance, or hostile.

In the political realm such a wide range of opinion must be expressed through a narrow range of policy alternatives. A vast complex of varying opinions held by many different individuals may result in a common pattern of support for a particular policy. One might conclude that both pollsters and politicians would be well advised not to infer too much about the underlying bases for responses to very simply structured policy opinion questions of the popular polls.

The ways in which attitudes toward the Soviet Union contribute to object appraisal, externalization, and social adjustment functions for the ten subjects were noted by the researchers. The functions of attitudes or opinions for each individual were a result of the role played by the attitude in mediating personal requirements. The personal requirement that predominates determines whether the individual is considered to be reacting rationally or emotionally. The method by which change in attitudes is effected is a result of which requirement predominates and what personal function is served by an attitude.[62] Although the research sample was much too small to adequately test the propositions, the research did generate a number of additional hypotheses and thereby contributed to the development of a functional approach to the study of attitudes and attitude change.

One can also approach attitude change as a consequence of learning processes[63] or as a consequence of perceptual processes. In the learning theory approach, one studies the relationship between the independent variable and aspects of learning; on the basis of study, one predicts a relationship between the independent variable and attitude change. Presentation of persuasive materials about a candidate is predicted to have an effect on attitude toward the candidate.

Psychological theories of attitude change have yet to be fully developed, and inconsistencies between aspects of the theories and research results are unresolved. Political scientists have not emphasized the study of change in attitudes, beliefs, and opinions. Their research also tends to be inadequately anchored in psychological theories about the formation of attitudes, opinions, and beliefs.

Research on the influence of peer groups on political attitudes indicates that peer norms have considerable influence on basic values and attitudes. Changes in attitudes among adults can be accounted for in part by peer-group influence. The upward social mobiles, for example, may change to conform to the values and attitudes of a new peer group. A young lawyer of working-class origin may become an active supporter of the Republican party after joining a Wall Street law firm. Geographical mobility may have the same effect, with a Yankee Republican who moves to the deep South becoming a Democrat to conform to his new peer group's political preferences. Conformity to the new peer group's political views is more likely to occur when politics is important to the peer group and when acceptance by the new peer group is important to the individual.[64]

A number of researchers have examined the influence of social groups on the creation, retention, and alteration of beliefs and values. An individual is more likely to work for group goals and to conform to group norms when he accepts and clearly understands the group goal and perceives the group as contributing to attaining his own goals. Conformity is more likely among individuals with average rather than high or low acceptance in the group. Conformity to group norms and goals will also be greater if the group perceives itself threatened by outsiders, and if group membership is highly attractive to the individual member. The higher the status of the group and the fewer the attractive alternative groups, the more attractive group membership is likely to become to the individual. Pressure to conform is usually greater in a small group than in a large one. Frequency of contact and degree of mutual liking also affect the degree of conformity to group norms. Research has also indicated that members are more likely to conform to group norms if they participate in making group decisions.[65]

Stimuli are more likely to be accepted or to be noticed if they come from trusted sources (e.g., friends as compared to strangers).

If stimuli appear reasoned and objective, rather than emotional and subjective, they are more likely to produce change. Individuals do not tend to perceive stimuli that arouse great fears; a message is more likely to be perceived if it is moderately threatening.[66]

Some individuals are highly susceptible to opinion change, and others are resistant to change. Those susceptible to change tend to agree with whatever suggestion or statement is made to them; those resistant to change give a negative response to whatever suggestion is made to them. The argument has been made that susceptibility to change is related to personality characteristics.[67] Certain personality types are more receptive to particular kinds of messages than other personality types. The authoritarian personality is characterized by submissiveness to authority, rigidity of opinions, concern with toughness and power, generalized hostility, conformity to conventional values, and projection of unconscious emotional impulses.[68] Authoritarians are likely to change their attitudes and opinions when someone accepted as authoritative endorses the position that would represent a change.

Generalizations about personality types can be used to account for variations in values, attitudes, and beliefs. For example, if we were to interview northern Republican migrants to southern cities or to interview central city Democrats who have moved to suburbia and to attempt to explain their change in party affiliation or lack of change, these generalizations would be useful because they are concerned with the processes by which changes in attitudes, values, and beliefs are brought about.

THE STUDY OF VALUES

Most political science research and theorizing has concerned attitudes and opinions, rather than values and beliefs. Public concern with public opinion on political and social issues—catered to by mass media—partly encourages this direction of research. It is easier to measure opinion than it is to measure attitudes, beliefs, and values. Methods and theories about attitude formation and change developed by psychologists have been borrowed by political scientists to study legislative, judicial, and mass voting behavior. The failure to focus on the study of values and their role in political behavior may also be a consequence of the scientific orientation of the discipline. The rejection of the idea that values can be scientifically proven to be superior or inferior can also be extended to the rejection of the study of the influence of differences in value patterns on political behavior.

Milton Rokeach, however, has suggested that greater understanding of political behavior can be achieved by determining the value systems associated with different patterns of behavior. Rokeach says that "values transcend specific objects and specific situations: values have to do with modes of conduct and end-states of existence. More formally, to say that a person holds a value is to say that he has an enduring belief that a particular mode of conduct or that a particular end-state of existence is personally and socially preferable to alternative modes of conduct or end-states of existence."[69] As such, a value provides a standard for motives, wants, actions, and attitudes; it justifies and rationalizes behavior. Values are organized into value systems, in which values are ranked according to their importance.[70] Individuals with different value systems have different attitude structures and behave different politically. Individuals with different value systems were found to differ in attitudes toward civil rights, toward liberalism and conservatism, and toward certain candidates.[71]

In a 1968 sample survey of the U.S. voting population, the mean ranking of the terminal value of peace was seventh for liberals, eleventh for middle-of-the-roaders, and fifteenth for conservatives. (Terminal values were defined as desired end-states.)[72] The terminal value of equality was ranked (among eighteen others) by supporters of different presidential candidates in 1968 as follows:[73]

Supporter of Candidate:	Rank of Equality
R. Kennedy	4
McCarthy	6
Johnson	4
Rockefeller	9
Nixon	12
Reagan	10
Wallace	14

Based on his analysis of a sample of the 1968 national electorate, Rokeach concluded that the overall terminal value system of Wallace supporters was closest to those of Nixon and Reagan supporters; Rockefeller adherents were closer to Senator Eugene McCarthy's supporters in terminal value systems; and Johnson supporters were closest to Robert Kennedy's supporters in terminal value systems. However, for both terminal and instrumental values, differences among supporters were not extreme. A study of differences in the value system of supporters of different parties or candidates in Italy, France, or Germany might show quite dissimilar value hierarchies between adherents of different parties in each country.

SUMMARY AND CRITIQUE

What arguments can be made for studying values instead of attitudes, beliefs, and opinions? The best argument, of course, would be that we can explain the behavior of individuals better if we know their value systems. However, that assertion can be made only after adequate research, and very little research has been done on the relationships between individual value systems and individual political behavior. Rokeach presents the following argument for emphasizing the study of values rather than the study of attitudes: First, value is a more dynamic concept because it includes the study of motivation. Second, values are determinants of attitudes, as well as of behavior; assuming an individual has fewer values than attitudes, it is more economical, in terms of research time and effort, to study values. Value is also a relevant concept in a greater number of academic disciplines. Therefore, a greater number of perspectives and more interdisciplinary efforts can be brought to bear on the research.[74]

The wide use of conceptual frameworks involving beliefs, attitudes, opinions, and values in political analysis indicates the utility which these concepts have in political analysis. Political scientists can research a number of problems using these concepts. Voting behavior,[75] political culture,[76] political recruitment,[77] comparative political elites,[78] and political and economic development[79] have been studied using one more of these concepts. The elaborate body of research and generalizations about attitudes, beliefs, and opinions in psychology and social psychology also enhances the attractiveness of using these concepts in the approach to the study of political behavior.

Concepts of attitudes, values, and beliefs can easily be used in combination with learning theory, communications theory, or decision-making theory to study very complex research problems. One can examine the process of legislative decision-making by studying the attitudes, beliefs, and values that the freshmen legislators bring to the legislature, the acquisition of new, or modification of existing, values, beliefs, and attitudes, and the response to certain types of cues in decision making.

Studies of the influence of attitudes, beliefs, and values on political behavior have been hampered and the development of useful theory has been impeded by a number of methodological problems. The multiplicity of definitions of essential concepts, differences in manipulation of independent variables, varying methods of measuring variables and of assessing the effects of manipulation, and variations in assumptions underlying research efforts have inhibited the development of a consistent, cumulative body of knowledge. For example, suppose we wish to find out the effects of a candidate's presentation of a message delivered in two different ways. In one method of presentation, the candidate makes the statement directly into the television camera, with the visual image of the candidate the only image on the screen. The other method presents scenes on the candidate at work, with his family, and campaigning, while a narrator presents the spoken message. The desired effects are an attitude change bringing about support for the candidate from those who did not previously support him and a reinforcement of support from those who do.

The task in such a study would include a measurement of the change that occurred. A number of ways have been used to measure attitude change in various studies; these include the percentage of subjects showing a change in attitude, those showing a positive change, those indicating a specified amount of change, indicators among subjects of net change, and the ratio of change occurring for all subjects. Although attitudes are sometimes defined as having affective and cognitive components, measurement usually focuses on only one. If we can discuss several different dimensions of attitude structures that have implications for behavior, then our measurement ought to take into account the different dimensions.

The impact of values, beliefs, and attitudes upon political behavior can be better studied and understood when relevant theories are developed. These theories should provide a common definition of the key concepts and criteria for operationalizing the concepts. Researchers then will be more likely to use a standard method of measuring change and variables affecting change and to use appropriate criteria to evaluate the effects of independent variables.

NOTES AND REFERENCES

1. Lewis A. Froman, Jr., *People and Politics* (Englewood Cliffs, N.J.: Prentice-Hall, 1962), p. 19. Milton Rokeach develops a different categorization of types of beliefs: descriptive ("I believe it is raining"); evaluative ("I believe Chrysler Corporation makes very dependable cars"); or exhortative ("I believe the New York Mets should win the pennant"). Regardless of their type, all beliefs are predispositions to act. *See* M. Rokeach, *Beliefs, Attitudes, and Values* (San Francisco: Jossey-Bass, 1968), pp. 115–16. *See also* Milton Rokeach, *The Nature of Human Values* (New York: The Free Press, 1973), pp. 6–7.

2. Rokeach, *Beliefs, Attitudes, and Values,* p. 112.

3. Theodore M. Newcomb, Ralph H. Turner, and Philip Converse, *Social Psychology* (New York: Holt, Rinehart and Winston, 1965), p. 40.

4. *Ibid.*

5. Carl I. Hovland, I. L. Janis, and Harold H. Kelley, *Communication and Persuasion* (New Haven: Yale University Press, 1953). Rokeach defines opinion as a verbal expression of an attitude, belief, or value (Rokeach, *Beliefs, Attitudes, and Values,* p. 125.) For a discussion of a variety of approaches, *see* William McGuire, "The Nature of Attitudes and Attitude Change," in Gardner Lindzey and Eliot Aronson (eds.), *Handbook of Social Psychology* (Reading, Mass.: Addison-Wesley, 1968), Vol. III, p. 152. McGuire argues that such a distinction cannot be made empirically.

6. Daniel Katz, The Functional Approach to the Study of Attitudes," *Public Opinion Quarterly* 24 (Summer 1960): 163–204.

7. Rokeach, *The Nature of Human Values,* p. 5.

8. *Ibid.*

9. *Ibid.,* pp. 7–10.

10. *Ibid.,* p. 18.

11. *Ibid. See also* Rokeach, *Attitudes, Beliefs, and Values.*

12. *See,* for example, Rokeach, *The Nature of Human Values,* chap. 6.

13. Lucian Pye, *Politics, Personality, and Nation Building* (New Haven: Yale University Press, 1962), pp. 177–86.

14. *See* Gabriel Almond and Sidney Verba, *The Civic Culture* (Princeton, N.J.: Princeton University Press, 1963), pp. 106–14.

15. *See,* for example, V. O. Key, Jr., *Public Opinion and American Democracy* (New York: Alfred A. Knopf, 1963); Harwood Childs, *Public Opinion* (Princeton, N.J.: D. Van Nostrand, 1965); Bernard Hennessy, *Public Opinion,* 3rd ed. (N. Scituate, Mass.: Duxbury Press, 1975).

16. Newcomb, Turner, and Converse, *Social Psychology,* pp. 48–50.

17. V. O. Key, Jr., *Public Opinion,* chaps. 3 and 10.

18. Newcomb, Turner, and Converse, op. cit., pp. 58–63; Key, *Public Opinion,* chap. 11.

19. Rokeach, *Attitudes, Beliefs, and Values,* pp. 116–18.

20. Milton Rokeach, "The Role of Values in Public Opinion Research," *Public Opinion Quarterly* 32 (Winter 1968–69): 547–59.

21. For a discussion of this *see* Philip Converse, "Constraint and Variety in Belief Systems," in David Apter (ed.), *Ideology and Discontent* (New York: Free Press, 1964), pp. 207–08; Newcomb, Turner, and Converse, *Social Psychology,* pp. 149–52.

22. Converse, "Constraint and Variety in Belief Systems," pp. 208–09.

23. Newcomb, Turner, and Converse, *Social Psychology,* pp. 50–66.

24. Philip Converse, "The Problem of Party Distance in Models of Voting Change," in M. Kent Jennings and L. Harmon Ziegler (eds.), *The Electoral Process* (Englewood Cliffs, N.J.: Prentice-Hall, 1966), pp. 175–207.

25. Clyde Coombs, *A Theory of Data* (New York: John Wiley and Sons, 1964), pp. 140–80.

26. Rokeach has emphasized the need for evaluating attitude toward the situation as well as attitude toward the object. *See* his *Beliefs, Attitudes, and Values,* pp. 126–28.

27. B. Kutner, C. Wilkins, and P. R. Yarrow, "Verbal Attitudes and Overt Behavior Involving Racial Prejudice," *Journal of Abnormal and Social Psychology* 47 (1952): 649–52.

28. Key, *Public Opinion,* chap. 11.

29. *Ibid.,* p. 265.

30. David B. Truman, *The Governmental Process* (New York: Alfred A. Knopf, 1951).

31. Bernard Berelson and Gary Steiner, *Human Behavior* (New York: Harcourt, Brace, and World, 1964), pp. 100–21.

32. *Ibid.,* p. 108.

33. *See* McGuire, "The Nature of Attitudes," in *Social Psychology,* for a review of determinants of attitudes and research on their effects.

34. Eleanor Maccoby, Richard E. Matthews, and Anton S. Morton, "Youth and Political Change," in S. Sidney Ulmer (ed.), *Introductory Readings in Political Behavior* (Chicago: Rand McNally and Company, 1961), pp. 75–85.

35. Kenneth P. Langton and M. Kent Jennings, "Political Socialization and the High School Civics Curriculum in the United States," *American Political Science Review* 62 (September 1968): 866.

36. McGuire, "Nature of Attitudes," in *Social Psychology*, p. 172.

37. *Ibid.*, p. 173. *See also* Milton J. Rosenberg, Carl I. Hovland, William J. McGuire, Robert P. Abelson, and Jack W. Brehm, *Attitude Organization and Change* (New Haven: Yale University Press, 1960); Muzafer Sherif and Carl I. Hovland, *Social Judgment* (New Haven: Yale University Press, 1961); and Carl I. Hovland, Irving L. Janis, and Harold H. Kelley, *Communication and Persuasion* (New Haven: Yale University Press, 1953).

38. McGuire, "Nature of Attitudes," in *Social Psychology*, p. 174.

39. For a discussion of this and other possible instances of attitude change where all five elements of attitude change may not be present, *see* McGuire, "Nature of Attitudes," in *Social Psychology*, pp. 174–75.

40. Muzafer Sherif and Carl I. Hovland, *Social Judgment* (New Haven: Yale University Press, 1961); Carolyn W. Sherif, Muzafer Sherif, and Roger E. Nebergall, *Attitude and Attitude Change* (Philadelphia: W. B. Saunders Company, 1965).

41. Fritz Heider, "Attitudes and Cognitive Organization," *Journal of Psychology* 21 (1946): 107–12.

42. Samuel A. Kirkpatrick, "Political Attitude Structure and Component Change," *Public Opinion Quarterly* 34 (Fall 1970): 403–07.

43. Gerald Pomper, *Voters' Choice* (New York: Dodd, Mead, and Company, 1975), pp. 166–73.

44. Samuel A. Kirkpatrick, "Political Attitudes and Behavior: Some Consequences of Attitudinal Ordering," *Midwest Journal of Political Science* 14 (February 1970): 14, Table 3.

45. Theodore M. Newcomb, "An Approach to the Study of Communications Acts," *Psychological Review* 60 (1953): 393–404.

46. Charles E. Osgood and Percy Tennenbaum, "The Principle of Congruity in the Prediction of Attitude Change," *Psychological Review* 62 (1955): 42–55.

47. For an example of an application of the congruity principle to analysis of changes in political attitude, *see* Denis Sullivan, "Psychological Balance and Reactions to the Presidential Nomination in 1960," in M. Kent Jennings and Harmon Zeigler (eds.), *The Electoral Process* (Englewood Cliffs, N.J.: Prentice-Hall, 1966), pp. 238–64.

48. Leon Festinger, *A Theory of Cognitive Dissonance* (Stanford: Stanford University Press, 1957).

49. *Ibid.*, p. 3.

50. *Ibid.*, p. 13.

51. *Ibid.*, pp. 12–15.

52. *Ibid.*, pp. 18–24.

53. *Ibid.*, pp. 28–29.

54. For a critique of cognitive dissonance theory, *see* Charles A. Kiesler, Barry Collins and Norman Miller, *Attitude Change* (New York: John Wiley and Sons, 1969).

55. *See* Leon Festinger, *Conflict, Decision and Dissonance* (Stanford: Stanford University Press, 1964); J. W. Brehm and A. R. Cohen, *Explorations in Cognitive Dissonance* (New York: John Wiley and Sons, 1962).

56. For a recent assessment of varieties of cognitive consistency theory, *see* Robert P. Abelson, Elliot Aronson, William J. McGuire, Theodore M. Newcomb, Milton J. Rosenberg, Percey H. Tannenbaum (ed.), *Theories of Cognitive Consistency: A Sourcebook* (Chicago: Rand McNally and Company, 1968). For other presentations of several varieties of attitude and attitude change theory, *see* Milton J. Rosenberg, Carl I. Hovland, William J. McGuire, Robert P. Abelson, and Jack W. Brehm, *Attitude Organization and Change* (New Haven: Yale University Press, 1960); Muzafer Sherif and Carl I. Hovland, *Social Judgment* (New Haven: Yale University Press, 1961); Charles E. Osgood and Percy Tannenbaum, "The Principle of Congruity in the Prediction of Attitude Change," *Psychological Review* 62 (1955): 42–55; Fritz Heider, "Attitude and Cognitive Organization," *Journal of Psychology* 21 (1946): 107–12; Dorwin Cartwright and Frank Harary, "Structural Balance: A Generalization of Heider's Theory," *Psychological Review* 63 (1956): 277–93; Chester A. Insko, *Theories of Attitude Change* (New York: Appleton-Century-Crofts, 1967); Roger Brown, *Social Psychology* (New York: The Free Press, 1965), chap. 11.

57. M. Brewster Smith, Jerome Bruner, and Robert W. White, *Opinions and Personality* (New York: John Wiley and Sons, 1964).

58. *Ibid.*, p. 33.

59. *Ibid.*, pp. 39–43.

60. *Ibid.*, p. 33.

61. *Ibid.*, pp. 253–79.

62. *Ibid.*

63. *See* Hovland, Janis, and Kelley, *Communication and Persuasion.*

64. For a more extensive discussion of these findings, *see* Sidney Verba, *Small Groups and Political Behavior* (Princeton University Press, 1961), pp. 22–45; A. Paul Hare, *Handbook of Small Group Research* (New York: Free Press, 1962); Clovis R. Shepherd, *Small Groups* (San Francisco: Chandler Publishing Company, 1964); Charles A. Kiesler and Sara B. Kiesler, *Conformity* (Reading, Mass.: Addison-Wesley, 1969); Robert E. Lane and David O. Sears, *Public Opinion* (Englewood Cliffs, N.J.: Prentice-Hall, 1964), pp. 34–42; Hovland, Janis, and Kelley, *Communication and Persuasion.*

65. Hovland, Janis, and Kelly, *Communication and Persuasion.*

66. Bernard Hennessy, "Public Opinion and Opinion Change," in *Political Science Annual,* Vol. I, edited by James A. Robinson (Indianapolis: Bobbs-Merrill Company, 1966), pp. 274–75. McGuire, "Nature of Attitudes," in *Social Psychology,* pp. 203–05, summarizes research which indicates the degree of relationship between fear arousal and attitude change may be curvilinear. Intervening variables may be the individual's level of anxiety (need or motive) and the complexity of the message.

67. *See* McGuire, "Nature of Attitudes," in *Social Psychology,* pp. 241–43, for a review of research findings.

68. T. W. Adorno, Else Frenkel-Brunswik, Daniel J. Levinson, and R. Nevitt Sanford, *The Authoritarian Personality* (New York: Science Editions, 1964), part I, p. 228.

69. Rokeach, "Role of Values in Public Opinion Research," p. 550.

70. *Ibid.,* p. 551.

71. *Ibid.,* pp. 556–60; "Voters and Value Systems," *Washington Post,* Aug. 11, 1968, p. B1.

72. Rokeach, "Role of Values in Public Opinion Research," p. 556.

73. Rokeach, "Voters and Value Systems."

74. Rokeach, *Beliefs, Attitudes, and Values,* pp. 157–58.

75. Angus Campbell, Philip Converse, Warren Miller, and Donald Stokes, *The American Voter* (New York: John Wiley and Sons, 1960); Donald R. Matthews and James W. Prothro, *Negroes and the New Southern Politics* (New York: Harcourt, Brace, and World, 1966).

76. Almond and Verba, *op. cit.*

77. David C. Schwartz, "Toward a Theory of Political Recruitment," *Western Political Quarterly* 22 (September 1969): 552–71.

78. Karl Deutsch, Lewis J. Edinger, Roy C. Macridis, and Richard L. Merritt, *France, Germany, and the Western Alliance: A Study of Elite Attitudes on European Integration* (New York: Charles Scribner's Sons, 1967).

79. Samuel Huntington, *Political Order in Changing Societies* (New Haven: Yale University Press, 1968); Daniel Lerner, *The Passing of Traditional Society* (New York: The Free Press, 1958).

STUDY QUESTIONS

1. Define the following:

belief	balance theory
attitude	opinion
value	cognitive consistency theory
value system	cognitive dissonance theory

Applications

2. What are the relationships between attitudes, beliefs, and values? In trying to explain the political behavior of individuals should political scientists concentrate on studying attitudes, or on studying beliefs, or on studying values? Why?

3. Can the behavior of individuals or groups of individuals be predicted from the study of attitudes?

4. How do attitudes and beliefs affect an individual's perceptions of political events?

5. To what extent do individuals change their attitudes over time? How can changes in attitudes be explained?

CHAPTER

6

Political Socialization

How do individuals learn the attitudes, beliefs, and values they hold about politics? How do they learn different political roles, such as voter, revolutionary activist, interest-group member, campaign worker, or legislator? By what processes do individuals learn patterns of political behavior? Is political behavior learned in a particular sequence? Are there urban–rural, north–south, or black–white differences in the way in which political attitudes are formed in the United States? If differences do exist, what factors can account for these differences?

Although interest in political socialization dates from the writings of Aristotle and Plato, it has been a subject of renewed interest in the past decades, particularly in the past fifteen years.[1] In part this interest has been stimulated by the recognition by new nations that they need to instill in their citizens support for the political community, which encompasses the nation, the regime (the political institutions and rules of the game), and the occupants of political roles. Nations that have undergone a sharp change in the nature of their regime, such as the countries of eastern Europe, or frequent changes in the structure of their regime, such as France, have also been faced with educating citizens, both young and old, to accept the regime and its political leaders. The riots, protests, and demonstrations directed against aspects of the American political system in recent years have also stimulated interest in the processes and consequences of political socialization.

DEFINITIONS OF POLITICAL SOCIALIZATION

A number of definitions of political socialization have been used by political researchers. One definition focuses on political learning by the individual.[2] From this perspective, political socialization is

> ... all political learning, formal and informal, deliberate and unplanned at every stage of the life cycle, including not only explicitly political learning but also nominally non-political learning that affects political behavior, such as learning of politically relevant social attitudes and the acquisition of politically relevant personality characteristics.[3]

Other definitions focus upon how the system acts upon the individual or on the socialization process as perpetuating or creating the learned patterns that are considered appropriate. For example,

> What do we mean by the function of political socialization? We mean that all political systems tend to perpetuate their cultures through time, and that they do this mainly by means of the socialization influences of the primary and secondary structures through which the young of the society pass in the process of maturation ... Political socialization is the process of induction into the political culture. Its end product is a set of attitudes, cognitions, value standards, and feelings—toward the political system, its various roles, and role incumbents. It also includes knowledge of values affecting, and feelings toward the inputs of demands and claims into the system, and its authoritative outputs.[4]

Definitions of political socialization have been criticized for tending to emphasize only learning that is supportive of the existing political culture and political system. To avoid this problem, perhaps political socialization is better defined as "developmental processes through which persons acquire political orientations and patterns of behavior."[5]

The different definitions of political socialization indicate some of the variations in direction which the study of political socialization has taken. One emphasis has been on the character of a country's political culture and its persistence or change over time.[6] Origins and development of individual political orientations are stressed by other researchers.[7] Political socialization has been used in the analysis of different political systems and in the analysis of individual political behavior.

THEORETICAL MODELS OF POLITICAL SOCIALIZATION

Social Learning Model

Theories on how learning occurs that are most often used by political scientists are social learning theory and cognitive development theory. Social learning theorists describe learning as the process of associating stimuli with appropriate responses. Social learning theories differ according to how they define the nature of the link between stimulus and response, the importance they give to variations in individual characteristics in learning, and the emphasis they place on rewards and reinforcement in the learning process. In one form of social learning theory, for example, an individual identifies with a model and imitates the model's behavior. A reward may be offered to induce imitation, such as the social approval of others. This type of explanation can account for children adopting the same party identification as their parents. A secondary reinforcement may occur through the value children attach to imitating their parents. Social learning occurs when a regime acts to foster public support through the creation of a sense of legitimacy for the regime. Legitimacy means that the government is viewed as having the moral right to exercise authority over the individual; obedience is given not because of fear of penalties such as imprisonment but because a citizen believes he or she has an obligation to accede to the rules and regulations enacted and enforced by the government.*

The development of legitimacy for a regime can be viewed as a six-stage learning process in which the regime provides the stimulus to create a public response. The first stage promotes an unconditioned response. The regime provides the stimulus for the populace in the form of material inducement, such as food, security, and shelter, or it creates situations in which these needs can be acquired. The population responds to the rewards these inducements offer. The second stage uses classical conditioning methods. The regime associates itself with the stimulus that provokes the behavior in the first stage; this association is made by pairing institutions or processes with the unconditioned stimulus of material inducements. The government thus becomes the cue for the stimulus and the reward. In

---

*Legitimacy is "the quality of 'oughtness' that is perceived by the public to inhere in a political regime. That government is legitimate which is viewed as morally proper for a society."[8]

the third stage, intermittent reinforcement, the government provides the reward only intermittently, which reduces the cost of providing the reward. In the fourth stage, secondary reinforcement, a new behavior pattern is demanded of the population by the regime; the response demanded is given because the government assures the citizens that if they respond the regime will produce the institutional processes that symbolize unconditional reinforcement. Secondary reinforcement is followed by reducing the cognitive dissonance. Compliance with the regime's demand for the new behavior pattern is accompanied by the conferring of legitimacy on the regime. This is done by the population to reduce the cognitive dissonance between gaining primarily symbolic rewards and having to learn new behavior patterns. The last stage of the legitimacy process is the development and use of condensation symbols, in which the symbols of legitimacy become substitute gratifications.

Condensation symbols may include the nation's flag, constitution, national heroes, and slogans such as "the American way of life" and "the law of the land." The regime must attempt to minimize the discrepancy between symbols and policy, to restrain the application of the symbol to the appropriate politics so as to maintain the symbol's credibility, and to generate new symbols of legitimacy, because over time symbols tend to be broadly applied and to lose their effectiveness. For example, President Lyndon Johnson used such symbols as "our national interest" and "protecting the right of a people to determine through democratic processes their own form of government" to justify escalation of the Vietnam War. Campaign rhetoric has generated new symbols such as the slogans "New Deal," "New Frontier," and "The Great Society."

Symbols can be used to increase the rate of learning, with the symbols conveying a negative or a positive sanction. Symbols can be used to oppose, to avoid, or to reward behavior.[9] For example, if an individual opposed the war in Vietnam, he was accused of acting against the national interest. A symbol could be used to avoid confronting a national issue, such as when the government said that all who supported the Vietnam War were acting in the national interest. National policy is usually formulated and presented to the public in terms of avoidance and escape symbols. The multistage process is not sequential; an individual accepts certain condensation symbols, as he simultaneously is in another stage relative to another problem of government policy that strives to bestow legitimacy.

Cognitive Theories of Socialization

Cognitive theorists emphasize the cognitions (beliefs, perceptions, or attitudes) held by the individual and the influences of these cognitions on the individual's interactions with his environment. To cognitive theorists, learning is the study of the acquisition and modification of cognitions. Cognitive and social learning theories have a number of variations.[10]

Jean Piaget's theory of cognitive development is widely used in research on political socialization.[11] Piaget says that children progress through several cognitive stages of learning. What a child is capable of learning is a function of the level of cognitive development that he or she has attained. The stages of cognitive development upon which most political socialization studies have focused are the ability to perform concrete operations involving accurate observation and manipulation of tangible objects, and the ability to perform formal operations requiring abstract reasoning and cause-and-effect analysis. Children between the ages of nine and twelve can usually perform concrete operations, and adolescents are usually capable of reasoning on abstract levels. Since much political thought uses concrete operations, and frequently abstract operations, the focus on this aspect of Piaget's work is understandable.

The use of cognitive development theory in political research is illustrated by the following series of studies. Samples of eleven-, thirteen-, fifteen, and eighteen-year-olds in three countries (the U.S., Germany, and England) were presented with a series of situations beginning with the following: A thousand people decide to leave their country to establish a new community on a Pacific Island. Once there, they must construct a government. The students were asked general questions, such as what is the purpose of government? what is the purpose of law? and then specific questions, such as should people without children pay taxes to support public schools? what should be done when members of a religious sect refuse to be vaccinated? The questions covered a range of topics, such as the scope and limits of government authority, civic obligations, the nature of law and freedom, political processes, and the role of political partisanship. These questions permitted an analysis of differences in political thought as it was formulated by individuals in different stages of cognitive development and in different countries. The study found that the youngest children rarely imagined that a law could be unfair or incorrect; they did not view law as functional, nor did they think it could be changed if it were not working properly.[12] Older children were more aware of the need for legal safeguards to maintain the right of privacy against intrusions by laws and the need to guarantee individual liberties. However, even by the age of eighteen the notion of protection of individual liberty as a reason for opposition to certain laws was advanced by only 40 percent of the children in the United States sample and by less than 25 percent of the children in the English and German samples.[13]

In the most advanced stage of cognitive development, children develop a sense of political community, an idea of the role of social institutions and of their structures and functions, and the ability to deal with abstract democratic concepts, such as authority, liberty, equality, freedom, representation, rights, and obligations. A sense of history also develops, although the temporal range does not usually reach its fullest extension until the end of adolescence. A more comprehensive understanding of human motivation also occurs. Deductive reasoning, which is characteristic of the last stage of cognitive development, is necessary for reasoned political thought. The evidence from this and other research is that the ability to reason deductively does not develop in most children until late adolescence.[14]

Indirect Political Socialization

A distinction can be made between direct and indirect political socialization.[15] Indirect socialization means the learning of non-political but politically relevant aspects of behavior; this involves personality characteristics and orientations toward various roles and role relationships, such as orientations toward figures of authority. In contrast, direct learning experiences are explicitly political in content.

One form of indirect learning is interpersonal transfer, in which explicit predispositions, such as orientations to authority, are developed. Patterns learned in other social roles are transferred to political roles. Orientations developed in family, school, and work experiences are transferred to the individual's role expectations for authority figures in the political system. A second form of indirect learning is apprenticeship, in which skills and values necessary for performance of political roles are developed. Children's organizations such as the Boy Scouts, 4-H clubs, church groups, and extracurricular activities in schools serve as agents of political socialization in this sense. The individual learns to accept the rules of the organization and to participate. A related type of indirect political socialization is the extension of general social values to the political system. The beliefs and values of the general culture are manifested in the political system; for example, a low value for equality in the general society would be transferred to a low value for equality in the political system.

The processes of indirect political socialization are continuous throughout life, changing and occurring as the individual's circumstances vary. A feedback process probably exists whereby the existence of democracy in one social system may result in increased demands for democracy in another, such as the work group or school or family. An example is the demand by students for more participation in university and college decision making. Awareness of this feedback process may have been present in the Soviet Union's fears of democratic reforms proposed by Czech liberals in the late 1960s. The existence of democracy in economic and social spheres probably would have stimulated demands for greater participation in the Communist party and the government.

Direct Political Socialization

A number of direct modes of political socialization exist.[16] Imitation of the political orientations and behavior of others is a major direct socialization process. Assuming the party identification of one's parents can be explained in these terms. A second type of direct socialization occurs in anticipation of a political orientation, role expectation, or role behavior appropriate to a future role that an individual wishes to acquire in the political arena, such as partisan voter, party official, or candidate for elective office. In high school and college, adherents of political parties who aspire to political roles develop orientations and behaviors appropriate to the desired future role through their participation in the Young Democrats, Young Republicans, or other political clubs.

A third type of direct socialization is provided by the educational system and other socializing agents, such as the family, church, or social groups that work directly to create political attitudes and patterns of behavior. The high school civics curriculum, with courses such as Problems of Democracy, American Government, and American History, is a deliberate attempt at political socialization. Such courses usually aim at developing support for the political community and the regime. In some nations, such as the People's Republic of China, support for incumbent political leaders is also a major objective of the educational system's efforts. Rituals such as saluting the flag, singing the national anthem, or studying major historical events or speeches of political leaders are used by the educational system to create desired political orientations. Expressions by teachers of their own attitudes may also have a direct but perhaps unintended effect on their students' political orientations. A fourth type of direct political education occurs through the impact of direct political experiences on the individual. A political campaign, an incident with a representative of the regime such as a policeman, legislator, welfare worker, housing inspector, zoning official, or highway worker, or an appearance in court affect the individual's political orientations toward the regime, its incumbents, or the political community.

Direct political experiences shape one's expectations, orientations, and future behavior in political roles. It is easier to study political orientations of individuals and the activities of socializing agents than it is to study the actual process of learning those political orientations.[17]

DISCONTINUITIES IN POLITICAL SOCIALIZATION

Individuals may be incorrectly socialized in the sense that the institutions and political cultures to which they are socialized may change over time, creating an incongruity between learned orientations and the actual political system. During the time lag between early learning of political orientations and actual entry into participation in the political system, political arrangements may change, the structure of institutions may alter, or a shift in political roles may occur. [18] Discontinuity may also arise when different stimuli are presented by various socializing experiences or by the agents of socialization. For example, one's family may support the Democratic party and its candidates, while one's friends are all Republicans. Another potential source of discontinuity is the variance between personal socializing experiences and impersonal situations in which political behavior may occur.[19] A source of discontinuity that has not been adequately explored is created by the presentation of an idealized version of the political system to children in the classroom and the home, which later personal experiences and observations of mass media contradict. This discrepancy may serve as a stimulus for political alienation or radical political activity by the disillusioned.

The nature of the political system itself may contribute to discontinuities in political socialization. Congruence between types of authority systems may vary inversely with the degree of social stratification, specialization, and stability of the community's political structures, and with the presence of secondary structures, such as schools and peer groups organized for political socialization. As one might anticipate, greater discrepancies in political socialization are likely to occur when a number of different socializing agents are present in the system.[20] In a developed country such as the United States, individuals are exposed not only to the family and the educational system but also to many other agents, such as several types of mass media, many social groups, and a variety of clubs, interest groups, organizations, religious institutions, and government agencies acting or attempting to act as socializing agents.

AGENTS OF POLITICAL SOCIALIZATION

Which agent or agents are the most important in creating and transmitting political orientations? What kinds of political behavior are learned from each agent? The findings of various studies do not present a consistent pattern. In part this may be a function of inappropriate research designs or different cultures.

The Family

The role of the family in political socialization may vary with the social and economic status of the family; children from working-class families who receive little exposure to politics or political information from the family may perceive the school as a primary source of political information.[21] The relative influence of the family may also vary with the pattern of paternal authority. Children from homes with disrupted family patterns, such as the absence of a father figure or presence of matriarchical dominance, have different attitudes than children from homes with more normal family patterns.[22] Children's levels of interest in politics may also be related to family structure; children who perceive their fathers as powerful have more interest in politics.[23] (The testing of these hypotheses has been limited and the evidence is not conclusive.)

Rather than the presence of a particular pattern of parental authority, the style in which authority is exercised may influence children's orientations toward authority. One test of the relationship between degree of parental punitiveness (as perceived by the child), children's levels of anxiety and authoritarianism, and their perceptions of presidential benevolence and strength found children's anxiety levels to be related to their level of authoritarianism, and levels of authoritarianism to be related to their perceptions of presidential strength. No relationship existed between the degree of authoritarianism and perceptions of presidential benevolence.[24]

Parental influence tends to be greater where a political object, such as an attitude or party identification, is important to the parent and where the child accurately perceives parental views.[25] Another study found that male children from maternal families (where the father is absent) tended to hold more authoritarian attitudes and to have lower levels of political interest than males from families where both parents were present. Both boys and girls from maternal families had lower levels of political efficacy.[26] Low political interest and high authoritarianism were also found in working- and middle-class nuclear families where the mother was dominant. One study of the relative influence of the father and mother in the transmission of political party identification and issue positions rejects the hypothesis that the father dominates in the transmission of values.[27]

In a sample of high school students surveyed in Jamaica, increased deviation from parental party identification accompanied the more autocratic parental authority patterns, except in the most autocratically run families. Children from the most autocratic families equalled the least autocratic families in low deviation from the parental norm of party identification.[28]

Children acquire basic orientations from parents, the most basic being a sense of belonging to a political community.[29] Basic orientations are largely affective or emotional. Through elementary school years and adolescence the child builds on this affective base a set of cognitive—or knowledge-based—orientations. Through the processes previously discussed, the school and peer groups become important in conveying cognitive orientations. Later, direct political experiences, the mass media, and secondary groups act as important socializing agents in establishing orientations toward political role incumbents and public policy concerns and may alter affective and cognitive orientations learned earlier. Agents of socialization who have initial contact also have direct authority over the child; agents operating in later periods tend to be peers or to be removed from direct personal contact with the individual.

Children's perceptions of political authorities have been extensively researched. During the early 1960s, children studied tended to have an image of the president as benevolent and strong, supposedly because children tended to view parental authority in this way.[30] Studies of minority and economically disadvantaged children, however, reported that these children were less trusting of government.[31] Research of the late 1960s and early 1970s also reported a more malevolent image of the president among economically advantaged white children.[32] The president was also viewed as weak and unable to force others to perform as he desired.[33] The image of political authority appears to reflect the changing political environment.

In examining the correlation of selected attitudes between parents and a national sample of high school seniors, one study found that the transmission of political orientations from parent to child varied extensively with the nature of the political orientations involved.[34] The orientations studied included party identification, political cynicism, political cosmopolitanism, opinions on four political issues, and evaluations of Catholics, blacks, and Jews. Except at the extremes of the political cynicism scale and generally for party identification, a high degree of correspondence was not present between the orientations held by parents and high school seniors.

Family influence on voter preference and partisan identification increases when family members agree on a party choice, political interest is high among family members, and the same family party identification has persisted over time. This is reinforced if family

167

members are in frequent contact, if they like each other, and if they have a similar life style. Affiliation with peer groups such as friends or coworkers who have a different party preference will weaken an individual's attachment to his parental family party preference. If children from a family of low social status rebel against rigid parental control, they may reject parental party identification. This pattern was not found among young voters from upper socioeconomic status backgrounds.[35]

The School

Although some researchers believe that an individual's primary socializing agent is the family,[36] others assign first significance to the school.[37] (These researchers do admit, however, that partisan identification is related to parental party identification.) A study of elementary and junior high school students found that children from low socioeconomic backgrounds and children with low intelligence both perceived that their teachers had a greater influence on their political socialization than did their families.[38]

The school accomplishes political socialization through its curriculum, classroom rituals, and values and attitudes unconsciously transmitted by its staff. The school's social climate, political and nonpolitical organizations, and extracurricular activities exert subtle socializing influences. The effects of being educated about political affairs, also a task of the school, bear on political socialization.[39] Noting the distinction between civic education—which seeks to inform children about the nature of political institutions, processes, and "rules of the game"—and political indoctrination—which attempts to instill in the individual a set of preferences for an ideology, party, or regime—research indicates that civic education efforts of the schools may have a greater impact on children from lower social status backgrounds.[40] However, a study of a French village indicates that where formal curriculum materials are highly incongruent with orientations presented by family and others in informal socializing experiences, the formal socialization effort is ineffective.[41] A national study of American high school seniors concluded that generally the high school civics curriculum had little impact on levels of political knowledge and sophistication, political interest, spectator politicalization, political efficacy, political cynicism, and civic tolerance.[42] This suggests that for most students the civics curriculum merely reinforces other socializing agents. Black students tend to score lower on scales of political knowledge, political efficacy, political cynicism, civic tolerance, political discussion, and media usage. The number and type of civic education courses taken have a greater impact on black students than on whites.[43] The research attributes this to a lesser degree of prior information among black students than among whites.[44]

Other socializing stimuli are presented by rituals observed in the schools, such as the salute to the flag, singing of the national anthem, celebration of national historical events, and displays of historical portraits or events on classroom walls. The teacher, through expression of opinions and display of interest in political events, may have an unconscious impact on the political orientations of students. However, a study of American elementary and junior high school students that evaluated the degree of congruence between children's and teacher's views concluded that congruence was greatest in areas with generally accepted orientations.[45] Another study indicated that the more democratic the classroom environment, the higher the sense of personal political competence. The school environment and extracurricular activities also serve to instill political values, such as participation, competitiveness, achievement, and observing the rules of the game.[46] The more educated may differ from the less educated in the following ways:

1. The more educated are more aware of the impact of government on the individual.
2. The more educated are more likely to follow politics in the mass media and to read communications about election campaigns.
3. The more educated have a greater store of political information.
4. The more educated hold political opinions on a greater range of subjects.
5. The more educated are more likely to take part in discussions of political subjects.
6. The more educated feel free to discuss more political subjects with a wider range of individuals than the less educated.
7. The more educated are more likely to consider themselves capable of influencing the government.
8. The more educated are more likely to be members of organizations.
9. The more educated are more likely to express a sense of personal competence and to trust others.[47]

Others have argued that the more highly educated possess greater competence even before acquiring a college education, and also tend to come from families with higher income, educational, and occupational levels. Conclusions about the influence of education may represent a confusion of education and socioeconomic background.[48]

Peer Groups

Another possible influence on political socialization is the peer group. A study of Jamaican children indicated that children of working class backgrounds whose best friends came from different social class backgrounds, tended to be resocialized in the direction of higher social class norms. Those whose peer groups were heterogeneous in respect to social class also tended to be more ambivalent and less supportive of the political system.[49] A study of the party identification of American high school students found that students attending a high school where most students held a party identification contrary to that of their family were more likely to deviate from family party identification than were students in high schools where their peers had partisan attachments similar to those of their family. The relevance of the political environment may vary with the youth's level of political interest and with his or her degree of psychological dependence on the family.[50]

Although several studies have examined the influence of family, peer group, and the school in the socialization of children, the relative influence of each has not been examined in detail. One exception is the study of the relative role of family, peer group, and school as politicizing agents on Jamaican high school students' levels of political efficacy. Using sophisticated data analysis techniques, which assumed that each of the three agents contributed additively to the development of high school students' political efficacy, the family was found to be four times more influential than the school or peer group along the entire range of levels of political efficacy. However, when controls for social class were applied, peer-group politicization was more influential among upper class children.[51] Among the children studied, a higher level of school politicization tended to be effective in moving students from a low to a medium level of political efficacy, but not in moving students from a medium to a high level of political efficacy.[52]

The Media

Little research has directly examined the relationship between children's consumption of mass media communications and their political orientations. The importance of the media as a socializing agent may vary among undeveloped, transitional, and modern societies; exposure to media is general and diffuse in traditional societies and more specialized and selective in developed nations.[53] What is absorbed from the mass media is a function of the individual's existing predispositions, which act as a perpetual screen on what is received from the mass media. Comparison of the consumption of mass media by a sample of American high school seniors and their parents indicates that consumption by seniors is lower than that of their parents. It has been suggested that consumption by the seniors will increase to approximate the level of their parents in the future.[54] High school seniors used the radio most and the television least to obtain information related to public affairs. However, the analysis does not assess the direct socializing effects of the mass media.

A frequently cited review of the effects of the mass media argues that mass media primarily reinforce—they do not create patterns of belief, nor do they convert.[55] However, more recent research sampling adults and children suggests that the mass media have a significant effect on political orientations.[56] Both news and entertainment can have an impact. Children may absorb role expectations about political and government figures from television, by watching shows about the FBI, policemen, or spy organizations. During election campaigns, they are exposed to commercials urging support and participation for a candidate or party. Children and adolescents are more likely to watch television news than to read news in newspapers and magazines.[57] Television is their most important source of information overall.[58] Print media use is usually more highly correlated with political knowledge and attitudes than is television news viewing.[59]

CHILDREN'S POLITICAL ORIENTATIONS

Young children's images of government are largely personal and charismatic, focusing on a few role incumbents such as the president or mayor. Political socialization begins at about age three; orientations at that age are primarily toward the political community and of an emotional nature. Later, prominent public figures or symbols, such as the president, policemen, and the flag, are recognized. Over time, orientations become more impersonal and more abstract, and children become interested in processes such as voting and law making.[60] As children grow older, they become more aware of the group and institutional character of government and they begin to conceive of government as process. Their own role in government as a participant also begins to be perceived. A distinction between president as law-executor and Congress as law-enactor becomes clear, and differentiation between private and public sectors develops by the eighth grade.[61] Children in the United States tend to approve of the scope of government to a greater degree than do adults and do not believe that the government exercises undue or excessive power over citizens.[62]

The key orientations for political participation as a voter—party identification, issue orientation, and candidate orientation—do not develop simultaneously; party and candidate awareness precede issue concerns. This may be true in the United States in part because parties are a stable organizing mechanism that persist over time. In a country such as France, which has experienced unstable party systems, children are oriented to politics through more stable social units, such as social class or religious affiliation.

Children first tend to view the rules of society as unchanging, but as they grow older the changeability of rules and the possibility that breaking the rules may not bring punishment becomes more evident. Early socialization processes result in the development of orientations of loyalty and of obedience to rules. The stress on participation develops later.[63]

We must remember that within any political system, political subcultures at variance with the total society's predominant pattern may exist. This variance places stress on the system and may result in its instability. If political socialization to the predominant cultural norms is effective, the stress on the system is considerably reduced.

Cultural variations in political socialization have been found in the United States.[64] Political socialization may vary with different group experiences (defined in terms of race, religion, ethnic origin, class, or place of residence), which are generalized into political orientations. For example, different experiences with authority figures in family or religious life may be generalized into perceptions of political authority figures.

ADULT SOCIALIZATION

Political socialization occurs throughout life, not only because political institutions and behavior patterns expected of the citizen in the political system may change, but for several other reasons.

As we have indicated, children are usually socialized to hold political values, such as to support the system and the regime, to accept the regime as legitimate, and to obey the rules and laws of the system. They are also taught orientations that relate to the citizen role, such as to participate in the system through voting. However, they cannot act on some of these orientations until they reach adulthood. Other relationships with the political system are not likely to be experienced until reaching adulthood; these include paying taxes, serving on a jury, dealing with government bureaucrats, or attempting to obtain a change in a rule or law. Most political roles are open only to persons who meet special qualifications, the most basic of which is a minimum age. To serve as a candidate for elected office, a party official, or an appointed member of a board or commission, the adult learns the role expectations and acquires the skills necessary to meet them. Few studies have been conducted of the processes of socialization to specialized political roles, although studies have been made of the orientations and expectations of those in a particular role. (*See* Chapter 7 for further discussion of specialized political roles.)

A variety of factors can influence recruitment to specialized political roles. Research has focused on social background characteristics, such as education, occupation, or social class; the prerequisites that provide competence for performance of a particular role, such as motivations, drives, needs, and other personality characteristics, have also been explored.[65] It has been argued that those who are recruited to activist roles have been highly exposed to political activity. This exposure may occur through membership in a highly politically active family, involvement in school politics or a reform movement, or employment in an occupation that coincides with the activities of government, such as the practice of law.[66] Evidence exists to indicate that these socializing experiences have not been experienced by some political activists.[67]

Certain forms of participation, such as taking part in demonstrations, riots, and various forms of civil disobedience, are open to those excluded from what are traditionally regarded as the more normal methods of expressing views and policy preferences in a democracy. These forms of participation also are learned through peer-group agents, the mass media, or formal instructional methods.

One author has suggested five changes that generally occur as a consequence of adult socialization; these changes would also occur as an adult becomes politically socialized. Adults shift focus from learning values to performing specific types of behavior. They synthesize what they have learned rather than acquire additional orientations. They modify their idealized expectations about role incumbents, the regime, and the political community, rather than completely change them. Increased awareness of conflicting demands of political roles, which is part of the maturation process, forces an adult to develop abilities or orientations to cope with these conflicts. An adult also continues to apply learned orientations both generally and specifically.[68] Adults who are geographically or socially mobile may be subject to more socializing agents who seek to impart new or different orientations. Roles that change as a consequence of maturation may also result in changed political orientations and behavior.

PROBLEMS IN RESEARCHING POLITICAL SOCIALIZATION

We must now consider three issues. (1) What approach should future efforts to develop a theory of political socialization take? (2) What methodological criticisms can be made of past research? (3) What methods are available to improve our knowledge of political socialization? A central issue in any discussion of political socialization is whether to explain individual political socialization or to focus on the implications of political socialization for the political system. Probably political socialization should be studied from both perspectives.

If political socialization theory is to be approached from the perspective of individual socialization, several sociological and social psychological theories can be utilized as a basis for analysis. Aspects of theories on learning, attitude change, personality, motivation, small groups and roles can provide a basis for improved understanding of political socialization. These approaches examine how political socialization occurs among individuals, focusing on the processes by which they learn and on what is specifically learned at each stage of political socialization.

An alternative approach is to focus on the relevance to the

political system of political socialization. Easton and Dennis have argued that this logically should be the first concern of those who study political socialization.[69] Three alternative theoretical approaches are feasible—allocative system stability, and systems persistence. By allocative theory is meant a focus on development of political value structures and on how values are allocated among members of a political community. The inadequacy of this approach to socialization is in part a consequence of the incompleteness of an allocative theory of politics. This approach can be attacked because it identifies the antecedents of existing adult behavior patterns and attitudes and ignores potential for change.[70]

An alternative approach is system stability, or structural—functionalism, which is implicit in many of the comparative studies of political socialization. A key assumption in this approach is that a system attempts to maintain stability, or, to state it very simply, to maintain a particular state of being over time. A constant state does not imply peace or order; for example, system stability to Mao Tse-tung apparently means permanent revolutionary fervor. The focus on stability or system maintenance may inhibit an adequate examination of the consequences of certain types of political socialization that produce change. Easton and Dennis advocate a systems persistence theory as a theoretical approach to the study of political socialization.[71] To ensure that a system persists, the system's members must be able to allocate values on a regular basis and to accept the allocative values as authoritative. This approach does not ignore the study of change in system patterns; it emphasizes the consequences of change in a system.

Even those who advocate a focus on the acquisition and development of individual political orientations are not satisfied with the knowledge we currently possess about the subject. One author has suggested that political scientists have not adequately studied learning processes or the development of political orientations in individuals.[72] Instead of studying development, they have examined the attitudes, values, and beliefs of children of different ages and assumed that any systematic differences among children of different ages can be attributed to development. This is faulty reasoning because older children may have been exposed to political stimuli different from the stimuli experienced by younger children. For example, because of different content in the mass media and in parental and school discussions to which they have been exposed and perhaps by observing the activities (such as strikes) of their teachers, younger children may be more likely than older persons to believe that strikes, demonstrations, and civil disobedience are appropriate ways of expressing political views and of obtaining changes in the structure of the system and its policies. The only way we can validly generalize about the development of political orientations is to study the same individuals over time.[73]

The published studies of political socialization generally focus on what individuals have learned, not the processes by which the individuals learn. One can study how children learn by examining the political, social, and physical conditions under which people learn, or by discovering psychological principles that explain how individuals learn.[74] Acquiring knowledge of both is necessary and not impossible, but political scientists have been quite slow in beginning the task. For example, we would anticipate that different stimuli are presented at home or in the outside environment to children in different social groups or from diverse subcultures. Their responses are not similarly rewarded or reinforced by the socializing agents to which they are exposed, and we might therefore reasonably anticipate that they would learn dissimilar orientations.

Studies of the same individuals over time are required if we are to understand how learning takes place both in the sense of understanding the social and psychological conditions under which it occurs and the psychological principles by which people learn. The interview method may be inadequate for longitudinal studies (studies conducted over time). Observation and in-depth interview methods would eliminate other problems, such as test anxiety created by the structured questionnaire, inability to ascertain the reasons given by individuals for their answers, the significance of their answers, or their conceptualization of the subject considered. Consideration should be given to projective techniques, such as Guttman scaling of attitude questions, and small-group experiments.[75]

Other criticisms can be made of the methods and theory used in socialization studies. The absence of theory resulting from these studies may be due to failure to examine the goals and values held by socializing agents and the values of persons being socialized.[76] Few researchers have examined the relationship between general cultural values and political values, although some work has been done.[77] It can be argued that manifest and later socialization experiences are more significant than latent and earlier experiences in influencing adult political behavior.[78] Researchers have emphasized the importance of childhood experiences in their studies. In the U.S., this emphasis may be due to the high degree of political stability; orientations established early in life often persist into and through adulthood to a greater degree in the United States than in other countries. Elite socialization, generational change, cultural differences, and discontinuities in socializing experiences have also been inadequately studied. Only through the study of variations in stimuli and response associated with different social groups and their environments can an adequate theory of political socialization be developed.

The data on which studies of political socialization have been based are not above criticism. The studies are few in number, and most have focused on one culture at one point in time in one small geographic area. Because of the limits of the universe from which the sample for a study is usually drawn and, in some cases, the methods used for drawing the sample, generalization from the studies to a broad population is not possible. Many more studies that test explicit hypotheses, based on theory appropriate to the research problem, are needed. Correct methods must be applied to explain learning and development of political orientations over time.

In order to develop adequate theories, the testing of hypotheses must contribute to an accumulation of knowledge; this is possible only if concepts are carefully defined and measured in a comparable fashion. Special problems in concept definition and measurement are present in political socialization studies of children, and particularly in studies of pre-high school children. In order for research results to be useful and comparable with results of other studies, a concept must be defined so that it can be used in a number of studies and measured in a fashion that produces reliable and valid results. Reliability, determined by testing and retesting, is somewhat impeded because children are constantly developing. A test–retest coefficient of .50 would not be unusual for an attitude scale administered to sixth-grade students, while the same scale might have a test–retest reliability coefficient of .85 when administered to high school seniors. Young children's cognitive structures are more likely to be latent or developing. Their political socialization has not yet resulted in the firm establishment of the attitude structures found in older children and adults. If this problem exists, can one even generalize about children's attitudes? Yes, if the researcher makes clear the reliability, both in terms of stability over time and homogeneity of items of the research instruments he is using.

Another problem is content validity; without content validity, construct validity is impossible. If one wants to study variations in attitudes, beliefs, and values of children of different ages at one point in time, how can one phrase a question so that young children can understand it and older children do not find it infantile? One has the same problem in studying the same set of children over time; a questionnaire item appropriate when the children are younger may appear too simple when the children have developed more sophisticated cognitive structures. The common use of structured, fixed-response questionnaires presents problems because the researcher assumes that he or she knows the significance to the child of the child's response and the context in which the child made the response. However, only when pretesting of a questionnaire on a sample of children similar to those in the study is done, can this be safely assumed. The pretest should use probing, open-ended, follow-up questions, presented orally. The questions should allow the researcher to evaluate the context and significance of the response to multiple choice questions.

Because of the contextual and significance problems, one can argue that socialization studies should use open-ended questions, obtain data by presenting problems or situations to be analyzed, or use only experimental methods. Most researchers have preferred to sacrifice the type of knowledge obtained through these data-gathering methods for the larger samples and greater number of variables that are possible with fixed alternative questions and paper-and-pencil questionnaires on which children can easily indicate their preferred response.

The problem found in other areas of inquiry is also lacking in political socialization studies. Although the objects of attention have been the same in several socialization studies, the operational definitions of the concepts, measurement techniques, and data-collection methods have not been the same. For example, several researchers have studied the perceived benevolence of the president. Using a paper-and-pencil questionnaire data-collection technique, Greenstein asked children in the fourth through the eighth grades, "What kinds of things do you think the president does?" The proportion of responses to this open-ended question coded as benevolence declined from 26 percent for fourth graders to 4 percent for eighth-grade children. Greenstein inferred that questions more specifically structured would uncover considerably higher benevolence ratings for the presidential role.[79]

Easton and Dennis used a different method to test children's image of the president. Each child was asked to respond to a number of statements about the president, each of which was stated with six wordings from positive to negative. For example, the child was asked to think of the president as he really is, checking one of the following:

1. Would always want to help me if I needed it.
2. Would almost always want to help me if I needed it.
3. Would usually want to help me if I needed it.
4. Would sometimes want to help me if I needed it.
5. Would seldom want to help me if I needed it.
6. Would not usually want to help me if I needed it.

The proportion who chose the first response declined from 67 percent in the second grade to 27 percent in the eighth grade.[80] The researchers designed another question to evaluate perceived benevolence: "Which do you think is most true?"

1. When you write to the president, he cares *a lot* what you think.
2. If you write to the president, he cares *some* what you think.
3. If you write to the president, he cares *a little* what you think.

The proportion in each grade selecting the first response declined from 75 percent in the second grade to 43 percent in the eighth grade.[81]

The concept of presidential benevolence has also been evaluated by Jaros, who designed a seventeen-item scale to measure presidential benevolence, with responses ranging from "agree very much" to "disagree very much." The scale was administered to a sample of Detroit area school children. Representative statements in the scale include "the president helps poor people," "the president helps us all to stay healthy," "the president does a great deal to help me," and "the president protects us from war." The attitude scale was converted to an index ranging from 0 to 100. The mean score on the scale for the sample of 746 Detroit school children was 72.5.[82]

Although all three measuring instruments are indices of presidential benevolence, they are not comparable. They do not use the same operational definition of the concept "presidential benevolence." However, research results from all these studies shows the same direction of the relationship, although the magnitude differs. Replicative studies using the same measurement procedures would be more persuasive in establishing the nature and magnitude of the relationship.

A second example of the problem of concept definition and the comparability of measures can be drawn from studies made of peer groups as agents of socialization. Differing conclusions about their effects as agents of socialization may be a result of methods used to measure their effects and of the political orientations on which the peer groups were hypothesized to have some consequence. A study of high school students in Illinois measured the effects of the social climate of the high school community on student deviations from parental party identification. An index of deviation was calculated by dividing the proportion of Republican-identifying students whose parents were Democratic by the sum of that figure and the proportion of Democratic students who were children of Republican identifiers. The association between the index of deviation and the high school community climate was then evaluated. [83]

To establish peer-group associations among Jamaican students, students were asked if their best friends were from the same social class or from a different social class. On the basis of their responses, students were categorized as belonging to either homogeneous or heterogeneous peer groups. Variations in support for democratic values, attitude toward voting, support for civil liberties, and level of politicization were examined. Students from working-class families generally scored low on these measures, but those whose peer groups were heterogeneous tended to hold political orientations more in keeping with middle-class norms. The study concluded that working-class students in heterogeneous peer groups were being resocialized toward middle-class norms, except for level of politicization. [84]

Another approach to the definition and measurement of peer-group influence was used to analyze peer-group influence on political orientations of high school seniors. Five variables that related to political orientation were considered: party identification, presidential candidate performance in the 1964 election, political efficacy, political cynicism, and support for the vote for 18-year-olds. Peer-group patterns were established by asking students to indicate the names of the five members of the senior class with whom they "went around most often." The basic assumption of this research is that the significant peer group is composed of members of the same class in the same school. Three different definitions of peer group were used: the five students named by each student; the set of individuals who named a specific senior as a friend; and the set of mutual friends (those who named a student and who had also been chosen by him).[85] Only moderate levels of association existed between high school seniors and their friends on the five different political variables. The level of association was lower for more basic orientations, such as party identification and level of political cynicism, than for current concerns, such as the most recent presidential election. For the sub-sample for which data were available, seniors' political orientations were closer to their parents for party identification and presidential vote preference, but more strongly associated with their peer-group for efficacy levels and preference for the 18-year-old vote.[86]

The methods used permitted considerable refinement of analysis because they allowed for the evaluation of independent, individual effects of such factors as student participation in extracurricular activities, sex differences, and social class of the student. However, research should also examine the cumulative effects of independent variables, patterns of orientations where conflict exists between parents and peers, and the effects of school atmosphere.

We have considered only three studies that examined peer-group influence on student political orientations. The political orientations that were examined in these studies varied, as did the methods used to assess peer-group influence. The direction of the findings is the same, but comparison of the findings and accumulation of a systematic body of knowledge are made difficult by different definitions and measurements.

How is the problem resolved? Through continued research, reliable and valid measures of concepts are developed. Over time, measures found to be reliable and valid are used by other researchers. A concept, such as presidential benevolence, comes to have an accepted operational definition and is similarly measured by researchers using the concept. Although this discussion is confined to the definition and measurement of two specific concepts, it is only illustrative; the problem is not unique to socialization studies or to political science research.

NOTES AND REFERENCES

1. Other academic disciplines concerned with the study of socialization have contributed to the study of political socialization. Cultural anthropologists and sociologists have studied the socialization of children and adults in different societies. Several approaches to psychiatry focus on childhood socializing experiences as a primary influence on the personality of the adult. The authors of a comparative study of political culture in five nations acknowledge the influence on their work of the psychocultural approach to studying political phenomena; see Gabriel Almond and Sidney Verba, *The Civic Culture* (Boston: Little, Brown, 1965). p. 11.

2. Herbert Hyman, *Political Socialization* (New York: The Free Press, 1959), p. 25. According to Robert Levine, "political socialization is the acquisition by an individual of behavioral dispositions relevant to political groups, political systems, and political processes. Examples of the kinds of behavior dispositions included are: attitudes concerning the allocation of authority, the legitimacy of a regime, and political participation; patterns of decision-making and deference; images of leaders and foreign nations; group loyalties, antagonisms, and stereotypes." Robert Levine, "Political Socialization and Cultural Change," in Clifford Geetz (ed.), *Old Societies and New States* (New York: The Free Press, 1963), pp. 280–81, footnote 1.

3. Fred I. Greenstein, "Political Socialization," in *International Encyclopedia of the Social Sciences,* vol. 14 (New York: Crowell-Collier and Macmillan, 1968), p. 551.

4. Gabriel A. Almond, "A Functional Approach to Comparative Politics," in G. Almond and J. S. Coleman (eds.), *The Politics of Developing Areas* (Princeton, N.J.: Princeton University Press, 1960), pp. 27–28.

5. David Easton and Jack Dennis, *Children in the Political System* (New York: McGraw-Hill, 1969), p. 7.

6. Almond and Verba, *Civic Culture;* Lucian Pye, *Politics, Personality and Nation-Building* (New Haven: Yale University Press, 1962); Henry W. Ehrmann, *France* (Boston: Little, Brown, 1968); Lewis J. Edinger, *Germany* (Boston: Little Brown, 1968); Easton and Dennis, *Children in the Political System.*

7. Hyman, *Political Socialization;* Lewis A. Froman, Jr., "Personality and Political Socialization," *Journal of Politics* 23 (May 1961); Fred I. Greenstein, *Children and Politics* (New Haven: Yale University Press, 1965); Robert D.

Hess and Judith V. Torney, *The Development of Political Attitudes in Children* (Chicago: Aldine Publishing Co., 1967).

8. Richard Merelman, "Learning and Legitimacy," *American Political Science Review* 60 (September 1966): 548.

9. *Ibid.*, p. 555.

10. For a discussion of various theories of learning, *see* Winifred F. Hill, *Learning: A Survey of Psychological Interpretations* (San Francisco: Chandler Publishing Co. 1963).

11. Jean Piaget's research is discussed in Henry W. Maier, *Three Theories of Child Development* (New York: Harper & Row, 1968), rev. ed.; J.H. Flavell, *The Developmental Psychology of Jean Piaget* (New York: Van Nostrand Rinehold, 1963); Jean Piaget and Barbel Inhelder, *The Psychology of the Child* (London: Routledge and Kegan Paul, 1971).

12. Joseph Adelson and Lynnette Beall, "Adolescent Perspectives on Law and Government," *Law and Society Review* 4 (May 1970): 495–504.

13. Judith Gallatin and Joseph Adelson, "Legal Guarantees of Individual Freedom: A Cross-National Study of the Development of Political Thought," *Journal of Social Issues* 27 (1971): 93–108.

14. Joseph Adelson, "The Political Imagination of the Young Adolescent," *Daedalus* (1971): 1013–50.

15. For a more extensive discussion of direct and indirect socialization, *see* Hess and Torney, *Development of Political Attitudes in Children,* pp. 19–22; Richard Dawson and Kenneth Prewitt, *Political Socialization* (Boston: Little Brown, 1968), chap. 5.

16. Dawson and Prewitt, *Political Socialization,* pp. 73–80.

17. *Ibid.*, p. 80.

18. A key focus in the five-nation study conducted by Almond and Verba was the degree of consistency between the orientations of the citizens and the political institutions of the society. Almond and Verba, *Civic Cultures,* chap. 1.

19. Dawson and Prewitt, *Political Socialization,* pp. 87–88.

20. Robert Levine, "The Role of the Family in Authority Systems: A Cross Cultural Application of Stimulus Generalization Theory," *Behavioral Science* 5 (October 1960): 295.

21. Hess and Torney, *Political Attitudes in Children,* pp. 100–01.

22. Dawson and Prewitt, *Political Socialization,* pp. 120–21.

23. Hess and Torney, *Political Attitudes in Children,* p. 101.

24. Dean Jaros, "Children's Orientations Toward the President," *Journal of Politics* 29 (May 1967): 383–84.

25. Kent L. Tedin, "The Influence of Parents on the Political Attitudes of Adolescents," *American Political Science Review* 68 (December 1974): 1579–92.

26. Kenneth P. Langton, *Political Socialization* (New York: Oxford University Press, 1969), p. 166.

27. *Ibid.*, p. 169.

28. *Ibid.*, pp. 26–28, 164–65.

29. Dawson and Prewitt, *Political Socialization,* p. 108.

30. Greenstein, *Children and Politics,* pp. 37–52.

31. Dean Jaros, Herbert Hirsch, and Frederick J. Fleron, Jr., "The Malevolent Leader: Political Socialization in an American Sub-Culture," *American Political Science Review* 62 (June 1968): 564–75; Edward S. Greenberg, "Children and Government: A Comparison Across Racial Lines," *Midwest Journal of Political Science* 14 (May 1970): 249–75; Edward S. Greenberg, "Orientations of Black and White Children to Political Authority Figures," *Social Science Quarterly* 51 (December 1970): 561–71; F. Chris Garcia, *Political Socialization of Chicano Children* (New York: Frederick A. Praeger, 1973), pp. 135–50; Dean Jaros and Kenneth L. Kolson, "The Multifarious Leader: Political Socialization of Amish, "Yank," "Blacks," in Richard G. Niemi and associates (eds.), *The Politics of Future Citizens* (San Francisco: Jossey Bass, 1974), pp. 41–62; James Lamare, "Language Environment and Political Socialization of Mexican American Children," in Niemi (ed.), *Politics of Future Citizens,* pp. 76–78; Sarah F. Liebschutz and Richard G. Niemi, "Political Attitudes Among Black Children," in Niemi, *Politics of Future Citizens,* pp. 83–102.

32. Christopher Arterton, "The Impact of Watergate on Children's Attitudes Toward Political Authority," *Political Science Quarterly* 89 (June 1974): 269–88; A. Jay Stevens and M. Margaret Conway, "Ethnic Children's View of the President and the Police: The Influence of the Family and the Mass Media" (Paper delivered at the Western Political Science Association meeting, Seattle, Washington, March 20, 1975).

33. Arterton, "Impact of Watergate"; Stevens and Conway, "Ethnic Children's View of the President."

34. M. Kent Jennings and Richard Niemi, "The Transmission of Political Values from Parent to Child," *American Political Science Review* 62 (March 1968): 169–84.

35. Herbert McClosky and Harold E. Dahlgren, "Primary Group Influence on Party Loyalty," in S. Sidney Ulmer (ed.), *Introductory Readings in Political Behavior* (Chicago: Rand McNally, 1961), pp. 221–37; Eleanor Maccoby, Richard E. Matthews, and Anton S. Morton, "Youth and Political Change," in Ulmer (ed.), *Political Behavior,* pp. 82–84.

36. Greenstein, *Children and Politics,* pp. 44–46, 72–74.

37. Hess and Torney, *Political Attitudes in Children,* p. 101.

38. *Ibid.*, pp. 100–01.

39. Dawson and Prewitt, *Political Socialization,* p. 146.

40. *Ibid.*, pp. 147–55.

41. Laurence Wylie, *Village in the Vaucluse* (New York: Harper & Row, 1964), pp. 207–09.

42. Kenneth P. Langton and M. Kent Jennings, "Political Socialization

and the High School Civics Curriculum in the United States," *American Political Science Review* 62 (September 1968): 857–59.

43. *Ibid.*, pp. 859–65.

44. *Ibid.*, pp. 866.

45. Hess and Torney, *Political Attitudes in Children*, pp. 114–15.

46. Almond and Verba, *Civic Culture*, pp. 284–94.

47. *Ibid.*, pp. 317–18.

48. Langton and Jennings, "Political Socialization and High School Civics Curriculum," p. 866.

49. Kenneth P. Langton, "Peer Group and School and the Political Socialization Process," *American Political Science Review* 61 (September 1967): 751–58.

50. Martin L. Levin, "Social Climate and Political Socialization," *Public Opinion Quarterly* 35 (Winter 1961): 596–606.

51. Langton, "Peer Group and the School," pp. 154–58.

52. *Ibid.*, pp. 140–60.

53. Herbert Hyman, "Mass Communications and Political Socialization: The Role of Patterns of Communications," in Lucian Pye (ed.), *Communications and Political Development* (Princeton, N.J.: Princeton University Press, 1963).

54. M. Kent Jennings and Richard Niemi, "Patterns of Political Learning," *Harvard Educational Review* 38 (Summer 1968): 448–49.

55. Joseph T. Klapper, *The Effects of Mass Communications* (New York: The Free Press, 1960).

56. John Robinson, "Perceived Media Bias and the 1968 Vote: Can the Media Affect Behavior After All?" *Journalism Quarterly* 49 (1972): 239–46; Steven Chaffee, L. Scott Ward, and Leonard P. Tipton, "Mass Communications and Political Socialization," *Journalism Quarterly* 47 (1970): 647–59, 666.

57. Margaret Conway, David Ahern, and Eleanor Feldbaum, "The Mass Media and Children's Regime Orientations" (Paper prepared for delivery at the American Political Science Association Meeting, Chicago, Illinois, August 29–Sept. 2, 1974); Herbert Hirsch, *Poverty and Politicization* (New York: The Free Press, 1971), chap. 7.

58. Neil Hollander, "Adolescents and the War: The Sources of Socialization," *Journalism Quarterly* 48 (1971): 472–79; Howard Tolley, *Children and War* (New York: Teachers College Press, 1973), pp. 104–12; Hirsch, *Poverty and Politicization*.

59. Conway, Ahern, and Feldbaum, "Mass Media and Children's Regime Orientations"; Tolley, *Children and War*; Hirsch, *Poverty and Politicization*.

60. *See*, for example, Greenstein, *Children and Politics*; Hess and Torney, *Political Attitudes in Children*; David Easton and Jack Dennis, "The Child's Image of Government," in Roberta Sigel (ed.), *Political Socialization*,

The Annals of the American Academy of Political and Social Science 361 (September 1965): 40–57. Roberta Sigel has suggested that the conclusion may be in part a function of inappropriate research instruments. *See* Roberta Sigel, "Political Socialization: Some Reactions on Current Approaches and Conceptualizations" (Paper delivered at the Annual Meeting of the American Political Science Association, New York City, Sept. 6–10, 1966).

61. David Easton and Robert Hess, "The Child's Political World," *Midwest Journal of Political Science* 6 (August 1962): 229–46. It should be noted that most studies have not examined the same children over time; they have assumed that differences among children of different ages studied at one time represent developmental differences rather than generational differences.

62. David Easton and Jack Dennis, "The Child's Image of Government," in Roberta Sigel (ed.), *Political Socialization, The Annals of the American Academy of Political and Social Science* 361 (September 1965): 52–53.

63. Hess and Torney, *Political Attitudes in Children*, pp. 91–92.

64. Joan Laurence, "White Socialization: Black Reality," *Psychiatry* 33 (May 1970): 174–95; Garcia, *Political Socialization of Chicano Children;* Hirsch, *Poverty and Politicization;* Jaros, "Children's Orientations"; Jaros, Hirsch, and Fleron, *The Malevolent Leader;* Greenberg, "Children and Government"; Liebschutz and Niemi, "Political Attitudes"; Lamare, "Language Environment," in Niemi (ed.), *Politics of Future Citizens.*

65. For a discussion of these various factors as a basis for political recruitment, *see* Lewis Bowman and G. R. Boynton, "Recruitment Patterns Among Local Party Officials: A Model and Some Preliminary Findings in Selected Locales," *American Political Science Review* 60 (September 1966): 667–76; Dwaine Marvick and Charles R. Nixon, "Recruitment Contrasts in Rival Campaign Groups," in Dwaine Marvick (ed.), *Political Decision-makers: Recruitment and Performance* (New York: The Free Press of Glencoe 1961), pp. 138–92; Rufus Browning, "The Interaction of Personality and Political System in Decisions to Run for Office: Some Data and a Simulation Technique," *Journal of Social Issues* 24 (July 1968): 93–110; Herbert Jacob, "Initial Recruitment of Elected Officials in the U.S.: A Model," *Journal of Politics* 24 (November 1962): 703–17.

66. Kenneth Prewitt, "Political Socialization and Leadership Selection," in Roberta Sigel (ed.), *Political Socialization*, pp. 96–111.

67. *See* Bowman and Boynton, "Recruitment Patterns"; Marvick and Nixon, "Recruitment Contrasts."

68. Orville G. Brim, Jr. "Adult Socialization," in *International Encyclopedia of Social Sciences,* vol. 14 (New York: Crowell-Collier and Macmillan, 1968), pp. 559–60.

69. Easton and Dennis, *Children in the Political System*, pp. 18–19.

70. *Ibid.,* pp. 21–24.

71. *Ibid.,* chap. 3.

72. Roberta Sigel, "Political Socialization: Some Reactions on Current Approaches and Conceptualizations."

73. Roberta Sigel and Marilyn Brookes, "Becoming Critical about Politics," in Richard Niemi and associates (ed.), *The Politics of Future Citizens* (San Francisco: Jossey-Bass, 1974), pp. 103–25.

74. Roberta Sigel, "Political Socialization: Some Reactions on Current Approaches and Conceptualizations," pp. 7–10.

75. *Ibid.,* p. 12.

76. *Ibid.,* pp. 7–10.

77. Almond and Verba, *Civic Culture,* Lucian Pye, *Politics, Personality.*

78. Almond and Verba, *Civic Culture,* p. 33; Donald Searing, Joel Schwartz, and Alden E. Lind, "The Structuring Principle: Political Socialization and Belief Systems," *American Political Science Review* 67 (June 1973): 415–32; David Marsh, "Political Socialization: The Implicit Assumptions Questioned," *British Journal of Political Science* 1: 453–65.

79. Greenstein, *Children and Politics,* p. 40.

80. Easton and Dennis, *Children in the Political System,* p. 179, Table 8–4c.

81. *Ibid.,* p. 184; p. 185, Table 8–5c.

82. Dean Jaros, "Measuring Children's Orientations Toward the President," University of Kentucky, Lexington, Ky., mimeo., n.d.; Dean Jaros, "Children's Orientations Toward the President," p. 379.

83. Levin, "Social Climate," p. 599.

84. Langton, *Political Socialization,* p. 126–32.

85. Suzanne Koprince Sebert, M. Kent Jennings, and Richard Niemi, "The Political Texture of Peer Groups," in M. Kent Jennings and Richard G. Niemi (eds.), *The Political Character of Adolescence* (Princeton, N.J.: Princeton University Press, 1974), pp. 232–33.

86. *Ibid., passim.*

STUDY QUESTIONS

1. Define the following:
   political socialization
   cognitive development theory
   direct socialization
   indirect socialization

2. What are the various ways in which direct and indirect socialization occur?

3. What kinds of research would one do to test the appropriateness of social learning theory in explaining the development of political party identification? In explaining change in a citizen's party identification?

4. What is the role of parents, schools, friends, and the mass media in the development of political orientations?

5. What kinds of research problems may be present in studying political socialization?

6. What have been the most important agents of socialization in your political development? Have the agents been important in: 1) development of your political attitudes? 2) your patterns of political participation?

7. Have you changed your political orientations in the past 5 years? If so, what has caused these changes?

CHAPTER
7

Role

The concept of role in sociology, psychology, and anthropology has several different meanings.

DEFINITIONS OF THE ROLE CONCEPT

Role can refer to a normative status in society, the rights and duties of which are part of a cultural pattern. This concept of role stresses the "attitudes, values, and behavior ascribed by the society to any and all persons occupying this status."[1] It also places an emphasis on society's definition of what is appropriate for each status, and so is dependent on an appropriate operational definition of status.

Role is also used to mean an individual's definition of his situation with reference to his and others' social positions. Role in this sense is the individual's orientation toward his situation with reference to his and others' social positions. His expectations act as stimuli for others with whom he interacts, and they present cues as to how others should respond to him.[2]

Role can apply to the behavior of an individual occupying a social position. Rather than referring to cultural definitions of what should be or to what an individual defines as model behavior or perceives others to define as model behavior, role in this sense is the actual behavior exhibited in a social situation.[3]

These three concepts of role predominate in the literature. The first is a normative application; it refers to what the individual ought to do, as defined by society; the second refers to the individual's orientations to a situation; the third defines role as the actual behavior of the individual. Common among all the definitions is the idea that an individual behaves with some reference and deference to the expectations that others have about how he should behave.[4]

Role expectation has several different aspects; these include generality or specificity, i.e., how rigidly the appropriate behavior is defined; scope or extensiveness, or the area of a person's life affected by the role; the sanctions applied to secure conformity to the role expectations; and the relationship of role expectations to other informal or formal role systems.[5] Several variables can affect the performance of a role; these include the nature of role expectations held by others, the location of a role in a network of roles, and the demands made for a specific role enactment. Other variables affecting role performance are the skills necessary for effective role enactment, the degree of congruence between the individual's perception of his identity and the requirements of a role, and the characteristics and impact of the audience.[6]

Other definitions of role are possible, and various aspects of the concept can be used in research. Sarbin has suggested that role is "a metaphor intended to denote that conduct adheres to certain parts (or positions) rather than to the players who read or recite them."[7] The focus of study can be on how people enact a role. The following questions aid in guiding analysis of political behavior: Has the individual selected the correct political role? Does the behavior conform to the normative expectations of the observers of the performance? Does the role enactment lead one to conclude that the occupant of the role is legitimately occupying the position?

To translate these questions into the political arena, we consider the style and policies the president of the United States should select as appropriate to his role. This is in part a function of the dominant role expectations in the society or in the part of society that provides his majority support. Where resources are not unlimited, is the president to be the defender of the free world or the leader in solving problems at home? The normative expectations of a president may change; a president who survives politically to run for re-election will adjust his performance to meet these changing expectations. A president who cannot perform or conform to the expectations of his constituencies is denied approval by being defeated in an election or by being forced not to run for re-election. President Lyndon Johnson found that his popular support declined as the Vietnam War continued and the role expectations of certain segments of the electorate about presidential behavior were not met.

Talcott Parsons has suggested that five dichotomous choices, which he terms *pattern variables,* are available to the individual to mediate his role orientations. These choices define how one relates to others. One can choose between *ascription* and *achievement;* i.e., one can evaluate and respond to others in a situation on the basis of presumed (or ascribed) qualities of the role occupant, or one can respond on the basis of another's actual achievements. Another choice is between *affectivity* and *affective neutrality:* Should personal emotions and feelings influence one's orientation or should emotions be controlled? The third choice is between *universalism* and *particularism:* Should general standards apply, or standards specific to the situation or the individual? The fourth choice is between *selfish interests* and *selflessness.* The fifth choice is between viewing another in a situation as having *specific* or *diffuse* properties. The contention of Parsons is that these five choices are always present and they are always either—or choices.[8]

The role expectations applicable to a particular position dictate what the choices of pattern variables should be. For example, in government bureaucracies or in any complex organization, the role expectations applied generally indicate that the following pattern variable choices by bureaucrats would be appropriate: achievement, affective neutrality, universalism, selflessness, and specificity. However, when dealing with a functionary—from government, a university, or a corporation—individuals would prefer to receive favorable treatment on the basis of special considerations, such as the characteristics of one's problem or friendship with the official. In such a case the pattern variable choices made by the bureaucrat would be ascription, affectivity, particularism, selfishness, and diffuseness.

Pattern variables have been used in analysis of political phenomena, such as the role expectations of public officials and their actual behavior, the strains placed by role expectations on American public officials, and the differences between dominant role expectations of several types of political systems.[9]

ROLE SYSTEMS

A role system is any set of related roles. This network of relationships may be focused on one role, which is the focal point of the relationships within the set. In any social system a set of role expectations tends to persist over time. The rights of the occupant of a role and the obligations or duties he has toward others in the role system acquire a relatively stable definition. Events, the acquisition of new roles, or the increased importance of some roles may result in a redefinition or a conflict over the definition of part or all of the set of role relationships.

A change in one relationship in the set has implications for others. If a legislator is appointed to a very important committee, such as the Appropriations Committee of the House of Representatives, certain relationships in his role set may become more important, others will decline in importance, and the nature of the mutual expectations between role members in the set may also change. For example, the representative may find that other representatives defer to him more often. The government agencies dependent on his committee for funds may become solicitous of his advice and respond more quickly to his requests for information or for assistance in resolving problems of his constituents. Lobbyists representing groups that would benefit from increased appropriations or funding of new government programs may besiege him with information, advice, and assistance.

Even if consensus generally exists on the expectations appropriate to a set of role relationships, variation in performance may and probably will occur. Because of the selectivity of perceptual processes, an individual may not correctly perceive the expectations others have for a particular role, and therefore he may perform it differently than expected. The attitudes of individuals who occupy a similar role may also vary. This could result in variations of motivation, which may be related to variations in role performance. The role expectations applied to party precinct leaders in a community may be the same throughout the community, but because of different motivations, the role incumbents may vary considerably in actual performance.

In each social system an individual occupies a particular position. Determinants of his social position are such factors as age, sex, family membership, occupation, and social group memberships. Positions must be viewed in context; one cannot describe a position without describing all positions related to it. The position under study is called the *focal position;* all positions related to it are called the *counter positions.* For example, if we study the American presidency, the presidency is the focal position, and the counter positions are congressman, senator, party leader, interest-group leader, executive bureaucrat, and White House staff member. All positions must also be considered in the context of the situation, which is defined by the specific scope of the social system under study.[10] The role expectations of the president probably vary with each situation he confronts; he feels different role pressures when he is considering a domestic and a foreign policy question, when his party controls the Congress, when he is up for re-election, and according to his current standing with the public and with his party leaders.

If we study presidents of institutions of higher education, the specific situation in which they occupy their role—in junior colleges, liberal arts colleges, or branches of a state university, for example—relates to their behavior in the role of president of a university or college. The term role then applies to the expectations applied to an incumbent of a particular position, and the expectation indicates how the incumbent of that position should behave. As such, it is a normative standard and cannot predict how he or she will behave.

ROLE CONFLICT

A role incumbent is subject to a number of expectations about how he or she should behave, expectations that may not be consistent with one another. Incompatible role expectations produce a *role conflict*, of which there are two types.[11]

One type of role conflict occurs when occupants of different counter positions within a role system have inconsistent or conflicting expectations about how an occupant of that position should behave. The president of the United States may be expected to encourage the conservation of natural resources by leaders of conservation groups; to maximize revenues by the Treasury Department, the Bureau of the Budget, and congressional finance committee members; and to promote the domestic economy by leaders of business and industry. If the issue in question is granting permission to drill for offshore oil, these three sets of expectations may pose conflicting demands to the president to grant or not to grant such permission. This type of conflict is *intra-role conflict*.

A second type of role conflict arises when an individual occupies two or more roles, and the expectations applied to him as the occupant of various roles conflict. A congressman may be expected to remain in the House to vote on a bill, while his family expects him to attend junior's performance in the senior play, or his district political party organization expects him to address an important fund-raising dinner. We can also illustrate role conflict by focusing on the president of the United States. As the leader of his political party, he is expected to be a partisan advocate of his party's views and a vociferous supporter of its candidates for public offices, speaking out to present the party's issue stands and campaigning for party candidates for office. On the other hand, in the role of the leading representative of the United States in making foreign policy and conducting world affairs, he is expected to be nonpartisan and a leader of all the country's citizens. This conflict arising from divergent expectations perceived by the president as occupant of two different roles is called *inter-role conflict.* Both inter-role conflict and intra-role conflict occur only when the incumbent of a role or roles perceives the expectations as conflicting.

To further illustrate the notion of role and the idea of role conflict, we can examine the role of United States senators. Matthews discussed the role expectations applied to senators during the late 1950s.[12] A "freshman senator" was expected to serve an apprenticeship when he or she first entered the Senate; the apprenticeship included presiding over the Senate when it conducted routine business in order to free the vice-president and other more senior senators for more important work. A freshman senator was not expected to participate in debate, because he or she was considered too ignorant of the legislative history of an issue and its details to make an intelligent contribution to the debate. The freshman senator was also expected to limit his or her discussion in committee sessions.

Generally, each senator was expected by others to do his or her legislative homework for the committees of which he or she was a member and to specialize in one or a limited set of problems so that the senator could contribute expert advice to colleagues. Each senator was also expected to limit participation in debate to discussing only issues on which he or she was an expert. Several of these expectations can be summarized under the rubric, "Be a work horse, not a show horse." Another expectation applied by senators to each other was to be courteous to one's fellow senators; this encompassed refraining from personal conflict over policy and conducting debate in a friendly form of discourse, flattering and praising one's opponents. If a senator were to strongly disagree with another senator during a floor debate, an opponent might be addressed as "my distinguished and esteemed colleague," before proceeding to shred the colleague's arguments. Another Senate role expectation found by Matthews was reciprocity; each senator is expected to help out colleagues whenever possible. Roll-call votes are scheduled so that members can vote on the issues about which they are concerned.

All of these expectations were held by senators about the behavior of other senators. Two kinds of role conflict are possible. The first, intra-role conflict, occurs when occupants of other focal positions have different expectations about the behavior of an individual senator; for example, the expectations held by the constituents of a large state about their freshman senator's behavior. He or she is expected to be active on issues of concern to constituents—without serving an apprenticeship. Party leaders in the senator's state also expect him or her to take part in many politically oriented activities that require frequent absences from the Senate and probably impair his or her conformance to Senate norms. In order to enhance their renomination and re-election possibilities, senators from large states frequently must conform more to non-Senate expectations than do their fellow senators, which might significantly reduce their effectiveness as senators.

Other senators cannot conform to Senate norms because of inter-role conflict. A senator who assumes the role of presidential candidate might experience conflict between the expectations appropriate to that role and the role of senator. As a presidential candidate, he is expected to speak on a number of important issues, not only a few on which he is considered an expert by his fellow senators. As a "show horse" he must play to the grandstand of mass media his opinions and activities and make frequent trips out of Washington, consequently neglecting routine Senate committee work.

In both the inter-role and intra-role conflict situations, the senator must make a choice as to which set of perceived role expectations he or she will conform. Several factors may influence that choice. One influence is the perceived legitimacy of the expectations; in other words, do those making demands on the senator have the right to make such demands? The senator may also evaluate the expectations in terms of how well others are conforming to them. A third factor, and perhaps the most important, is the sanctions that can be applied to him if he fails to conform to the role expectations of someone in a counter position. If a person's ambitions are primarily centered on being elected president of the United States, attaining a Senate committee assignment is of considerably less importance to him than earning public acclaim and delegate votes.[13]

Frequently an occupant of a role attempts to meet expectations that are beyond his or her capabilities, resulting in role strain. Mitchell has pointed out that the sources of strain are likely to be presented to all incumbents of a political role, but perception of the sources of strain and reaction to them vary with the individual role occupant. Of course, role occupants may try to restructure their environments in order to alter the expectations of others and thereby minimize the sources of role strain.

Sources of political role strain are: "(1) insecurity of tenure; (2) conflict among public roles; (3) conflict of private and public roles; (4) ambiguities in political situations; (5) diffused responsibility and limited control of situations; (6) time and pressure of demands; (7) and status insecurity."[14] Elected officials facing the possibility of defeat in seeking re-election may try to reduce this possibility (and thus the strain it brings) by gerrymandering electoral districts or eliminating party rivals by securing appointive jobs for them. A politician may try to reduce the frustration induced by role strains by eliminating its sources through such punitive activities as harassing investigations or unfriendly treatment of perceived sources of strain. Efforts may also be directed at obtaining compensations, such as high salaries and fringe benefits, lucrative pensions, or access to financial rewards that directly or indirectly arise from the official's role occupancy. Access to financial rewards can be attained through association with a law firm or a corporate directorship, or by purchasing stock based on a favorable price or an inside tip about future profits.[15]

ROLE SOCIALIZATION AND RESOCIALIZATION

A role is a learned set of expectations; in the socialization process, learning the expectations others hold about a role can occur in several ways. Role expectations are explicitly taught in courses in American history and U.S. government in schools. Political roles are learned by imitation; in this way one may acquire aspects of political roles such as party identification, or in the case of legislators, appropriate orientations toward their districts, an interest group, or their fellow members. One may identify with a position one wants to assume and acquire the orientations appropriate to the role before one actually achieves it.

Socialization to political roles is promoted by serving as an officer in a business association or service club. One gains experience in bargaining, forming coalitions, making decisions and dealing with the public; in short, organizational service provides training in skills and orientations appropriate to political roles. (Other methods of socialization to political roles are discussed in Chapter 6.)

After one assumes a particular role, he or she engages in further interaction during which the expectations applied to that role may change. The development of new expectations and the learning of roles appropriate to newly assumed positions are sometimes referred to as *resocialization.* We should not assume, however, that this is an easy process for individuals. For example, as a situation changes, the role occupant may find it difficult to adapt to new role expectations that develop. A librarian who has learned to view her role as protecting the library's collection may be unable to adapt when she is told her main task will be to promote interest in reading among disadvantaged children. The librarian may be unable to accept resocialization.

Resocialization may be experienced by any occupant of a political position, whether he or she occupies an executive, legislative, or judicial role. By using role theory and examining factors contributing to resocialization, one can evaluate the impact of selected experiences on the attitudes, values, and behavior of people in specific roles. The influence of assignment to a tour of duty at the United Nations on representatives from various countries has been studied. The role expectations applied to U.N. delegates by those with whom they come in contact, such as reporters, delegates from other countries, and members of the permanent U.N. secretariat, altered in a number of ways the role expectations perceived by the delegates and, correspondingly their role behavior.[16] For example, a French specialist in health care, interacting with delegates from more than a hundred countries on a special committee organizing a world-wide attack on malaria, acquires new perspectives as a result of his experiences, and may modify his role orientation. The health care expert operates in an atmosphere that emphasizes expertise and attack on an international problem. He or she works in an international, rather than a national, system; internationalism may be emphasized in the role expectations held by his or her fellow experts. Role conflict may arise when persons occupying positions counter to the French expert's request or expect behavior at odds with the expectations of his superiors and coworkers in the French government.

Resocialization occurs when one acquires a new status for which no appropriate role model previously existed. This commonly occurs in a developing nation, as the political system and the economy evolve into more complex institutional arrangements. It is also common in a developing country such as the United States. The creation of quasi-governmental community action programs financed and sponsored by the Office of Economic Opportunity created new roles for indigenous community leaders and for the paid organizers of federal community action programs, setting into motion the process of resocialization. Attacks on community action programs by local politicians, who frequently tended to perceive these programs as a threat to their control of local politics, is symptomatic of conflicting expectations about what community organizers should do, as perceived by the local community, the organizers, and the local politicians.

POWER AND ROLE BEHAVIOR

Some treatments of the concept of power are stated in terms of role expectations. This is not a new approach to the study of power. In a "how to succeed" handbook for autocratic rulers, written by a sixteenth-century Florentine politician–bureaucrat for a Renaissance prince, role expectations and role behavior to be followed by the prince in order to survive as a ruler are examined. Machiavelli said that princes should make appointments on the basis of merit, encourage craftsmen to improve themselves, and mingle with the people while maintaining the dignity and majesty expected of a ruler. [17] The prudent prince was also counseled to establish himself as a powerful but not hated individual.[18] In the ruler–subject relationship, a number of role expectations exist. For example, the prince expects his subjects to be loyal, while the subjects expect the prince to rule justly and provide them with good government. If his subjects expect him to be cruel if they act against him, they are more likely to be faithful to him.[19] Discussing coalitions and alliances, Machiavelli noted that one's friends preferred one to be an active ally, while nations or rulers who were not friends expected one to be neutral in a conflict.

The concept of power has remained a central concern of writers on politics. It is frequently discussed in terms that indicate power in effect is based on the interaction of role players. "Power is a relation . . . among people."[20] Power relationships can be described in terms of a number of factors, including the source of the holder's power, means or instruments used to exert it, the amount or extent of power, and the responses of the subject. For example, we could examine a governor's power base and the means he or she would use in a power relationship with the state legislators. The amount of power can be represented by a probability statement of the chances of the governor obtaining the responses he or she prefers in voting on key issues. If one wanted to compare the relative power of several governors, one would calculate the base, means, and scope of their power and the number of people each governor could affect. Measurements must also be made of the costs to the power wielder of attempting to exert influence over another and of the cost to the intended object of resisting the exertion of power.[21]

Referring to the dimensions of role expectations discussed at the beginning of this chapter, we see certain similarities with aspects of power. Consider Dahl's statement that A has power over B to the extent that he can get B to do something that B would not otherwise do. The exercise of power may be conceptualized as the resolution of a conflict between role expectations; when a power relationship exists, the role prescriptions that are accepted are defined by the power wielder. Power from this perspective is conceived of as an individual role rather than a group phenomenon; it is one approach to more precise consideration of one type of role relationship.

USES OF THE ROLE CONCEPT IN THEORY BUILDING

The concept of role can be used in analysis of political behavior in three ways: as an independent variable, as a dependent variable, or as an intervening variable. Most writing about politics utilizing the concept of role has focused extensively on describing the distribution of role orientations among political actors, rather than using the concept in testable hypotheses.

Role has been used as a dependent variable, with the emphasis on accounting for the choice made among alternative role orientations or on the distributions of political role orientations in different environments. For example, are county chairmen in political party organizations more likely to be campaign-oriented in competitive districts or in those in which their party is in a dominant or subordinate position? Using the role concept as an intervening variable helps to explain and specify the relationship between an independent and a dependent variable. For example, a legislator may oppose an increase in his state's sales tax, but vote in favor of a bill raising the tax. The legislator's role orientations toward his party leadership, his constituency, the governor, or an interest group may account for behavior at variance with his basic attitude on the issue.

An example of the development of a descriptive typology using role concepts was provided by a study of the state legislatures of California, New Jersey, Tennessee, and Ohio. The authors argue that the role concept is particularly useful for political science because it ties together the concerns of institutional, functional, and behavioral analysis.[22] The focus of their study was on the norms of behavior perceived by occupants of the role of legislator; the study also distinguished among different legislative roles. One type of role applies to a legislator in his relations with all other legislators; using this concept of role, one can elaborate the norms or "rules of the game" to which legislators expect other legislators to adhere.

Among other roles is the purposive role, which refers to behavior the legislator perceives as appropriate to the accomplishment of legislative goals. Five purposive role types are identified: the *ritualist* who perceives the legislative process in terms of the technical aspects of committee work, rules, and procedures for enacting legislation; the *tribune*, who views his job as acting as the spokesman for popular opinion; the *inventor*, who perceives his role as creating and initiating public policy; the *broker*, whose role perceptions focus on achieving compromises between conflicting interests; and the *opportunist*, who meets only minimum requirements of the role and uses his legislative office to maximize his nonlegislative interests, either personal or political.

Another set of legislative roles focuses on orientations toward interest-group activity. The roles include *facilitators*, those knowledgeable about group activity and supportive of it; *resistors,* those knowledgeable about group activity and hostile to it; and *neutrals,* those who either have little knowledge or no strong reaction to group activity.

Other role relationships are based on the way a legislator believes he should decide on an issue; these are labeled representational role orientations. A legislator who considers himself a free agent deciding on the basis of his principles is termed a *trustee.* A legislator who believes he should always vote according to his district's will is a *delegate.* A legislator expressing both trustee and delegate role orientations is a *politico.* Role orientations toward party, executive, and bureaucracy also operate.[23] Together, these form a system of role orientations for the legislator. Of course, occupants of positions counter to the legislator have sets of role orientations also.

These role typologies are based on legislators' perceptions of their role enactments, rather than on their perceptions of others' role expectations. A more recent study examined role expectations of legislative behavior held by the mass public and by attentive constituents (defined as persons nominated by legislators as district residents who were politically knowledgeable and to whom the legislator would turn for advice). Four types of role orientations— procedural, purposive, representational, and policy oriented—were found to exist, but the distributions of role expectations were different in the attentive public and the mass public. Only a general evaluation was obtained of the extent to which respondents' expectations of legislative role enactments were satisfied. The samples of attentive constituents and mass public were asked if they thought the legislature had done an excellent, good, fair, or poor job. This question, however, does not directly assess the extent of perceived compliance with the respondents' explicit legislative role expectations.[24]

There are problems in analyzing political behavior using the role concept. For example, we must ask whether a legislator's role orientations are consistent over time and apply to all issues or to all who occupy the counter position. Does a member of a legislature serving his fourth term have the same set of role orientations as he had in his first term? A legislator's role orientations also may evolve over the course of a legislative session. A state political leader implies this by asserting that it was difficult to manage a legislature with a large number of freshmen legislators in it. When the session started the freshmen were aware of their ignorance and did as instructed. However, after a few weeks—at about the time important legislation was being reported out of committee—freshmen legislators could find their way around and thereupon started acting as if they had all the answers. An evolution of the relative importance placed by freshmen legislators on different role orientations among the role set (representational, purposive, interest group, party, etc.) and of the freshman's selection of the appropriate role with respect to the party leaders in and outside of the legislature had occurred.

As a legislator develops ambitions for higher political office, do his role orientations change? Does he perceive the same representational role orientations, whatever the nature of the issue at hand? A representative from a middle-class, suburban, Republican district may have one interest-group orientation toward representatives of the state AFL–CIO and a second toward representatives of the state manufacturers association. The ability of role theory to contribute to predictive theory, whereby we could predict legislative behavior and policy decisions, is being questioned. The four-state legislative study referred to previously did not attempt to formulate such a theory. What is needed is an elaboration of the scheme in order to make it useful for predicting role enactment or role behavior. Most researchers have focused on norms and expectations and have not attempted to predict behavior from knowledge of role expectations. For example, in the four-state legislative study and in a study of the Canadian Parliament, the legislators' own generalized expectations—and, to a limited extent, their perceptions of the expectations held by others—were the research focus.[25] Where the actual expectations of others were evaluated, as in the legislative study, expectations were evaluated only in vague and very oversimplified terms. Role expectations are undoubtedly specific to both situation and object, although this idea has been ignored in political science research using the role concept. However, several problems are engendered by increasing specificity of roles. First, a proliferation of role types will result. Also, one cannot assume that role orientations are stable over time. Role orientations are altered and elaborated through the ongoing process of interaction with others. However, studies tend to be cross-sectional, concentrating on political actors at only one point in time.

Francis has suggested that the concept of role be elaborated and made useful for political science research by developing role typologies defined in terms of attitude dimensions, with which one can build a set of probability statements to define the role set. Using three of the sets of role orientations elaborated by the four-state study, Francis has indicated the form such a theory would take. [26] Using the district, representational, and interest-group orientations, a probability model of role behavior was developed. This model specified the probability that a legislator will accept instruction, consult interest-group leaders and leaders at the state and district level. From legislators' general orientations toward the three counter positions, a model was developed to predict the probability of seeking instruction. Role typologies were used to specify attitude dimensions; attitude dimensions were then translated into probability statements. In order to predict the probable pattern of a series of interactions, one must know the legislator's cognitive structure, i.e., "the way in which people, events and ideas are organized in his own mind." [27] Whether and who a legislator consults is then a function of his or her cognitive structure.[28] Legislators could be expected to initiate interactions and consult others according to their priorities. In order to account for role behavior, then, one must have knowledge of their relevant priorities.

Problems of operational definitions and research procedures are encountered when roles are translated into attitude dimensions and then expressed through probability statements. What attitude dimensions are appropriate for the definition of particular political roles? In more practical terms, can one collect the data necessary for testing hypotheses utilizing this approach to role theory? In practice, it could be done as Francis has demonstrated. The role approach used in the legislative studies also ignores the total environment within which political behavior occurs. One must study the expectations and cognitive structure of those occupying positions counter to the political actor.[29]

The role concept and typologies of role orientations can describe the characteristic role orientations of political actors in different political systems. A recent study of predominant political role orientations of citizens in five western democratic countries (United States, West Germany, Great Britain, Italy, and Mexico) found substantial differences in the distribution of orientations in these countries.[30] The concept has also been used in comparative analyses of political recruitment and party organization.[31] In a study of local party officials in five communities in Massachusetts and

North Carolina, an emphasis on campaign-related activity was found, with 60 percent describing this kind of activity as the most important job.[32] This type of analysis reflects the individual's definition of his role—not his behavior or others' expectations about his behavior. Considerably less emphasis on campaign activities was documented among precinct leaders in Detroit.[33] Precinct leaders from both parties in the precincts controlled by the county's minority party were much more likely to emphasize getting-out-the-vote activity. [34] Detroit precinct leaders who were party regulars were also much more likely to focus on promoting voting turnout. Apparently the career pattern of the activist within the party contributed to the activist's role definition; those who held other party offices or aspired to them tended to place less emphasis on voter mobilization. Differences in role perceptions also existed between the Republicans and Democrats.[35] A study of county party organizations in North Carolina also found a tendency for leaders' reported role behavior to vary with the majority or minority status of their party.[36]

One of the pressing problems of political science is to develop methods for studying the processes of social change. This is crucial if political science is to contribute to the development of public policy. Much of the government's concern is with stimulating or channeling social change, whether that change is concerned with alleviating poverty through promoting job training, black business ownership, and educational advancement, or with adopting technological innovations in education, health care, transportation.

How can role theory aid in the study of social change? How can it be useful in bringing about social or political change? Role theory provides a perspective from which we can study varieties of political and social change. The political modernization of a country such as Iran, the change in a government's institutions, such as occurred in France from the Fourth to the Fifth Republic, or the slow development of a competitive party system in the South are all topics to which role theory can be applied. Using role theory, we can examine the development of new role expectations, the sanctions bestowed for violation of norms, and the consequences of role changes. For example, the political role system of a country tends to become more differentiated as a country modernizes. (In a tribal society, the political leader may also be the religious, economic, and social leader.) As political development occurs, new roles and role relationships develop and the political system tends to become more independent of the economic and social system. Study of the secularization of the political system would show the evolution of political positions and the development of role expectations applied to those positions. This does not mean, of course, that all developed political systems have a similar role structure.[37]

The fight against poverty in the United States has focused on the development of particular role orientations among the victims of the cycle of poverty. The acquisition of general and specific orientations and their accompanying skills have been promoted and related to the role of the worker in general and to more specific worker roles, such as television repairmen, electrician, or mechanic. The role orientations appropriate to a trainee are emphasized first. Much of the policy debate has centered around the most effective methods and the best bureaucratic organization to use to develop these orientations. It has been difficult to decide how to develop appropriate role orientations for bureaucrats, corporate officials, and instructors administering job-training programs for the poor. The part played by role expectation, and the interest in knowing how to influence or change these expectations, is obvious.

The role concept has proved useful in developing typologies of political actors in different types of political systems. However, one cannot say that it has been substantially used in the development of explicit, predictive propositions. One definition of theory is "a set of interrelated constructs [concepts], definitions, and propositions that presents a systematic view of phenomena by specifying relations among variables, with the purpose of explaining and predicting the phenomena."[38] Such a role theory of politics does not exist.

Role expectations can be used as independent variables to explain variations in the dependent variable of role enactment. Differences in legislators' style and interests could be accounted for in part by differences in the role expectations perceived by legislators. Role expectations could be used to develop predictive theory if adequate measures of variables affecting the perception of role expectations and appropriate measures of dimensions of role expectations were developed. The model of legislative instruction-seeking created by Francis indicates that the possibility exists. Much greater attention to formulating researchable hypotheses and operationally defining concepts is required, however.

What is the relationship between role and other concepts used to study individual behavior? A link between role and personality has been suggested. The importance of the relationships of roles and personal attitudes is a function of the behavior implied by the role. It has been argued that attitudes should be treated as intervening variables in behavior where the same initial conditions are present, but political behavior varies. Resulting theories should have greater predictive values and also be stated more simply. Research results have not always supported the thesis that personality characteristics are an important intervening variable.[39] Role theory can help account for this finding. The expectations others have about behavior of an occupant of a social role may explain the discrepancies. "Role is related to the individual to the extent that he internalizes appropriate attitudes and behavior, and it is related to the society in that group expectations exist, however ambiguously."[40]

NOTES AND REFERENCES

1. A status is a polar position in patterns of reciprocal behavior; certain rights and duties are associated with status. Ralph Linton, *Cultural Background of Personality* (New York: Appleton-Century, 1936), p. 77, quoted in Neal Gross, Ward S. Mason, and Alexander W. McEachern, *Explorations in Role Analysis: Studies of the School Superintendency* (New York: John Wiley and Sons, 1958), p. 12.

2. Cotrell's use of the role concept is an example of this type; the term means an internally consistent set of conditioned responses of one member of a situation, which represents a stimulus pattern for a consistent set of conditioned responses of another member of that situation. *See* the discussion in Gross, Mason, and McEachern, *Explorations in Role Analysis*, p. 13.

3. Biddle and Thomas have identified the three main variations in meaning of the term "role": (1) "a set of standards, descriptions, norms, or concepts held (by anyone) for the behaviors of a person or position"; (2) "a position"; and (3) "a behavioral repertoire characteristic of a person or position." *See* Bruce J. Biddle and Edwin J. Thomas (ed.), *Role Theory: Concepts and Research* (New York: John Wiley and Sons, 1966), pp. 11–12.

4. Gross, Mason, and McEachern, *Explorations in Role Analysis*, p. 17.

5. Theodore Sarbin and Vernon L. Allen, "Role Theory," in Gardner Lindzey and Elliot Aronson (eds.), *The Handbook of Social Psychology*, vol. 1, 2nd ed. (Reading, Mass.: Addison-Wesley, 1968), pp. 499–502.

6. *Ibid.*, pp. 503–14.

7. *Ibid.*, pp. 489; 514–34.

8. Parsons has defined a social system as a system where a plurality of actors interact and in which the action is guided by rules that are part of a complex of complementary expectations concerning roles and sanctions. Role

expectations are defined by patterns of evaluation by Parsons. Talcott Parsons and Edward Shils (ed.), *Toward a General Theory of Action* (Cambridge, Mass.: Harvard University Press, 1962), pp. 23–24.

9. William Mitchell, "Occupational Role Strains: The American Elective Public Official," *Administrative Science Quarterly* 3 (September 1958): 210–28.

10. Gross, Mason, and McEachern, *Explorations in Role Analysis,* pp. 48–69.

11. Neal Gross, A. W. McEachern and Ward Mason, "Role Conflict and Its Resolution," in Eleanor Maccoby (ed.), *Readings in Social Psychology,* 3rd ed. (New York: Holt, Rinehart and Winston, 1958), pp. 447–59.

12. Donald Matthews, *U.S. Senators and Their World* (Chapel Hill, N.C.: University of North Carolina Press, 1960), chap. 5.

13. *Ibid.*

14. Mitchell, "Occupational Role Strains," p. 212.

15. *Ibid.*

16. Chadwick Alger, "Non-Resolution Consequences of the United Nations and Their Effect on International Conflict," *The Journal of Conflict Resolution* 5 (June 1951): 128–45.

17. Niccolo Machiavelli, *The Prince* (New York: The Modern Library, 1950), p. 85.

18. *Ibid.,* p. 63.

19. *Ibid.,* p. 60.

20. Robert A. Dahl, "The Concept of Power," *Behavioral Science* 2 (July 1957): 203.

21. John Harsanyi, "Measurement of Social Power, Opportunity Costs, and the Theory of Two Person Bargaining Games," *Behavioral Science* 7 (January 1962): 67–80.

22. John C. Walhke, Heinz Eulau, William Buchanan, and Leroy C. Ferguson, *The Legislative System* (New York: John Wiley and Sons, 1962), p. 7.

23. *Ibid.; see also* chaps. 11–15.

24. G. R. Boynton, Samuel C. Patterson, and Ronald D. Hedlund, "The Missing Links in Legislative Politics: Attentive Constituents," *Journal of Politics* 31 (August 1969): 700–02. *See also* G. R. Boynton, Samuel C. Patterson, and Ronald D. Hedlund, "The Structure of Public Support for Legislative Institutions," *Midwest Journal of Political Science* 12 (May 1968): 163–80; Samuel C. Patterson, G. R. Boynton, and Ronald D. Hedlund, "Perceptions and Expectations of the Legislature and Support for It," *American Journal of Sociology* 75 (July 1969): 62–76; Samuel C. Patterson and G. R. Boynton, "Legislative Recruitment in a Civic Culture," *Social Science Quarterly* 50 (September 1969): 243–63.

25. Walhke, Eulau, Buchanan, and Ferguson, *Legislative System;* Allan Kornberg, *Canadian Legislative Behavior* (New York: Holt, Rinehart, and Winston, 1967).

26. Wayne Francis, "The Role Concept in Legislatures: A Probability Model and A Note on Cognitive Structure," *Journal of Politics* 27 (August 1965): 567–85.

27. *Ibid.*, p. 582.

28. *Ibid.*, pp. 583–84. The elaboration of the role has not gone uncriticized. For one critique, *see* Benjamin Walter, "Of Complements and Empirical Probabilities: A Critical Note on Francis' Paper," *Journal of Politics* 28 (May 1966): 419–24. *See also* Francis' rebuttal, "The Utility of Probabilities in Models: A Reply to Walter's Critical Note," *Journal of Politics* 28 (May 1966): 425–28.

29. Harmon Zeigler and Michael Baer, *Lobbying: Interaction and Influence in American State Legislatures* (Belmont, Calif.: Wadsworth Publishing Co., 1969), pp. 6–8.

30. Gabriel Almond and Sidney Verba, *The Civic Culture* (Princeton: Princeton University Press, 1963).

31. Louis Bowman and G. R. Boynton, "Activities and Role Definitions of Grassroots Party Leaders," *Journal of Politics* 28 (February 1966): 121–40; William J. Crotty, "The Party Organization and Its Activities," in William J. Crotty (ed.), *Approaches to the Study of Party Organization* (Boston: Allyn and Bacon, 1968), pp. 217–46; James David Barber, *The Lawmakers* (New Haven: Yale University Press, 1965).

32. Bowman and Boynton, "Activities and Role Definitions," p. 128.

33. Samuel J. Eldersveld, *Political Parties: A Behavioral Analysis* (Chicago: Rand McNally, 1964), p. 254.

34. *Ibid.*, p. 259.

35. *Ibid.*, p. 260.

36. Crotty (ed.), *Approaches*, pp. 266–67; 273.

37. Gabriel Almond and G. Bingham Powell, *Comparative Politics: A Developmental Approach* (Boston: Little, Brown, 1966), pp. 306–10.

38. Fred Kerlinger, *Foundations of Behavioral Research* (New York: Holt, Rinehart and Winston, 1965), p. 11.

39. Kenneth P. Langton, *Political Socialization* (New York: Oxford University Press, 1969), pp. 13–14.

40. *Ibid.*, pp. 14–15.

STUDY QUESTIONS

1. Define the following:

role	role system
inter-role conflict	power
intra-role conflict	role socialization

2. What inter-role and intra-role conflict do you experience in your roles as student, citizen, family member, and employee? What are the sources of these role conflicts?

3. Describe the role system in which the governor of your state or a member of your legislature operates.

4. How does role resocialization occur? Describe the role resocialization that is likely to occur when a legislator, such as Gerald Ford, becomes vice-president and then president.

CHAPTER
8

Group-Level Analysis

How are people organized for political action? Is it profitable to examine political behavior in units larger than the individual but smaller than the political system? Does group membership have a bearing upon political values, attitudes, beliefs, and opinions? Does group membership influence political action? Are broad membership groupings mere conveniences used for unjustifiable generalizing by pollsters and by those prone to shallow political analysis?

The group-level approach to political analysis has had a long and honorable tradition in political science, although it has undergone extensive revision and refinement in recent years. The importance of this approach lies not so much in the convenience it affords in categorizing individuals, but in the ways in which it can be used to draw together diverse research from several areas and lead us toward more useful explanation and prediction. We know that the group concept "implies that the members . . . have something in common; they share, perhaps, a set of values or they have identifiable characteristics which distinguish them from the rest of the population of a social system."[1]

One of the most common approaches classifies groups according to their proximity to the individual member. The *primary group* is the group with which an individual has the most frequent face-to-face contact. Included are one's family, neighbors, work associates, and friends. The contact need not be on a day-to-day basis, but a member of a primary group interacts regularly with other members of the group on a personal basis. *Secondary groups* are affiliative groups in which the relationship is usually of a less personal nature, with considerably less personal interaction and contact. The American Medical Association, the AFL–CIO, and the American Political Science Association serve as secondary groups for doctors, union members, and political scientists. *Categoric* or *tertiary groups* such as race, sex, age, or ethnic groups, have no organization but are merely conveniences for classification. By this definition, everyone belongs to several categoric groups. Certain secondary groups organize along categoric lines, such as the Congress for Racial Equality (CORE), the National Organization of Women (NOW), the American Association of Retired Persons, and the Italian-American Anti-Defamation League.

All three of these group classifications can be subsumed by a *reference group,* "a group to whose standards people refer" in developing their opinions, attitudes, and beliefs.[2] This is usually a group from which one seeks approval, in which case we refer to it as a *positive reference group.* If one seeks the approval of one's family, the family acts as a *primary positive reference group.* If one is rebellious toward one's family, then the family acts as a *primary negative reference group,* providing cues as to how *not* to act. For conservative Republicans who are in business for themselves, the National Association of Manufacturers or the Chamber of Commerce may act as *secondary positive reference groups,* whereas these two groups may act as *secondary negative reference groups* for union members. Membership, formal or otherwise, does not necessarily mean that a group will influence the organization of a member's perceptions.[3] A reference group can be of a categoric or tertiary nature as well. For those who "don't trust anyone over 30," the so-called generation gap is a very real idea, symbolized by the negative cues supplied by the categoric group of those over 30. Ethnic groups are prominent examples of positive and negative reference groups.

INFLUENCES OF GROUPS ON INDIVIDUALS

Political scientists have expended considerable effort analyzing group influences, particularly upon individual members and nonmembers. Others have concentrated on intergroup relationships or influences of groups upon the political system itself. We have already paid much attention to group influences upon members (*see* Chapter 6). We turn now to considerations of why individuals join groups, following which we discuss group influences upon members and nonmembers, upon other groups, and upon the political system.

Many people tend to join organizations that express attitudes and values consistent with their own. By joining such an organization, a new member receives a reinforcement of his values and opinions, and may also have latent beliefs awakened, as new information and opinions are brought out by respected members of the group. The interaction of group members is likely to lead to the expression of values and opinions of which the new or old member might have been only dimly aware, if aware at all. Discussion of new issues and events may be based upon previously expressed opinions or upon beliefs that are fundamental to the group's purpose or membership.[4] For example, if the government announces a program to tax cars based on their gas mileage, a group member might mention it in passing, with some critical comment, pro or con. This in turn could lead to further discussion (informed or not), which would act as a cue for other group members, even if they do not participate in the discussion. The issue might not even be germane to the group's purpose. Members of a bowling team, who meet primarily for athletic and social purposes, could briefly mention the federal government's new energy tax program in the course of an evening, awakening and crystallizing beliefs that the members might never have discussed before.

One does not necessarily make a conscious effort to seek out and join groups that hold values and opinions similar to one's own. However, it is fairly easy for individuals to ascertain if a group is "like us" and whether or not it would be pleasant to affiliate with the group. In other words, people tend to seek out homogeneous group memberships.[5] An individual rarely consciously affiliates with a group because he enjoys a good argument. Most of us prefer receiving reinforcement of our positions, political and otherwise, and group memberships tend to reflect this.

Factors operating to increase conformity to group standards and norms are smallness of size, frequency of contact, homogeneity of opinion, and internal cohesion (*see* Chapter 5). If a group is small, meets frequently, is comprised of individuals who generally hold the same beliefs, and has a great deal of solidarity, it can be expected that pressures to conform will be present to a high degree. Another factor affecting conformity relates to democratic decision making: if an individual feels that he has participated in making some decision, he is likely to be more committed to the group's opinion, even if he has lost, than one who has merely been a bystander. Similarly, if an issue is ambiguous and the results of a position are difficult to predict, the group supplies cues to form opinions and take actions.[6] For example, it is difficult to predict every four years which presidential candidate might take positions and actions basically in accord with one's position. Although the outcomes are ambiguous and distant in time, one generally relies upon the political party of the candidate as a source of positive or negative reference cues before one casts a ballot.

An example of the importance of groups in forming and crystallizing opinions is found by examining the characteristics of those who most often answer survey questions with a reply of "no opinion." Although they may be classified by categoric or tertiary group discriptions, such as "poorly educated" or "rural residents," they often have no primary and secondary group memberships to which they refer for cues. They may also be unaware of the stand that their appropriate reference group has voiced on an issue or are unable to predict how that group might feel.[7]

This is not to suggest that there are no individual differences within groups or that differences that may exist are unimportant. The Supreme Court is a primary group with considerable differences between members. The nine justices meet regularly with each other, hear cases, and consult with one another individually and as a group. It would seem that a functional group of as few as nine men would have considerable influence upon its individual members, but 9–0 decisions have been uncommon.

Groups or cliques do exist within the Court: one given to broad interpretations of the Constitution; another to somewhat restrictive interpretations; and a third pivoting between the first two, depending upon the issue or case at hand.[8] But there is little evidence to suggest that any of these cliques, comprised of just a few persons, determine behavior of their member justices. Rather, a new member "tended to be 'ingested' by the Supreme Court through the pivotal clique and then, after a period of functioning with the Court, found his place in the group by joining one of the two opposing cliques."[9] As numerous studies have developed the theme, it would appear that justices are guided in their decisions by ideology, presumably acquired in pre-Court days and further developed through Court experience. Although one might impute a single ideological leaning to a justice, this would be a rather simplistic approach. A justice might presumably have a liberal attitude on certain broad issues (civil rights, civil liberties, etc.) and still be consistently conservative on other issues (property rights, federal expansion of powers, etc.). In other words, although groups may affect opinions, attitudes, values, and beliefs, they are not necessarily pervasive in their influence, and considerable latitude exists for individual variation; this is a basic weakness of the group-level approach to political analysis.

The group concept has been employed in the study of voting behavior. In a sense, this type of study is a bridge between group influences on individuals and group influences on politics. An early such study considers several demographic variables, such as race, sex, religion, and education.[10] Predictably, these variables are strongly related to voting patterns, although party identification is a more valid indicator of future political action than demographic variables alone.[11] Related to this is the phenomenon of ethnic voting behavior. Several studies show what many political candidates have known or should have known for some time: ethnic voting continues to be a persistent and important theme in American politics.[12] Although the last major waves of immigration ended just before the First World War, "national origins continue to be a salient dimension in many people's perceptions of themselves and of others."[13]

The melting pot thesis has been largely dispelled by political scientists and sociologists who have investigated the impact of immigration and ethnic groups in this country.[14] We speak of the "black vote" or the "Jewish vote" quite frequently in describing the support provided by these groups to one party or another. Although it is ridiculous to imply that all voters of ethnic or categoric groups will and do vote for an "ethnic" candidate, these and other groups may throw their support to a single party or aspirant. Among the more extreme examples are the 92.1 percent vote by Jews for Roosevelt in 1944[15] and the NBC sample precinct analysis that showed 97 percent of blacks voting for Johnson in 1964.[16] The same patterns are present to some extent in many identifiable ethnic groups in America, and political parties are not insensitive to this. For years, New York City parties have attempted to have a "balanced ticket," with a clearly identifiable candidate of Irish, Italian, and Jewish extraction on the ballot. Lately they have added blacks and Puerto Ricans to their slates, and citywide candidates take the mandatory "Three-I" tour (Ireland, Italy, and Israel) immediately before the election.

A major body of literature suggests that ethnic voting and politics will continue for some time. Despite non-homogeneity of residential patterns, different socioeconomic levels within each group, and other factors that seemingly work toward assimilation, ethnicity is still a major force to be reckoned with in political behavior:

> That many urban and suburban politicians persist in giving attentive consideration to minority social groupings in American-born constituencies . . . may be due less to their inveterate stupidity than to the fact that ethnic substructures and identification are still extant, highly visible, and, if handled carefully, highly accessible and responsive. The political practitioner who chooses to ignore the web of formal and informal ethnic substructures on the presumption that such groupings are a thing of the past does so at his own risk.[17]

The Republican blueprint for victory beyond the end of this century is based largely on expanding appeals to regional and ethnic blocs.[18]

GROUP INFLUENCES ON POLITICS

The concept of a majority is pertinent to the study of groups. What *is* a majority? Do majorities rule? Are majorities related to a single issue? A candidacy? If a majority exists, does its composition or preferences change over time?

In considering the political process in America, it has been said that "the making of governmental decisions is not a majestic march of great majorities united upon certain matters of basic policy. It is the steady appeasement of relatively small groups."[19] If this is so, how are groups heard in the first place, and why do governments feel the necessity to appease them?

Intensity of opinion, which is relative to individuals as well as groups, affects political participation. "All other things being equal, the outcome of a policy decision will be determined by the relative intensity of preference among the members of a group."[20] If a few members feel quite intensely about their side of an issue, it is expected that their preferences will prevail in a discussion. If a particular group engaged in pressuring the government feels and acts intensely about its position, the intensity is a valuable resource to use to impress legislators and administrators. A casual approach lacking in conviction cannot be expected to impress government decision makers with the urgency or necessity of solving a problem. Hence, groups that operate on the basis of ideology may have a distinct advantage, if they are competing with groups that are not impelled to action with intensity.

Before intensity of conviction and action can be brought to bear upon the political system, a group must have *access* to those in power. Formal and informal means of gaining access to a legislature are used. Formal means include rules governing apportionment or the structure and operation of the legislature. Informal means are those in which the "effect is somewhat more subtle but of at least equal significance."[21] If a representative is uncertain of the potential effects of a "yes" or "no" vote on a bill, he may ask groups to supply him with information about the political consequences of his vote. The groups he chooses to consult would have greater access to him, although on an informal basis.[22] In short,

> The degree of access to the legislature that a particular group enjoys at a given moment is the result of a composite of influences. . . . Depending on the circumstances and the relative importance of these factors in a given situation, some groups will enjoy comparatively effective access, and others will find difficulty in securing even perfunctory treatment.[23]

We should not accept the point of view that government in general or a legislature in particular is "just a sounding board or passive registering device for the demands of organized political interest groups."[24] Groups can be highly effective in obtaining certain ends from government, although there are variables that they may be unable to control. Groups essentially contribute to, rather than determine, government policy and direction, generally because they compete with other groups in the system.

The conventional approach used to study group influence on politics is the case study. Case studies have explored in depth the making of a particular bill, such as a campaign finance act,[25] a civil rights act,[26] and ratification of the nuclear test ban treaty.[27] The researcher must carefully weight the effects and contributions of individuals and groups who have contributed to the final decision, bill, or policy. The contribution of the tobacco industry in hindering and resisting legislation requiring effective labeling of cigarette packages is a case study of group influence.[28] Other groups, supporting either side of the issue, participated in this decision-making process, including doctors, the Surgeon General's office, and citizens who were aroused to write or otherwise petition their representatives.

PRESSURE TECHNIQUES OF GROUPS

The popular idea of pressure group activists is of slick-talking people representing big-money interests who buttonhole legislators and bribe them with huge sums to do the bidding of those who are, more likely than not, corporate "fat cats" who puff on big cigars and manipulate political power.[29] Although this image may be overdrawn, it is the impression one receives from the occasional revelations that presumably sell newspapers. It would be simplistic, however, to assume that this is the only way in which groups bring their influence to bear upon the government, or that it is a necessarily effective way. Most pressure activity does tend to be obscured from the national headlines. Lobbyists do not openly solicit votes from representatives in the presence of reporters. Because a great deal of legislation is relatively minor, affecting few persons or groups, the popular press generally has little reason to publicize lobbying efforts.

An average individual is not concerned with government activity that does not directly affect him. Because of this phenomenon, we speak of "attentive" and "general" publics.[30] The attentive public is defined as persons who normally follow the course of government closely, or persons who are aware that they may be directly affected by potential or actual government activity. These persons and groups are more likely to have an interest in pressure group activity and to participate in such activity.

Legislatures are not the only bodies of government subject to group pressure. The executive and the judicial branches of government are not immune to influence. The activity of groups with no constitutional foundation, such as political parties, are also objects of political pressure and influence. Courts are particularly susceptible to pressure from groups, usually in the form of litigation brought before them. A group brings a case before the courts when an issue directly concerns the group. They may also enter court cases on behalf of individuals, where a fundamental principle is at stake that affects more people than the person directly bringing a case before the court. Test cases and *amicus curiae* ("friend of the court") briefs can also be used to spell out a particular position held by a group in an attempt to influence the courts.[31]

> The activities of the judicial officers of the United States are not exempt from the processes of group politics. Relations between interest groups and judges are not identical with those between groups and legislators or executive officials, but the difference is rather one of degree than of kind.[32]

Interest groups bring pressure to bear upon the bureaucracy that is charged with carrying out legislative intentions and policies. For instance, the American Medical Association would find it in its own best interest to cooperate with the Department of Health, Education, and Welfare in promoting specific policies most favorable to the medical profession. Interests opposing integration and black militants favoring a separatist position might approach the U.S. Office of Education to argue against integration, despite Supreme Court decisions.

Lobbying or pressure activity is not restricted to groups outside of government. When the administration transmits a position to Congress in the form of a presidential special message, the executive branch is acting as a lobby. Most major government agencies maintain what are euphemistically known as "legislative liaison officers," whose nominal function is to keep Congress and executive agencies informed about what the other is doing and thinking on specific legislation. These officers perform as a pressure group for their agency, seeking to persuade the Congress to enact legislation in accord with administration or agency wishes.

Further, lobbying need not be restricted to legislative concerns. An agency in the executive branch can pressure another agency to act in a certain way. This is best illustrated by the pressures exerted by the Nixon Administration on the Internal Revenue Service to reveal confidential tax returns and to subject Nixon's "enemies" to unusual scrutiny. Thus, the interaction of government departments and agencies are actually pressure activities. In this case, the pressure group can be classified as a primary group because it functions on a daily, face-to-face basis.

There are three basic categories of lobbying techniques: (1) *direct personal communication,* which presents arguments, research results, and testimony personally to the objects of pressure activity; (2) *intermediary or indirect approaches,* such as contacting constituents and close friends, waging mass letter and telegram campaigns, public relations activities, and publicizing voting records; (3) *opening communications channels,* a euphemism covering methods such as bribery (seldom if ever used, according to the lobbyists), entertaining, campaigning, and collaborating, or log-rolling, with other groups.[33]

Pressure activities are not restricted to lobbying. Groups can make their wishes known, consciously or unconsciously, through a variety of other techniques. An example is the mass demonstration, violent or nonviolent. When protesters march on the Pentagon or on the Justice Department, they are engaging in a form of group pressure that has had a long history. In the United States, violent protests have been traced back to the early seventeenth century, when Indians sought to prevent white settlers from invading their property. Farmers, city dwellers, slave owners, women, and others have occasionally resorted to protest, violent and otherwise, to press their demands for recognition and to stress the legitimacy of their positions.[34] When protest becomes violent, special problems are raised for the political system. Some official solutions result in the dissolution of the protesters as a group.

> . . . the official approach to the problem of mass revolt has been to offer the rebels the benefits of individualism—reforms which promise members of the insurgent group fairer treatment, more votes, more jobs, and so on—provided only that they give up "unrealistic" demands for control of territory, recognition of collective political and economic interests, and the like. Naturally, such offers are rejected by the insurgents.[35]

Since conflict is occasionally used by groups as a technique to achieve their ends, we now turn to the role played by groups in political conflict.

GROUPS AND POLITICAL CONFLICT

One school of thought in political science considers the group the primary political unit:

> ... even in its nascent stages government functions to establish and maintain a measure of order in the relationships among groups for various purposes. ... Unless one denies ... that the notion of differentiations in the habitual interactions of men is synonymous with the notion of groups and ... that government is made up of just such patterns of habitual interaction, acceptance of groups as lying at the heart of the process of government is unavoidable.[36]

The school that views politics as an allocation process is especially concerned with group conflict.[37] In their view, conflict occurs because resources, advantages, and values are scarce. Groups actively compete for rewards distributed by the political system, on their own behalf and on behalf of individuals.

Coleman has examined the roles played by groups in political and social conflict.[38] By examining the ways in which conflict has occurred in American communities in recent years, Coleman developed a theory of conflict largely based on the role of groups in competition for scarce resources and values. Four issues raised in local communities were examined by Coleman: school policy, fluoridation, industrialization, and libraries. Although these issues may appear prosaic to the average reader, they are frequently typified by high intensity and involvement of the local citizenry. Beyond the immediate ones he selected for study, Coleman says that there are essentially four types of issues with which communities are concerned. These issues concern economics, the power or authority of public officials, cultural values, and personality. The type of issue that becomes controversial is generally related to the nature of the city: central or self-contained cities are more prone to economic issues; satellite or suburban cities tend to have disputes over cultural issues; and "service cities," such as resorts, frequently have personality disputes.

According to Coleman, the size and nature of the community also have a bearing on how individuals participate. In large cities, individuals tend to express themselves through intermediary organizations; in small communities, where more personal arguments take place, voluntary associations frequently act on behalf of the individual.

Coleman notes that major changes occur in issues over time. A specific issue tends to give way to a more general one. If a dispute arises over placing certain books on library shelves, the more general issue of censorship or First Amendment freedoms emerges shortly.

However, political issues, especially those involving few people, tend to remain specific. "Political controversies, for example, exhibit the pattern much less than do disputes based primarily on differing values or economic interests."[39] The reasons for this are unclear, but one of the more consistent findings is that there is a notable tendency in the United States toward minimal popular involvement in politics. Milbrath cites a considerable body of literature on this point:[40]

About one-third of the American adult population can be characterized as politically apathetic or passive; in most cases, they are unaware, literally, of the political part of the world around them. Another 60 percent play largely spectator roles in the political process; they watch, they cheer, they vote, but they do not do battle.[41]

Controversy over an issue may also spawn other issues, sometimes unrelated to the original issue. This may happen because the relationships within a community are susceptible to change when the original issue is raised. If relationships are upset, issues previously suppressed or accepted may arise. The equilibrium of the community then becomes disturbed. Especially with political issues, "the diversification of issues is more a purposive move on the part of the antagonists, and serves quite a different function: to solidify opinion and bring in new participants by providing new bases of response."[42] Issues change as the controversy progresses from disagreement to hostility and from fairly reasoned argument to less rational forms of discourse.

The progress of an issue in a community proceeds as follows:

1. Initial issue arises
2. Disrupts equilibrium of community relations
3 Previously suppressed issues (against opponents) appear
4. Opponent's beliefs increasingly enter into the disagreement
5. Opponent appears totally bad
6. Charges made against opponent as a person
7. Dispute becomes independent of initial disagreement[43]

Groups and group roles were found by Coleman to be central to the entire community conflict process. They formed the basis for the community's social organization and also acted to upset local equilibrium by performing several of the steps outlined above.[44] For instance, as a controversy begins to expand in scope, individuals seek allies, and ad hoc organizations emerge that are polarized on the initial and then on subsequent issues.

According to Coleman, the controversy serves to create groups because groups provide a voice for shared values and attitudes which might otherwise be suppressed. New leaders are brought into the controversy by group formation, particularly as highly charged partisan organizations emerge. New leaders

> . . . often . . . are men who have not been community leaders in the past, men who face none of the restraints of maintaining a previous community position . . . In addition, these leaders rarely have real identification with the community.[45]

As existing community organizations are drawn into the controversy, they frequently become polarized against the new militants. Organizations in the North and South that had not taken an overt position on school integration, for example, found themselves drawn into the controversy, whether or not it was fundamental to their purpose. For instance, such groups as the American Legion or the Lions, normally looked upon as social-interest organizations, were not founded to take positions related to national interest, with the exception of patriotism and national social norms. They may have been drawn into the school segregation controversy in some communities because of other interests of their leaders and members.

Community organizations are not necessarily drawn into a controversy. There may be significant pressures from within a community and from within a group to remain neutral or to disengage from a conflict. If this happens, a group is maintained, but at some cost, since the newer or "combat" ad hoc groups may pre-empt functions or roles of the community organization. Whatever happens, the controversy is likely to be expressed by groups that become important new means of communicating views and shared attitudes. If the conflict gets out of hand, organizations and elements in the community that might normally play a conciliatory role are neutralized.[46]

Overlapping group memberships minimize tension.[47] We use the term *cross-pressured* to refer to situations in which individuals are subjected to two or more sets of attitudes, opinions, or beliefs that conflict with one another. One's father might be a die-hard Democrat and a union member with a strong penchant for political activism. If one's mother is equally intense and active as a Republican, extreme cross-pressures will bear on the individual. Belonging to two or more primary groups with different views on the same issue creates cross-pressures.

"Persons belonging to two or more groups which pull in opposite directions (cross-pressured persons) are likely to have diminished political interest."[48] If one lives and works in a homogeneous situation, cross-pressures are usually not present to a significant degree. If this is the case, reinforcement of existing positions might occur, which would intensify political participation and political conflict. In a heterogeneous situation, cross-pressures are more likely, and they serve to diminish participation and perhaps to minimize conflict. But, when individuals allow themselves to be pressured out of participating in a conflict, they forfeit the chance to voice their usually moderate positions to those who are not cross-pressured, and who are more prone to take extremist positions. In suppressing and raising issue stands, the role of groups in community conflict can be fundamental to community equilibrium and conflict patterns.

Conflict essentially creates and helps to identify groups.[49] All groups are not formed by conflict situations, but shared interests do provide a rallying point. Conflict within a group can also take place, despite a common basis of shared attitudes or interests. Formal or informal provisions within a group for the expression of hostile viewpoints perform a "safety-valve" function and act to preserve the group. "Conflict is thus seen as performing group-maintaining functions insofar as it regulates systems of relationships."[50] Groups that are relatively flexible and loosely structured are more likely to have some provision for expressing conflict, rather than suppressing it. Such groups "institute safeguards against the type of conflict which would endanger basic consensus and thereby minimize the danger of divergences touching core values."[51]

Conflict with other groups can increase internal cohesion and solidarity.[52] As conflict helps to identify groups for others, internally it increases group identification of its members. Under such conditions, centralization of group authority may occur, if the conflict is protracted or violent, and if the nature of the group requires differentiated labor. For example, when a nation is at war and must mobilize its resources, greater authority is necessary at higher levels. Rationing by a central authority may take place, temporarily displacing a free market economy.

Another example can be drawn from the experience of black groups in the United States during the 1960s. Many black organizations grew and disbanded during this decade, some more militant than others. Older and less militant organizations, such as the NAACP or the Urban League, were challenged by newer groups for not being militant enough. The newer organizations, such as the Congress of Racial Equality (CORE), tended to have greater militancy and a higher degree of centralization of effort. Probably the most militant of the new black organizations, the Black Panthers, explicitly stated that they were engaged in combat, although not necessarily violent combat. The militancy of their attitudes is revealed in the group's tight, almost paramilitary organization, whose centralization of command exceeded that of other black groups. When conflict did become violent, such as when Fred Hampton, chairman of the Illinois Black Panthers, was shot by Chicago police in 1969, the entire black community responded in various ways to increase their identification with the Panthers. Groups engaged in continuous struggle, such as the Panthers, become quite intolerant of deviations by members. "Such groups tend to assume a sect-like character: they select membership in terms of special characteristics and so tend to be limited in size, and they lay claim to the total personality involvement of their members."[53] Groups of this nature are also more inclined to seek out "enemies," or to create them if need be.[54] Because their internal cohesion and unity in part rests upon the existence of opposing groups, they may view other groups as enemies when there is no reason to do so. Such a view may actually create opposing groups, whether or not they existed in the first instance. An example of this might be the way in which "law and order" forces in the U.S. have occasionally created a picture that suggests that the poor, blacks, and the young are forces of social dissolution. If members of these categoric groups feel they are attacked unjustifiably, they may coalesce to form primary and secondary organizations to express their point of view. They may suggest that it is the "law and order" advocates in society who

225

choose to ignore basic social and moral obligations and who ignore First Amendment protections of free speech and assembly.

The constant forming and reforming of groups is fundamental to political and social conflict. The means by which such conflict takes place will occupy political scientists for years to come.

CRITIQUE OF GROUP ANALYSIS

Group-level analysis has provided some important clues to the study of political behavior. For example, there is evidence that the family, as a primary group, can have a meaningful influence upon the political behavior of its members. The study of attitudes is refined by the use of categoric groups, such as age, sex, and regional groups. Political activity often finds expression through group activity, as individuals coalesce with others to achieve political and social ends. The literature of political science frequently depends on group analysis. When we discuss parties, legislatures, courts, and bureaucracies, we are discussing groups, not isolated individuals. Political science cannot afford to ignore the group. Any discussion of political conflict inevitably involves the group concept, because conflict often finds its expression through groups, and may have its roots in group antagonisms.

However, we have not been dealing with an operational definition of "group." We have defined "group" in the sense of memberships (primary, secondary, and categoric) and perceptions (positive and negative references). These definitions do not comprise a theory of politics or human behavior. The study of ethnic politics, for instance, relies upon the group *approach*, employing basic sociological concepts to understand how and why ethnicity is manifested in voting behavior or in different styles of political participation. It would be fallacious to assume that this approach is embodied in a group *theory* of politics, however.

How is the group concept operationalized? An alternative approach has been that taken by a large school of political scientists, who look upon the group as a collectivity of interests and action:

> Politics is the process by which social values are authoritatively allocated; this is done by decisions; the decisions are produced by activities; each activity is not something separate from every other, but masses of activity have common tendencies in regard to decisions; these masses of activity

are groups; so the struggle between groups (or interests) determines what decisions are taken.[55]

The above approach to groups involves too many intangibles to be empirically verified. However, considerable research has been done in the name of group "theory" from this frame of reference. A common error has been to assume that the referent of "interests" implies that group theory, if it is a theory, must concern itself with pressure groups.[56]

What other groups operate to influence politics? In what circumstances? What are their characteristics? And what are their interests? Group theorists have failed to come to grips with these definitional problems, and critics of group theory have demonstrated tautologies and imprecisions in the group approach. "Equilibrium" is used in the context of several different arguments by group theorists, without any clear empirical reference.[57]

If group theory is to be regarded as a theory, then the group concept must be sufficiently clear. That it is not clear is the main thrust of the criticisms directed at what passes for group theory. If we define groups in terms of sociological characteristics, such as primary, secondary, and tertiary groups, we are assuming that some form of activity or shared interests and attitudes defines a group. The shared activity may be nothing more than overt hostility toward another group. In other words, group members are identified on the basis of something that they do, or something that they are. Even when we can clearly identify the nature of the activity that justifies a group's existence, does that mean we have a group theory of politics? It may be useful to study political behavior by categorizing individuals into a number of groups, but such an endeavor

> ... gives little information as to the pattern of group politics in a given society. Thus, it cannot tell us why and how individuals will do or behave politically. The superficial plausibility of the group approach rests upon a certain partial reading of American politics which enables group theorists to ignore the real premises from which they operate. If this is so, there is no warrant to assume that the study of politics is the study of groups. Rather groups are reduced to the status of one kind of political actor.[58]

Some critics think that group "theory" can never be empirically tested because "it does not relate any variables to one another, nor specify any relations between variables."[59] Group "theory" cannot both explain and predict. For example, the group approach cannot tell us when a group such as the Symbionese Liberation Army will emerge.

If we cannot precisely define the nature of an activity that characterizes a group, we cannot assume that such activity characterizes a group, nor can we assume that such activity is common to other groups; i.e., we cannot generalize. If a group activity is poorly defined, we can never be certain that similar patterns of political behavior and action exist in other groups, or that any pattern exists, even within the group under study. Fundamental to the approach of group theorists is the assumption that some form of interest provides a raison d'être for a group. But, if interest and activity are given circular definitions, what is left to examine? And, can we assume that an interest is similar enough to that held by other groups to warrant generalization and prediction?

Group theorists have overinterpreted their own findings and approaches. If the group is an essential component of politics, as writers since Aristotle have maintained, can we really assert that groups are anything more than components? Are they really "the stuff of politics"? In other words, the nature of the beast is such that it is necessarily limited to the status of an organizing concept, and is not a broad theory. "The fundamental perspective of group theory precludes any substantial deviation from a subsystem orientation." [60]

One can examine why people join organizations to possibly determine the group basis of politics. But this can be overinterpreted. A large body of evidence shows that Americans are not "joiners" in the popular sense of the word. Further, since group politics are not necessarily pressure politics, we are left with "very little evidence that these associations have an appreciable effect upon the attitudes of their membership."[61] In short, the claims made for group "theory" far outweigh any empirical evidence offered on its behalf.

Another criticism of the group approach is that it has been mainly applied to the United States and almost exclusively to problems involving American politics. An empirical theory must also apply to non-American and non-Western nations. When cross-national studies of groups have been done, there has been little attempt at replication. One work dealing with pressure groups on a cross-national basis reports studies that are essentially single-nation, non-comparative studies that do not have a set of propositions that were tested uniformly in each of the nine countries studied.[62]

Groups can be used as an organizing concept, and as a starting point for the study of politics. Ignoring the group concept is not the answer, although this has been done by researchers. In political science, there has been an almost cyclical history of the group concept. It becomes the focus of a number of researchers until its problems become evident, and is then laid aside only to be rediscovered again at some later date.[63] Why is this so? What has caused political scientists to periodically ignore this organizing concept which supposedly "takes us right to the very heart of the discipline"?[64] Political scientists are no less prone than members of other disciplines to jump from one field of exploration to another as the occasion warrants. However, another explanation might lie in some of the fundamental problems of the group approach, which we have elaborated above.

At this point, the group approach has no standing as a theory; it is a set of poorly defined concepts, with little basis for comparison between them in the development of more elaborate models or theories of political behavior. The group approach is a major tool of descriptive analysis, and it thus plays an important role in the development of other models and theories. It will continue to be used to classify individuals into categories useful for description. Its potential is circumscribed, but it can play a major role in the development of paradigms for political science.[65]

NOTES AND REFERENCES

1. Don R. Bowen, *Political Behavior of the American Public* (Columbus, Ohio: Charles E. Merrill Publishing Co., 1968), p. 41.

2. Bernard R. Berelson and Gary A. Steiner, *Human Behavior: An Inventory of Scientific Findings* (New York: Harcourt, Brace, and World, 1964), p. 558.

3. Robert E. Lane and David O. Sears, *Public Opinion* (Englewood Cliffs, N.J.: Prentice-Hall, 1964), p.34.

4. Berelson and Steiner, *Human Behavior*, pp. 331–39. *See also* James Q. Wilson, *Political Organizations* (New York: Basic Books, 1973), p. 26–27.

5. Berelson and Steiner, *Human Behavior*, pp. 327–31.

6. Lane and Sears, *Public Opinion*, pp. 34–36.

7. *Ibid.*, p. 40.

8. Eloise Snyder, "The Supreme Court as a Small Group," *Social Forces* 36 (March 1958): 234.

9. *Ibid.*, p. 238.

10. Angus Campbell and Homer C. Cooper, *Group Differences in Attitudes and Votes* (Ann Arbor, Mich.: Center for Political Studies and Institute for Social Research, University of Michigan, 1956).

11. *Ibid.*, p. 35–37.

12. *See* especially Raymond E. Wolfinger, "The Development and Persistence of Ethnic Voting," *American Political Science Review* 59 (December 1965): 896–908, and Mark R. Levy and Michael S. Kramer, *The Ethnic Factor: How America's Minorities Decide Elections* (New York: Simon and Schuster, 1972).

13. Wolfinger, "Development and Persistence of Ethnic Voting," p. 896.

14. In addition to Levy and Kramer, *The Ethnic Factor,* two good examples of different approaches are: Nathan Glazer and Daniel Patrick Moynihan, *Beyond the Melting Pot* (Cambridge: M.I.T. Press and Harvard University Press, 1963), and Edgar Litt, *Ethnic Politics in America* (Glenview, Ill.: Scott, Foresman and Company, 1970).

15. Wesley Allinsmith and Beverly Allinsmith, "Religious Affiliation and Politico-Economic Attitudes," *Public Opinion Quarterly* 12 (Fall 1948): 387.

16. Levy and Kramer, *The Ethnic Factor,* p. 229.

17. Michael Parenti, "Ethnic Politics and the Persistence of Ethnic Identification," *American Political Science Review* 61 (September 1967): 725.

18. Kevin P. Phillips, *The Emerging Republican Majority* (New Rochelle, N.Y.: Arlington House, 1969).

19. Robert A. Dahl, *A Preface to Democratic Theory* (Chicago: Phoenix Books, The University of Chicago Press, 1956), p. 146.

20. *Ibid.*, p. 147.

21. David B. Truman, *The Governmental Process: Political Interests and Public Opinion* (New York: Alfred A. Knopf, 1951), p. 322.

22. *Ibid.*, p. 335.

23. *Ibid.*, p. 350.

24. *Ibid.*

25. Robert L. Peabody, Jeffrey M. Berry, William G. Frasure, and Jerry Goldman, *To Enact a Law: Congress and Campaign Financing* (New York: Praeger Publishers, 1972).

26. Daniel M. Berman, *A Bill Becomes a Law: Congress Enacts Civil Rights Legislation,* 2nd ed. (New York: Macmillan, 1964).

27. Ronald J. Terchek, *The Making of the Test Ban Treaty* (The Hague: Neijhoff, 1969).

28. A. Lee Fritschler, *Smoking and Politics* (New York: Appleton-Century-Crofts, 1969).

29. A sensationalized report along these lines is Robert N. Winter-Berger, *The Washington Pay-off* (New York: Dell Publishing Co., 1972).

30. Gabriel A. Almond, *The American People and Foreign Policy* (New York: Frederick A. Praeger, 1960), p. 138.

31. Clement A. Vose, "Litigation as a Form of Pressure Group Activity," *Annals of the American Academy of Political and Social Science,* 319 (September 1958): 20–31.

32. Truman, *The Governmental Process,* p. 479.

33. Lester W. Milbrath, "Lobbying as a Communications Process," *Public Opinion Quarterly* 24 (Spring 1960): 32–53.

34. *The Politics of Protest,* a Report Submitted by Jerome H. Skolnick, Director, Task Force on Violent Aspects of Protest and Confrontation of the National Commission on the Causes and Prevention of Violence (New York: Clarion Books, Simon and Schuster, 1969), pp. 10–15.

35. *Ibid.,* p. 20.

36. Truman, *The Governmental Process,* pp. 45–46.

37. Harold Lasswell, *Politics: Who Gets What, When, and How* (Cleveland: Meridian Books, World Publishing Company, 1958). Similar accepted definitions are that politics is "concerned with the distribution of advantages and disadvantages." (Lewis A. Froman, Jr., *People and Politics* [Englewood Cliffs, N.J.: Prentice-Hall, 1962], p. 6.) The political system is defined "as those interactions through which values are authoritatively allocated for a society. . ." (David Easton, *A Systems Analysis of Political Life* [New York: John Wiley & Sons, 1965], p. 21.)

38. James S. Coleman, *Community Conflict* (Glencoe, Ill.: The Free Press, 1957). The following discussion relies heavily upon Chapter 2 of this work, "The Dynamics of Controversy," p. 9–14.

39. *Ibid.,* p. 10.

40. Lester W. Milbrath, *Political Participation: How and Why Do People Get Involved in Politics?* (Chicago: Rand McNally and Company, 1965), pp. 16–22.

41. *Ibid.,* p. 21.

42. Coleman, *Community Conflict,* p. 10.

43. *Ibid.,* p. 11.

44. *See also* George C. Homans, *The Human Group* (New York: Harcourt, Brace, and World, 1950), pp. 459–60.

45. Coleman, *Community Conflict,* p. 12.

46. *Ibid.,* pp. 12–13.

47. *Ibid.,* p. 13. *See also* Seymour Martin Lipset, *Political Man: The Social Bases of Politics* (Garden City, N.Y.: Anchor Books, Doubleday and Company, Inc., 1963), pp. 75–82. "The available evidence suggests that the chances for stable democracy are enhanced to the extent that groups and individuals have a number of crosscutting, politically relevant affiliations." p. 77.

48. Milbrath, *Political Participation,* p. 55.

49. Lewis A. Coser, *The Functions of Social Conflict* (Glencoe, Ill.: The Free Press, 1956), pp. 33–38.

50. *Ibid.*, p. 39.

51. *Ibid.*, p. 80.

52. *Ibid.*, pp. 87–95.

53. *Ibid.*, p. 103.

54. *Ibid.*, pp. 104–10.

55. Harry Eckstein, "Introduction: Group Theory and the Comparative Study of Pressure Groups," in Eckstein and David E. Apter (eds.), *Comparative Politics: A Reader* (New York: The Free Press, 1963), p. 391.

56. *Ibid.*

57. Peter H. Odegard, "A Group Basis of Politics: A New Name for an Old Myth," *Western Political Quarterly* 11 (September 1958): 296–97. The arguments put forward by Odegard on this point were apparently ignored by various systems analysts as well, who use and change the meaning of this term extensively.

58. Stanley Rothman, "Systematic Political Theory: Observations on the Group Approach," *American Political Science Review* 54 (March 1960): 32.

59. Eckstein, "Introduction," p. 392.

60. Oran R. Young, *Systems of Political Science* (Englewood Cliffs, N.J.: Prentice-Hall, 1968), p. 92.

61. Rothman, "Systematic Political Theory," p. 22.

62. Henry W. Ehrmann (ed.), *Interest Groups on Four Continents* (Pittsburgh: University of Pittsburgh Press, 1958).

63. Robert T. Golembiewski, William A. Welsh, and William J. Crotty, *A Methodological Primer for Political Scientists* (Chicago: Rand McNally and Company, 1969), p. 122.

64. *Ibid.*, p. 121.

65. Wilson, *Political Organizations,* p. 26, is even more blunt in discussing why people join groups. ". . . little in the way of a highly predictive theory is likely to emerge . . ." However, it should be pointed out that Wilson's own work may serve as a bridge for those engaging in conventional group studies and those of the rational decision-making school. *See* especially Chapter II in Wilson.

STUDY QUESTIONS

1. What do the following mean? How do they relate to political behavior?
   primary group
   secondary group
   categoric or tertiary group
   reference group

2. How can the study of groups encompass the following approaches?
   personality
   attitudes, beliefs, opinions, and values
   political socialization
   role

3. How do groups influence politics?

4. How do groups contribute to or diminish conflict?

5. What data-collection techniques are pertinent to the study of groups? Specify, indicating the level at which groups can be examined using a particular technique.

CHAPTER
9

Decision Making

Decision making is used as the basis for analysis by some political scientists who attempt to deal with politics on a broad level. This approach considers a decision and the events surrounding it as the basic, stable unit of analysis and as the act that is fundamental to political life. As one advocate of this approach says, decision making is not a question of

> dealing with some special aspect of the political process, but with its central core. Voting, legislating, adjudicating, and administering have always been conceived of as decision-making processes. The tools of political analysis—legal, historical, and behavioral—have always been adapted to the analysis of decision. The use of a decision-making framework for political research is not novel; rather, it represents continuing development along paths that stretch back to the beginnings of political science.[1]

The concern of most in the decision-making school is not necessarily to establish exactly how individuals arrive at decisions, although this may be implied from some of their classificatory schemes. Rather, these political scientists are concerned with how whole systems operate in making a decision or in bearing the effects of one. The system may be an administrative agency, a community, or the foreign policy apparatus of a nation. Whatever level of a political regime is being studied, the fundamental category of the research is the decision.

One approach characterizes decision making as a process of fulfilling seven functions:

> Think of any act of decision. We conceive it as beginning in an influx of information from sources at the focus of attention of participants in the decision process, some of whom perceive that their goal values have been or may be affected in ways that can be influenced by community decision. We refer to this as the *intelligence phase.*
>
> The next phase is *recommending,* or promoting, which refers to activities designed to influence the outcome. The *prescribing phase* is the articulation of norms; it includes, for instance, the enacting of enforceble statutes. The *invoking phase* occurs when a prescription is provisionally used to characterize a set of concrete circumstances. When a prescription is employed with finality, we speak of *application.* The *appraisal phase* characterizes the relationship between policy goals and the strategies and results obtained. The *terminating phase* involves the handling of expectations ("rights") established when a prescription was in force.[2]

These classifications are used not only for the convenience they afford in delineating the decision process, but to describe structures particularly pertinent to the fulfillment of the functions. For example, a field worker in the Head Start program might be involved in gathering and processing information about the effects of the program on preschool children. He is not limited solely to the intelligence function, but might make recommendations and preliminary evaluations for consideration by Head Start officials in Washington. He would then be in the position of applying a new policy that could be adopted on the basis of the information he and others had gathered, and would naturally be involved in the appraisal function as well. Although his position as a field worker for Head Start nominally requires that he be primarily involved in the application phase, he would inevitably perform several other functions as well.

Decision-making analysis is dynamic, involved as it is with "time plus change—change in relationships and conditions."[3] The decision-making approach affords a researcher the opportunity "to help identify and isolate the 'crucial structures' in the political realm where change takes place—where action is initiated and carried out, where decisions must be made; and to help analyze systematically the decision-making behavior which leads to action and which sustains actions."[4] The process by which decisions are made may be generally described as involving a sequence of "(a) pre-decisional activities, (b) choice, and (c) implementation."[5] Thereafter, the classificatory scheme becomes more elaborate. These three events relating to a decision may be used for the systematic analysis of behavior.

Concern with behavior characterizes most decisional analysis. In one work, careful attention was paid to the development of a conceptual scheme whereby one could account for influences on national actors—those who engaged in the actual decision process relative to foreign policymaking. Included in this analysis was the importance of perceptual processes and how members of policymaking groups individually and corporately defined a problem with which they were faced.[6]

The role perceptions in decision making, particularly as it relates to foreign policymaking, are illustrated in a model of the foreign policy decision process. This model shows how information flows between actors and agencies. Information is not received or processed value-free. Instead, individuals and groups involved in the decision process were found to pay attention selectively to information and engage in an unconscious process of selective recall.[7]

Classification and categorization can assist in developing empirical theory in the approach to decision making that defines politics as "concerned with the distribution of advantages and disadvantages among people."[8] This definition places decision making at the core of any political process. Political systems can be defined in light of the means by which decisions are arrived at and in terms of who participates in making decisions. Four types of decisional systems are possible; they involve the interaction of leaders with leaders (bargaining), leaders with followers (hierarchy and democracy), and followers with followers (discussion).[9] Each process can then be characterized according to the concerns of the actors involved, their attitudes, the rewards involved, and the direction in which the decision evolves, as shown in Table 9–1.

This decisional system model of politics obviously has applications to the study of group and system behavior; the sequence models discussed earlier accommodate studies of individual behavior. One of the more striking recent developments in political science has been an approach concentrating on individual behavior, but which can have serious implications for groups and political systems. We turn first to analysis of individual behavior, and then to studies of

TABLE 9–1. A General Model of Politics

Type of Decision Making	Actors	Interest and Information	Issue Orientation	Type of Issue Concern	Type of Attitudes	Type of Rewards	System Changes
Bargaining	Leaders	High	High	Position	Utilitarian and Knowledge	Material	Hierarchy and Democracy
Discussion	Non-leaders	Low	Low	Style	Value-expressive and Ego-defensive	Symbolic	Hierarchy
Democracy	Leaders and non-leaders	High for leaders; low for non-leaders	High for leaders; low for non-leaders	Style	Utilitarian and Knowledge for leaders; Value-expressive and Ego-defensive for non-leaders	Material for leaders; Symbolic for non-leaders	Hierarchy
Hierarchy	Leaders and non-leaders	High	High	Position	Utilitarian and Knowledge	Material	Bargaining

Source: Lewis A. Froman, Jr., *People and Politics: An Analysis of the American Political System* (Englewood Cliffs, N.J.: Prentice-Hall, 1962), p. 79. Reprinted by permission.

local decision making. These varied approaches show two strikingly different ways in which we may build empirical theory to both explain and predict.

RATIONAL DECISION MAKING

A major approach to the study of decision making derives from mathematics and economics.* Within the discipline of economics are specialists in decision making, a curious overlap of that discipline and political science, but not at all unusual. The economists' approach to analysis of decisions is highly useful to political scientists and has received increased attention and respect. In the following pages we introduce some of the major considerations of political scientists who take the rationalist approach.

Assumptions and Concepts

There are several assumptions that underlie the rationalist approach. As with other approaches to political science, there is the assumption that *behavior is not random*. In effect, it is assumed that there are *decision rules* by which individuals and groups take action. Whether implicitly or explicitly, decisions are arrived at by some fixed means, often arbitrary. One hardly ever questions the countless everyday decisions in our lives. Upon arising, one gets dressed, has breakfast, goes to work, and so forth. These "decisions" are taken for granted, and the rule governing each one is fairly implicit, unless one is given to anguish over the simplest things in life.

An example of a decision rule with which we are all familiar is the "majority rule." In the American political scene we often rely on this rule without question. But even this basic rule of democratic societies sometimes needs clarification. Do we mean an absolute majority—a majority of all those eligible to vote? A simple majority—a majority of those present and voting? A plurality—the most votes received? An extraordinary majority—some fixed percen-

---

*For those who have been warned about these two disciplines, there is nothing to fear in the following pages. There will be no mathematical notation whatsoever!

tage over 50% + 1? For any situation, it is assumed that there is a decision rule that can be invoked to guide the decision process.[10]

It is also assumed that there are *costs* to be borne in making decisions and that these costs derive in part from the number of individuals involved in the process, as well as from the decision rule. For instance, the time and attention in gathering information about an issue on which to vote (decide) are costs. Can one ever be fully informed, or have complete knowledge? This is unlikely, but one can still seek as much information as possible. At what point does it become too costly to seek information? Can a U.S. senator concerned about an upcoming vote directly affecting his constituents devote an entire day to the issue? How many staff members must be diverted from their routine duties to help inform him? Can his office routine be interrupted for days on end? Or will the senator ultimately have to reach a decision because other equally pressing issues demand his attention?

Costs from decision rules must be considered as well. In 1975 the Senate moved to change its rule governing cloture, the term used to indicate the cutting off of debate. This rules change was a fundamental consideration in the Senate, since there has generally been an informal rule allowing senators the right of uninterrupted debate. This rule allowed filibusters to take place, debates in which organized minorities attempted to prevent a vote on which they were certain to lose. The formal rules of the Senate operated in such a way that of those present and voting, one-third of the Senate, plus one member, could defeat a cloture vote. In early 1975, the Senate debated changing the rule so that an extraordinary majority of two-thirds of those present and voting would be reduced, which would make it more difficult for minorities to block a final vote on the Senate floor. The new decision rule finally arrived at was a requirement that cloture be voted by at least 60 percent of the total membership of the Senate. Whether this new decision rule will increase the costs to minorities has yet to be seen.

Costs can be defined as internal and external. *Internal costs* are essentially psychological in nature: Is one likely to participate in elections if the act of participation is self-defeating or worthless? Another way of putting this is in terms of individual stress. For instance, if Jones feels a low sense of political efficacy (feels that participating in politics is not worthwhile), he probably cannot be counted upon to participate in an election. There may be *external costs* as well, which derive from interaction with others. The more people one interacts with, the larger the costs become. External costs can also be psychological in nature. Assume that Jones has a low sense of political efficacy but lives in a household that otherwise values political participation and pressures its various members to vote. In this situation, we have a case of cross-pressures, where internal preferences clash with external preferences. If the costs of participating, despite low feelings of efficacy, are seen as lower than those of not participating, Jones may go to the polls to vote. Another example of external costs is the stress imposed by the urbanization process. As an area becomes increasingly urbanized there are increased costs to the polity, in the form of more taxes for improved streets, schools, and sewage systems. There can also be psychological costs as old and familiar environments change as a consequence of urbanization.[11]

Costs are not willingly borne unless there are benefits from the decision. The benefits are frequently referred to in terms of their *utility.* Costs are borne until the actor or group sees that further participation is worthless. In Figure 9–1, the costs are borne as long as there is something to be gained from participation—as long as it is profitable or advantageous to continue participating. Using a simple analogy, if one were to participate as a bidder in an auction, one might continue bidding up to the point where *marginal costs* (which economists define as the cost of purchasing the last item) equal the *marginal utility* (the worth of the last item). One does not happily continue to participate if the costs of participation exceed the benefits. At an auction, one might happily pay $20 for an old lamp if it were worth that much or more. However, if its real worth were $15, marginal costs would exceed marginal utility. And the bidder might stop offering bids at some fixed point, such as $12, because savings of anything less than $3 do not constitute a bargain.

Using Figure 9–1, we can apply the example of the senator who was greatly concerned with a piece of legislation. At some point, his costs (in terms of hours expended, an arbitrary unit) might equal or exceed the benefits or utility of his decision. Thus, if he sees that devoting time to the bill is worth up to 10 hours of his time and no more, he will turn to other matters at least by the 10th hour because by that time he is no longer getting a "bargain" for the expenditure of his time. In the first hour he learned a lot about the bill, in the second hour less, and in the third hour even less. He might then

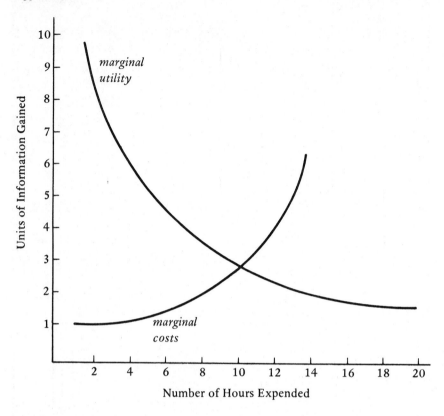

FIGURE 9–1

Marginal Costs and Marginal Utility in Gaining Information

decide that at some point before the 10th hour the time he expended was not worthwhile. By relying on his party affiliation for a voting cue at some arbitrary point, perhaps the third hour, he is able to cut costs significantly, should he decide to do so.

Even in its collective and deliberative aspects, the process of decision making is of a purely individualistic nature.[12] According to this interpretation, there can be no room for an organic view of the state, as espoused by several classical political theorists. However, it is not a statement of rampant individualism, in a Hobbesian or Darwinian state of nature, where individuals prey on each other and only the fittest survive. Rather, individuals are bound by the state and by the constitution, which is a set of decision rules under which the state operates. Since we are concerned in political science with actions of the state, we must also comprehend the individuals who are part of the polity.[13] In the rational decision-making approach, therefore, there is no room for broad concepts such as the "general will" espoused by Rousseau. There is no mysterious process by which individual choices are aggregated into a higher (and perhaps different) order. Decision rules, as found in constitutions and laws, indicate how, when, and what preferences will prevail. With this approach we can analyze individual actors and groups (courts, legislatures and their committees, the electorate, etc.).

According to the rationalists, decisions are not made in a random manner. *Decisions are purposive.* People are assumed to be goal-oriented in their decision making. Further, some goal-oriented choices may be preferable to others. Behavior is assumed to be rational when people know their own preferences and can place them in logical order. Another way of stating this idea is that "rational behavior is, then, the choice of that alternative which maximizes expected utility."[14]

Although there are numerous other assumptions in the rationalist approach to decision making as the focus of political behavior, we can summarize the points made thus far: Individuals are studied in order to gain insights into their own decision preferences. Preferences are rank-ordered by each individual. The rank-ordering is done on the basis of implicit or explicit calculations of the costs and benefits. Rational individuals attempt to impose their own preferences on society through the mechanisms allowed by their constitution or decision rules. In sum,

The center of attention becomes the mental calculus of the individual as he is confronted with a choice among alternative rules for the reaching of subsequent political decisions. . . . Simple self-interest dictates that the individual will try to rank alternative rules and institutions for collective decision making.[15]

Methods and Applications

The approach taken by the rationalist school of decision making is quite different from that of most behavioralists. Behavioral researchers usually attempt to operationalize concepts in the development of testable hypotheses. Behavioralists begin with an inductive process of reasoning, proceeding from specific to general statements.

This is followed by the deductive phase in which specific logical consequences are derived from the general statement, or hypothesis. Finally, the verification process occurs, in which one attempts to determine whether the logical consequences of the hypothesis are present to an acceptable degree.

By contrast, the rationalist approach is claimed to be highly deductive in nature and to generate specific consequences from broad statements that are axiomatic in nature. We have already stated some of these axioms; they boil down basically to the rational ordering of preferences by individuals who seek to minimize costs and maximize utility or benefits. The scientific method as discussed in Chapter 2 seeks to develop theories based upon the empirical *observation of behavior,* noting regularities and uniformities. The deductive and axiomatic approach of the rationalists can be reconciled with the scientific approach inasmuch as it is based upon *postulated behavior.* Starting from these postulates, specific logical consequences can be derived and then tested.

We can explore the consequences of postulated rational behavior with deductive reasoning. Assume, for instance, that a decision must be made by an individual who acts according to assumed rationality. There will be considerations of cost (time, money, or some other resource) and benefit. For the sake of simplicity, the costs can be viewed as low or high. The benefits can be seen as positive or negative, the latter implying wasted time and effort.

Figure 9–1 diagrams the possible decisions that would be made given the variables of cost and benefit. According to rational behavior assumptions, one would expect box A to yield a positive or favorable decision since costs are low and there are positive benefits to be gained from a favorable decision. If benefits are seen as negative, it would not be rational to expect a decision that would be of no benefit and would be detrimental to the individual making the decision. Hence, in boxes B and D a negative decision is made. In box C the decision maker is faced with a problem of marginal cost and marginal utility. If the cost is less than the benefit to be gained, we might expect a favorable decision. On the other hand, if the cost exceeds the expected benefit, a negative decision would be made. [16] Thus, in Figure 9–2, there are five possible outcomes deriving from cost and benefit. Of those five, only two are positive in nature; the other three are negative.

	Positive Benefit	Negative Benefit
Low Cost	A *Favorable Decision*	B *Unfavorable Decision*
High Cost	C *Favorable Decision,* if cost is less than benefit *Unfavorable Decision,* if cost exceeds benefits	D *Unfavorable Decision*

FIGURE 9–2

Hypothetical Decision Possibilities

Extending this further to a consideration of the perceived likelihood of receiving positive or negative benefits, we can determine that the likelihood of a favorable decision being made under such conditions of cost, benefit, and probability of occurrence is only 3 in 10, or 30% (*see* Figure 9–3). Through such analysis we *may* gain insight into the ways in which political institutions, such as the congress or the presidency, arrive at decisions. This of course is predicated on the assumption that rational behavior prevails. If this assumption can be made, we might be able to explain the relative lack of speed of governmental processes as a result of the difficulty of arriving at decisions when costs, benefits, and the likelihood of receiving those benefits are not known. In sum, the rationalist school of thought does not assume that decision makers can ever possess complete or perfect information. Since our hypothetical decision-making model includes a "forecast"—or expected probability of receiving benefits—information is obviously less than perfect.

How can the consequences of postulated rational behavior be tested? One frequently used method is simulations or games. These might involve limited numbers of persons playing bargaining games. In a sense, these games constitute experiments as we described them in Chapter 3; that is, the fact that the research is being conducted is known to the subjects involved, although the purpose of the research

	Positive Benefits		Negative Benefits	
	Likelihood of Receiving Benefits			
	High	*Low*	*High*	*Low*
Low Cost	*Favorable*	*Favorable,* if it is believed that costs are less than benefits *Unfavorable,* if it is believed that costs exceed benefits	*Unfavorable*	*Unfavorable*
High Cost	*Favorable,* if it is believed that costs are less than benefits *Unfavorable,* if it is believed that costs exceed benefits	*Unfavorable*	*Unfavorable*	*Unfavorable*

FIGURE 9–3

Likelihood of Receiving Benefits According to Hypothetical Decision Possibilities

may not be immediately clear. Although the researcher can only manipulate the rules of the game, he can determine the consequences of decision making by observing the progress and outcomes of games. Games may played with two or more individuals. When played with only two persons, we frequently refer to them as *zero-sum games;* i.e., the net gain of the winner is equal to the net loss of the loser. The sum of the two yields a score of zero. The children's game of guessing what someone has in their hand provides an illustration. A correct guess of the object yields a net gain (of the object) for the winner, and a net loss (of the object) for the loser. Whether games are considered zero-sum depends on the number of players involved, whether or not coalitions can be formed according to the rules of the game, and the availability of resources to the players.

Consider a game in which there are only three players. Although the game situation only simulates the "real world," there is an implied assumption that it reflects the real political world. Since rationalists assume that politics often require coalition formation, rules may be established to encourage two players to form a coalition against the third. Games are considered to be only analogous to politics.[17]

One three-person game sought to find out what types of coalitions would take place, and whether or not players would attempt to act in a rational manner to gain maximum benefits. Participants had no previous acquaintance with each other before the experiments began. They were all briefed about the rules and goals of the game. Negotiation situations were provided, so that player A had a chance to bargain with player B and then later with player C. Players B and C were also given an opportunity to negotiate with each other. Since there was a real monetary reward for successful negotiation and coalition-building, the players attempted to strike bargains that would net them the highest possible benefit in terms of dollars received. The researcher conducted the game as follows:

> At the end of the conversations the experimenter asks each person privately if he has formed a coalition and, if so, how the payoff is to be distributed within the coalition. If two players agree on their answers to these questions and if their answers are compatible with the value of the coalition, the experimenter pays each person in the coalition the appropriate amount.[18]

The result of this game and others like it show that making coalitions that cannot produce maximum benefits is not likely in game situations. "Observing the frailty of human wit, it is foolish to deny the possibility of error."[19] The frequency of error might provide some insight into the limits of rationality, and here the data strongly suggest that the assumptions of rationality are often met. In more than 90 percent of several hundred attempts at playing this game, a coalition was formed between two players, at the expense of the third. Further, these coalitions were highly efficient since they came quite close to achieving the optimal dollar amounts possible through the game playing.[20]

Although game playing has been a major means by which rational decision making has been tested, it has been shown that survey research can be applied in this area as well. To set the stage for this, consider a situation in which three or more choices are afforded three or more decision makers. Assuming three choices—X,

Y, and Z—and three or more choosers, who if anybody can win? For instance, we might have evenly divided preference orders for candidates for a job. In one example, it is assumed that a political science department of fifteen members has interviewed candidates X, Y, and Z for a position.[21] The fifteen divide evenly:

	Group I	Group II	Group III
Preference Orders	X Y Z	Y Z X	Z X Y

In this situation, it is impossible for a majority to win:

> If X is chosen, then a majority (II, III) that prefers Z to X is frustrated; if Y is chosen, then the majority that prefers Z to X is frustrated; finally, if Z is chosen a majority composed of groups I and II, that prefers Y to Z, is frustrated. Thus no matter what the choice, a majority is dissatisfied.[22]

In this situation, where there are three or more choices and three or more choosers, what is known as Arrow's Paradox, after the economist Kenneth Arrow, may result.[23] How likely is this possibility? Will the department have to allow the dean to decide? Will it lose its new faculty position? Or is it possible that other preference orderings that can produce a majority will take place?*

> Most investigations of the paradox of voting suggest, however, that all may well be lost. Under a variety of theoretical assumptions, it has been determined that the probability of majority frustrations is an increasing function of both the number of choosers and the number of choice alternatives, and is especially sensitive to the latter. For example, with five or more alternatives and large electorates, the probability is at least one quarter, and may be as large as .8, that a voters' paradox arises.[24]

In the United States, we commonly accept the notion of a majority, usually a simple majority of those actually voting. In some southern states, it is necessary to receive a majority of those casting ballots in the primary election. Since these primaries frequently have

---

*This assumes that majorities are "best," a normative conclusion, not an empirical one.

three or more individuals running for the Democratic nomination, no clear winner can emerge. A run-off primary must take place between the top two vote-getters of the first primary. Most states outside the South do not have such provisions, because this degree of competition may not necessarily take place in the primary or the general election. In New York, a three-candidate race took place in 1970 for the U.S. Senate seat. A survey asked college students what they perceived as a candidate's position on various issues. Their responses were weighted in order to predict an individual's vote. The weighting procedure was rather complex, as was the formal means of calculating the respondent's likely vote. No consideration was given to the respondent's perception of which candidate was likely to win. Using this model and the assumptions of rational ordering of preferences, it was possible to correctly predict the vote of 83 percent of those surveyed. This study was conducted with assumptions of rationality; it did not use parental preferences for candidates and parties or social background factors such as age, sex, religion, or socioeconomic status.[25] There thus seems to be a high degree of predictive value in properly applied survey research grounded in rationalist assumptions.

Critique

Rational behavior theorists in political science have been able to muster considerable evidence for their position that *homo politicus* is not the blind, instinctive, visceral individual so many others claim him to be. The rational person is conceived as:

> one who behaves as follows: (1) he can always make a decision when confronted with a range of alternatives; (2) he ranks all the alternatives facing him in order of his preference in such a way that each is either preferred to, indifferent to, or inferior to each other; . . . (4) he always chooses from among the possible alternatives that which ranks highest in his preference ordering, and (5) he always makes the same decision each time he is confronted with the same alternatives.[26]

When a predictive model achieves an accuracy of the level reported in the example of the New York election research (83 percent) or in the three-person bargaining situation (92 to 95 percent), it is obvious that it commands serious attention. What are the problems with the rational behavior school of decision making?

One problem is attitudinal and behavioral intensity. Can a single intense individual have preferences that prevail over mildly held preferences of others? In the example of the three groups of faculty members with preferences for candidates X, Y, and Z, it is possible that the intensity of one group might persuade another group to reorder its own preferences, and the dean need not intercede nor will the new faculty position be lost. However, it would seem that the models employed by rational decisionalists cannot account for preference intensity, because levels of intensity are so highly individualistic.*

There is also a problem of error in decision making. It is possible that persons will make less than optimal selections. However, careful study has shown that most of these errors result from a lack of information, or from a miscalculation of those studied. The assumption of rationality, however, cannot be rejected on grounds of error.

> Much, if not most, error results from misinformation and reasoned rejection of the cost of correction, not from simple stupidity. And if we are right in these conjectures, then error, if properly accounted for, does not interfere with explication by means of the notion of rationality.[28]

Finally, a major problem derives from the individualistic approach employed. If one conceives of a polity as something less than a dictatorship, and where there is no General Will divorced from the interests of an individual or set of individuals, how are system-wide decisions really made? Certainly, we can examine individual decision making using the rationalist approach, and we can find high levels of predictive capacity through survey research of large groups. However, the same problem faces rationalist theorists as faces other schools of thought in political science: the problem of linkage between rulers and the ruled. To state that the "political structure is conceived of as something that *emerges* from the choice processes of individual participants"[29] is to say both a lot and very little. We are left with wondering how "emergence" ever takes place, if at all. Articles of faith are somewhat hard to swallow if we claim rationality in the individuals we study.

---

* Rational theorists admit that their approach is individualistic. Although intensity is usually thought of as an individual trait, they say it cannot be considered![27]

Despite these problems, there is obviously much to be said in favor of the rationalistic approach to decision-making analysis. Rationalist theories are being used increasingly because they have demonstrated a great ability to explain and to predict, which is what we demand of empirical theories. The interdisciplinary nature of this approach suggests that it will be used extensively and continue to expand in use as fresh insights are gained from other fields of inquiry.

THE COMMUNITY POWER CONTEXT

In the proliferating study of community power structures, we can study decision making itself, in a readily recognizable and relevant context. It is not uncommon in our society to make assumptions about "the Establishment," or to fail to take decisive individual action because "you can't fight city hall." The assumption underlying these examples of conventional wisdom is that power, as a political phenomenon, rests outside of oneself, but is associated with making binding decisions on oneself.

By a close reading of the literature on community decision making, we can also see the development of several conceptual schemes, created by scholarly interaction. In fits and starts over the last several decades, the ways in which we conceive of and examine our political environment have changed drastically in a continual process of refinement.

The link between theory and methodology is also well illustrated in this line of development. Knowing quite little about the various research methods employed, we can see how theory tends to lead methodology and to demand innovative techniques to assist in the verification of theory. We can also, however, find far too many examples of the way in which method and approach can virtually dictate findings that are presented as conclusive, when indeed they are not so at all. The study of community power is a prime example not only of methodological refinement, but of methodological failure as well.

The conceptualization of community power also leads us to an examination of the way in which normative and empirical works differ in their assumptions of values. Certain early approaches implicitly ask the question, who should rule? In what ways should power be exercised, and for whose benefit? Later approaches seek to determine who actually rules. In the conflict between normative and empirical approaches, we see a classic example of the very real differences that can and do emerge in scholarly debate on descriptions of and prescriptions for the real world.

First Generation Models: Reputational/Elitist

The study of community power is not necessarily a uniquely American phenomenon; scholars have for centuries commented on apparent tendencies for power to concentrate in the hands of a few instead of many. However, a coherent picture of the ruling elite model, as it may be called, began to emerge in studies conducted by American sociologists starting in the 1920s. The landmark studies of this era were conducted by Robert S. and Helen M. Lynd.[30] Conducted in Muncie, Indiana, these studies became classics that pointed not just to elite control, but to virtual monopolistic control—by a single family. The Middletown reports were not intended to be an examination of only control processes at work, although this was a central theme of their undertaking. They were a comprehensive attempt to examine a community in depth, and to examine the culture of a single community and how the culture interacts with its members. The dominance of a single family controlling a small business elite, however, has a fascination that is hard to lay aside. There is little doubt today that methodologically their work was unsound because it drew unevenly from a wide variety of observations, records, and interviews.

In a conceptual sense, there is much to be desired in the work of the Lynds and in other studies of elites. There is a tendency to assume that *reputed* power is *actual* power.[31] The reputational/elitist school assumes that if people feel a person or persons have power or its resources then the power is actually possessed and employed. As tenuous as their work may appear to be, however, the impact of a single family upon a total culture is not easy to ignore, if valid. For instance, one of the more striking passages in the Middletown studies shows how the "X family" either owns, operates, or reputedly influences virtually all industrial and essential services. These include a bank, hospital, department store, brewery, churches, political parties, and the newspaper, to name a few.[32] However questionable the methodology appears to be, this early portrait of a single town gives a picture of a small, coherent, and presumably cohesive elite with an all-pervasive impact on the life of a community. If this description has any value, the X family had a control over various decisional and allocative processes and institutions which is scarcely short of total. Even if the study is not entirely accurate, the attribution of such power to a single elite may, if held widely enough, provide sufficient latitude for that elite to attempt to influence the decisional processes of the town. In short, other potentially competitive groups that feel ineffective in the face of such real or imagined power may not participate by default.

Numerous other studies of community power, defining power on the basis of reputation, result in elitist findings. Hunter's work is of special importance in the development and refutation of elitist theory. Hunter may have been overinterpreted by his critics. There is a tendency to take his elitist findings of political power and generalize them to a pervasive picture of power, à la Middletown. Hunter's examination of "Regional City" (Atlanta) began with a reputational methodology. Four lists of leaders were provided by the Chamber of Commerce, the League of Women Voters, "newspaper editors and other civic leaders," and the community council.[34] In other words, the findings were begged in advance by starting with these closed lists, limited to those who were described by the four groups as potentially powerful in the community.

A panel of fourteen persons selected forty individuals, presumably the preeminent leaders of Regional City in business, politics, society, and general community leadership. As Polsby says:

> . . . consider the question Hunter asked, first of his original list-makers, then of the panel. He wanted them to name the community's top leaders which presupposed that a group of top leaders exists . . . this presupposition causes great methodological difficulties. First, how many "top leaders" are there? Second, what differentiates "top" from "nontop" leaders? Third, how do we know the judges are applying standards of "topness" consistent with one another and with Hunter? Fourth, how do we know the judges are correct, that in fact there are "top leaders" in the community, and that, if there are, they have been correctly identified?[35]

In short, the methodology presumed in advance that an elite did exist, and the research simply identified this elite and its characteristics. Alternative assumptions apparently were not considered or included in the research design, and findings of elitism were literally dictated by the methods.

The findings are therefore obvious, but bear at least a brief repetitition here. A relatively permanent set of individuals, comprising a power elite structured in a pyramidical fashion, was found to dominate the life of Atlanta. Largely derived from the business and commerce world, this group had no blacks and only four members from local government, including two from the school system. Another criticism concerns the extent to which

> Hunter limits the role of the alleged decision makers to the relatively innocuous task of "getting consent." He specifically denies that the top members of the pyramid had special opportunities either to innovate or to execute policies.[36]

This criticism, which refers to the means by which a researcher operationally defines power and its use, is central to the criticism of the pluralists, to whom we now turn.

Second Generation Models: Decisional/Pluralist

As part of the attack on the elitist model Dahl proposed that Hunter's definition of "ruling elite" lacked the requisites for complete operationalization. He claimed the definition is normally embedded in an implicit hypothesis, to the effect that

> Such and such a political system (the U.S., the U.S.S.R., New Haven, or the like), is a ruling system in which the ruling elite has the following membership. Membership would then be specified by name, position, socioeconomic class, socioeconomic roles, or what not.[37]

Such an hypothesis is particularly susceptible to improper tests, such as confusing "a ruling elite with a group that has a high potential for control," assuming that the elite is "a group of individuals who have more influence than others in the system," and that the elite generalizes "from a single scope of influence."[38] On the other hand:

> The hypothesis of the existence of a ruling elite can be strictly tested only if:
>
> 1. The hypothetical ruling elite is a well-defined group.
> 2. There is a fair sample of cases involving key political decisions in which

the preferences of the hypothetical ruling elite run counter to those of any other likely group that might be suggested.

3. In such cases the preferences of the group regularly prevail.[39]

Dahl essentially tests the ruling elite hypothesis in New Haven by the means which he had earlier proposed.[40] The examination of political decision making is implicitly part of the second point above; it was the core of his approach, instead of reputationally derived models such as those employed by the elitists. In the examination of decision making, the pluralists are subject to the same criticism of the elitist research. A subjective bias must inevitably arise in selecting key political decisions for study. How are issues to be considered key or central? Cannot groups disagree over what is important? One group may consider an issue to be vitally important, perhaps even essential to its own continuance or survival, while another group may choose to ignore the issue entirely.[41]

Returning to the means by which Dahl attempted to study decision making, we find that he adopted what he refers to as an eclectic methodology. He used the following considerations—instead of merely limiting himself to an examination of the "key political decisions" to which he had earlier referred. He determined the nature and extent of "changes in socioeconomic characteristics of incumbents in city offices"; examined a single category of individuals, the "Social and Economic Notables, to define their nature and extent of participation in local affairs"; surveyed "samples of participants in different issue areas in order to determine their characteristics"; surveyed registered voters for the same purpose; and studied changes in voting patterns among varying community strata, such as ethnic groups.[42]

The result of such a comprehensive approach to community power was a sweeping rejection of not only the methods but the conclusions of the elitists as well. According to Dahl, different issues tend to evoke participation of different individuals and groups; there is some degree of overlap, but not noticeably so. Central to this finding is the conclusion that decision making is a group process, where different groups are concerned with different issues. Thus, the major issue areas Dahl chose to examine—urban renewal, education, and nominations for office—tended to involve different groups, with only a minimal overlap. Decision making was considered by Dahl to extend beyond the loose definition of ruling offered by the elitists.

To Dahl, it involved the processes of initiation, modification, and veto; this greatly expanded the potential for inclusion of individuals and groups ignored by the elitist school of thought. This broadened definition of decision making, along with the varied approaches used, led ultimately to the finding that political officeholders participated to a greater degree than suggested by Hunter.

Following in Dahl's footsteps, the pluralist school argues that power is necessarily tied to issues, especially to real issues. The pluralists claim that in order to study power we must at least examine the actual decisions and determine who was involved in the entire process. It is not enough to claim, as do the reputational/ elitists, that certain individuals have the potential for control. One must find out whether or not they actually engage in the decision-making process. This approach was also used in the Atlanta study, in an attempt to replicate the findings of Hunter using the decisional approach.[43] As might be expected, the elitist conclusions of Hunter were rejected in favor of decision-making patterns similar to those in New Haven. A decisional approach was also taken in an Oberlin, Ohio, study with similar results again, reinforcing the claims of the pluralist school that New Haven was not unique in its dispersion of authority and that economic notables do not play the central role claimed for them by Hunter.[44]

A different methodological approach, employing primary documents such as public records, memoirs, personal letters, and biographies, revealed that even large cities, such as New York, may be characterized as pluralistic in nature.[45] New York might be the ultimate case for pluralism because political power and decision making are highly fractionated there through diverse political and nonpolitical influences.

> The city's political system is, in fact, vigorously and incessantly competitive. The stakes of the city's politics are large, the contestants are numerous and determined, the rules of the competition are known to and enforced against each other by the competitors themselves, and the city's electorate is so uncommitted to any particular contestant as to heighten the competition for the electorate's support or consent. No single ruling elite dominates the political and governmental system of New York City.[46]

With the volume of replicative attempts of the pluralists, one might expect that the debate over community power, who rules, who governs, or who makes decisions might have ended, and that social scientists would have moved on to other areas of concern. However, the same questions might be asked of the pluralists as were asked of the elitists: Did anything in the methodology ultimately prejudice or bias the findings? Does the examination of decisions, with the broad interpretation of decision making, necessarily imply that political notables, as well as political and nonpolitical groups, would and should participate? Is there a normative bias to the decisional approach created by the implication that decision making is diversified, an impression one receives from reading the works of this school? In other words should the decisional process involve shifting groups rather than coherent elites?

Critics of the pluralist model question the fundamental assumptions about power that appear to underlie this model. The pluralists

> . . . begin with a view of society (or community, or any other social unit) as an aggregation of different individuals motivated by self-interest, predominantly rational (in the sense that they are conscious of their interests and active in seeking their fulfillment), and free from any permanent relationships with anyone or anything else.[47]

Further,

> . . . there is the question of whether persons using pluralist methodology could recognize issues. Issues can be defined either by the observer's commitment to an ideological outlook that defines important problems or by his ability to comprehend fully the issue definitions of the people he studies. The pluralist literature, however, claims no ideology, other than commitment to empirical science—a commitment which emphasizes that which is rather than that which ought to be. And interestingly enough, pluralist ability to get "into the heads" of its subjects appears to be hampered by a similar acceptance of the existing political order.[48]

This attack is not entirely without justification, and serves to point up some of the weaknesses of the decisional/pluralist school of thought.[49]

There are additional difficulties involved in accepting the work of the pluralists. The attention paid to overt decisions requires one to decide subjectively the issues that are central to the political process, thus lending an immediate bias to the research. As the

257

researcher looks for such issues, he inevitably excludes some issues. Decisions alone will not locate community leaders. If an issue is suppressed from emerging in the public arena, then power is exercised through a "nondecision."

> Of course power is exercised when A participates in the making of decisions that affect B. Power is also exercised when A devotes his energies to creating or reinforcing social and political values and institutional practices that limit the scope of the political process to public consideration of only those issues which are comparatively innocuous to A. To the extent that A succeeds in doing this, B is prevented, for all practical purposes, from bringing to the fore any issues that might in their resolution be seriously detrimental to A's set of preferences.[50]

In a discussion of politically potent issues in Baltimore involving race and poverty, it is shown how effective a "nondecision" may be in stopping real grievances from emerging in the public forum. In one particular instance, organizers from the Congress of Racial Equality (CORE) announced that Baltimore was to become a focus of their activity. Acting with unusual speed, the mayor organized biracial "task forces" to make recommendations on programs that could be developed for the city's black population.

> Whatever his motives, the Mayor made an extremely effective nondecision. Before CORE's organizers stepped off the train in Baltimore, their planned campaign was aborted. Whatever hope they may have had of forming a local alliance with local liberals, black and white, was shattered by successful pre-emptive co-optation on the Mayor's part . . . CORE thus found itself without access to the political system and with no resources, other than the inert mass of impoverished Negroes, for the exercise of power.[51]

Used alone, the decisional approach is subject to serious faults that cannot be ignored. Conceptual and methodological refinement is found in the study we next consider.

Third-Generation Models: Combined Approaches

The refinement of concepts and methods to study community power is well illustrated in a study conducted by Presthus.[52] Rather than accepting or rejecting *a priori* either of the two previously used approaches, Presthus chose instead to test them simultaneously in a comparative study of two small upstate New York communities. The decisional approach involved the selection of five decisions, each broadly affecting the appropriate community, with concentration on those primarily involved in the initiation phase of decision making. Attention was also paid to those who assisted in implementation or who opposed the decision.[53] The reputational method was employed by asking respondents in a sample survey to name persons whom they would include in a group of leaders to make a decision on some communitywide project.[54] Two methods, asking who has power and tracing decisions, were thus conceived of as *mutual supports* in the determination of relationships between overt (decisional) and potential (reputational) power.[55] Finally, Presthus employed "a combination of intellectual and subjective frames of thought in . . . synthesizing, weighing, and modifying the evidence provided by the two methods. . . ."[56] The use of this technique, while methodologically appalling to those who prefer to let the data speak for itself, is an admission of the necessary and ultimately subjective role of interpretation in even the most complex data analysis.

The approaches taken resulted in findings that do not support either the elitists or the pluralists exclusively; Presthus found something of merit in both schools of thought. A small number of individuals, representing .005 percent of the populations, was found to "play the central active role in initiating and directing major community decisions."[57] At first glance, the limited proportion of participating individuals would appear to support the elitist school, especially since Dahl's expanded definition of decision making, encompassing the initiation phase, is included within the finding. However, there are essentially two decision-making centers in the towns studied by Presthus. One of these is political and largely related to the electoral process. The other deals with economic affairs, largely in the private sector, and draws its membership from those holding high positions in local business and society. As might be expected, the economic group has a firmer grasp on their necessary resources than politicians have on votes, and so experiences a greater continuity of leadership and position. The political and economic elites do not exist in a vacuum, but compete and cooperate with each other on matters of mutual interest. Further, these two elites compete with and rely upon the expertise of specialists, those concerned with single issues, such as education or welfare. Such specialists must be counted upon to participate in the total decision process, although they lack the continuity and cohesiveness of the other two bodies of participants. The comparative approach taken by Presthus also suggests that no single pattern of decision making or dominance by a single group can be expected to occur from town to town; nor does each elite play the same role from community to community. [58]

A substantial proportion of the leaders identified by the two methods were found to be involved in more than one decision. Considering the size of the towns studied (6,000 and 8,500), contrasted to the size of other cities of community power studies, Presthus determined that "there is an inverse association between overlapping [elitism] and size."[59] Thus, the larger the city, the more likely one is to make a case for pluralism, because of the "existence of multiple competition among leaders, i.e., little overlapping among the local elites in terms of their participation in major issues. . . ."[60] A generally low rate of participation by the citizenry-at-large was found; the low rate held for normal electoral channels of influence such as referenda, elections, and public meetings. Participation through group membership was also sharply limited. After studying fifty-two voluntary organizations, it was found that approximately 40 percent of the groups were active in decision-making processes affecting the community, and most of these were single-issue concerns. The notion of Americans as "joiners" is dispelled by this study that found that about half of the individuals surveyed in both communities belonged to no voluntary organizations at all or only one (excluding churches). Hence, the potential for participation through group organizations is sharply curtailed by limited memberships and minimal participation by voluntary organizations in communitywide decision making, and because most of the groups that do participate concentrate on single issues only. It was further suggested that the extent of social integration in a community is positively related to the ability of a wider-based citizenry to participate in decision making. Communities low in social cohesion and characterized by sharply variant values are more prone to have limited or elitist decision centers.[61]

On a methodological level, Presthus found that his assumptions about the utility of the reputational and decisional methods were largely borne out. The reputational method, based primarily upon the potential for power, was able to include 52 percent of the list arrived at by the decisional method, which focused upon behavior alone. The use of both methods also provides clues as to why individuals, who may be legitimately reputed as having the potential for participation, fail to exercise that potential or are not identified by the decisional method. The two approaches are not to be considered mutually exclusive; they are more complementary than contradictory.

Fourth-Generation Models: New and Expanded Concerns

Presthus also addressed research to the distribution of ideological positions within the communities he studied. This was more of a central concern of research published in the same year as Presthus's work.[62] This study, like Presthus's, was comparative, examining four communities, two in "Western State" and two in "Southern State." The communities studied varied widely in size, history, politics, and life style. In addition to these variables, the authors introduced another variable—change over time. This is a highly critical element in empirical studies that frequently focus on a single event or point in time. The authors were able to determine the relative stability of the community power structures studied, instead of concluding that a community was necessarily and immutably elitist. In elaborating a six-stage decision-making model, the authors in a sense also operationalized the sequence model to which we referred earlier, although there are distinct differences between the two. By referring to their model as relating to political decision making, the authors suggest that the process involved "is political only in the sense that those engaged in action at any stage are acting consciously, in some measure, in reference to the scope of government."[63]

But what is the scope of government? The authors suggest that determining the scope of government is fundamental to the study of leadership and citizenry ideologies, which they consider the central question in community power structures. Thus, the ways in which leaders and others normatively view the role of government—in either "expansionist" or "contractionist" terms—operationally define political ideologies.

By political ideology we mean a system of interrelated ideas about the polity that includes general answers to the following questions:

1. What sorts of general interests exist in a community, person, or group?

261

If the latter, are the interests community-wide public interests or are they those of less inclusive sectors of the community?

2. Who ought to make the decisions about the proper scope of government and in whose interests?

3. What share of available socioeconomic and cultural values is a person currently being allocated relative to others in a community?

4. What role should the government play in allocating values produced in the economy, in the society, and in the governmental institutions themselves?[64]

According to the implications of these questions, we can describe political leaderships as either agreeing on preferences about the scope of political activity—in which case they are "convergent"—or as disagreeing, in which case they are "divergent." Similarly, the distribution of political power among citizens can be classified as broad or narrow, particularly regarding opportunities to participate meaningfully in the decision-making process. The various types of possible power structures emerge as in Figure 9–4.

Given this typology, it is easy to see why time must be counted as an important variable. To assume that a community is, and must be for all time, a single form of power structure, is to

	Broad Distribution of Political Power Among Citizens	Narrow Distribution of Political Power Among Citizens
Ideology of Political Leadership is Convergent	*Consensual Mass*	*Consensual Elite*
Ideology of Political Leadership is Divergent	*Competitive Mass*	*Competitive Elite*

FIGURE 9–4

Types of Power Structures (Robert E. Agger, Daniel Goldrich, and Bert E. Swanson, *The Rulers and the Ruled: Political Power and Impotence in American Communities* [New York: John Wiley & Sons, 1964], p. 73. Reprinted by permission.)

assume a totally static situation. If Hunter's Regional City were to be pictured as a consensual elite structure, can we assume that it is fixed and unchanging? To do so would be to ignore the potential impact of events, powerful leaders, and changes in the political climate that might act to redistribute political power. This would be true even if we were to assume Hunter's findings as valid for the point in time when he studied Regional City. Recognizing the limitations of any typology, we can still posit the conditions under which decisional structures in communities may vary over time. We can also suggest some characteristics of these structures, as well as of the communities themselves.

The authors take an analytic approach, derived from some of the considerations we have raised. To present only a summary of their findings would do an injustice to their impressive work. However, we might include a brief summary of the primary perspectives they used, which they suggest be used for future analyses. These include:

> ... viewing a community as a polity: (1) the patterns of decisional preferences; (2) the patterns of political participation; (3) the patterns of political influence relations; (4) the patterns of power relations that constitute the community's power structure; (5) the patterns that constitute the formal institutions of local government; (6) the patterns of decisional outcomes produced by the power structure; and (7) the type of regime.[65]

Given these considerations, and the properly guarded and tentative nature of their conclusions, we can suggest that these researchers have indeed laid the groundwork for future empirical studies of community power structures and the complex interactions that occur within political decisional structures.

CRITIQUE OF DECISION-MAKING APPROACHES

The concern with decisions as stable units of analysis offers several distinct advantages in the development of empirical theory. For one, attention is paid to the centrality of decision making in the value-allocative process. By focusing on the decision, it is easier for the concerned student of politics to sweep away the superfluous and begin to answer the questions imposed by the formulation of politics as "who gets what, when, how." Several approaches may be taken in this context. One can trace a decision through the steps outlined by Lasswell (from intelligence through termination), examining the individuals and agencies involved. With this method, it is possible to determine if each of the functions is performed optimally or whether minimal performance by involved agencies may lead to inadequate decisions. In any analysis of policymaking, this approach appears to have much to commend it, because it offers analytically distinct operational categories of performance in the political arena.

The nascent stage of political science is evidenced by its multiplicity of decision-making schemes. The concern of some with behavior, especially in the foreign-policy process, is highly suggestive of the ends to which decision-making analysis may be applied. The relationship of leaders and followers suggests that decisional analysis may provide the information to develop a macro theory of politics. But certain problems remain.

If decision making is to serve as the focus for the study of political behavior, can we afford to ignore external influences? If we restrict our attention to the legally defined government, we run the risk of assuming that there are no individuals elsewhere who are concerned with decisional outcomes, and that they might not apply pressure to achieve their ends. But we know that pressure groups play an important role in the formulation of public policy at all levels of government. What function do they play, and how? Do pressure groups facilitate or obstruct formation of public policy? These questions have been asked and answered elsewhere, but decisional analysis has not thus far integrated these findings.

On the other hand, rational decision-making analysts have shown how individual decisions are arrived at. Considerations of cost and utility enter the preference-ordering of individuals who seek to maximize their goals in an uncertain world. In situations where plurality or majority does not necessarily govern a decision, the linkages between individual and group decisions are unclear, however. An alternative approach—considering "nondecisions"—shows that power can be exercised in meaningful ways by actors who are not always visible to the public eye. "Nondecision" may also gratify the needs of those who are certain that someone, somewhere, must be wielding power. By acting on issues before they emerge publicly, power can be exercised by nondecision making.

Although the Baltimore study of nondecisions is revealing and offers some fascinating insights, it is a case study, from which it is impossible to generalize. Case studies require replication to lend validity to their findings. But is this possible? Can one study something that is essentially a "nonevent," something that in effect does not happen?[66] If a nondecision was made, it is assumed that it was made by an elite.[67] Are nondecisions by nature nonempirical? If conflict is not present, can one go behind the scenes to observe nondecisions?[68] The problem is obviously moot.

THE PROBLEM OF INTEGRATING APPROACHES

The various approaches to studying decision making show the strengths and weaknesses of decisional analysis. We have presented several approaches to the study of politics, all of which use the decision as the central focus. Two of these were sequence models. This approach has been taken by numerous scholars, who have not hesitated to devise more classification schemes, attempting to uncover the novel.[69] Although the contributions of these scholars have been welcome and are not without merit, there is frequently a sensation of tasting old wine in new bottles, as fresh labeling schemes are suggested.

The broad model of politics illustrated in Figure 9–1 is very provocative because it attempts to classify decisional systems according to the principal actors, their interest and information, issue orientation, concerns, attitudes, and rewards. It suggests that a dynamic exists in making decisions. It shows how the systems themselves can change. It would appear from a close reading of this model that changes to hierarchy occur more than for any other decisional system,

Discussion ⟶ Hierarchy ⟶ Bargaining

Democracy

a suggestion which is neither unique in the study of politics[70] nor comforting to those who normatively admire and would preserve democracy.

The community power studies suggest that there are situations where bargaining occurs among leaders to arrive at decisions, which are imposed on those below them. Other studies, however, suggest that these tendencies of elites are not always present; instead these studies depend on other factors, such as control of resources by bureaucrats, ideologies of the leadership, the distribution of power, and the nature of the decisional environment. The best of these, the fourth-generation model, shows that theory can be grounded in solid empirical work and that theory can be operationalized. This approach not only seems to have demonstrated the utility of the decisional focus in analysis, but may have laid groundwork for the formulation of a macro theory.

The decisional approach is commonly criticized for the incoherent findings it produces.[71] The decision or the decision maker has been central to analyses of foreign policy, legislators, the military, and the press. Because the concerns of political scientists have broadened, little theory has emerged. Empirically testable theory of the sort that suggests that *"if* certain circumstances are operative, *then* certain decisions and actions are likely to ensue,"[72] has emerged from few decisional analyses.

However, this criticism cannot hold for all approaches to decision making. The rationalist approach is a deductive form of analysis, which tests very specific consequences (phrased as hypotheses) of a broad and axiomatic theory of human behavior. This approach is receiving increasing use and serious attention. Although it seemingly flies in the face of much empirical research that suggests that rational behavior is not the norm, a coherent body of knowledge on individual and collective decision making may be emerging from this approach. If some of its inherent problems can be resolved—e.g., dealing with attitudinal intensity, explaining environmental influences on individuals and groups, and showing how collective decisions can emerge from individual preferences—it might be possible to integrate findings with those of other scholars, especially scholars concerned with system changes and problems raised in the fourth-generational model of community power. Until such time, it seems that in any of its several forms decision-making analysis cannot serve as a paradigm. We turn now to another approach, systems analysis, in which decision making is also a central concern.

NOTES AND REFERENCES

1. Herbert A. Simon, "Political Research: The Decision-Making Framework," in David Easton (ed.), *Varieties of Political Theory* (Englewood Cliffs, N.J.: Prentice-Hall, 1966), p. 15.

2. Harold D. Lasswell, *The Future of Political Science* (New York: Atherton Press, 1963), pp. 15–16.

3. Richard C. Snyder, "A Decision-Making Approach to the Study of Political Phenomena," in Roland Young (ed.), *Approaches to the Study of Politics* (Evanston, Ill.: Northwestern University Press, 1958), p. 10.

4. *Ibid.,* p. 15.

5. *Ibid.,* p. 20.

6. Richard C. Snyder, H. W. Bruck, and Burton Sapin, *Decision-Making as an Approach to the Study of International Politics* (Princeton, N.J.: Foreign Policy Analysis Series, No. 3, 1954).

7. Karl Deutsch, *The Nerves of Government: Models of Political Communication and Control* (New York: The Free Press, 1963), pp. 258–61.

8. Lewis A. Froman, Jr., *People and Politics: An Analysis of the American Political System* (Englewood Cliffs, N.J.: Prentice-Hall, 1962), p. 6.

9. *Ibid.,* pp. 49–66.

10. On several questions that concern the majority rule model, *see* James M. Buchanan and Gordon Tullock, *The Calculus of Consent: Logical Foundations of Constitutional Democracy* (Ann Arbor: University of Michigan Press, 1962), chaps. x–xii; xv; xvii.

11. Frank B. Feigert, "Conservatism, Populism, and Social Change," *American Behavioral Scientist* 17 (November/ December 1973): 272–78.

12. Buchanan and Tullock, *Calculus of Consent,* pp. 11–15. *See also* William H. Riker and Peter C. Ordeshook, *An Introduction to Positive Political Theory* (Englewood Cliffs, N.J.: Prentice-Hall, 1973), pp. 33–37.

13. Riker and Ordeshook, *Positive Political Theory,* p. 37.

14. *Ibid.,* p. 20. This position of rationality and preference-ordering is distinct from the views held by other students of human behavior. Learning theorists, for example, "assert choosers choose by habit and discovery rather than by analysis of preference." Some psychoanalysts would assert that fundamental instincts dictate behavior, which is rationalized only later. William H. Riker and William James Zavoina, "Rational Behavior in Politics: Evidence from a Three Person Game," *American Political Science Review* 64 (March 1970): 49–50.

15. James M. Buchanan, "An Individualistic Theory of Political Process," in Easton (ed.), *Varieties of Political Theory,* p. 29.

16. There is always the possibility of self-defeating behavior, whether

deliberate or not. On this point, *see* Riker and Ordeshook, *Positive Political Theory,* p. 21.

17. Riker and Zavoina, "Rational Behavior in Politics," pp. 51–52.

18. William H. Riker, "Bargaining in a Three-Person Game," *American Political Science Review* 61 (September 1967): 647.

19. Riker and Ordeshook, *Positive Political Theory,* p. 24.

20. Riker and Zavoina, "Rational Behavior," p. 53.

21. Kenneth A. Shepsle, "Theories of Collective Choice," in Cornelius P. Cotter (ed.), *Political Science Annual: An International Review,* 5 (Indianapolis: The Bobbs-Merrill Company, 1973), p. 35.

22. *Ibid.,* pp. 35–36.

23. *Social Choice and Individual Values,* 2nd ed. (New York: John Wiley & Sons, 1963).

24. Shepsle, "Collective Choice," p. 36.

25. William C. Stratmann, "A Concept of Voter Rationality" (unpublished Ph.D. dissertation, University of Rochester, 1971).

26. Anthony Downs, *An Economic Theory of Democracy* (New York: Harper & Row, 1957), p. 6.

27. Riker and Ordeshook, *Positive Political Theory,* pp. 110–12. There is a paradox here as well.

28. *Ibid.,* p. 31.

29. Buchanan, in Easton (ed.), *Varieties of Political Theory,* p. 26.

30. Robert S. Lynd and Helen M. Lynd, *Middletown* (New York: Harcourt, Brace and World, 1929); idem., *Middletown in Transition* (New York: Harcourt, Brace and World, 1937).

31. Peter Bachrach and Morton S. Baratz, *Power and Poverty: Theory and Practice* (New York: Oxford University Press, 1970), p. 5; *see also* Nelson Polsby, *Community Power and Political Theory* (New Haven: Yale University Press, 1963), pp. 480–81.

32. Lynd and Lynd, *Middletown in Transition,* p. 14.

33. Floyd Hunter, *Community Power Structure* (Chapel Hill: University of North Carolina Press, 1953).

34. *Ibid.,* p. 269.

35. Polsby, *Community Power,* pp. 48–49.

36. Polsby, *Community Power,* p. 55.

37. Robert A. Dahl, "A Critique of the Ruling Elite Model," *American Political Science Review* 52 (June 1958): 465.

38. *Ibid.*

39. *Ibid.,* p. 466.

40. Robert A. Dahl, *Who Governs?* (New Haven: Yale University Press, 1961).

41. Bachrach and Baratz, *Power and Poverty,* pp. 10–16.

42. Dahl, *Who Governs?*, p. 331. A detailed and useful guide to Dahl's methodology is on pp. 330–40.

43. M. Kent Jennings, *Community Influentials: The Elites of Atlanta* (New York: The Free Press, 1964).

44. Aaron Wildavsky, *Leadership in a Small Town* (Totowa, N.J.: Bedminster Press, 1964).

45. Wallace S. Sayre and Herbert Kaufman, *Governing New York City: Politics in the Metropolis* (New York: Russell Sage Foundation, 1960).

46. *Ibid.*, pp. 709–10.

47. Thomas J. Anton, "Power, Pluralism, and Local Politics," *Administrative Science Quarterly* 7 (March 1963): 447. Emphasis added.

48. *Ibid.*, p. 454.

49. Other useful critiques of the pluralist position are in Charles A. McCoy and John Playford (eds.), *Apolitical Politics: A Critique of Behavioralism* (New York: Thomas Y. Crowell, 1967). *See* especially the selection by Todd Gitlin, "Local Pluralism as Theory and Ideology."

50. Bachrach and Baratz, *Power and Poverty*, p. 7.

51. *Ibid.*, p. 71. *See* especially chapters 5 and 6 of this work for practical applications of the nondecision concept.

52. *Men at the Top: A Study in Community Power* (New York: Oxford University Press, 1964).

53. *Ibid.*, pp. 52–57.

54. *Ibid.*, p. 57.

55. *Ibid.*, pp. 59–60. Emphasis in original.

56. *Ibid.*, p. 37. Emphasis in original.

57. *Ibid.*, p. 405.

58. *Ibid.*, p. 407.

59. *Ibid.*, p. 408. Emphasis in original.

60. *Ibid.*

61. *Ibid.*, pp. 409–12.

62. Robert E. Agger, Daniel Goldrich, and Bert E. Swanson, *The Rulers and the Ruled: Political Power and Impotence in American Communities* (New York: John Wiley & Sons, 1964). For a useful review of the Hunter, Jennings, Presthus, and Agger works *see* Lyman Kellstedt, "Atlanta to Oretown: Identifying Community Elites," *Public Administration Review* 25 (June 1965): 161–68.

63. Agger, Goldrich, and Swanson, *Rulers and the Ruled*, p. 40.

64. *Ibid.*, p. 16.

65. *Ibid.*, pp. 112–13.

66. Richard M. Merelman, "On the Neo-Elitist Critique of Community Power," *American Political Science Review* 62 (June 1968): 451–60. *See also* the reply by Bachrach and Baratz, and Merelman's rejoinder, *Amer. Pol. Sci. Rev.* (December 1968): 1268–69. In his rejoinder, Merelman suggests "the

situation is analogous to a jury forced to convict on circumstantial evidence. It is always nice to have a corpus delecti around. We must otherwise make leaps of faith that are usually too great for most political scientists—as scientists and not as citizens—to attempt." (*Ibid.*, p. 1269). At a later date, Bachrach and Baratz are accused of introducing a concept that lacks practicality. This charge is based on the grounds that their analysis blurs "the useful distinction that can be made between covert control and mobilization of bias . . ." Geoffrey Debnam, "Nondecision and Power: The Two Faces of Bachrach and Baratz," *American Political Science Review* 69 (September 1975): 889–99. In "Power and Its Two Faces Revisited: A Reply to Geoffrey Debnam," *ibid.*, pp. 900–04, Bachrach and Baratz defend their analysis by saying:

> For us . . . the test of a construct's worth is the contribution it makes toward gaining an understanding of the nature and uses of power in a polity. Empirical verification is much to be desired but it is not foremost in importance.

It almost seems that besides "nondecisions" we may be forced to cope with nonverification.

67. Merelman, "On the Neo-Elitist Critique of Community Power," pp. 453–55.

68. Bachrach and Baratz, *Power and Poverty,* p. 46.

69. *See,* for instance, Herbert A. Simon, "Political Research: The Decision-Making Framework," in Easton (ed.), *Varieties of Political Theory,* esp. pp. 18–21, and the operationalization of this approach in Karl A. Lamb and Paul A. Smith, *Campaign Decision-Making* (Belmont, Calif.: Wadsworth Publishing Co., 1968).

70. *See,* for instance, Robert Michels, *Political Parties: A Sociological Study of the Oligarchical Tendencies of Modern Democracy,* trans. by Eden Paul and Cedar Paul (New York: The Free Press, 1962).

71. James N. Rosenau, "The Premises and Promises of Decision-Making Analysis," in James C. Charlesworth (ed.), *Contemporary Political Analysis* (New York: The Free Press, 1967), pp. 189–211.

72. *Ibid.*, pp. 208–09. Emphasis in original.

STUDY QUESTIONS

1. How can the sequence models of decision making be used to study political behavior? What are their strengths and limitations?
2. What are the assumptions of the rational decision-making school of analysis?

3. What do the following mean?

   decision rules
   marginal costs
   marginal utility

4. How does rational decision-making theory differ from a more conventional approach to the study of political behavior? How can it be integrated with conventional approaches?

5. Discuss the principal findings of each of the major approaches to community power. How might the methods used have biased the findings? What are the conceptual weaknesses of each of the approaches?

6. What data-collection techniques may be pertinent to the study of decision making? Specify, indicating the level at which decisions are examined.

CHAPTER
10

Systems Analysis

Classification and categorization occupy behavioral analysis to an unusual degree. This is due to the necessity of developing guidelines for research and of tying together the research findings of the behavioral movement in some orderly fashion. The several models and theories examined thus far show a progression of ability to generalize. Systems analysis is an even more general scheme. It is sufficiently general to subsume the various models and theories discussed in chapters 4 through 9.

In the early 1960s, Thomas Kuhn argued for the necessity of a *paradigm,* or working model, to incorporate research assumptions and to guide further research in physics, the branch of science to which Kuhn belonged. Although Kuhn's plea was not specifically directed to the problems of the social and behavioral sciences, his words have particular relevance for political scientists at this time.[1] In the view of some, political science has experienced a dramatic change in the direction of its concerns and the means of answering the questions raised by those concerns.[2] For others, the success or the desirability of this change is yet to be determined.[3] But it is apparent that major changes in the discipline are under way. In recent years, one of the hallmarks of this change has been the emergence of systems theory as a possible paradigm for organizing knowledge and for generating hypotheses.

Systems theory owes a considerable intellectual debt to the work done in cybernetics. Systems theory has also drawn heavily from a biologist who first began exploring the possibilities of broad explanations of behavior in the 1920s.[5] Following the New Deal and

World War II, it became increasingly apparent to a number of academicians that various disciplines need not stand in splendid isolation from one another, and that the artificial restraints imposed by rigid disciplinary boundaries hinder rather than aid research. Increasing attention was paid to means by which disciplines might be drawn together. Among many formal and informal conferences held by researchers in various areas was a series at the Reese Hospital in Chicago. The scope of their concerns was broad indeed.[6] A major contributor in the direction of these conferences, which started in 1951, was David Easton, a political scientist whose work has been highly influential in the discipline.

EASTONIAN ANALYSIS

We will not provide a complete statement of the theory and implications of Eastonian systems analysis. For the sake of simplicity, as well as for clarifying the relationships between Easton and other systems theorists, we shall deal with the main burden of his argument and with the principal concepts he has elaborated.

Political systems are defined by Easton as "a set of interactions, abstracted from the totality of social behavior, through which values are authoritatively allocated for a society."[7] Underlying this straightforward definition are a number of assumptions that lend direction to systems analysis. For one, the emphasis is upon interaction as a variable. Interactions may take place between individual actors, institutions, or actors and institutions collectively interacting with others. Easton does not specify which actors or institutions interact in the value-allocation process. If we stress interactions in Easton, we must therefore stress process as well; Easton's is not a stable but a dynamic model, in which the system and its individual actors engage in processes designed to secure the maintenance and dynamic equilibrium of the system itself.

Easton recognizes that no single way of conceptualizing human behavior can properly encompass the variety and complexity of that behavior, at least for the time.[8] Any attempt to conceptualize and describe behavior, therefore, must be quite general and broad in nature. This being the case, Easton's model uses as its major unit of analysis the political system itself, in which political life is viewed as a system of behavior. A system is presumed to be analytically distinct from its environment. Although an analytical distinction is made between the system and its environment, the system is open in varying degrees to influences from the environment. Indeed, the nature of environmental influences and the ways in which the system responds to them is one of Easton's major concerns.

In separating a system from its environment, however, we refer symbolically to the system's *boundary*. The nature of systemic boundaries, how they are defined, and their degree of flexibility or rigidity are major problems facing systems theorists. There is a distinct parallel between the controversy over the proper boundaries or scope of political science and the problem of defining boundaries in systems theory. Do the boundaries of the political system encompass a broad or narrow portion of the whole social system? Are they subject to change? Do they respond to external influences and, if so, to what degree? Should boundaries be defined legalistically? Are some forms of behavior isolated as systems from the environment?

It is useful to look at the boundary problem as one of mutual perceptions; i.e., the outlooks of the internal actors of the system who interact with themselves, the actors in the environment—who may belong to other political systems or interlocking systems such as economic and cultural spheres of activity—help to define the boundaries. An example of this is shown in Figure 10–1, in which the

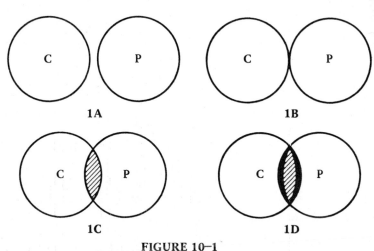

FIGURE 10–1

Boundary Relationships between Congressional and Presidential Systems

Congress and the presidency are viewed as distinct but related systems. In Figure 10–1A, we see a virtual nonsystem; that is, the Congress and the presidency do not interact with each other at all. This is a situation which exists in real life infrequently. An example of a nonsystem might be congressional consideration of its own organization (procedural rules, committee chairmanships, member ethics, etc.), in which there is no evidence that the president or his executive office has communicated preferences to the Congress. Figure 10–1B represents a tangential relationship, in which provision is made for minimal contact between the two systems. Such a situation might arise in purely legal or constitutional relationships, such as fulfilling the legislative function. There is no direct constitutional provision for the president's role as "chief legislator," although it is a role often imputed to him.[9] The only constitutional provision for presidential involvement in the legislative process is approval— signing a bill into law or vetoing it. The "advise and consent" provision relating to presidential appointments might nominally fit this category, but only in a purely legal sense.

In Figure 10–1C we see a relationship that is probably closer to a real life situation between the two systems; i.e., there is a degree of constitutional and legal overlap between them, involving considerable interaction. The shaded area of the circle in Figure 10–1C represents the potential for political conflict and compromise, in legal and constitutional terms alone; the term "checks and balances" is another way of saying this. Presidential appointments may lead to considerable political conflict. In the constitutional sense, the Senate gives its "advice" by approving or disapproving of the presidential nominees. However, as President Johnson found out in 1968 and President Nixon in 1969, the appointment of a Supreme Court justice is not necessarily a *pro forma* process. The Fortas, Carswell, and Haynesworth nominations led to considerable political conflict before they were rejected by the Senate.

In Figure 10–1D, we make allowances not only for legal boundaries but for behavioral and perceptual boundaries as well. In Figure 10–1D, both the president and the Congress may view their own proper scope of action in quite flexible terms through broad interpretations of the powers legally granted them. They may see their scope of action in these terms because of their own proclivities, or because the nation is in a state of crisis that requires greater freedom of action on their part.[10] Continuing our example of the

Supreme Court nominations, if presidents Johnson or Nixon felt that the Senate was obliged to merely bestow a *pro forma* approval of their nominee, they might have increased the tension of the conflict in a concerted attempt to secure approval when they met with resistance. President Nixon's attempt to define for the Congress what was an impeachable act is an instance of trying to limit the boundaries of a subsystem. The potential for political conflict (represented by the darkened area in Figure 10–1D) is considerably broadened through the perception of boundaries by one of the actors or both. Such conflict does not always occur; this is especially true in a period of crisis when other actors may feel that an expansion of boundaries is required. The first one hundred days of Roosevelt's New Deal, the months immediately following President Kennedy's assassination, or President Ford's brief "honeymoon" were periods of expanded executive action.

However, it can generally be assumed that there will be actors present in one system or the other who will view such boundary interpretations with a jaundiced eye. Strict constructionists of constitutional prerogatives of the president are highly critical of executive proposals of major extensions of federal or presidential powers. Civil rights legislation inevitably leads to extended rhetoric by some congressmen and senators who view it as an expansion of the federal system's boundaries.

Inputs and Outputs

If we assume that systems are susceptible to varying degrees of influence from the environment, and that systems may affect their surroundings, we must make reference to the *inputs, outputs,* and *feedback* variables. A political system cannot exist unto itself. Surrounded as it is by a physical, cultural, and economic environment, and by other political systems, it must interact with these potential sources of influence. Inputs from the environment and from the system are *demand* or *support* inputs. Without inputs, the system can do no work and cannot sustain itself. An analogy may be made to the human biological system.[11] It is difficult for a person to survive for long without such basic physical supports as food, clothing, and shelter. Clothing and shelter are needed in varying degrees, as determined by the physical environment, and sometimes by the cultural

277

one. Minimal caloric requirements must be met in order for the human system to continue functioning. Demands are also necessary as they lend purpose and direction to the system. Excessive support, such as too many calories, would ultimately lead to organic breakdown, because the internal demands generated by such an existence would place too great a strain upon the body. Thus, external demands, in the form of exercise, may place a required and desirable form of stress upon the system.

Likewise, the political system receives demand inputs from its environment; it reacts to cultural and economic problems and to problems within its own system. Demands are generally concerned with the allocation of resources, material or positional. Demands are made by individuals and groups within or without the system who are likely to have different views on how resources should be allocated. There is never any assurance that demands will be met in a one-for-one ratio to outputs or to allocations of resources. The system is not as mechanistic as it might appear at first glance. This is especially the case if the resources to be distributed by the system are scarce and highly valued by competing groups; it is then less likely that demand input X will result in output X—especially if the sources of demand possess sufficient and relatively balanced resources to promote alternative demands as well. For instance, demands for tax reform do not arise from one sector of the economy alone. Those favoring an excess profits tax on major oil corporations must compete with the oil industry before Congress. The result (the output) may be a temporary but protracted stalemate, which is to the advantage of the oil industry that opposes any tax increases. Or, after extended conflict on the matter, the result may be a compromise, such as increased federal regulation of the domestic energy industry.

Therefore, demand inputs result in stress upon the system, which may be functional if it activates the system to allocate resources. However, stress can only go so far in any system. A physician may recommend jogging to an overweight patient, but he will also recognize that jogging a minimal distance represents healthy stress. Advising the obese patient to run a four-minute mile could lead to total collapse. In living or political systems, overreaction to stress generally follows a lag in response, and may precede collapse, if stress is increased over time.[12]

Stress can, however, be functional to the system. "While extreme stress always worsens performance, moderate stress can

278

improve it above ordinary levels."[13] In the Eastonian model (*see* Figure 10–2), system maintenance or survival is a primary goal, one that supercedes all others. In discussing demand or support inputs, we therefore consider such additional variables as the substance, source, intensity, and quantity of demands. Because they are related to the demands and supports, these variables will be indicative of the ability and capacity of a system to modulate stress, which in turn will suggest the ability of the system to perform its tasks and survive.

> ... when a system is subjected to a disturbance which materially affects the performance of its identifying function, some of its variables will be momentarily displaced but each tends to return to its respective *status quo ante*. In other words, implicit in systems analysis is the proposition that some of the system's variables must be maintained within specified boundaries or the system will not be able to continue to perform its identifying function.[14]

Questions of system equilibrium and survival are implicit in all systems theory.

Crucial to the consideration of input/output analysis is the learning and corrective capacity of a system; we refer to this as *feedback*. System outputs or decisions do not automatically solve all problems. Indeed, they may create problems that were not seen in initially making decisions. Those to whom Easton refers as the *authoritative decision makers*—or the allocators of values—must receive information on the effect and effectiveness of their decisions. This information, or feedback, acts as new input to the system, whether the information comes from outside the system or from other actors within the system. Feedback can have several results. It may provide increased or altered demands, in which the process continues somewhat cyclically. It may provide information that the

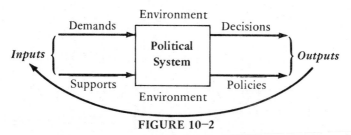

FIGURE 10–2

Basic Eastonian System (David Easton, "An Approach to the Analysis of Political Systems," *World Politics* 9 [April 1957], p. 384. Reprinted by permission.)

outputs have essentially solved a problem, in which case feedback would be a potential source of support. Feedback may also reveal that the outputs are not accomplishing the purposes desired by the authoritative decision makers, and corrective action may thus be suggested.

It appears that there is little overt concern in the Eastonian model for support inputs. However, no system can survive if it is subject only to demands. Support inputs for the political system can assume many forms. A system needs material resources to support itself. Material values can be transformed into resources that can be allocated. Earlier we pointed out that the human system has several basic needs, such as food, clothing, and shelter. Intangible supports may be needed as well, such as affection, respect, and acceptance by others. A political system also requires intangible supports, such as a recognition of legitimacy by environmental actors, and by those internal to the system. Tangible supports for a political system may include money and personnel, derived from taxes and recruitment processes. In attempting to derive such resources, the system may unwittingly provide sources for dysfunctional demand inputs; for instance, demands by taxpayers to ease their burden may reduce government services in certain areas. Feedback from these areas could result in the necessity for greater resources. For example, a reduction in welfare services, including those related to public health and sanitation, could result in an increase in disease. The government might then have to expend even more funds in order to abate the problem. Similarly, the U.S. government may have become accustomed to compliance with the Selective Service System. Related to pursuit of a policy that became increasingly unacceptable to the American public in the 1960s, the draft, as a normal vehicle for supports, posed problems for the government which might never have been expected.

Critique of Eastonian Analysis

The Eastonian systems model stresses boundaries by helping to define and isolate a system from its environment through analysis. Provision is made for feedback, although not explicitly. Easton's systems model is heuristic rather than predictive, and lends itself to comparative analysis. Because Easton has elaborated a carefully refined model, with definitions and classifications of variables, then he must bear the burden of specifying why and how certain functions are performed. The system is denoted by its ability to allocate values authoritatively, but Easton spends comparatively little time and space suggesting testable hypotheses about the nature of the allocative process or the actors involved.

Specifying the institutional arrangements by which the system is governed is a problem related to this. The feedback process is crucial to Eastonian analysis. It is the mechanism by which a system can learn of reactions to its policies and practices. Easton is seemingly convinced that "a democratic institutional framework can handle the feedback process in the best possible manner."[15] This may or may not be the case, but it reveals a normative bias on Easton's part, much as we accept majority rule as the most appropriate means of settling controversies.

However, the problems inherent in a broad theory can also be of value. We suggested earlier that systems analysis subsumes approaches such as group theory and decision-making theory. If we examine Easton, we see that the considerations raised by various schools of thought can be properly applied to the questions Easton poses. Decision theory, for instance, may "flesh-out" the bare bones of the resource-allocating function of the political system. Group theory can more explicitly specify sources of demand and support inputs, as well as reactions to outputs. These approaches are complementary, which may lead to a broader theory of political life to explain and predict at a high level of accuracy.

PARSONIAN STRUCTURAL—FUNCTIONALISM

Another theorist who has addressed himself to the major task of developing a broad theory of behavior, although not specifically political, is the sociologist, Talcott Parsons. His works are landmarks in the development of such theory, and they helped to lay the foundations for the so-called school of structural–functionalism.[16] Without intending to slight other important members of this school, we shall concentrate on Parsons's relationship to Easton, which is developed at a relatively workable level by Gabriel Almond, with whom we deal later in this chapter.

281

Basic Concepts of Structural—Functionalism

Readers familiar with the works of Parsons will recognize the difficulty of abstracting his work in a few pages, as he is generally recognized as not only one of the most influential contemporary social theorists but also one of the most abstruse. In a brief overview, we start by taking Parsons' basic scheme and relating its various parts, before we detail its specifics.

To begin with, Parsons asserts that all systems have four basic *functions* to perform (see below). These are performed by *structures,* within which are *actors,* each of whom has *roles* to play, which are performed according to five *pattern variables.* This basic scheme is considered operative for all macro and micro social systems. Thus, the total social system has the same basic functions as do social or political subsystems.

Parsonian Functions. A common way of looking at the functions Parsons ascribes to systems is the so-called G-A-I-L approach, an acronym for the four Parsonian functions necessary for system survival. *Goal attainment* is the first function; it is most concerned with the preservation of the society or the system. In the total social system, this function is performed primarily by the polity. If the system is to survive, resources must be mobilized in support of specified goals. This is the function of *adaptation* and, in the social system, is performed primarily by the structure we call the economy. Certain functions are performed primarily by structures; no single structure performs all functions alone, nor is any structure necessarily uni-functional. Because structures and individual actors tend to be *multi-functional* (to deal with functions other than the one with which they are primarily concerned), a third major function, *integration,* must be performed. Because no agency can perform all functions equally well, a means must be found to integrate the performance of individual actors and institutions. This is a function performed by institutions of society or of the system, such as educational institutions, through which information and norms are passed on. Distinctly related to integration is the function of *latency,* or *pattern maintenance,* which deals with the maintenance of conformity to the norms of the cultural system. Values are passed to succeeding generations, and sanctions are applied for not observing values or norms. In the social system, this function is performed primarily by the family.

These constructs can be examined schematically, as in Figure 10—3 where the basic Parsonian scheme of functions and structures in the total social system is illustrated. (In this and succeeding figures relative to Parsonian structural—functional analysis, we do not take into account the concepts of actors, roles, and pattern variables. These will have to be assumed as given. For more extensive discussion of these, *see* especially the works cited in note 16 of the Notes and References section.)

Multifunctionality and interaction between various structures is indicated by the arrows between the functional quadrants in Figure 10—3.

A problem with this form of conceptualization is understanding the relationship of functions and structures to other systems. One approach to this is shown in Figure 10—4, in which we can more clearly see not only the relationship of particular functions to selected environments, but the central positions of two of them—goal attainment and integration. The complexity of the environment is also suggested more clearly by this schematic representation. It offers some idea of the problems that face actors in the central goal-setting arena, who may be likened to Easton's "authoritative decision makers" and to other actors.

The Parsonian approach is not restricted to analyzing the total social system; it can also be adapted to examining subsystems. For instance, as political scientists we are most concerned with examining the polity, the structure concerned primarily with goal

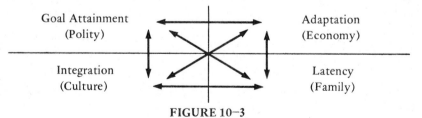

FIGURE 10—3

Parsonian Scheme for a Total System (Adapted with permission of Macmillan Publishing Co., Inc., from *Economy and Society: A Study in the Integration of Economic and Social Theory,* Talcott Parsons and Neil J. Smelser. First published in the United States of America in 1956 by the Free Press.)

FIGURE 10–4

Relationship of Parsonian Functions with Environment (From *The Political Basis of Economic Development* by Robert T. Holt and John E. Turner. Copyright © 1966, by Litton Educational Publishing, Inc. Reprinted by permission of D. Van Nostrand Company.)

attainment. Figure 10–5 shows how this structure, supposedly concerned primarily with a single function, is actually multi-functional. In pursuing its major function of goal attainment on behalf of the total system, the polity performs other functions, and it has more specialized structures to assist in this task. The generalized function of goal attainment is not only supported by institutions such as the economy, culture, and family, which are concerned with supporting the total system, but with specialized structures that assist in this endeavor as well, such as the judiciary and the administration. The idea of multifunctionality is demonstrated still further in Figure 10–6, which shows how the legislative subsystem, that assists in performing the latency function within the polity may be further

Goal Attainment (Executive Functions and Roles)	Adaptation (Administrative Functions and Roles)
Integration (Party-Political Functions and Roles)	Latency (Legislative-Judicial Functions and Roles)

FIGURE 10–5

Parsonian Functions in the Political System (Adapted from William C. Mitchell, *Sociological Analysis and Politics: The Theories of Talcott Parsons* [Englewood Cliffs, N.J.: Prentice-Hall, © 1967], p. 104. By permission.)

subdivided. From Figures 10–5 and 10–6, we can also develop an idea of the complexity of the Parsonian scheme, since actors can occupy several quadrants, to greater and lesser degrees. Using Figure 10–6, we can assume that a congressional leader, such as the Speaker of the House, readily operates in all four quadrants. As a party leader, he is concerned with goal attainment. His role as speaker is clearly not limited to one function, for he may be an invaluable source of information and a major resource in Congress. Because he is a party member and a member of various blocs and cliques, he is therefore involved in the integration function. When he applies

Goal Attainment-Leadership party leaders committee chairmen bloc leaders delegation deans	Adaptation:Information committees office and committee staff informal study groups
Integration:Ideological ideological blocs friendship cliques political parties	Latency informal groups formal procedural rules friendship groups

FIGURE 10–6

Parsonian Functions in the Legislative Subsystem (David Leege [Unpublished seminar paper, Indiana University, 1960]. By permission of the author.)

formal procedural rules and invokes sanctions, he is fulfilling the latency function. The ways in which he fulfills each function are indicated in part by the five pattern variables (*see* page 191).

Problems and Applications

Although we have barely skimmed some of the essential concepts of the Parsonian approach, it should be apparent that we have no simple classificatory scheme of demonstrable utility. Parsons and his interpreters offer numerous definitions of concepts, which are often conflicting and often confusing. The essential step of classification is provided for in the Parsonian scheme, but with definitions that may be difficult to apply in empirical analysis.

Some utility of the approach, however, is evident; in delineating functions and in suggesting the institutions that might perform those functions, Parson has contributed to a more fruitful form of comparative analysis. If we can properly define the meaning and implications of the integration function, we might then ask what institutions in Western and non-Western countries perform this function. Ascribing a function to an institution may be wrong, and we may find that different societies perform the same function (if a function is universal) through different structures. If this is the case, we may be able to infer why some societies or polities are more or less prone to internal stability. In examining the adaptation function on a cross-cultural basis, we would expect to find that some polities are more prone to become involved in economic planning than others, a factor that could aid or hinder the goal-attainment function.

An examination of the Parsonian approach illustrates additional problems and promises of structural–functionalism as it is here conceived:

> First, Parsons does not adequately deal with a stratum of behavior that operates at a subcultural level and does not recognize the impact that this level of behavior may have on the culture and performance of systems . . . Second, political analysis should proceed at both the systemic and individual levels of analysis. Generalizations about the operation of systems must be supplemented with generalizations about individual decision-making. The behavior of individuals cannot always be inferred from data on the culture of social systems. . . . [however] Parsons' image of

social structure can be used with considerable effectiveness both as a foil and as a systemic statement about the cultural-institutional sources of social behavior.[17]

ALMOND'S SYSTEMIC STRUCTURAL—FUNCTIONALISM

There are many approaches that fall under the general rubric of systems analysis, in part because the approach is still in a developmental stage, but also because systems analysis is a synthesis of the approaches previously discussed in this book. Gabriel Almond, whose work has been primarily in comparative politics, sought to suggest "how the application of certain sociological and anthropological concepts may facilitate systematic comparison among the major types of political systems operative in the world today."[18] In so doing, he helped to lay the groundwork for not only a more comprehensive analysis, but for systems analysis as well. He also delineated the conceptual components of political systems, such as role, which he describes as "the unit of the political system."[19] He describes structures, or patterned interactions among roles, and other characteristics of the political system, such as concern with the "scope, the direction, and the conditions affecting the employment" of *"ultimate, comprehensive,* and *legitimate* physical coercion" which is "the monopoly of states."[20] He also directs his attention to *political culture,* i.e., the "pattern of orientations to political action."[21] He examines the role structure of several types of political systems, such as the Anglo-American, pre-industrial, totalitarian, and European systems. Almond's approach is significant for systems analysis because it provides more substantive definitions.

Almond later provided a clearer statement of his approach. He reiterated some of his earlier statements and then proceeded to explore their meanings, consequences, and applications:

> . . . the political system is that system of interactions to be found in all independent societies which perform the functions of integration and adaptation by means of the employment, or threat of employment, or more or less legitimate physical compulsion . . . legitimate force is the thread which runs through the inputs and outputs of the political system.[22]

According to Almond, all systems share certain characteristics. They all have structures, which can be compared for their degree of specialization. The same functions are performed in all systems; we can examine the frequency with which they are performed, which structures perform them, and the style or manner in which they are performed. As with Parsons, all structures are multifunctional. Further, all systems are culturally mixed and can be examined for their levels of development, as well as for the extent to which they can be considered modern.

Input functions in Almond's analysis are "political socialization and recruitment, interest articulation, interest aggregation, and political communication." Output functions are "rule-making, rule-application, and rule-adjudication." Output functions may appear to be a restatement of the classic legalist approach to political science. Indeed, they almost seem like Montesquieu revisited. However, if the political system is concerned with the specification of goals (Parsons), or the allocation of values (Easton), then the performance of these functions cannot be ignored. The statement of output functions is a clear illustration of the multifunctionality argument. Courts not only adjudicate, but legislate, in a very real sense. The bureaucracy initiates legislation, and it also administers its own rules.

Each of the seven functions enumerated by Almond is performed by special structures, according to the pattern variables outlined by Parsons. For example, the input function of political socialization and recruitment can be considered. This function is "the process of inculcation into the political culture," which results in "attitudes, value standards, and beliefs towards the political system."[23] In a sense, this function can be considered analogous to Parson's latency function, which is performed in the total social system by the family. Almond recognizes the institution of the family, along with others such as the church, schools, and voluntary associations. These perform a pre-political socialization function by introducing the individual to patterns of authority and decision making. Among the pattern variables Parsons enumerates is the dichotomy of *affective neutrality*. This pattern variable is especially important in political socialization, because the individual will presumably learn certain norms, such as loyalty towards his political system (the affective aspect of the variable). He may also learn to be objective and to judge his system by its performance rather than by its presumed attributes (affective neutrality). Similarly, political socialization is *universal* or *particular*; an individual is an occupant of many roles, each with specific claims and demands upon the actor. The style of socialization may be *specific* or *diffuse*. Almond suggests that primitive and/or parochial systems tend to be diffuse, whereas totalitarian systems tend to be rigid about the ways in which socialization is carried out.

Concern with the means by which a system carries out socialization and recruitment (input functions) and the consequences of such performance is reflected in a major study. In this work, an empirical examination of attitudes and belief structures in the United States, Great Britain, Germany, Italy, and Mexico, the authors seek to examine some of the preconditions of the civic culture, a "pluralistic culture based on communication and persuasion, a culture of consensus and diversity, a culture that permitted change but moderated it."[24]

The work is not without conceptual or methodological faults, although it is a ground-breaking study in both of these areas. On a conceptual basis, the authors address themselves to a series of questions about the political cultures of the nations studied and about the input processes that relate to the orientations of the citizenry of these nations. As an application of systems analysis, certain variables previously posited by Almond are examined empirically. This work represents a new methodological direction for comparative analysis; it employs survey research with questions and phraseology that are comparable, given the problems of language and meaning posed by studying five diverse countries.

Almond has paid even more detailed attention to some of the questions raised in his earlier essays.[25] Interest articulation, interest aggregation, and political communication, earlier regarded as input functions, are examined in regard to their styles, means, consequences, and effects on political modernization. Government structures are examined not from a purely legalistic or historical standpoint, which characterizes so much of early political science, but for the output functions which they perform (rule making, rule application, rule adjudication) and the effects various structures have upon the political culture.

Critique of Almond

Almond is not without his critics. His systems approach to structural–functionalism has yielded a classification of input and output variables highly useful to a researcher, especially one concerned with comparative analysis. Difficulties of operationalization abound, but this does not mean that they are insurmountable. However, does his work really represent a comprehensive theory of how systems operate? This is doubtful; Almond himself maintains that it really represents instead "a proposed first step towards constructing a theory of the political system and of the development of political systems."[26] Shortly after Almond set forth his scheme of inputs and outputs, it was noted that

> Almond's "seven-function system" (really neither functionalist nor a system), despite its advance over institutional description, may be praised as interesting or perceptive, without compelling further attention. It will be useful, indeed, to those seeking a better way to define the problems they want to study, but it cannot serve as a foundation for the study of whole political systems.[27]

Almond's approach is a significant contribution to a systems model for political science. As he and his followers continue to operationalize his categories and concepts, we will be better able to determine whether systems analysis can serve the functions of theory, explanation, and prediction.

STABILITY AND CHANGE

The three theorists mentioned here are all concerned with systems stability. Easton in particular is concerned with stress upon and within the political system, and its sources, mechanisms, and outcomes.[28] Although some analysts have recently become concerned with the total system, others have turned in recent years to an examination of political development and change, or to the role of violence in our social and political life. While nominally different, these concerns actually present an excellent opportunity for linking micro and macro theories of politics.

Almond has suggested that essentially four different types of groups perform the input function of interest articulation. These groups are institutional, associational, nonassociational, and anomic.[29] The *institutional interest group* is formed for purposes other than interest articulation, although it performs this function from time to time. It is characterized as having a relative degree of permanence and formal organization. An example of this type of group is the professional bureaucracy; although created for other purposes, it has definite interests and articulates them from time to time.

Associational interest groups approximate to some degree the pressure groups with which we are familiar. They are formed specifically to articulate their interests and do so on a much more frequent basis than the other types of groups. They also have a relatively high degree of organization and permanence and can serve as a major source of demand inputs to the political system.

Nonassociational interest groups are most similar to the categoric or tertiary groups referred to Chapter 8. They have no organization or structure, although their interests are expressed by individuals or groups who claim to speak for the larger group. For example, a senator can claim to speak for the disenfranchised, the poor, the black, and the young, although he is not a member of any of those nonassociational groups.

Anomic interest groups are those most likely to contribute to system instability. These are temporary groups, coalescing without any real structure as the result of an event, personality, issue, or combination of these factors. Their particular importance to the political system lies in their essential "normlessness," that is, their lack of attachment to the social or political system. In a sense, the presence of such groups in the system suggests a basic weakness in the system that might lead to greater instability or ultimate overthrow of the system. The degree to which anomic interest groups are present may be one of the keys to violent political change. "The vulnerability of a traditional regime to revolution varies directly with the capability of the regime for modernization."[30] If institutions created for specific ends cannot adapt themselves to changing conditions, then the system must expect change to take place, which may be violent.[31]

An increasing concern of political scientists in recent years has been the incidence of violent and nonviolent disruptions of political systems. Nonviolent tactics are viewed as tools to gain access to government leaders and resources and to lead to bargaining situations. For instance, the Gandhian approach in India contributed to the eventual displacement of the colonial system with independence. In contemporary India, however, nonviolence has often been superseded by the articulation of "nonnegotiable demands," which are opposed to the spirit and practice of the Gandhian ideal. These demands have met with less success than that experienced in colonial days. Political campaigns modelled on the Gandhian ideal were led by the late Dr. Martin Luther King, Jr., whose Birmingham, Alabama, bus boycott had a substantial economic impact on the bus company. Although the nonviolent approach has been used with considerable success in the South, there is not yet enough evidence on its potency in the North. In Czechoslovakia, nonviolent resistance to the Soviet invasion of August 1968 did not repel the Soviet armies. It is questionable whether the techniques were completely unsuccessful because they served in part to limit the Soviets. Although they had an obvious military disadvantage, the Czechs were able to stop the Soviets from dividing their country and to assume a bargaining posture, however unequal, through nonviolent tactics. [32]

A similar approach examines protest in political systems by viewing such activity as an attempt to mobilize resources. A specific target of protest is assumed; political protest groups attempt to win rewards, generally of a material nature, by forming coalitions with other groups that are as powerless as the protest group or with groups that control resources or that have access to the media. Protest by groups with little political power is not very likely to lead to success, especially within a short time span. The activity itself, however, can be useful in building more coherent groups who have a greater chance of acquiring and managing their own resources.[33]

A successful attempt has been made to deal with analysis of civil strife by developing a model that might predict system instability.[34] In an analysis of 114 polities, various measures are employed, such as political and economic deprivation, level of institutionalization of the polity, and past history of instability. There is a direct relationship between the potential size and previous history of coercive forces and the magnitude of eventual violence. When coercive forces are so large that they are utterly repressive, then and only then does strife diminish. "The adage that force solves nothing seems supported; in fact, force may make things worse."[35] Considerable work remains to be done in this area of research, but it is apparent that long strides are being taken that may have eventual importance for scholarly work and for public policy.

CRITIQUE OF APPROACHES
BASED ON SYSTEMS ANALYSIS

We may be faulted for combining under the general rubric of systems analysis several approaches that are superficially quite different.

However, we see from Easton to Parsons to Almond a distinct line of development. No single theorist has the "best" model, but each has contributed to a process of intellectual development. We have purposely confined our description of each approach to its highlights. In so doing, we do not intend to oversimplify, nor to do injustice to each theorist. We previously criticized some of the more salient points of each model, and we now begin to tie these criticisms together as they relate to the current state of systems analysis.

The type of analysis posited by Easton, Parsons, and Almond is considerably broader than that offered by group and decision analysts. Each of these three theory-builders has constructed an analysis broad enough to accommodate some of the same concerns of theorists of schools with theories that are less broad. Indeed, systems analysis and structural–functionalism are often described as "broad" or "middle-gauge" theory.

Do approaches based on system analysis have an empirical foundation? As far as empiricists are concerned, none of the models we have described contain testable hypotheses. The normative bias that underlies systems analysis and structural–functionalism is also considered a problem. Systems theory may be a fine pedagogical tool for offering a taxonomy of how a political system operates. As such, it is really what Easton meant by describing it as a *Framework for Political Analysis.*[36] The problem with frameworks or any bare-bones approach is that although a lot of wind can whistle through them, they afford no protection to their inhabitants. This is not to say that systems theorists have made no effort to give substance to their various systems, for they have paid great attention to detail.

However, one searches in vain for testable hypotheses in the works of systems and functional analysts.[37] Applying our earlier definition of hypotheses—"general statements, suggestions of the connections between concepts"—we might incorrectly assume that systems analysis provides testable hypotheses. Easton posits a system in which demand and support inputs operate with hypothetical relations; but are they testable? Emphatically, "no." For example, one can use input/output analysis only to describe current poverty programs in the ghetto and to raise questions about empirical phenomena. If one were to observe that the infusion of federal dollars for a job-training program in the ghetto was followed after some time by a reduction in crime, one might infer a relationship between the federal aid (input) and the decreased crime rate (output). But this is a simple causal analysis, testable in its own right. One might ask, why bother to put this in a systems framework in the first place? We have repeatedly said that the functions of theory are twofold: to explain and predict. The overly simplified systems model example relating crime and job-training programs might help to explain such relationships, but it does nothing to predict future relationships, or to explain how these relationships might occur elsewhere.

In this light, it is more accurate to think of systems analysis not as a theory, but as a model. As such, it may help to generate hypotheses, although it does not contain hypotheses itself.[38] Systems analysis proceeds under the assumption that "it is useful to view political life as a system of behavior."[39] Proceeding from this, Easton and others constructed elaborate models of the political process, some of which we have reviewed in this chapter. These models can serve the highly useful purpose of generating hypotheses, although systems analysts generally do not do so. Further, these models can provide an interesting and useful taxonomy for the political process, a sort of conceptual ledger for the presence or absence of variables that presumably enter into politics. A thoughtful and concise critique of systems analysis suggests that:

> A theory is not merely an "approach" to a discipline or topic—a suggested framework for explanation. . . . theories can function with any kind of generalization, whatever the terms they employ. But theories are definite and particular; they are attempts to explain real phenomena. . . . systems theories are research strategies, or statements about the content that political generalizations ought to include.[40]

Although perhaps useful as an approach to research problems, systems analysis suffers from a lack of substantive content. Whether it is a useful taxonomy is a moot point, dependent upon the preferences of each student. Readers of this work may be familiar with two texts for American government courses that follow the systems approach.[41] Others with more advanced training may have seen applications of systems analysis in other fields, such as comparative politics[42] or international relations.[43] As useful as the operationalization of systems analysis might be to some problems, there is no evidence to suggest that it is the best approach available to researchers.

More specifically, Eastonian analysis is immediately suspect because it never attempts to define "political" in any meaningful sense.[44] "System" is defined by interactions, but it is described in terms of its human components or actors, without reference to the interactions that supposedly define it in the first place.[45] In short,

> . . . one would really expect that criticism of a conceptual structure would be based largely on its adequacy or inadequacy in relating to the phenomena. Easton has no phenomena! The "political system" which he so busily dissects exists nowhere except in his mind; the closest empirical approximation is probably the sovereign national state.[46]

Parsonian analysis is similarly open to criticism. By aiming for a general theory to explain and predict human behavior in all fields, Parsons essentially requires a static system, incapable of meeting change. This fundamental error does not mean that his work is entirely without value. However, although Parsons prepares an elaborate taxonomy, one can search in vain "for adequate explanations of concrete phenomena."[47] Furthermore, there is a bias present toward the collectivity in his four-fold system. He ignores the individual and thus raises serious questions about the ultimate values upon which his work and others are premised.[48]

In Almond's seven-function system, which is a meld of Eastonian and Parsonian analysis, we have another example of an attempt at an all-encompassing theory. Almond also can be criticized for producing an elaborate taxonomy or a model that fails to meet the requirements of theory. Although Almond's approach has been used in comparative analysis, because systems analysis appears to offer some points on which useful comparisons can be made, this is not sufficient to warrant the label of theory, as is made clear below:

> . . . specialists in comparative government have for years taken it for granted that comparisons are always worth making even when there is no specific end in view. Now, inquiry may aim at description, explanation, or evaluation, or all three; and comparative government, as presently conceived, seems primarily concerned with description. But it is pointless to make endless comparisons unless the similarities and differences uncovered by the comparison are explained, and explanation does not necessarily depend on still further comparisons.[49]

If political science seeks to be more rigorous and empirical, it must be divested of biases in its approaches. Does systems analysis leads us closer to this goal? From the works of the three theorists we have examined, there is considerable evidence that the reverse is true.

Concerns with "steady states," "equilibrium," and "system maintenance" all have a heavily loaded bias toward maintaining the status quo and toward group behavior, to the neglect of individual behavior. If something is dysfunctional for the system in which it operates, does not that carry a negative connotation? To describe variables as functional or dysfunctional appears to place a higher value on system maintenance than on system change or displacement. The function of a variable, person, or event is measured against whether it assists a system or one of its subsystems in performing other functions. Implicitly, then, systems analysis states that maintenance of the system has a higher value. If we continue this line of reasoning, stability to the systems analyst becomes a prime requisite, and variables described as "functional" take on a positive value. Further, what is "functional" in the eyes of one analyst at one time might not be functional to another elsewhere, which might lead to unforeseen results, some of which may be patently "dysfunctional."

A somewhat morbid example of this might be the occasional crop failures in China. To the more paranoid individuals in this and other countries who are fearful of the "yellow peril," a famine killing five or six million Chinese might be considered functional, since it lessens the imminent menace. Leaders in the People's Republic of China who are forced to deal with the many problems of a famine, may consider the famine entirely dysfunctional to the economy and to the regime.

The time element also casts some doubt upon the utility of such concepts as functional and dysfunctional. One could argue that in 1933 rabid anti-Semitism was entirely functional to the Third Reich because it provided a convenient scapegoat for Germany's ills and gave a coherence to the ideology of National Socialism. Strictly avoiding any reference to human values, the loss of a significant element of Germany's professional and mercantile population in a short time, without adequate replacements, could have contributed in part to the eventual German defeat in the Second World War. What was perceived as functional by the German regime at one time may have been dysfunctional to the German nation at a later time.

In short, by considering system maintenance or stability as a prime goal, by measuring variables against artificial and system-biased constructs such as functionality, analysts may fall prey to using a heavily value-laden scheme that ultimately interferes with the goals of explanation and prediction. Functionality can take on the hue of a purely normative *theology* instead of an empirical social *theory*. Much depends on the operationalization of systems models, of course, but the danger is no less there because systems analysis uses abstract concepts with a seemingly empirical tone. There is little empirical orientation in the work of the three model builders, a criticism to keep in mind in evaluating such approaches in terms of whether they do or do not contribute to theory building.

Considerably greater information is required at all levels, as we have suggested in chapters 4 through 9 dealing with specific substantive topics of political science. Theory and method must go hand-in-hand. The questions posed by the systems analysis school are perhaps too broad, although they could suggest new concerns for political scientists. An inescapable difficulty in the systems approach is the lack of clear empirical references. Some of the variables discussed by the systems school are taken further and operationalized by communications analysts in the development of more adequate prediction and more comprehensive explanation. Systems analysis, which has been in vogue in recent years, may be supplanted by the communications approaches discussed in the next chapter. The constant interaction between theory and empirical findings will test the constructs of systems analysis and structural–functionalism and may either refine or replace them. This constant process of development in political science is both exciting and frustrating.

NOTES AND REFERENCES

1. David B. Truman, "Disillusion and Regeneration: The Quest for a Discipline," *American Political Science Review* 59 (December 1965): 65–66.

2. Robert A. Dahl, "The Behavioral Approach in Political Science: Epitaph for a Monument to a Successful Protest," *American Political Science Review* 55 (December 1961): 763–72.

3. For instance, Herbert J. Storing (ed.), *Essays on the Scientific Study of Politics* (New York: Holt, Rinehart and Winston, 1962); Christian Bay, "Politics and Pseudopolitics: A Critical Evaluation of Some Behavioral Literature," *American Political Science Review* 59 (March 1965): 39–51.

4. Norbert Wiener, *Cybernetics* (New York: John Wiley and Sons and the M.I.T. Press, 1948).

5. Ludwig von Bertalanffy, "General Systems Theory," *General Systems, I* (1956), pp. 1–10.

6. Roy R. Grinker (ed.), *Toward a Unified Theory of Human Behavior* (New York: Basic Books, 1956).

7. David Easton, *A Framework for Political Analysis* (Englewood Cliffs, N.J.: Prentice-Hall, 1965), p. 57.

8. *Ibid., passim*. The following discussion relies heavily upon this work as well as upon Easton's *A Systems Analysis of Political Life* (New York: John Wiley and Sons, 1965).

9. Many works on the presidency follow the pattern of describing the office in terms of possible roles. *See* Clinton Rossiter's *The American Presidency* (New York: Harcourt, Brace and World, 1960).

10. *See* Rexford Tugwell, *The Enlargement of the Presidency,* 1st ed. (Garden City, N.Y.: Doubleday, 1960), for an extended statement on this point.

11. In this light, *see* John D. Astin, "Easton I and Easton II," *Western Political Quarterly* 25 (December 1972): 726–37.

12. James G. Miller, "Toward a General Theory for the Behavioral Sciences," *American Psychologist* 10 (September 1955): 527–28.

13. *Ibid.*, p. 528.

14. J. S. Sorzano, "David Easton and the Invisible Hand," *American Political Science Review* 69 (March 1975): 91.

15. *Ibid.*, p. 103.

16. Notably *The Social System* (Glencoe, Ill.: The Free Press, 1951), and edited with Edward A. Shils, *Toward a General Theory of Action* (Cambridge: Harvard University Press, 1951). Also, with Robert F. Bales and Edward A. Shils, *Working Papers in the Theory of Action* (New York: The Free Press, 1953).

17. Harold Kaplan, "The Parsonian Image of Social Structure and Its Relevance for Political Science," *Journal of Politics* 30 (November 1968): 903–08.

18. Gabriel A. Almond, "Comparative Political Systems," *Journal of Politics* 18 (August 1956): 391.

19. *Ibid.*, p. 393.

20. *Ibid.*, p. 395. Emphasis in original.

21. *Ibid.*, p. 396.

22. Gabriel A. Almond, "Introduction: A Functional Approach to Comparative Politics," in Gabriel A. Almond and James S. Coleman (eds.), *The Politics of the Developing Areas* (Princeton: Princeton University Press, 1960), p. 7. The discussion that follows relies upon this work.

23. *Ibid.*, pp. 27–28.

24. Gabriel A. Almond and Sidney Verba, *The Civic Culture: Political Attitudes and Democracy in Five Nations* (Princeton: Princeton University Press, 1963), p. 8.

25. Gabriel A. Almond and G. Bingham Powell, Jr., *Comparative Politics: A Developmental Approach* (Boston: Little Brown, 1966).

26. Gabriel A. Almond, "A Developmental Approach to Political Systems," *World Politics* 17 (January 1965): 205.

27. Leonard Binder, *Iran: Political Development in a Changing Society* (Berkeley: University of California Press, 1962), p. 10.

28. *See* especially *A Systems Analysis of Political Life,* pp. 57–69; 220–340.

29. Almond, in Almond and Coleman (eds.), *Politics of Developing Areas,* pp. 33–38.

30. Samuel P. Huntington, "Political Development and Political Decay," *World Politics* 17 (April 1965): 422; *idem., Political Order in Changing Societies* (New Haven: Yale University Press, 1968).

31. *Ibid.,* p. 397.

32. Ronald J. Terchek, "Theory Application of Gandhian Tactics in Three Disparate Environments: India, the United States, and Czechoslovakia" (Paper prepared for delivery at the annual meeting of the American Political Science Association, New York City, August 31–Sept. 4, 1969).

33. Michael Lipsky, "Protest as a Political Resource," *American Political Science Review* 62 (December 1968): 1144–58.

34. Ted Gurr, "A Causal Model of Civil Strife: A Comparative Analysis Using New Indices," *American Political Science Review* 62 (December 1968): 1104–24.

35. *Ibid.,* p. 1124.

36. *Ibid.*

37. We specifically exempt from this criticism the recent work by Alfred Kuhn, *The Logic of Social Systems: A Unified, Deductive, System-Based Approach to Social Science* (San Francisco: Jossey-Bass, 1974). This work is exactly what its subtitle says it is, and is also a rich source of testable hypotheses, all related to one another. There is no evidence brought to bear in testing the hypotheses, a project suitably left for others. This work is more general and more specific than any of the theoretical systems analyses we have examined. Its recent publication has limited the opportunity for scholars in the social sciences to test the hypotheses that deductively flow from Kuhn's model. However, it would be no surprise if systems analysis receives increased currency through the logical analysis Kuhn brings to bear on the examination of individual and collective behavior.

38. Henry Teune, "Models in the Study of Political Integration," in Philip E. Jacob and James V. Toscano (eds.), *The Integration of Political Communities* (Philadelphia: J.B. Lippincott Company, 1964), pp. 294–97

39. Easton, *Framework,* p. 24.

40. Eugene J. Meehan, *The Theory and Method of Political Analysis* (Homewood, Ill.: The Dorsey Press, 1965), p. 147.

41. Marian D. Irish and James W. Prothro, *The Politics of American Democracy,* 5th ed. (Englewood Cliffs, N.J.: Prentice-Hall, 1971); and Stephen

299

V. Monsma, *American Politics: A Systems Approach* (New York: Holt, Rinehart and Winston, 1969).

42. Andrew J. Milnor, *Elections and Political Stability* (Boston: Little, Brown, 1969).

43. Morton A. Kaplan, *System and Process in International Politics* (New York: John Wiley and Sons, 1957).

44. Eugene J. Meehan, *Contemporary Political Thought: A Critical Study* (Homewood, Ill.: The Dorsey Press, 1967), p. 172.

45. *Ibid.*, pp. 172–73.

46. *Ibid.*, p. 174.

47. *Ibid.*, p. 145.

48. *Ibid.*, p. 150.

49. *Ibid.*, pp. 180–81.

STUDY QUESTIONS

1. What do the following mean? What is their importance in the study of political behavior?

policial systems	input and output functions
system boundary	feedback
inputs and outputs	multifunctionalism

2. How can systems analysis encompass the following approaches?

personality	role
attitudes, beliefs, opinions, and values	groups
political socialization	decision making

3. What are the value biases in the systems approach to the study of politics?

4. What data-collection techniques could be pertinent to the study of political systems? Specify, indicating the level at which systems could be examined.

CHAPTER
11

Communications Analysis

Communications analysis is a major step toward the development of broad theory in political science. A fundamental assumption of the communications approach is that "society can only be understood through a study of the messages and the communication facilities which belong to it. . . ."[1]

In this chapter we shall consider the various levels of communications analysis and discuss some studies that have applied this approach. Before we discuss the means by which communications analysis has been applied, it is necessary to first clarify some basic concepts.

DEFINITION OF CONCEPTS

The fundamental unit of analysis in communications analysis is the *message,* i.e., "any thought that is complete or stands by itself."[2] Messages contain information, which is

> . . . a name for the content of what is exchanged with the outer world as we adjust to it, and make our adjustment felt upon it. The process of receiving and using information is the process of our adjusting to the outer environment, and of our living effectively under that environment.[3]

Information also shows a "patterned relationship between events."[4] The concept of pattern, either of relationships or interactions, is fundamental to communications analysis.

Encoding and Receiving Messages. Messages are *sent, received,* and *stored.* Before they are sent, they must be *encoded.* The process of encoding by an individual or a group is an attempt "to select and execute a response (R) to the environmental event (S). . . ."[5] This suggests the way in which communications analysis can encompass other approaches, such as decisional analysis. The response requires several steps, all related to the heart of the decisional process—how one reacts to stimuli. If one receives a stimulus, the response is necessarily a decision.

Several steps in the encoding process are required before the message or response can be sent or transmitted.[6] Encoded messages are transmitted in a variety of ways; we refer to their passing through a *communications channel,* i.e., "a transmission medium over which messages flow."[7] The messages may not arrive at the intended recipient; they may be *blocked* or intercepted by others.[8] Distortion can occur within the channels, or because the message was improperly *encoded* or *decoded.* Encoding and decoding depend on one's perceptions of the message or stimulus, a subjective element that increases the possibility of misunderstanding or distortion.[9] Further, since encoding or decoding involves human brain activity— "A combination of electrochemical phenomena occuring within [individual] human evaluators, decision makers, and the like, together with sign and symbol communications"—the entire communications process involves something less than objective reality.[10]

In the process of transmitting messages over channels, a channel, such as face-to-face oral communication, the mass media, or diplomatic couriers, ultimately has a given "capacity, which, if exceeded, creates a condition called *overload.*"[11] In this case, the communications channel becomes totally ineffective because messages may not get through at all.

An example of the use of these concepts in political analysis is helpful. Assume, for example, that action in a combat zone requires the immediate attention of the president. The collapse of the forces of the Republic of South Vietnam in spring 1975 will serve as our illustration. For this example, we will also assume that members of the U.S. armed forces were not in the combat zone. Sensory information (visual and aural) was perceived by South Vietnamese intelligence teams and newsmen in such a way as to suggest that unusual conditions existed. However, our concern is with a hypothetical single message that ultimately reached President Ford.

Each intelligence officer and each newsman in the combat zone could not gather all the objective facts about the situation. They did not know the effects of North Vietnamese units on South Vietnamese operations.

On the basis of preliminary reports filed with army headquarters and newspapers, Saigon officials began to get a picture of what was happening in the combat zone. Officials at the U.S. Embassy, who were not skilled in military tactics and strategy, were briefed by Vietnamese officials fluent in English. These briefings involved a translation process and required that the reports be collated and interpreted, so that some pattern might emerge. U.S. Embassy officials then composed a wire for President Ford. Information had to be selected for the message on the basis of a preliminary evaluation. The selection process involved recalling some information, from memory as well as files, in order that pertinent information be transmitted. Action that appeared routine and did not fit the pattern of a coordinated enemy offensive was rejected as unrelated. The message was written using ordinary language and symbols, all of which could be subjected to varying interpretations. The possibility of distortion of objective reality was thus introduced at several stages, even before the message was transmitted. Since it was a classified message, it was then probably put into a top secret code for electrical transmission. This process could again introduce distortion, because a code clerk could incorrectly encode certain letters or words. We will assume that the communications channel used was one normally reserved for high-priority messages by radio-telegraph facilities. If enemy agents had been able to identify the channel and had wanted to block the message from reaching the president, they could have jammed the radio frequency with overriding noise. Assuming that this was not done, the message could have been received over a special teletype machine that converts electrical energy into mechanical energy and a typed message. Communications personnel would then have had to alert the officers in charge, one of whom presumably had the wisdom (or "stored" instructions) to notify the president. The president received a message composed thousands of miles away by people he had never met, a message compiled on the basis of information provided by still other unknowns. In consultation with his advisers, all of whom had to read and interpret the message through their own value screens, the president made a response (decision). The cycle was then resumed as presidential messages were sent to officials in Vietnam, the Congress, the Pentagon, the press, and the average citizen.

We have not detailed all the steps possible in this example, but it is easy to see how distortion can take place at any point in the message flow. For instance, if there were only one channel for presidential messages from Vietnam and many messages had to be passed, the equipment might break down. The abilities of the president and his advisers to assess a high number of messages with complex information in a short period of time also could cause distortion of the message.

Feedback. Essential to the entire communications process is *feedback,* defined as:

> . . . a communications network that produces action in response to an input of information, and includes the results of its own action in the new information by which it modifies its subsequent behavior.[12]

Expressed in another way, feedback refers to the process by which an individual, group, or a system learns the consequences of its action(s), so that corrective behavior may be instituted. In the feedback process, four other concepts are involved. *Load* refers to the amounts of information involved in feedback and other channels. *Lag* is the delay involved in responding to information transmitted by feedback channels. *Lead* is the inverse of lag; it indicates the ability of a system to act on predicted and anticipated events. *Gain* is literally the amount and speed of reaction to information.[13]

We can relate feedback processes to our example of communications between Vietnam and the U.S. by examining other channels involved in the presidential decision-making process. Load is a critical factor because the channels carrying information have a limited capacity. How did the president respond to the initial messages? Did he delay until further information was forthcoming? Did he request this information from Saigon? How detailed were his requests, and did they ask for the sort of information needed to make a command decision? In other words, was there a lag in the decisional process introduced by faulty use of communications? Or, was the president prepared by having received advance warning and prediction of the event, so that only his formal order to implement a planned response to the offensive was required? What was the reaction to the initial message from Saigon? Was it treated casually or overlooked by those responsible for alerting the president? Or did the lights burn overtime at the White House, as the meanings of the message were explored by the president and his advisers?

The use and elaboration of these concepts might seem at first glance to be superfluous and merely descriptive of what any astute political observer could apprehend. However, by specifying the details of the communications process, it may be possible to develop more refined predictors of political behavior. The communications analysis of behavior is fairly well established, but has only recently been developed in the context that we have outlined.

LOW-LEVEL ANALYSIS:
INTERPERSONAL COMMUNICATION

Long before communications analysis in its modern form became the focus for many analysts, social scientists had been paying attention to the effects of interpersonal communications on behavior and attitudes. A considerable body of research on behavior and attitudes has focused on aspects of political behavior that most easily relate to interpersonal communications. Chapter 5, which discusses values, attitudes, opinions, and beliefs, derives in part from studies exploring interpersonal communications and relationships. Chapter 6, which considers political socialization, is also based on such work. To consider studies of socialization or attitude without understanding the necessary role played by communications is impossible.

A necessary antecedent for political action is that "the political actor must pick up relevant stimuli from the environment. Stimuli likely to be perceived as political make up only a small part of the total available."[14] There is little doubt that stimuli are available to some degree to most individuals, but the amount present is a function of one's environment, needs, and training. An individual in a situation requiring little knowledge of current affairs might make little attempt to seek out political information, unless it was personally relevant (e.g., if he is unemployed and the government is considering a new job-training program). Selective attention and selective perception are therefore crucial if the communications process is to be at all effective in altering or reinforcing behavior and attitudes.

The way in which the *communicator* is perceived has a direct relationship on the effectiveness of the communication. "*Who* says something is as important as *what* is said in understanding the effect of a communication on an attitude."[15] The source of a message or stimulus, as perceived by the recipient, can be the major reason a message is understood properly. If one feels that the communicator is an untrustworthy or otherwise unattractive source, the message may be consciously or unconsciously screened out.

> The source's believability reflects the extent to which his message is perceived as being correct and in accord with empirical evidence. Hence, it depends on the recipient's perception of the source as knowing what is correct and being motivated to communicate what he knows—or, more briefly, his perceived expertise and objectivity.[16]

The attractiveness and similarity (to the recipient) of the source also affect how the message is received. If one carries out an order given by a person whom one *dis*likes, a considerable rationalization process is necessary. If we perceive a source as similar to ourselves, the message is more likely to be accepted.[17]

Group membership also affects the communications process. We have examined in Chapter 8 some of the means by which group membership leads to resistance to communications. If a group member receives messages that run counter to his group's norms, whether he accepts or rejects that message depends on the extent to which he values group membership. Counternorm messages are therefore rejected by those with a high regard for their group and by those who rely upon their group for status or a feeling of "belonging." The more one values a group membership, the more probable it is that one will not only reject messages opposing group norms, but also rely more strongly on communications with other group members.[18]

Status within a group can be associated with resistance to counternorm messages. Members with only average status in a group are likely to be more resistant to external stimuli than are those with a high status. Popularity within a group is "positively correlated with conformity and resistance to counternorm communications," and conformity is to be expected of those aspiring to leadership positions.[19]

However, those holding leadership positions might be more prone to occasionally deviate from group norms, and these persons could also be highly influential in changing group attitudes.[20] Evidence for this is shown by a pioneering study of group leaders and followers.[21] Two national cross-sections were matched against a special sample of about 1,500 local leaders, including mayors, county party chairmen, American Legion post commanders, and regents of the Daughters of the American Revolution. The study was concerned with how the American public and its local leaders viewed civil rights and civil liberties. (This study was undertaken in the 1950s, prior to campus rebellions, ghetto uprisings, and the activist mood that dominated the next decade; however, the questions the study asked and their answers are of intrinsic importance today.) For those concerned with the persuasive effects of communications and how to interpret them, there are some suggestions from this study. Perhaps most importantly, the study found that civic leaders were more prone to holding pro-civil liberties positions than was the national sample. [22] Although this was not directly related to group membership, the study concluded that leaders holding high formal status in their organizations may be more susceptible to communications campaigns than are the members of their associations.

The evidence for this is murky and inferential at best. For instance, conformity to group norms may be essential for those who seek leadership positions and wish to maintain them.[23] Another study reports that the group members most successful in effecting attitude change or influencing others were those with high status or power in the group.[24] Although group leaders tend to resist change in their attitudes and beliefs, once persuaded, they can become successful message carriers.[25] Formal and informal leaders therefore operate as opinion leaders," and assist in the "two-step flow of communications." They tend to expose themselves to more media than do most people and to pass on to others their own perceptions and interpretations of media messages. In this way, they can reinforce existing opinions or assist in changing them.[26] Personal contact, therefore, is probably the most important phase of any communications process. A distinct advantage of personal contact is its flexibility; it can be more effective in meeting resistance and adapting to arguments or passivity than can the mass media.[27]

As used by group leaders or opinion leaders, personal communication can provide stimuli of sufficient intensity that a listener's attitudes may be increased and he or she may be mobilized to action. In a political campaign, for example, personal persuasion may be at least as effective as mass media campaigns in arousing voters to go to the polls.

MIDDLE-LEVEL ANALYSIS: THE MASS MEDIA

The role of mass media in influencing attitudes and behavior is shown by the 1960 televised debates between Richard Nixon and John F. Kennedy. The first telecast had a national audience of almost seventy-five million viewers. The three succeeding broadcasts drew smaller audiences, but in no case less than forty-eight million persons watched the third and fourth debates. The television debates were apparently one of the deciding factors in Kennedy's victory. A survey by the Roper organization showed that about 57 percent of the voters admitted to having been influenced in one way or another by the debates. About 6 percent, representing potentially four million voters, "decided to cast their ballots on the basis of the television performances, and their verdict was three-to-one for Kennedy, providing him with considerably more votes than the two one-hundredths of one percent by which he won the popular count."[28] Although it is questionable whether the debates actually were the cause of the Kennedy victory, there is no doubt but that they played a large part. They also suggest the importance of the mass media in a striking and dynamic way.

From this example, it is possible to overstate the case for mass media. Influence of the mass media is limited by the fact that a listener, viewer, or reader is not an "automaton actuated by impulses transmitted by anonymous rulers" of the media.[29] There is little evidence to support the idea that people are manipulated by mass media. Television news in particular has been singled out by many as having a bias and an ability to distort a candidate's image. An intensive study of this problem provides scant support for this position:

... during the 1972 presidential election compaign, the direct effects of television news exposure on voters' reactions to campaign issues were minimal. Perhaps over a longer period of time, in a noncampaign atmosphere, in another presidential election, or in campaigns for lower level offices, television news exposure would show different effects. But in the 1972 presidential campaign, television news had few *direct* and *independent* effects on voters.[30]

Lest we throw out the baby with the bathwater, it must be conceded that the media often has an enormous effect, a point well understood by leaders of societies in the process of nation building or by leaders who use the media for mass persuasion. Although there are limits on the effects of the mass media, it does play a significant role in politics, and an examination of that role is essential to understanding political behavior.

Roles Played by the Media

What roles do the media play? The mass media—radio, television, newspapers, and magazines—are transmitters of information. They gather information through their own channels, encode it in styles peculiar to their own medium and particular format, and transmit it to viewers, listeners, and leaders. Besides the means by which they gather information, the means by which they encode their messages is the most crucial.[31]

The media can be expected to give vastly different treatment to an event, such as a campus sit-in. They may report different aspects of the same event. A radio reporter can roam about with his tape recorder, reporting the facts as he sees them or has been given them by the campus public relations office, and comment with or without editorializing. Television camerapersons are somewhat more restricted, but their filmed report of the event, with voice commentary, is a radically different means of encoding information. Viewers may have the sit-in "brought into their homes," but only those scenes recorded by the camera are received. The visual effect may heighten viewers' involvement, but objectivity in encoding and decoding is severely limited. If the cameras record the presence of shouting long-haired students, even if they are a distinct minority, one receives the impression that only "hippie-types" are involved, that they are the only students at that college, or that all students are like that.

Newspapers have to rely primarily on the written word, with a photograph or two of the event. The headline for the story cues the reader about whether or not he wants to read the story and what he may get out of it. On the basis of a quick reading, a member of the paper's staff may provide a capsulized description of the story. Weekly magazines have more time to cover the story and to provide an indepth report, although they may allocate less space to the event. Encoding involves considerable condensation, when one is attempting to put more information in less space. Monthly magazines, or those that hold some expressed viewpoint, may not cover the story at all, but instead make some passing reference to it in the context of a broader article on student unrest. Each station, paper, or magazine may have a distinct style of reporting. It is possible to read accounts of an event in *The New York Times, Chicago Tribune*, and *Berkeley Barb* and wonder if the reporters covered the same event.

Considerable distortion is thus unintentionally present in the mass media. There is no assurance that messages are read or viewed by large audience or that once received they are decoded in the manner desired by those reporting the event. The variety mass media offers can inhibit its potential overwhelming influence; for example, one can usually select three evening news programs, all of which may express different viewpoints. In larger cities, there may be some choice of newspapers, although this option has been declining in recent years. National news magazines of different persuasions are also available.

In addition to varying vehicles within each medium, a viewer or reader can also choose several types of media by subscribing to a newspaper and magazine, listening regularly to the radio, or watching television. It is important to distinguish among the media in terms of the amount of reliance the public places on them for political information. A 1972 national sample was asked which media source they used for information about the 1972 campaign; they responded as follows:[32]

Newspapers	57%
Radio	43
Television	88
Magazines	33

Since television was by far the most widely used source of political information, one is led to wonder to what extent the public relies upon more than one source. The same national sample was asked whether or not they used each of the media, and the following cumulative index was derived.[33]

Number of Media Used
by National Sample

None	5%
One	21
Two	33
Three	27
Four	13

Although there is a strong tendency for the American public to receive political information primarily from television, there is no evidence to suggest that this is the single source for a significant number of people. The variety of media is apparently operative, and there is an overlap between the audiences (or receivers) of communications channels.

Can media audiences be differentiated? Magazine users are found to have the greatest familiarity with issues, to participate to a greater degree in the electoral process, and to be more internationally oriented. Next in order in each of these variables are newspaper readers, television viewers, and radio listeners.[34] Those who rank highest in media exposure—those who use three or four media for political information—tend to have a higher educational level and to be more involved in politics.[35] Reliance upon the mass media for political news increases noticeably after high school. And there are considerable differences between which medium students and their parents choose, parents tending to pay greater attention to all four media:

Although students watch a good deal of television, they pay attention to its news broadcasts much less regularly than parents. Daily attention to the newspapers is also much less frequent among the students, while the differences in the use of radio and magazine news are smaller but in the same direction. As with political interests, there are rather similar proportions of nonusers among students and parents. For the most part, increased media usage in adulthood means shifting from irregular to regular use.[36]

If we find associations between mass media use and political behavior, can we properly infer that behavior is *caused* by the

311

mass media? We have already suggested that there are tendencies to emphasize the influence of mass media, almost to the exclusion of other factors; or to discount the media almost entirely in accounting for political behavior. In part, the effects of mass communication may be summarized as follows:

> Mass communication ordinarily does not serve as a necessary and sufficient cause of audience effects, but rather functions among and through a nexus of mediating factors and influences.
>
> These mediating factors are such that they typically render mass communication a contributory agent, but not the sole cause, in a process of reinforcing . . .
>
> The efficacy of mass communication, either as a contributory agent or as an agent of direct effect, is affected by various aspects of the media and communication themselves or of the communication situation . . .[37]

A demagogue works his audience up to fever pitch by using appeals of fear and hatred to get his message through. We can document such successes, but there are numerous cases in which such appeals have lost an audience. A speaker who insists that sex education in the schools signals the presence of a communist menace may get his message through to certain audiences. But if he were to deliver the same message to other groups, he might be laughed off the stage. Audiences may be totally different and subject to entirely different types of appeals. In a similar fashion, audiences of the mass media can be stratified by a number of variables, such as age, education, sex, or region. To have a significant impact, the mass media must develop highly differentiated means of obtaining the attention of categoric groups and then of finding the effective means of holding that attention and having their message accepted. This is not an easy task, and it may contribute to a diminished effect of the mass media. Because mass media are pluralistic and address themselves to a wide variety of audiences, it cannot be assumed that they have an inordinate effect on behavior and attitudes.

The mass media play an important role in providing information about the political world to the citizen and often in mediating between the individual and the political system. However, the means by which they do this and the behavior and attitudes they produce are still a subject for continued research.

UPPER-LEVEL ANALYSIS:
COMMUNICATIONS AND THE POLITICAL SYSTEM

In their concern with building broad empirical theory, communications analysts have come the closest to providing a theory that is operational and serves the purposes of explanation and prediction. There are several reasons why communication is such an important object of study at the system level.[38]

The functions performed by and required of the political system must be accomplished by communicating. This alone justifies the attention paid to communications. Communication is itself a function, not merely a vehicle for the performance of other functions. We can thus compare nations on the basis of how the function of political communication is carried out and what effects it has. Suggested as variables for comparison between political systems are the following:

1. Homogeneity of political information
2. Mobility of political information
3. Volume of political information
4. Direction of the flow of political information.[39]

Conceptualization at this level can incorporate specifics such as those entailed in low- and middle-level analyses and still allow for greater generalization.

Borrowing heavily from cybernetics, one researcher postulated that control requires communication or the transmission of messages and information.[40] Since politics is concerned with questions of power and control, a necessary condition for examining these intangibles is an understanding of the central role of communications.[41] The fundamental assumption of the control approach, linking theory to substantive research, is that by viewing

> ... nations and governments as communications systems, impersonal, verifiable evidence can be obtained to check general descriptive or qualitative assertions about nationalism, about sovereignty, and about the merger of states.[42]

By extension, we can also use this approach to examine the ways in which other systems and groups behave in the political world.

Nationalism has been studied in light of communications.[43] This topic, which has absorbed political scientists for years, can be profitably broken down for study by determining the actual importance of concepts such as "consciousness" or "will," which frequently emerge in discussions of nationalism. These terms can then be operationalized and given empirical referents, so that they can be measured for relevance, as well as for the extent to which they actually reflect communications patterns. By so doing, it might be possible to

> ... identify pathological or self-destructive developments in nationalism where they occur, and perhaps to predict them in their early stages, as well as to suggest approaches to policies that might tend to prevent nationalistic conflicts from leading to national and social destruction.[44]

Other aspects of nationalism are similarly operationalized and quantified, such as the process of national assimilation or differentiation and the efficiency of communication among a nation's people. This could determine a nation's unity to some degree.

Although communications media are not all-powerful, their role has been integral in the process of nation building. Although one can measure increased communication flows (such as the flow of mail within a country),[45] the media can be employed to heighten national integration.[46] Totalitarian societies are noted for central control of the mass media. The position of Joseph Goebbels as Propaganda Minister of the Third Reich ensured direct and immediate government control over the content of the mass media, in which the Fuehrer's message took precedence.[47]

Although totalitarian regimes are usually forced on the populace, public opinion in these countries is still perceived by their leaders as essential to mobilizing support.

> Nazism, fascism, communism, and indeed all totalitarian movements have thus differed from classical authoritarianism in that they have sought to impose their dictatorial authority by means of the controlled mobilization of the masses. Public opinion, propaganda, and mass communication were always of central concern to them.

> The interest of totalitarian regimes in influencing public opinion is manifested by their large investment of resources and energy in the instruments of communication. The proportion of the gross national product devoted by totalitarian countries to literacy, newspaper publication, radio and

television expansion is, in general, substantially higher than the proportion spent by nontotalitarian countries which are at the same level of GNP per capita.[48]

Besides developing and maintaining their own positions, leaders of totalitarian societies are concerned with building a nation from geographically and ideologically disparate elements. Mao Tse-tung used mass media of every variety, from the simplest to the most complex, to integrate a nation that had been torn apart by years of civil war, in which a common language was lacking, and where fundamental transportation facilities were lacking. Posters, loudspeakers, public theater performances, and more conventional media have all been employed to develop a national Chinese consciousness.[49] The success of these media is not subject to firm conclusions, since evidence on activity in China is sorely lacking. We rely in part upon observations of travellers and defectors, but such evidence must remain suspect. It is obvious, however, that the leadership of several countries has perceived the necessity of communications to develop an integrated nation. In sum, the mass media may be a necessary condition for national cohesion, but they cannot be considered a sufficient condition. As with election campaigns, if communications are perceived to be important, they assume a more significant role, although their effectiveness remains in doubt.

INTEGRATING THE LEVELS OF ANALYSIS

One study of how Supreme Court decisions are communicated and implemented integrates different facets of political science and other disciplines.[50] Its concern was with how the Supreme Court decisions abolishing prayer in the schools were arrived at, transmitted, implemented, and accepted at the local level.[51] Decision making, groups, attitudes, values, role expectations, and leadership are considered by the study. All of these variables are cast in the context of a communications network, used as a consistent explanatory framework. This research is not only an interdisciplinary work by a political scientist, but an effective demonstration of how the levels of communications analysis can be linked together.

One of the most complex problems facing political scientists is the means (or linkages) by which attitudes and decisions are

315

communicated, complied with, or distorted. Linkages can be studied well in a communications framework, and the study can help us to understand how decisions are arrived at, transmitted, and perceived by the citizenry-at-large.

Considering the Supreme Court as the highest level in the decisional process, the researcher defined decision making

> . . . in a relational sense. Activity is entailed not only on the part of those attempting to affect the behavior of others but on the part of those whose acts are to be affected. As for Supreme Court decision-making, it is compliant behavior on the part of others that gives substance to the Court's determinations. If the Court announces a policy and no compliant behavior ensues, then there is no decision.[52]

This definition implies a power relationship, where power is viewed as requiring communication to exist and maintain itself.

It was hypothesized that "pressures of a very specialized kind are brought to bear upon a wide range of actors motivating them to alter activity to make it consistent with rulings of the United States Supreme Court."[53] The types of pressures upon policy implementers and those affected by the decisions of the Court are explained as relating to cognitive consistency—the means by which people attempt to bring their attitudes into balance with their cognitions. This implies that individuals with attitudes that conflicted with the Court's would have to change their attitudes or behavior; if they did not, their perceptions of public policy or the Supreme Court would lead to noncompliance. How are these changes brought about?

The Court is portrayed as a highly regarded source of messages; although it lacks formal coercive power, it achieves a high degree of compliance nonetheless. The manner in which the Court "presents itself invokes responses which are congruent with the substance of its policies."[54] The content of the messages (or decisions) is especially important, because the Court lacks effective sanctions to ensure compliance. Reviewing the five major cases involving religion and the public schools to come before the Court since World War II, the research concluded that message cues were based upon the persuasiveness of the arguments presented. The Court also relied upon effective symbols such as Madison and Jefferson.[55]

Messages are transmitted to and through a large number of individuals, who vary with the content of the decision. In the cases involving school prayers, communications recipients and channels included "state attorneys general, superintendents of public instruction, school superintendents, principals, teachers, and school-board members."[56] All these individuals have a host of roles to play, and their perceptions must be taken into account in determining whether compliance or noncompliance will result.

The message or decision is eventually received at the local level, where it is implemented or challenged. The prevailing attitudes and norms of one local environment, "Eastville–Westville," and the ways in which the prayer decisions were eventually accepted and implemented by that community are described. Using a variety of techniques, including content analysis of the media and surveys of "influentials" and a cross-section of the community, a comprehensive picture is drawn of a poorly understood and complex phenomenon—linkage between government and citizen. The communications framework used by the researcher adds greatly to an understanding and appreciation of the processes involved in cutting through levels of government and society in order to implement official policy.

CRITIQUE OF COMMUNICATIONS ANALYSIS

Communications theory is one of the best examples of the ways in which political scientists, drawing heavily from other disciplines, have attempted to integrate theory and content at the most narrow and broad levels. Basic concepts have been defined and operationalized in a considerable body of literature and are incorporated in models for a generation of further research and theory building. In this sense, communications theory might be the developing paradigm of which we spoke earlier (*see* pages 30–40).

In the narrowest sense, communications theory allows the researcher to examine the means by which individuals receive and transmit information, how perception and socialization condition communication, and how this tends to integrate an individual into a group. The group approach to the study of politics can be improved by turning to constructs used in communications theory for an enhanced understanding of how groups operate internally and with reference to other groups or to the political system. Decision-making studies and systems models can also profit from the detailed questions posed by communications theory. We have shown how communications analysis can be applied at various levels, such as interpersonal communication, mass media, or broad units of the political system. What remains to be done?

Although scientific inquiry stresses objectivity, it is difficult to treat the objects of communications analysis as impersonal processors of information. It is also difficult to query individuals about their values, attitudes, opinions, and beliefs and accurately infer their perceptual processes. To make inferences about the means by which individuals process, encode, and decode information is even more demanding—if not impossible—if carried to its logical extreme. For instance, the communications approach deals with units of information. If we take a sentence as our "unit," then we may ultimately be called upon to analyze in the area of 10^{50} possible sentences in the English language alone. No formal mathematical structure can handle that order of complexity.[57] Communications theory cannot readily develop constructs that are easily operationalized and are capable of generalization. In this effort, political scientists will have to pay greater attention to the findings and techniques of biologists and psychologists. If we learn how the human mind physically copes with problems and apply these findings to political behavior, bold—and perhaps frightening—new strides in the science of politics will be made.

As in systems analysis, communications theory is criticized for a tendency to be more mechanistic than is customary in studies of human behavior. The impersonal view of individuals supposedly inherent in the communications approach seems to imply that, in groups or alone, people are nothing more or less than participants in a process about which they have nothing to say—that they are indeed automatons. Yet, no communications theorist has taken this point of view. We cannot assume that artificial distinctions between mechanisms and organisms are necessarily real. Communications theory can show how individuals react to demands placed upon them by others and by their environment,[58] but this does not substantiate the charge that the communications approach is as cold and impersonal as it might appear at first glance.

The communications approach especially lends itself to operationalization and the opportunity to quantify and to measure. In this respect, communications theory offers testable propositions, in which formal relations between variables can be measured to determine cause and effect. This is not true of group theories of behavior. More so than the other approaches we have studied, communications analysis can both explain and predict.

Figure 11–1 shows the role of communications in scientific endeavor. Assume that "Concept Y" is a message. In Figure 11–1A, the message is caused by variables such as a decision or a series of attitudes held by certain people. The message caused or created by other events must be communicated, possibly with effects on others, as in Figure 11–1B. The complete analysis in Figure 11–1C shows the central role of the hypothetical message. Since all human political activity is grounded in communications, and the activity itself must be communicated, communications is thought by some to be

A. Causal Analysis of Concept Y

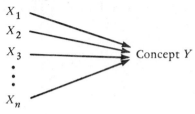

B. Effect Analysis of Concept Y

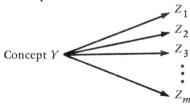

C. Complete Analysis of Concept Y

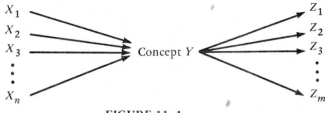

FIGURE 11–1

Hypothetical Cause-and-Effect Relationships of Communications
(From *The Study of Human Communication* by Nan Lin, copyright ©
1973, The Bobbs-Merrill Company, Inc. Reprinted by permission of the
publisher.)

the obvious way to integrate other approaches.[59] The problem of operationalization, however, remains.

The communications approach is very much concerned with "indicators" of performance. The concepts of *lead, load, lag,* and *gain* can be operationalized within a communications situation to indicate the relative efficiency and effectiveness of a system. This might ultimately lead to "the dangers of false counting and distorted quantification in the search for performance indicators."[60] This can happen, and has been detected in published research. But this danger is not limited to communications theory alone, nor to any other approach of behavioral scientists. False quantification or undue haste to give an empirical referent to one's work can emerge in any scientific endeavor. The fact that Lysenko counted missing tails on rats and concluded that environment, not genetic makeup, determines heredity did not dismiss the validity of the entire field of genetics. When he was ultimately found out, his work was derided and dismissed, as it should have been. The same can happen to specialists in communications approaches to behavior as well. The ultimate test of any work is its acceptance by those are professionally qualified to evaluate it. The "Communications to the Editor" section in any issue of the *American Political Science Review* will develop an appreciation of how grudgingly acceptance is granted by fellow scientists.

The content of communications is at least as important, if not more so, than the actual number of messages.[61] Obviously, a considerable amount of gibberish would not be considered of greater significance than an important "yes" or "no." The communications approach cannot be considered so mechanistic that it ignores content. If a communications analyst were concerned solely with communication flow, then distortion and noise would be thoroughly irrelevant. Examples of empirical applications of communications theory used in this chapter do not substantiate the charge of merely counting or ignoring content. White House correspondents can and do make inferences about the conduct of our nation's affairs merely by scanning the list of visitors the president will receive on a given day. A popular parlor sport after President Nixon's re-election and before the content of the Watergate tapes was made available was to assume his culpability merely from the fact that he received calls from certain people. It has been demonstrated that content can be used effectively in a communications analysis of events by relating values, attitudes, and communication patterns to explain an outcome, namely enforcement of the Supreme Court's school prayer decisions.

We have faulted other approaches that supposedly offer a genuine theory of politics. In each case we found the approaches wanting in one respect or another. Is communications analysis sufficiently capable of explanation and prediction to warrant the status of a theory? In most respects, it would appear it does. One can operationalize and relate variables that are at once broad and specific and avoid many of the pitfalls offered by other approaches. It is still too early to reach a definite statement that this approach meets all the requirements of theory, however. Too little work has been done employing the approach, although it appears to be rapidly gaining favor. The variables considered by communications analysts are exciting at this time because they serve to fill in some of the gaps in research. Studies of political development can profit greatly by accounting for variables related to communications analysis. However, this does not necessarily mean that all studies should be cast in the communications framework. The communications approach may simply offer a new and more highly refined model that is capable of generating more useful concepts and testable hypotheses.

Communications theorists have given us a new and potentially useful means of examining interactions at higher levels, such as those involving the media, political parties, pressure groups, and other informal institutions that may act as intermediaries between the individual and the political system. It will be necessary to determine to what degree political scientists can profitably use such analysis, and whether they will abuse the tools provided by communications analysis. In other words, can we possibly make too much of a good thing? In attempting to quantify relevant variables in a communications context, we must pay increasingly critical attention to the ways in which we operationalize and quantify, as well as determine the necessity or desirability of doing so at all levels and in all instances. Political science cannot be limited to communications theory alone. One advocate of the communications approach warns those who see that approach as the final paradigm for political science.

Currently, the communications approach—and appropriate, still developing techniques of measurement—looks extremely promising. At this point it would appear to be premature, however, to settle upon any single model, paradigm, pretheory, or particular set of tools. The most rewarding procedure seems to require, for the time being, at least, the encouragement of alternative models and alternative methods and techniques. . . . It is almost self-evident that communication approaches and general systems and decision-making approaches are complementary. In the long run several competing measurement devices are likely to prove reciprocally reinforcing in somewhat analogous ways.[62]

NOTES AND REFERENCES

1. Norbert Wiener, *The Human Use of Human Beings: Cybernetics and Society* (Boston: Houghton Mifflin Company, 1950), p. 9.

2. Lester W. Milbrath, *The Washington Lobbyists* (Chicago: Rand McNally and Company, 1963), p. 187. Emphasis in original.

3. Wiener, *The Human Use of Human Beings,* p. 124.

4. Karl Deutsch, *The Nerves of Government: Models of Political Communication and Control* (New York: The Free Press, 1966), p. 84.

5. Robert C. North, "The Analytical Prospects of Communications Theory," in James C. Charlesworth (ed.), *Contemporary Political Analysis* (New York: The Free Press, 1967), p. 304.

6. *Ibid.,* pp. 304–05.

7. Milbrath, *Washington for Lobbyists,* p. 307.

8. *Ibid.*

9. North, in Charlesworth (ed.), *Contemporary Political Analysis,* p. 307.

10. *Ibid.,* p. 306.

11. Milbrath, *Washington Lobbyists,* p. 188. Emphasis in original.

12. Deutsch, *Nerves of Government,* p. 88. Emphasis in original.

13. *Ibid.,* pp. 187–90.

14. Lester W. Milbrath, *Political Participation: How and Why Do People Get Involved in Politics?* (Chicago: Rand McNally and Company, 1965), p. 39.

15. Arthur R. Cohen, *Attitude Change and Social Influence* (New York: Basic Books, 1964), p. 23. Emphasis in original.

16. William J. McGuire, "Persuasion, Resistance, and Attitude Change," in Ithiel de Sola Pool, Wilbur Schramm, *et al.* (eds.), *Handbook of Communication* (Chicago: Rand McNally, 1973), p. 230.

17. *Ibid.,* pp. 231–32.

18. Carl I. Hovland, Irving L. Janis, and Harold H. Kelley, *Communica-

tion and Persuasion: Psychological Studies of Opinion Change (New Haven: Yale University Press, 1953), pp. 134–44.

19. *Ibid.*, p. 153.

20. *Ibid.*, p. 154.

21. Samuel A. Stouffer, *Communism, Conformity and Civil Liberties: A Cross-Section of the Nation Speaks Its Mind* (Gloucester, Mass.: Peter Smith, 1963).

22. *Ibid.*, especially chap. 2.

23. Elihu Katz and Paul F. Lazarsfeld, *Personal Influence: The Part Played by People in the Flow of Mass Communications* (New York: The Free Press, 1955), pp. 51–53.

24. *Ibid.*, p. 105.

25. Lewis A. Froman, Jr., *People and Politics: An Analysis of the American Political System* (Englewood Cliffs, N.J.: Prentice-Hall, 1962), pp. 41–42.

26. Katz and Lazarsfeld, *Personal Influence,* pp. 309–20; *see also* Paul F. Lazarsfeld, Bernard Berelson, and Hazel Gaudet, *The People's Choice: How the Voter Makes Up His Mind in a Presidential Campaign,* 3rd ed. (New York: Columbia University Press, 1968), pp. 151–52. For a critique of the two-step model of communications, *see* Everett M. Rogers, "Mass Media and Interpersonal Communication," in Pool, *et al.* (eds.), *Handbook of Communication,* pp. 294–95. The fundamental criticism of this model is that communications flows are more complicated than the two-step process implies. An explication of a "multi-step flow model" is found, *ibid.,* p. 296.

27. Lazarsfeld, Berelson, and Gaudet, *The People's Choice,* pp. 153–54.

28. Earl Mazo, *The Great Debates* (Santa Barbara: Center for the Study of Democratic Institutions, 1962), pp. 4–5.

29. V. O. Key, Jr., *Public Opinion and American Democracy* (New York: Alfred A. Knopf, 1964), p. 344.

30. Robert D. McClure and Thomas F. Patterson, "Television News and Voter Behavior in the 1972 Presidential Election" (Paper delivered at the Annual Meeting of the American Political Science Association, New Orleans, September 4–9, 1973, p. 19). Emphasis in original.

31. A popular work that treats this aspect of communications extensively is Marshall McLuhan and Quentin Fiore, *The Medium is the Massage* (New York: Random House, 1967).

32. Data Source: Center for Political Studies, University of Michigan.

33. *Ibid.* Does not equal 100% because of rounding.

34. Key, *Public Opinion,* pp. 347–50.

35. *Ibid.,* pp. 348–49; 357–58.

36. M. Kent Jennings and Richard G. Niemi, "Patterns of Political Learning," *Harvard Educational Review* 38 (Summer 1968): 450–51.

37. Joseph T. Klapper, *The Effects of Mass Communication* (New York: The Free Press, 1960), p. 8. *See also* Walter Weiss, "Effects of the Mass Media of Communication," in Gardner Lindzey and Elliot Aronson (eds.), *Handbook of Social Psychology,* vol. 5 (Reading, Mass.: Addison-Wesley, 1968), pp. 77–195.

38. Gabriel A. Almond, "Introduction: A Functional Approach to Comparative Politics," in Almond and Coleman (eds.), *Politics of Developing Areas,* pp. 45–52.

39. *Ibid.,* p. 50.

40. This term derives from the Greek root, suggesting "steersman" or "governor." *See* Norbert Weiner, *Cybernetics: Or Control and Communication in Animal and the Machine* (New York: The Technology Press of M.I.T. and John Wiley and Sons, 1948), p. 19.

41. Karl W. Deutsch, "Communication Theory and Political Integration," in Philip E. Jacob and James V. Toscano (eds.), *The Integration of Political Communities* (Philadelphia: J.B. Lippincott Company, 1964), pp. 49–51. A more elaborate description of the linkage between control and communications may be found in Deutsch, *The Nerves of Government,* pp. 75–142.

42. Deutsch, in Jacob and Toscano (eds.), *Integration of Political Communities,* p. 49.

43. Karl W. Deutsch, *Nationalism and Social Communications: An Inquiry Into the Foundations of Nationality* (New York: The Technology Press of M.I.T. and John Wiley and Sons, 1953). For a thorough critique of the means by which Deutsch imputes different meanings to nationalism and related concepts, *see* Walker Connor, "Nation-Building or Nation-Destroying?" *World Politics* 24 (April 1972): 319–55.

44. Deutsch, *Nationalism and Social Communications,* pp. 139–40.

45. Karl W. Deutsch, "Transaction Flows as Indicators of Political Cohesion," in Jacob and Toscano (eds.), *Integration of Political Communities,* pp. 75–97.

46. For a thorough review, *see* Frederick W. Frey, "Communication and Development," in Pool *et al.* (eds.), *Handbook of Communication,* pp. 337–461.

47. *See* Leonard W. Doob, "Goebbels' Principles of Propaganda," *Public Opinion Quarterly* 14 (Fall 1950): 419–42.

48. Ithiel de Sola Pool, "Communication in Totalitarian Societies," in Pool, *et al.* (eds.), *Handbook of Communication,* p. 465.

49. *See* especially Alan P. L. Liu, *Communication and National Integration in Communist China* (Berkeley: University of California Press, 1971).

50. Richard M. Johnson, *The Dynamics of Compliance: Supreme Court Decision-Making from a New Perspective* (Evanston, Ill.: Northwestern University Press, 1967).

51. *Engel* v. *Vitale*, 370 U.S. 421 (1962); *Abington School District* v. *Schempp*, 374 U.S. 203 (1963).

52. Johnson, *Dynamics of Compliance*, p. 8.

53. *Ibid.*, p. 16.

54. *Ibid.*, p. 42.

55. *Ibid.*, pp. 55–57.

56. *Ibid.*, p. 58.

57. Eugene J. Meehan, *Contemporary Political Thought: A Critical Study* (Homewood, Ill.: The Dorsey Press, 1967), p. 329. The estimate of 10^{50} by V. H. Yngve is cited by Mortimer Taube, *Computers and Common Sense* (New York: McGraw-Hill Book Co., 1961), p. 29.

58. Deutsch, *The Nerves of Government*, pp. 79–80.

59. A work that stresses this in a broader focus than politics alone is Nan Lin, *The Study of Human Communication* (Indianapolis: Bobbs-Merrill, 1973).

60. Oran Young, *Systems of Political Science* (Englewood Cliffs, N.J.: Prentice-Hall, 1968), p. 60.

61. *Ibid.*

62. North, in Charlesworth (ed.), *Contemporary Political Analysis*, pp. 315–16.

STUDY QUESTIONS

1. What do the following mean? What is their importance in the study of political behavior?
   message
   encoding and decoding
   communications channels
   two-step flow

2. How can the study of communications relate to the following approaches?

personality	groups
attitudes, beliefs, opinions, and values	decision making
political socialization	systems
role	

3. What is the relevance of the mass media to political behavior?

4. What can the study of political communications tell us about political systems?

5. What data-collection techniques may be pertinent to the study of communications? Specify, indicating the level at which communications may be examined.

CHAPTER

12

Theory and Politics

How does political science advance from approaches to theory to genuine theory?* If we wish to develop theories of politics that describe and explain political behavior, how might we best proceed?

At some point, the connections between generalizations developed by studying specific research problems become apparent, and broader generalizations result. Careful and comparative consideration of explicit problems is the most appropriate theory-building strategy. The first step toward building a theory is to repeatedly test specific hypotheses in order to establish scientific laws. Middle-range theories then could be developed by combining related generalizations into a set of generalizations of broader scope.[2]

We have considered eight major approaches to the development of theory in political science. How can they be used in the study of specific research problems? What is the utility of each? Each cannot be used to study all problems; the appropriate theoretical approach is dictated by the nature of the research problem. Systems analysis and decision-making analysis are more appropriate for studying the behavior of social systems, while attitude or personality approaches are generally more useful for study of individual political behavior. One can be interested, however, in comparing political systems in terms of the distribution of attitudes among individuals who are its members. The political socialization of individuals is

---

*We have previously suggested that "a theory is a group of laws, usually rather few in number, from which others, usually a larger number, have actually been deduced and from which one expects to deduce still further ones. The laws that serve as the premises of these deductions are called axioms of the theory; those which appear as conclusions are called theorems."[1]

studied because it has consequences for the political system. (For example, subcultural variations in how people learn to support the political regime and community are related to political stability.)

The *data-collection method and the conceptual approach used depend on the research problem.* A limiting factor is the nature of the available data that can be collected to test hypotheses. Attitudinal data are not available to study patterns of support for an extremist political position in an election held 100 years ago, but census data do exist that would indicate residential patterns, allowing the researcher to examine group patterns of voting.

By what criteria should political scientists evaluate approaches to political analysis? Several guidelines can be stated. The most general is the *capability of the approach to contribute to the development of empirical theory,* theory that can explain and predict events or processes. Within this context, several other criteria have been used in criticism of various approaches. An approach must have well-defined concepts that are unambiguous but comprehensive. The *concepts should be operationally defined in a consistent manner.* Appropriate indicators should be used. Although we emphasize formulation of hypotheses, emphasis must also be placed on the *appropriateness of the data-collection method to the relevant concepts.* It should also be possible to make inferences in testing propositions, without referring to theory or concepts outside the approach being used. If that becomes necessary, then the approach needs to be reformulated.

Other criteria for evaluating an approach include its *capacity to stimulate research.* For example, little research has been based on the highly regarded group theory of politics.[3] Its heuristic value in stimulating empirical research and further theorizing has been limited. One therefore questions whether the group approach can significantly contribute to the development of empirical political theory. Finally, an approach should explain as much as possible as simply as possible.

A distinction was made earlier between macro theory and micro theory. Micro theory is used for analysis at the individual level; macro theory is used in the study of larger social units. One could argue that the primary focus of political science should be on the political system, that we should be concerned about individual behavior only if it helps to explain differences in system behavior over time or variations between different political systems. The need to relate micro-level analysis to macro-level concerns is acknowledged here.

An example of the problem of relating micro- to macro-level concerns is the attempt to correlate individual voting behavior to policy outputs and system processes. We can focus first upon variables such as an individual's interest in politics, sense of civic duty, sense of political effectiveness, party image, identification with a party, and social group characteristics. These individual characteristics can then be related to generalizations about system-level differences.

One work focuses on the extent to which the connection between class position and voting behavior is reinforced by loyalties based on religion or region.[4] Region was defined as a subnational territory with potential to create loyalties and to become the focus of political conflict. Regional loyalties, rather than social-class ones, were the focus of political loyalty in this study. The South in the United States, Wales and Scotland in Great Britain, and Quebec in Canada are examples of such regions. To examine the class basis of voting, the author used party preferences in voting in national elections; he obtained data for this variable from survey interviews conducted between 1936 and 1960 for the United States and for shorter time periods for Australia and Great Britain.[5] Occupation was used as a measure of social class, divided into manual and nonmanual occupations.[6] This categorization is an objective one; i.e., it does not measure the individual's perception of his social class, or the possibility of incongruence between other indicators of social class.

The author views policy differences between parties on a representative left–right continuum, and he categorizes political parties as parties of the left or of the right in each of the four countries studied. The measure of class voting, then, is the difference in support given by nonmanual workers to parties of the left.* For example, if 75 percent of the manual workers vote for parties of the

---

*The author of this study had to resolve several definitional problems. One was the definition of nonwage earners who were included in the survey samples, such as retirees, housewives, and students. Another was to establish criteria for defining parties of the left that could be applied cross-nationally. A third was to determine which political office was to be used as a measure of the dependent variable, "party voted for."

left and only 35 percent of the nonmanual workers support left parties, the index of class voting is 40 percent. The study had the following results:

	Percent Supporting Parties of the Left
Manual Workers	75%
Nonmanual Workers	35
Index of Class Voting	40%

The level of class voting over time within each country and between countries was examined, as well as the level of class voting by region and by religion in the four countries studied. The highest level of class voting was found in Great Britain, followed by Australia, the United States, and Canada. The level of class voting in the United States has fluctuated over time; for the period studied, it was lowest in the South. Class voting varied with religious affiliation, with class voting occurring least often among Catholics.

The relationship between a number of other variables and levels of class voting show several interesting patterns. For example, localism and informal bases for political action are seemingly greater in countries with lower levels of class voting. Countries with higher levels of class voting have mass-based, bureaucratic parties. The degree of centralization of control is positively associated with the level of class voting; as class voting increases, so does centralized control. Which is the cause and which is effect are other questions. Differences between social classes in the sense of political efficacy and levels of political participation are greater in countries with low levels of class voting. The nonrational, particularistic aspects of politics, such as patronage, graft, and voting on the basis of a candidate's race or religion are more prevalent in countries with low levels of class voting.

This study collected information about individuals through surveys of samples of eligible voters in order to construct indicators of group behavior (i.e., patterns of voting by occupation, religion, and region). These indicators were used to explain differences in other aspects of political behavior at the system and the individual level. Of course, the generalizations are limited to the time span and to the countries studied.[7]

An error in inference must be avoided when moving from the micro-level of analysis to the macro-level, and vice versa. One cannot infer that the relationship among individual characteristics is the same as that present in group data. Aggregate data may show that counties with higher levels of blue collar workers are also more supportive of a particular candidate in an election. But this does not necessarily mean that blue collar workers were the most supportive of that candidate. Other inferential fallacies are also possible, such as generalizing from individual relationships to collective ones. One cannot assume that the nation with the most persons ranking high in achievement motivation will have the most rapid economic development.

Other inferential fallacies include the selection of data to substantiate one's preferred findings. Generalizing findings from one historical period, geographical situation, or environmental context to another also cannot be valid. One cannot assume that all the relevant conditions prevalent in the first period, situation, or context are present in the situation with which it is being compared. For example, the conditions surrounding the undeclared war in Korea in the 1950s were not precisely the same as the conditions surrounding the undeclared war in Vietnam in the 1960s and 1970s.

APPLYING APPROACHES TO RESEARCH PROBLEMS

How can various approaches be used to study policy and political problems? To illustrate, we will examine their use or potential for use in the study of the following problems: (1) the variations between policies at different levels of government; (2) the development of and change in party systems and voter alignments; and (3) political power and poverty in modern society.

Research Problem: Comparative Policy Outputs

How can one account for policy differences between units of government? What are the effects of legislative malapportionment, absence of party competition, or a low tax base on state or local politics? Can the methods and theoretical bases used to study such problems in the

United States be used for cross-national analysis or for studies of policy outputs in other countries?

Until recently, political scientists tended to assume that policy outputs—such as type of support for education, welfare, or transportation programs—differed between states such as Mississippi and Ohio in part because Mississippi was a one-party state and Ohio had strong two-party competition. These assumptions have been challenged by research indicating that variations in policy outputs of the states are in large part a product of the level and pattern of economic development of the state, rather than of its political system or political process.

Research on policy patterns uses systems theory. Figure 12–1 is a systems model formulated by Dawson and Robinson to show the "flow" involved in making policy.

In their definition of concepts in the model, policy includes the goals of the political system, the means by which the goals are implemented, and the consequences of the means selected. Process is the interaction between subsystem components over time. The political system is the "group of functionally interrelated variables whose task is the authoritative allocation of values for a given society."[8] The explicit hypothesis tested by Dawson and Robinson was "the greater the degree of inter-party competition within a political sys-

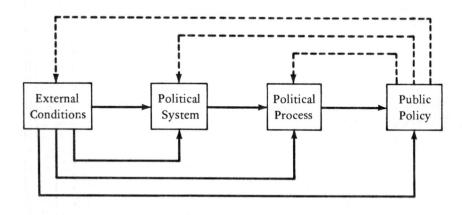

- - - - - Feedback

FIGURE 12–1

The Development of Public Policy (Richard Dawson and James Robinson, "Inter-Party Competition, Economic Variables, and Welfare Policies in the American States," *Journal of Politics* 25 [1963], p. 266. By permission.)

tem, the more liberal the social welfare measures that system will adopt."[9]

The next step in the research process was to specify the operational definitions of the concepts. The political systems examined by Dawson and Robinson were forty-six of the fifty states. Interparty competition was viewed as having three components: the time span over which competition is studied; the significant offices for which the degree of competition is evaluated; and the way in which competition is measured. The time span selected for their study was the period from 1938 to 1958, and the significant offices were the governorship, the upper house, and the lower house of the state legislature. Three variables were used as indicators of interparty competition: states were ranked in terms of the percentage of popular vote for governor received by the predominant party in the state, and the percentage of seats held by the majority party in both houses. The three percentages were then averaged and each state assigned a rank on the basis of that average. For each of the three institutions (governor, House of Representatives, and Senate), the percentage of the times that the majority party was in control was obtained, the three percentages were averaged, and a rank assigned. The percentage of time that control of the three institutions was split between the two parties was computed, and a rank order assigned. These three variables were the indices of interparty competition.

To measure social welfare policies, nine measures of revenue and expenditure patterns for each state were ranked, such as the percentage of state revenue derived from death and gift taxes, average per-pupil expenditure for education, and average payment per recipient of aid for the blind. Three ordinal measures of external conditions were used: the rank order of each state's per-capita income; the rank order of the percentage employed in occupations other than agriculture, forestry, and fishing; and the rank order of the proportion of the state's population residing in urban areas.

To test the hypotheses, rank-order correlation measures were used to examine the association between each of the measures of party competition and the measures of policies, between measures of external conditions and of party competition, and between external conditions and welfare policies. The relationship implied by their research findings is presented in Figure 12-2. In other words, policy and party competition were functions of external conditions.[10]

Now let us return to Figure 12-1. Does the hypothesis state a relationship implied in the theoretical model? If it does, is interparty

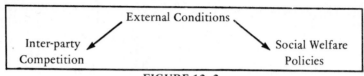

FIGURE 12–2

Party Competition and Social Welfare Policies

competition a measure of the political system or of the political process? The authors say that process is the interaction of the system's subcomponents, and that the political system refers to "that group of functionally inter-related variables whose task is the authoritative allocation of values for a given society."[11] An intervening set of variables (external conditions) is left out of this analysis. A complex system of interacting relationships also has been left out of the analysis, since feedback processes are ignored completely.

Critique of the Research.   Have the researchers operationally defined and measured the concepts in their hypothesis? Why measure party competition at an ordinal level when the variable can be measured at a higher level? When one averages several separate measures of interparty competition, to what extent are the phenomena distorted? The authors also assume that the three component parts contribute equally to interparty competition, and this assumption is questionable.

The findings of Dawson and Robinson stimulated a number of other studies of policy outputs and their relationship to environmental and political characteristics of government units. These studies illustrate the problems of theory building through careful, rigorous, and replicative hypothesis-testing. Most studies continue to be based on an oversimplified systems model, which incorrectly identifies socioeconomic variables as input variables (*see* Figure 12–3).

Inputs must be measured in terms of demands made, not in terms of potential for demands and supports that may be reflected by socioeconomic characteristics of government units. One must question whether environmental conditions are operationally mea-

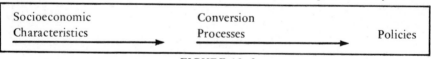

FIGURE 12–3

A Simple Systems Policy Model

sured by standard indices such as income level, occupational and urbanization pattern, educational attainment, and ethnic composition. Significant intervening variables, such as social structure, political culture, institutional arrangements, elite attitudes, values, and perceptions also are ignored in the policy studies.

Furthermore, systems models emphasize the role of many feedback processes, but feedback is virtually ignored in the policy studies. With few exceptions, studies of policy outputs have also ignored the time dimension. Studies of change in policy over time can help clarify the nature of the relationships between environment, system, process, and policy. For example, one study has examined the relationship of socioeconomic variables to policy outputs in the states over a seventy-year span. Two relatively stable socioeconomic indices emerged, one reflecting industrialization and the other cultural enrichment. However, these two indices varied in their relationship to expenditure patterns during the seventy-year period, with the industrialization measure fluctuating not only in magnitude, as did the cultural enrichment variable, but also in the positive and negative nature of the relationship.[12]

The relationships between theory, hypothesis, concept, data measurement, and inference are subject to other criticisms. Operationalization of political system characteristics is inadequate; among the system aspects that should be more extensively considered are the organization of the executive and the legislature, the roles and strength of interest groups, intergovernmental linkages among federal, state, and local systems, and party system characteristics.[13] Community power research also has indicated that the same policy processes probably do not operate in all policy areas.[14] Studies of the budgetary process also indicate that budgetary changes are incremental; major shifts occur as a result of change in control of significant political positions, such as the assumption of office by a president or governor with different policy priorities.[15]

Problems are presented by the statistical methods frequently used in data analyses. Inferences of causality cannot be made from correlation and regression analyses of cross-sectional data. State policies undoubtedly have consequences for state politics. If a state votes special tax preferences to industry of such a level that the state achieves a competitive advantage over other states, it can attract industry and increase its industrial development. This would probably also result in increased urbanization. Making causal inferences from correlational analysis of cross-sectional data is statistically and logically fallacious. Methods do exist to derive causal inferences, and more sophisticated studies have made use of these.[16]

Another problem in policy outputs studies, which probably contributes to different findings, is the failure to use a common definition of expenditure variables. Some studies focus only on state expenditures, while others include state and local expenditures for such services as education. Critics have suggested that both types of expenditures be considered.[17] The distribution of benefits also has an impact on policies, but this has not generally been considered in research efforts. For example, is a state's gasoline tax revenue based on miles of existing state highways, which might tend to be more beneficial to rural counties, or is it based on population density, which benefits urban core areas more? Is state aid to elementary and secondary education based on need or on a local area's ability to match state monies? Expenditures, which are policy outputs, must be considered in terms of who benefits from that policy.

Environmental variables may set the boundaries within which expenditures or other policy outputs can vary, but the actual policy alternatives that exist are a consequence of other factors. For example, the revenue-raising structure of a state is a most significant and politically potent element of a state's policy outputs. The income levels and distribution of income, amount and structure of real and personal property, and retail sales set boundaries, but the extent of the state's reliance on any of these for revenue is a political choice. Socioeconomic characteristics establish boundaries; political values determine which revenue sources will be selected.

Other criticisms have been made of comparative state and local policy studies. State expenditure increases found by studies are logically and statistically invalid. The existence of a correlation between expenditures at Time 1 and expenditures at Time 2 is not adequate evidence of an incremental strategy by decision makers. Decision makers may allocate funds to state agencies as an increment over what the agency received the preceding year. What is needed is precise analysis of year-to-year changes in state expenditures and not a gross analysis of changes for every five- or ten-year period. A state's relative capabilities and its actual allocations may vary considerably from year to year. Incrementalism must be established, not assumed, and established by analysis of year-to-year changes in allocations to particular agencies or programs. A pattern of incrementalism is descriptive of a process of change, but it does not explain major changes in expenditure levels. Changes in environmental variables may not be strongly related to changes in outputs. This raises further questions regarding conclusions about incrementalism in state policy outputs.[18]

Studies of policy outputs have relied almost exclusively on data, such as census data or state budget and revenue data, collected for aggregated populations. Are aggregate data adequate for testing the systems models underlying policy outputs? Some researchers have concluded that they are not and have incorporated other types of data into their research. Demand measures, based on sample survey studies of elite perceptions, attitudes, values, or behavior can be used to measure process variables or to evaluate intervening variables.[19]

Although policy includes the type and quality of programs a government unit operates, policy studies have tended to rely too heavily on revenue and expenditure patterns as indicators of the kind and quality of programs. This probably has been overemphasized because of the problem of measuring program characteristics. How, for example, can one measure state differences in civil rights programs? One proposed solution is to measure them as one would a set of attitudes, treating the absence of a particular program as a negative response to an attitude. The resulting configuration can be examined to see if it forms a pattern and, if so, variables associated with the pattern can be found.[20] The importance of various factors to account for policy differences between government units is also a function of the type of policy being evaluated. Revenue and expenditure patterns may vary more with economic development or tax base, while policies, such as election laws, protection of civil rights, uses of police power, or permissible forms of local government, vary more with the political system or the political process.

One researcher has argued that distinctions should also be made between public policy, policy outputs, and policy impacts. He distinguishes among them in this way:

> Public policy represents actions taken by the government; policy outputs represent the service levels which are affected by these actions; and policy impacts represent the effect which the service has on a population.[21]

337

The environment thus represents the "social, economic, and political surroundings," which supply the impetus for public policy and are affected by its impact.[22]

Other examples can be cited. Suppose that a state government fails to enact policies demanded by a particular group. If the issue is salient to the group and its members become sufficiently aroused, the group might support candidates of another political party. For example, Catholic white collar workers who normally support the Democratic party in a northern industrial state have lobbied unsuccessfully for years with the Democratic-controlled legislature for state aid to children attending parochial schools. A number of Republican candidates support the Catholics' position and gain substantial and continuing support from Catholic white collar workers. These Catholics gradually come to consider themselves Republicans. In effect, policy outputs have affected the political process by causing party realignment.

Although our primary focus has been on outputs at the state level, others are possible. One can compare cities, states and cities, and government units in different countries. Such analyses could explain the effects on policy outputs of variations in environment, policy demands, and government processes and institutions.

Other approaches to comparative policy outputs have been used in conjunction with systems theory. The progression from theory to hypothesis statement to hypothesis testing has been accompanied by a number of problems involving concept definition, operational measurement, data analysis, and inference. The appropriateness of a theoretical approach to the study of policy patterns can be adequately evaluated only when these problems are resolved and further research is conducted.

Research Problem: Party Systems and Voter Alignments

How can we best describe and explain the development and activities of political parties? What accounts for the differences in party systems in developed nations? What variables can explain differences in participation rates, party types, and party systems of nations that have come into being since World War II? How can we account for changes in the American party system?

A number of different approaches have been used with varying degrees of success to explain the evolution of party systems. One set of analyses of party system development and voter alignments combines Parsons' structural–functional analysis, group theory, and attitudinal analysis. Parsons asserted that four functions must be performed by any social system: adaptation, integration, goal attainment, and pattern maintenance.[23] Four subsystems perform these functions, and six types of interchanges exist. The party system's evolution is a consequence of three of these interchanges: between the integrative and goal attainment subsystems, between the integrative and pattern maintenance subsystems, and between the pattern maintenance and goal attainment subsystems.[24] The first involves patterns of competing parties; the second, membership in various groups in society and the readiness of these groups to be mobilized; and the third, representative processes.

The process of nation building presents four institutional problems that must be overcome in the development of a modern nation-state. The first of these, legitimation, refers to effective recognition of the right to criticize, oppose, petition, and demonstrate against a regime. The second, incorporation, refers to granting to the political opposition the right to participate in political processes. Representation, the third institutional problem, is overcome when those who oppose the regime obtain the right to serve in the legislature. The final problem, majority power, refers to overcoming the immunity of the executive from legislative influence. The timing of overcoming the barriers to solving these problems and the magnitude of the barriers have considerable influence on the nature of the party system. For example, a nation with few barriers to legitimation and incorporation of political opposition, but with many barriers to representation of political opposition, tends to have a separation of executive and legislative power and a competitive party system that rewards successful alliances. This describes the American party system. Low thresholds for legitimation and incorporation, a high barrier to representation, and a moderate barrier to legislative influence over the executive describes the system in Great Britain.[25]

The development of political parties in Western European nations can be viewed as a result of the timing, sequence, and intensity of effects of four critical conflicts in the process of nation building. These four conflicts were between the dominant and one or more subcultures; between the church and the interests of the state; between the primary elements of the economy, such as agriculture, and the secondary elements of the economy, i.e., industry; and between workers and employers, a final outgrowth of the Industrial Revolution. Nation building was a three-phased process in Western Europe; during the first phase, efforts were made by a nation-building elite to penetrate and standardize areas of disputed control between the state and the church interests. Conflict in the society ensued from such efforts. In the second phase, a variety of alliances were formed to support and to oppose these efforts at centralization. The outgrowth of these efforts at national integration was a shifting focus to goal attainment, with efforts focused on gaining some measure of political control to achieve specified ends. Accompanying these efforts were reforms and extensions of the right to vote, changes in electoral procedures, and extensions of the area in which the national legislature exercised its law-making power. The nature of Western European party systems is a function of the timing of various conflicts and the way in which conflicts were assimilated by the political system.[26]

The conflicts between elites and peripheral powers and between church and state characterize national revolutions in Western Europe, and the conflicts between urban and landed interests and between employers and workers characterize the Industrial Revolution. The most crucial conflict in the development of party systems in Europe was between the nation-state and the church; in most modern countries, the key conflict has been between workers and employers, or in the adaptive subsystem. Another modern conflict has been in the goal attainment sector of society, primarily focusing on an attack on the elites of the society. One can view the rise of National Socialist and Fascist parties in these terms.[27]

The scheme used to analyze the development of party systems in Western European countries does not provide operational definitions of the key concepts, thus impeding application of this analytical approach to the study of the development of non-Western European party systems. The utility of the scheme is also limited by the failure to consider the functions of parties and political movements, other than considering them as vehicles for the expression of conflict.

Another approach to analysis of the development of party systems focuses on structural characteristics alone. Expansion of suffrage, the complexity and divisiveness of a social structure, the existence of a unitary as opposed to a federal political system, the structure of legislative and executive power, and the nature of the electoral laws are viewed as determining the number and type of political parties and the ease with which new parties arise within a political system.[28]

Group and attitudinal approaches have been used to study party systems and voter alignments in the United States. Attitudinal studies have focused on character and extent of attachment to specific political objects, such as political parties and office-holders or candidates for office. The frequency with which certain issue stands are held, as well as their saliency and intensity, are also studied. Beliefs and attitudes of individual citizens have been used to analyze voter alignments. Key variables are a voter's party identification, his party image, his concerns with issues and policy preferences (his issue orientation), and his preferences for a candidate or set of candidates (his candidate orientation). Other attitudes, such as sense of political effectiveness, trust in others, the responsiveness he attributes to different levels of government, and his sense of civic duty also explain voter alignments and levels of political participation.

Concepts and propositions of group theory are also used, such as distribution of dependent and independent variables in the voter populations.[29] The relationship between historical events, their attitudinal consequences for groups in the population, and for voter alignments are also considered by some studies.[30] However, most research prior to the 1950s did not infer from data derived from survey research.

Earlier survey research on voting behavior conducted by sociologists focused on the group as a basis for analyzing political behavior. Research examined political affiliations, voting turnout, and the vote of categoric groups organized according to age, sex, region of the country in which a voter was raised, occupation, income, education, ethnic background, and religion. Small group theory also served as a basis for analysis, focusing attention on patterns of communication, opinion leadership, and voting cues.[31]

Attitudinal analysis of voter alignments presents certain problems. Behavior and attitudes may not be congruent; for example, a person may identify himself as a Republican, but consistently support the Democratic party's candidates. Electoral laws and the competitive nature of state party systems may distort the patterns of

341

party affiliation. The existence of a closed primary in a state may result in a disproportionate part of the population registering as party members. Hence, party identification would not reflect relevant attitudes. An individual may have different party identifications at the state, local, and national levels.[32] The data base for attitudinal studies is available only for a limited number of countries and only for more recent history. Data-based research using an attitudinal approach cannot be used for research into the origins and development of party systems.

Can Easton's system approach be used to analyze party systems and voter alignments? Does the input–output–feedback model permit one to incorporate political, social, legal, and personal variables to account for variations in party systems, which could not otherwise be integrated into an explanatory system? Easton's examination of the political system of the American South illustrates the usefulness (or lack of it) of a systems approach. What criteria are provided by Easton for the change-producing inputs of southern political systems? What testable hypotheses are presented about the relationships of types and levels of inputs and outputs, in this case, party systems and voter alignments?

Easton sees parties as structural mechanisms for handling conflicts within a society. Where competition is permitted by a regime, maximum inclusiveness of the population in the parties is encouraged by the party system. Electoral rules are considered a device to facilitate inclusiveness (or exclusiveness) of parties and to reduce support stress.[33] However, no testable hypotheses or operational definitions of key concepts are present. Making inferences about relationships on the basis of Easton's systems model is not possible.

Independently of Easton's conceptual framework, one can hypothesize that legal, economic, and political factors can limit or structure the inputs of supports and demands into the political system. Thus the use of literary tests and the poll tax and economic sanctions kept black voter registration low in the South. Another device used to exclude blacks from political participation was the white primary. The southern primary was essentially an activity of a private club, and the club had the right to limit participation to those it wished to admit as members. Other limiting factors on the input of demands into the southern political system were the commanding positions of southerners in national congressional and senatorial power structures. The chairmen of key committees controlling legislation that could effect changes in the structure of southern politics tended to be southerners. Federal intervention was excluded from the South by a party rule that required that the nomination for president by the Democratic convention be by a two-thirds majority. In effect until 1936, this rule gave effective veto power to the southern delegations over any candidate. These legal and political barriers to participation in the South began to be dissolved in the 1930s and 1940s. The white primary was overturned by the Supreme Court in 1944, the Twenty-fourth Amendment prohibiting poll taxes became effective in 1964, and the use of literacy tests as a discriminatory device to keep black citizens from registering to vote was successfully attacked by the Voting Rights Act of 1965. The filibuster as a means of keeping civil rights legislation from coming to a vote in the Senate was overcome during the process of enacting the Civil Rights Act of 1964. The ability of southern congressional committee chairmen to use their powers to prevent passage of civil rights legislation has been inhibited by writing legislation so that it can be sent to a committee that supports it; in the Senate, this has been curtailed by sending legislation to a committee with instructions to report it out by a specific date. Southern votes in the Electoral College ceased to be a factor when Franklin Roosevelt and other Democrats succeeded in obtaining a majority without the support of all the southern states. The legal and political factors that worked to keep the federal government from intervening in southern politics on behalf of the civil rights of blacks were removed by the late 1960s. Legal and political devices used by state and local governments in the South to prohibit black participation in politics have been thwarted by federal law and Supreme Court decisions. Supports and demands of black citizens can now enter the political system through electoral and political party activity.[34]

The input of demands by black citizens was not only inhibited by legal devices inhibiting their right to vote, but the malapportionment in southern and most other state legislatures worked to limit effective representation of blacks. The apportionment of the southern states tended to favor the more rural counties and particularly counties with the highest proportion of black citizens.[35] In counties with large black populations, concern for keeping the black man out of the political system was greatest.

Competition between the two parties was suppressed in the South because party competition would broaden the electorate, and racial segregation would be maintained by limiting party competition. Hence, southern politics had a different focus and a different pattern of voter alignment. Conflict occurred only within the Democratic party. In the absence of party competition in the general election, how was conflict structured in southern politics?

V. O. Key's classic study of the southern political systems, published in 1949, found several different patterns of southern politics. One pattern was personalism, a division of a state Democratic party into one dominant faction, with a changing coalition of interests and individuals opposing the dominant faction. The dominant faction generally centered around one individual such as Huey Long of Louisiana or Eugene Talmadge of Georgia. A second pattern was multifactional politics in the Democratic party; in this pattern coalitions were highly unstable, forming and regrouping in succeeding elections. Multifactional politics had a friends-and-neighbors aspect, with voting support based on personal acquaintance or name familiarity. A third pattern of southern politics was bifactionalism; in three southern states (Virginia, Tennessee, and North Carolina), there was a dominant faction with a minimum amount of issue orientation, and some semblance of Republican opposition. In Virginia the Byrd machine was opposed by a shifting coalition of interests based on ambition or issue opposition. Also present in these states was an active, but generally unsuccessful, Republican minority. Thus, prior patterns of political conflict structured a continuing pattern of party system characteristics, based on the presence or absence of personalities, issues, and party opposition.[36]

This study concluded that the alignments of voters in the South could be explained in part by the emphasis on one issue—race—rather than on economic issues. Economic issues dominated politics outside of the South and promoted competitive two-party politics.

When political and legal devices were overcome during the 1960s, minorities entered into political participation. Voting registration of black citizens increased from 250,000 in 1940 to 3,112,000 in 1968 or from 5 percent of the black voting age population to 62 percent in 1968.[37] As the South continues to industrialize and urbanize, race will be neutralized and no longer be the issue around which southern party politics is structured. The structuring of southern politics on the same bases as other areas of the country is also influenced by Supreme Court decisions striking down discriminatory practices that exist throughout the United States—practices including *de facto* school segregation and racial discrimination in housing, transportation, employment, and public accommodations. The enforcement of such decisions may increase the political impact of the issue in the short run, as demands to overturn decisions are presented by groups. In the long run, such decisions destroy the basis for an exclusionary and unique party politics in the South and bring to the front issues of concern to other areas of the country.[38]

Striking down southern laws and practices excluding black citizens from southern politics can be conceptualized as inputs from the environment and outputs of the larger political system (the United States) occurring as inputs into southern political systems. The consequences are the restructuring of southern politics, open access to southern political systems, new patterns of demands, and a further reshuffling of the patterns of conflict and of voter alignments.[39] We might expect changes to occur at different rates in southern political systems or different patterns of participation and voter alignment to result from lowering of legal barriers to participation, but no testable hypotheses are provided by Easton concerning the relationship between patterns of measured changes in inputs and measured changes in outputs (party systems and voter alignments).

Easton's systems theory has not contributed significantly to the analysis of party system development and change. The absence of operational definitions of key concepts and testable hypotheses in Easton's systems analysis does not qualify systems analysis to be a theory. The relationship between reductions of barriers to participation, increased political participation, and changes in southern political systems can be stated and tested without recourse to Easton's conceptual apparatus. The shifts in party systems and voter alignments can also be conceptualized as involving changed perceptions, cognitions, and attitudes on the part of actual and potential political participants. Patterns of reference group identification and group interaction change, and new party alignments occur. Analysis of the party system must also consider the impact of shifting campaign responsibilities from the party organization to professional campaign managers and increased reliance on manipulation of the mass media as a principal campaign technique. Other institutional changes, such as methods and mechanisms of campaign finance, have also occurred. These have significant consequences for the structure of the party and for the relative importance of political parties as linkage mechanisms between the government and the people.

345

Eastonian conceptual apparatus contributes little to the analysis of party politics. The specific types of demands and supports that result in party realignments are not suggested by Eastonian analysis, and no criteria for selection of relevant variables are presented. If an Eastonian-based analysis of inputs of demands and supports to southern political systems can be a focus, cannot one also concentrate on economic patterns of development, urbanization, and changes in mass media distribution and consumption as political and legal barriers to participation? In sum, Easton's systems approach does not adequately identify relevant variables, suggest and define useful concepts, provide operational definitions of the concepts, or provide testable hypotheses for research.

POLITICAL ANALYSIS AND PRACTICAL POLITICS

But, so what? By now the reader has been exposed to a host of elaborately overworked concepts, hypotheses, and analytic frameworks. Is there any practical use for all of this? Or is political science in an ivory tower, losing contact with reality, and slipping into a jargon and verbiage unique unto itself, with its own arcane mysteries fathomed only by the initiates?

A verbal anesthesia seems to have been developed by political scientists, who use terms that are not in the lexicon of the layman. *Rotated factor matrix, regime affect, stochastic models,* and *cognitive dissonance* are not terms bandied about in normal conversation, nor in the news media. Criticisms of the increasingly scientific approach to politics come from all sides and from within the discipline. One work focuses on such verbiage as we have described.[40] Every discipline develops its own jargon, whether justified or not.

"Questions for a Political Science Recruit" aptly concludes:

> Come now, can you operationalize,
> Quantify and conceptualize?
> Can your output be machine-read?
> Have you a code in your head?
> Are you adept at research design—
> Brother, can you paradigm?[41]

Actually, there are some very practical uses for the scientific approach to political science.*

Policy Planning as Applied Political Science

Empirical theory has been shown to be applicable to policy planning. All governments wish to ensure success for their policies, so they carefully scrutinized plans for cost, benefit, and long-range implications. This is one reason why the U.S. Census is so valuable to government planning experts. If one were developing an all-out attack on the problems of the inner-city, census data would be required to understand how many people might be affected, the number of inadequate housing units, the extent of unemployment, illiteracy, and disease. In short, it is better to argue from data than from mere conjecture.†

Planning also involves considering the possible outcomes of a policy. What has happened when such programs have been attempted elsewhere? Were the desired results achieved, and if not, why?

Data also can be used to enable policymakers to better predict what might happen, through the use of explanatory variables. An example of this might be the study of the impact on attitudes and behavior of a massive Office of Economic Opportunity anti-poverty program. The study was funded in an attempt to discern the various payoffs of such a program.[42] Of related interest is the study of the means by which the 1963 Community Health Center Act was implemented in several metropolitan areas. This study set forth the need for developing measures of effectiveness.[43] Planning of community programs should obviously try to take into account existing attitudes in the "target" community, before programs are imposed. Black attitudes in Watts after the 1965 riots were compared to those of white respondents to a survey. Blacks felt a greater disaffection with the government, and lowered feelings of political efficacy. Although there was no notable tendency toward "revolution," the riots apparently led to a greater pragmatism in the community,

---

*The one president of the United States who resigned his office in disgrace was reputedly fond of advising college students *not* to study political science.

†The *Pentagon Papers* and the results of policy planning for the Vietnam War reveal that the nature of data, as well as the values of the planners, can be open to question.

particularly in terms of the necessity of getting more blacks into positions of government responsibility.[44]

Planning with the assistance of empirical research need not be limited to domestic policies. "Deterrence," or the means by which one or more nations seek to deter another nation or group of nations from entering into armed conflict, has been studied.[45] The study examined factors that might make a credible deterrence policy by reviewing all cases over a three-decade period where a major power threatened to attack a small ally of another powerful nation. Using objective measures of importance to the major power, such as the minor nation's Gross National Product as a percentage of the major nation's GNP, economic and political interdependence of the minor nation, and the extent of major nation and smaller nation military cooperation, the researcher tested several extant hypotheses about deterrence. No single factor, such as strategic balance, was found to be "essential to deterrence. But as more [factors] are present the stronger mutual interdependence becomes, and the greater is the attacker's risk in pressing onward."[46] The research shows the distinct advantages of an empirical approach that uses inductive and deductive reasoning in order to legitimately test hypotheses.

A significant document on the making of foreign policy in the 1960s, by a political scientist who primarily uses inductive reasoning, offers a strategy for deterrence.[47] But is the research credible? Can the work be accepted on its face value, or should it be tested? When it has been tested, it has been found to lack validity.

In recent years, we have seen the development of numerous forecasting or prediction devices for domestic elections, such as the "Vote Profile Analysis," developed by pollster Louis Harris, and the National Broadcasting Company's election eve "projections." However, the candidate needs guidance in planning his campaign, which will give him the maximum number of votes to win. This guidance must come very early in the campaign, so that necessary adjustments in tactics and strategy can be made. In 1959, the Democratic Advisory Council engaged a group of political scientists from the Massachusetts Institute of Technology for that purpose. They formed a private corporation known as "Simulmatics"[48] and set about simulating the 1960 presidential election long before it took place, in order to advise Democratic planners.[49] They used poll data that were not current, but based upon voter preferences and perceptions on fifty-two "issue-clusters" in 1958. Voters were divided in 480 groups, based upon regional and socioeconomic characteristics. Their reactions were "simulated" on computers, using a statistical model to "predict" the election several months before it was held. Thirty-two states were ranked on the basis of how well Kennedy would do in the election. Democratic planners were especially interested in the extent to which Kennedy's religion would affect his chances. The researchers' examinations of voter perceptions of the religion issue were far more accurate than the state-by-state polls taken during the campaign. The simulation's results had a correlation of .82 with the actual results as compared to a much lower correlation (.53) between poll forecasts and the election returns.[50] And this was done using two-year-old data. After the election, the Simulmatics researchers found that their results were amazingly close to what actually happened; Kennedy received 322 electoral votes in the simulation, only eight more than he actually received.

> The mean deviation of the postdicted Democratic percentage of the party vote from the actual is but 9/10 of 1 percent in the 32 states of the North and but 6/10 of 1 percent for the country as a whole.[51]

The applicability of theoretical models and empirical political research to predicting election results seems legitimate, at least for those who can afford to pay for simulations. However, simulation techniques are not limited to elections. They are dependent upon the nature of a problem and the availability of data.

Simulation of elections may call for resources beyond the means of the average individual. Is there any practical use to which the reader of this text can put some of the recent developments in political science? We believe that this is entirely possible, and we turn now to how one may directly influence policy at a level that does not call for a great deal of resources.

In recent years, journals have reported results of significant research employing the role and systems approaches and focusing on attitudes, perceptions, and behavior of city councils. City councils have a great deal to say about the making of local policy. They are a logical starting point for those who want to confront urban problems. What knowledge can political science contribute to those who use pressure tactics on such a body?

A major study conducted over several years employed survey research, involving interviews with incumbent city councilmen in eighty-four cities of the San Francisco Bay area. From this study we can draw some useful information and suggestions on pressure tactics. The authors initially say that "there has been remarkably little cumulative knowledge about the components of group influence on policy outcomes."[52] Their preliminary report on this question is based on information from twenty-five cities. They hypothesize that the success of interest groups is highly dependent upon predispositions of councilmen and that access to these individuals is in large part a function of those predispositions. When asked why some groups are influential in the policy process, 84 percent of the councilmen responded on the basis of some characteristic connoting respect, such as intelligence or good name of the group, or the common sense displayed by the group. Only 31 percent mentioned a characteristic based upon an objective strength, such as the wealth or voting power of the group.[53] On the basis of their attitudes toward pressure groups, the councilmen were classified as "pluralists," "tolerants," or "antagonists." The "pluralists," those who most highly valued group contributions to the legislative process, felt interest groups contributed useful information and had the potential to mobilize support for proposals before the council. However, roughly 75 percent of the legislators were described as neutral or hostile to interest group activities, and the authors suggest that:

> It does not appear to matter greatly, in terms of the behavior we are describing, whether the councilman is neutral and relatively unaware, or hostile and highly aware, of the groups. *Unless groups are both salient and valued,* the political actor in the local community makes little effort to modify his behavior on their behalf.[54]

These orientations are not always a product of early socialization. They are apparently acquired as a result of personal experience with the legislative body, constituency, and party.[55] We may assume for the time that pressure activity offers no guarantee of success unless certain preconditions exist. Councilmen have to deal with their fellows as well as outside groups, and they are ultimately accountable to someone other than the interest group attempting to secure some end.

A major problem for urban planners is the increased involvement of all levels of government, that often work at cross-purposes. Governments often reflect entirely different styles because their constituent members differ; suburban governments may pursue policies contradictory to those of metropolitan governments. Using a broad variety of data relating to policy development in the Bay Area, one researcher again found that councilmen's perceptions play a key role in the process.

> There is in the councils of a metropolitan region such as that around the San Francisco Bay a satisfactory level of agreement on what the problems are that cities in different stages of development face, and there is very high agreement on what the city's future should be like. There is less agreement, as one might expect, on the specific policies that should be adopted to obtain the goals that are envisaged . . . [56]

A multiple approach to metropolitan problems would be concerned not only with what *ought* to be done, but with what *can* be done. Such an approach would have to account for the numerous preferences and biases among city councilmen throughout the region, in order to find a common ground within each council and within the region. To what extent is such an approach likely to succeed? Its success or lack of success is in part a function of the type of community involved. In larger cities, councilmen were more receptive to interest group activity than were their counterparts in smaller and more homogeneous cities.[57]

A strategy for influencing representative bodies is suggested by this study:

> It appears that members of the public dissatisfied with their representative assembly can intrude into its deliberations and force attentiveness in two ways at least, (1) by playing a role in determining who is selected to the representative body, and (2) by defeating incumbents when they stand for re-election . . . When, however, citizens do not exercise that control, allowing the assembly more or less to determine its own members and seldom unseating an incumbent, they thereby permit the representative group the privilege of defining for itself the goals and programs of the community.[58]

This is the conventional approach to electoral accountability. But does it work quite that simply? Individuals who leave office voluntarily may be unresponsive to normal electoral pressures. The reasons why councilmen or other officeholders might leave office without being instructed by the electorate to do so are many and complex. In such circumstances, those who leave office are often replaced by a

351

person who essentially agrees with his predecessor about public priorities.[59] Such individuals cannot be influenced through electoral processes. Pressure activity may be the only means by which the public can voice its demands.

Researchers in political science are constantly testing new hypotheses and new techniques and challenging old ones in areas of inquiry never considered amenable to empirical research. The development of scientific knowledge in any discipline proceeds by theory building and hypothesis testing. There are problems in organizing political science research across diverse fields such as international relations, voting behavior, comparative governments, and public administration. But the increasing relevance of political science bodes well for the future of the discipline. As knowledge accumulates and is further aggregated into a coherent whole, we can be better prepared to comprehend the subtleties of politics, to predict the consequences of alternative actions, and perhaps even to contribute to making better public policy.

NOTES AND REFERENCES

1. Gustav Bergmann, *Philosophy of Science* (Madison: University of Wisconsin Press, 1957), pp. 31–32.

2. Robert Merton, *Social Structure and Social Theory*, rev. ed. (Glencoe, Ill.: The Free Press, 1957), p. 280.

3. The group theory to which we refer may be found in David B. Truman, *The Governmental Process: Political Interests and Public Opinion* (New York: Alfred A. Knopf, 1951). *See also* the intellectual progenitor of Truman: Arthur F. Bentley, *The Process of Government* (Chicago: University of Chicago Press, 1908).

4. Robert R. Alford, *Party and Society* (Chicago: Rand McNally, 1963).

5. *Ibid.*, p. 71.

6. *Ibid.*, p. 74.

7. For a summary of this research and inferences based on it, *see* Alford, *Party and Society*, chaps. 10 and 11.

8. Richard Dawson and James Robinson, "Inter-Party Competition, Economic Variables, and Welfare Policies in the American States," *Journal of Politics* 25 (1963): 267.

9. *Ibid.*, p. 270.

10. *Ibid.*, p. 289.

11. *Ibid.*, p. 267.

12. Richard I. Hofferbert, "Socio-Economic Dimensions of the American States: 1890–1960," *Midwest Journal of Political Science* 12 (August 1968): 401–18.

13. Herbert Jacob and Michael Lipsky, "Outputs, Structure, and Power: An Assessment of Changes in the Study of State and Local Politics," *Journal of Politics* 30 (May 1968): 510–38.

14. *See* Robert Dahl, *Who Governs?* (New Haven: Yale University Press, 1961).

15. Otto Davis, M. A. H. Dempster, and Aaron Wildavsky, "A Theory of the Budgetary Process," *American Political Science Review* 60 (September 1966): 529–47.

16. James C. Strouse, "Politics, Economics, Elite Attitudes, and State Outputs: A Dynamic Analysis Using a Block Recursive Model" (Unpublished Ph.D. dissertation, University of North Carolina, 1970.)

17. James Dyson and Douglas St. Angelo, "Persistent Methodological and Theoretical Problems in Analysis of Policy Outputs," pp. 5–6; 10–11 (Paper presented at the Southern Political Science Association Meeting, Miami Beach, Florida, Nov. 8, 1969.) The failure to control for the impact of federal aid in certain areas of state expenditures, such as mass transportation, highways, education and welfare, also distorts the evaluations of the impact of state economic and political system variations on patterns of state expenditures.

18. *Ibid.*, p. 25.

19. *See* Strouse, *Politics, Economics, Elite Attitudes,* for the incorporation of measures of elite attitudes into analysis of expenditure patterns.

20. This method has been used in the analysis of state civil rights laws by Donald J. McCrone and Charles F. Cnudde. *See* their "On Measuring Public Policy" in Robert E. Crew, Jr. (ed.), *State Politics* (Belmont, Calif.: Wadsworth Publishing Co., 1968), pp. 523–30.

21. Ira Sharkansky, *Policy Analysis in Political Science* (Chicago: Markham Publishing Co., 1970), p. 63.

22. *Ibid.*

23. Stein Rokkan and Seymour Martin Lipset, "Cleavage Structures, Party Systems, and Voter Alignments: An Introduction," in Lipset and Rokkan (eds.), *Party Systems and Voter Alignments* (New York: The Free Press, 1967), pp. 1–64; Stein Rokkan, *Citizens, Elections, Parties* (New York: David McKay, 1970), chap. 3.

24. Rokkan and Lipset, "Cleavage Structures," in Rokkan and Lipset, *Party Systems,* pp. 6–9.

25. *Ibid.*, p. 27.

26. *Ibid.*, pp. 33–43.

27. *See* Rokkan and Lipset, "Cleavage Structures."

28. Leon Epstein, *Political Parties in Western Democracies* (New York: Frederick A. Praeger, 1967), chap. 2.

29. *See* Angus Campbell, Philip E. Converse, Warren E. Miller, and Donald E. Stokes, *The American Voter* (New York: John Wiley & Sons, 1960); Angus Campbell, Gerald Gurin, and Warren E. Miller, *The Voter Decides* (Evanston, Ill.: Row, Peterson and Co., 1954); Donald R. Matthews and James W. Prothro, *Negroes and The New Southern Politics* (New York: Harcourt, Brace, and World, 1966); Angus Campbell, Philip E. Converse, Warren E. Miller, and Donald E. Stokes, *Elections and the Political Order* (New York: John Wiley & Sons, 1966).

30. *See* Gerald M. Pomper, *Elections in America* (New York: Dodd, Mead and Co., 1968); V. O. Key, Jr., *Southern Politics* (New York: Random House, 1949).

31. *See* Paul Lazarsfeld, Bernard Berelson, and Hazel Gaudet, *The People's Choice* (New York: Columbia University Press, 1948); Bernard Berelson, Paul Lazarsfeld, and William N. McPhee, *Voting* (Chicago: University of Chicago Press, 1954); Lester Milbrath, *Political Participation* (Chicago: Rand McNally, 1965), chap. 5.

32. Philip E. Converse, "On the Possibility of Major Political Realignment in the South," in Campbell, Converse, Miller, and Stokes, *Elections and the Political Order,* p. 219.

33. For a discussion of the effects of the legal, social, and political impediments to political participation in the South and the types of political systems extant in the South in the mid-1940s, *see* V. O. Key, Jr., *Southern Politics.*

34. An excellent summary of the laws and decisions that effected these changes is contained in *Revolution in Civil Rights,* 4th ed. (Washington, D.C.: Congressional Quarterly Service, 1968).

35. V. O. Key, *Southern Politics,* pp. 308–09, footnote 12.

36. *Ibid., passim.*

37. Joe R. Feagin and Harlan Hahn, "The Second Reconstruction: Black Political Strength in the South," *Social Sciences Quarterly* 51 (June 1970): 47, Table 2.

38. For development of this argument, *see* James L. Sundquist, *Dynamics of the Party System* (Washington, D.C.: The Brookings Institution, 1973).

39. Samuel Lubell has argued that one cannot eliminate race as a basis for southern politics because court decisions, new laws, and social conflict have made desegregation the basic issue for politics throughout the country. The South has not acquired northern political patterns; rather, the North has acquired southern political patterns. *See* Samuel Lubell, *The Hidden Crisis in American Politics* (New York: W. W. Norton and Co., 1970). Argument can be made that party realignment involves redistributive issues. (Redistributive issues are issues that say that some people should gain advantages at the expense of other people.) Some authors reason that party realignments have been necessary to bring about redistributive government policies. With the growth of presiden-

tial power, however, party realignment may be less likely, because attention is beginning to focus largely on the presidency rather than congressional and state elections. This makes a thorough realignment of party orientation by voters less likely. *See* Carl D. Tubbesing, "Predicting the Present: Realigning Elections and Redistributive Policies," *Polity* 7 (Summer 1975): 478–503.

40. Betty H. Zisk, "The Compleat Jargoner: How to Obfuscate the Obvious Without Half Trying," *Western Political Quarterly* 23 (March 1970): 55–56.

41. Inis L. Claude, Jr., *P.S.*, III (Winter 1970): 47.

42. At this writing, the results of this type of study are still fragmentary and reported largely by unpublished papers delivered at annual meetings of professional associations. They include: Lester W. Milbrath, "The Nature of Political Beliefs and the Relationship of the Individual to the Government" (Midwest Political Science Association meeting, Chicago, Ill., May 2–3, 1968); *idem.*, "The Impact of Social Change Problems upon the Poor" (American Political Science Association meeting, New York City, Sept. 2–6, 1969); Everett M. Cataldo, Richard M. Johnson, and Lyman A. Kellstedt, "Political Attitudes of the Urban Poor: Some Implications for Policy Making (American Political Science Association meeting, Washington, D.C., Sept. 3–7, 1968).

43. Robert H. Connery *et al.*, *The Politics of Mental Health: Organizing for Community Mental Health in Fragmented Metropolitan Areas* (New York: Columbia University Press, 1969); Charles H. Backstrom, "Social Indicators: Local Community Response to National Programs" (Unpublished paper prepared for delivery at the annual meeting of the American Political Science Association, Washington, D.C., Sept. 3–7, 1968.)

44. David O. Sears, "Black Attitudes toward the Political System in the Aftermath of the Watts Insurrection," *Midwest Journal of Political Science* 13 (November 1969): 515–44.

45. Bruce M. Russett, "The Calculus of Deterrence," *Journal of Conflict Resolution* 7 (June 1963): 97–109.

46. *Ibid.*, p. 109.

47. Herman Kahn, *On Thermonuclear War* (Princeton, N.J.: Princeton University Press, 1960).

48. This group's work served as the basis for a rather sensationalized novel by Eugene Burdick, *The 480* (New York: McGraw-Hill, 1964).

49. *See* Ithiel de Sola Pool, Robert P. Abelson, and Samuel L. Popkin, *Candidates, Issues, and Strategies: A Computer Simulation of the 1960 and 1964 Presidential Elections* (Cambridge: The M.I.T. Press, 1964), especially chap. 1, upon which the following discussion is based.

50. *Ibid.*, pp. 56–57. A correlation of .82 is quite high, the upper limit being 1.00.

51. *Ibid.*, p. 109.

52. Betty H. Zisk, Heinz Eulau, and Kenneth Prewitt, "City Council-

men and the Group Struggle: A Typology of Role Orientations," *Journal of Politics* 27 (August 1965): 618–46. The following discussion relies upon this article. *See also* Betty H. Zisk, *Local Interest Group Politics: A One-Way Street* (Indianapolis: Bobbs-Merrill, 1973).

53. Zisk, Eulau, and Prewitt, *Typology of Role Orientations*, p. 628.

54. *Ibid.*, p. 645. Emphasis in original.

55. Kenneth Prewitt, Heinz Eulau, and Betty H. Zisk, "Political Socialization and Political Roles," *Public Opinion Quarterly* 30 (Winter 1966–67), pp. 569–82.

56. Heinz Eulau and Robert Eyestone, "Policy Maps and Policy Outcomes: A Developmental Analysis," *American Political Science Review* 42 (March 1968): 143.

57. Kenneth Prewitt and Heinz Eulau, "Political Matrix and Political Representation: Prolegomenon to a New Departure from an Old Problem," *American Political Science Review* 63 (June 1969): 427–41.

58. *Ibid.*, p. 441.

59. Kenneth Prewitt, "Political Ambitions, Volunteerism, and Electoral Accountability," *American Political Science Review* 64 (March 1970): 14.

STUDY QUESTIONS

1. What approaches can be used to analyze public policy outputs and their impact within a country? To compare countries?

2. What approaches can be used to analyze changes in political systems within a nation and to compare nations?

3. Drawing from material covered in chapters 4 through 11, discuss the distinctions between micro theory and macro theory.

4. How, if at all, can political science contribute *to* the political world, without simply describing it? Will such a contribution bias a political scientist's findings?

Glossary

aggregate data Data that describe persons or events collectively

attitude A relatively enduring organization of interrelated beliefs that describe, evaluate, and advocate action with respect to an object or situation

behavioral approach An approach to the study of politics that advocates the development of systematic empirical theories of human behavior to explain political behavior

belief A generalization by an individual that describes or evaluates an object or a situation; for example, "I believe that all swans are white," or "I believe that single-member legislative districts are more fair than are multi-member districts."

boundaries Legal or permissible limits of action for any system or subsystem

categoric group An unorganized group whose members all share an attribute such as age, sex, or race

cognitive consistency Refers to the organization of beliefs, attitudes, and values in a meaningful, rational way: i.e., organized into structures that appear to be consistent to the individual holding beliefs, attitudes, and values

cognitive development theory Theory that views learning as the acquisition of cognitions (beliefs, attitudes, perceptions) and the modification of already acquired cognitions

cognitive dissonance theory A theory of attitude change that says that an individual will seek to avoid information and situations that reveal an inconsistency between his or her cognitions and what actually exists

component analysis A method used to examine the components of the independent variable of communication and the components of the dependent variable of attitude change

357

computer program A set of instructions for a computer, indicating what and how information is to be processed and how the results will appear (usually on a page printed by the computer)

concept A term that expresses in abstract form the essential characteristics of something or the relationship between things that are being studied. Examples of concepts used in political science include justice, power, vote, attitude, conflict, and decision.

content analysis The rigorous application of classification and description to textual material appearing in print

cross-pressures Attitudes, opinions, or beliefs that an individual perceives as conflicting

decision rules The implicit or explicit rules that guide the making of decisions

dependent variable The variable for which we seek an explanation. It may be an event, an attitude, or an aspect of behavior.

fact An empirically verifiable observation about the nature of reality on which agreement, at least in principle, can be achieved

feedback The process by which the consequences of actions, plans, and decisions are communicated so that corrective action can be taken, if necessary

generalizations See *propositions*

hypothesis The suggested relationship between variables. *See also* **null hypothesis**

inter-role conflict A conflict that occurs when an individual occupies two or more roles that have different role expectations

intra-role conflict A conflict that occurs when different role expectations are applied to an occupant of a role

longitudinal analysis The examination of a particular problem over time

marginal costs The costs of purchasing the last item, such as acquiring the most recent piece of information

marginal utility The worth or value of the last item, such as the most recent piece of information gained

message Any thought which is complete or stands by itself

motivation The process of energizing, regulating, and directing behavior

null hypothesis A statement of no relationship between variables

opinion A verbal expression of an attitude

paradigm A set of assumptions that structure the way a science studies its subject matter The paradigm defines the nature of the problems the science will study, the methods it will use, and the criteria for evaluation and judgment of the acceptability of research results.

personality An integrated set of emotional and behavioral characteristics that dispose an individual to act a certain way

political socialization The process of learning politically relevant attitudes or roles. Also, the process by which a political system or a group within the political system indoctrinates its members.

political system A system that consists of the government—which is the formal institutions and processes that make, execute, and enforce laws for a society—and of the activities of individuals, groups, and other institutions that affect or are related significantly to the government

politics The activities within the scope of and related to the political system

power A role relationship among two or more people, such that one can get the other or others to do that which might not otherwise be done

primary group A group in which there is relatively persistent face-to-face contact, such as one's family or work group

primary source An information source that provides raw data or information with which to make analyses

probability sample A type of sample often used in social research, in which all persons in the group under study have an independent and known chance of being included; that is, the probability of any one person being selected is known, and that probability is independent of the selection of any other person

propositions Statements of the relationships between concepts

reference groups A group to which people refer in developing their own opinions, attitudes, and beliefs

reliability The extent to which a measuring instrument produces consistent, precise, and accurate results

research design The written outline or guide to research that defines the problem to be studied, sets forth hypotheses, and says how the hypotheses will be studied

role A set of socially prescribed expectations that define how an individual holding a particular role should behave

role conflict The conflict that results when incompatible role expectations are applied

role socialization The process of learning expectations that others hold about a role

role system A set of related roles

salience The importance or significance of an object that is related to an attitude

scientific explanation The deduction of phenomena from a general theory and a set of facts known independently of the phenomena to be explained

secondary group An affiliative group in which there is little frequent, face-to-face contact

secondary source A source that repeats or analyzes information that has appeared elsewhere

social judgment approach An approach to attitude-change theory that says that an individual evaluates communications in terms of how closely the message conforms to his or her existing attitude position

social learning theory A theory that says learning is the process of associating stimuli with appropriate responses

statistical significance An arbitrary level of probability, usually set at .05 (5 times in 100), indicating the extent to which an observed relationship is likely to have occurred by chance

structured interview A type of interview that uses detailed questions, oriented toward specific topics

symbol An object of feelings or of actions directed not toward the object itself but toward that for which the object stands. A symbol may be verbal (such as "no taxation without representation" as a symbol for the right of self-government) or visual (such as the United States flag as a symbol for the nation).

tertiary group *See categoric group*

theory A set of laws that are related in a deductive manner, some having been deduced from others

unstructured interview A purposive interview of a probing nature, allowing follow-up on responses, according to the discretion of the interviewer

validity The extent to which accuracy is achieved in results of an empirical situation under study

value A belief that a particular goal or the means of achieving a goal is preferable to other goals, or to other means of achieving goals

value system A set of beliefs in which the relative worth of different goals and the means of achieving different goals is ranked

variable A property to which numbers can be assigned and which can stand for a concept in a theory

Author Index

Abelson, Robert P., 153, 154, 355
Adelson, Joseph, 183
Adorno, T. W., 127, 155
Agger, Robert E., 263, 269
Ahern, David, 185
Aiken, Michael, 125
Alford, Robert R., 352
Alger, Chadwick, 207
Alker, Hayward S., Jr., 94, 125
Allen, Vernon L., 206
Allinsmith, Beverly, 230
Allinsmith, Wesley, 230
Allport, Gordon, 123, 124
Almond, Gabriel, 126, 152, 155, 182, 184, 185, 187, 208, 231, 298, 299, 324
Anton, Thomas J., 269
Applegate, Albert A., 94
Apter, David, 152, 231
Aronson, Elliot, 126, 151, 154, 206, 324
Arterton, Christopher, 184
Asch, Solomon E., 127
Astin, John D., 298
Atkinson, J.W., 126

Bachrach, Peter, 41, 268, 269, 270
Backstrom, Charles H., 64, 95, 355
Baer, Michael, 208
Bakke, Wright, 124
Bales, Robert F., 62, 95, 298
Baratz, Morton S., 41, 268, 269, 270
Barber, James David, 124, 126, 127, 128, 208
Bay, Christian· 297
Beall, Lynette, 183
Bentley, Arthur F., 17, 352

Berelson, Bernard, 126, 152, 229, 323, 354
Bergmann, Gustav, 40, 41, 352
Berman, Daniel M., 230
Berry, Jeffrey M., 230
Bertalanffy, Ludwig von, 298
Bettelheim, Bruno, 124
Biddle, Bruce J., 206
Binder, Leonard, 299
Blalock, Hubert M., Jr., 16
Bowen, Don R., 229
Bowman, Louis, 186, 208
Boynton, G.R., 186, 207, 208
Braithwaite, R.B., 40
Brehm, Jack W., 153, 154
Brim, Orville G., Jr., 186
Brookes, Marilyn, 187
Brown, Roger, 126, 127, 154
Browning, Rufus, 126, 186
Bruck, H.W., 267
Bruner, Jerome, 96, 154
Buchanan, James M., 267, 268
Buchanan, William, 207
Bullitt, William C., 127
Burdick, Eugene, 355
Burnham, Walter Dean, 94
Burns, James MacGregor, 93

Campbell, Angus, 96, 125, 127, 128, 155, 230, 354
Carey, George W., 16
Cartwright, Darwin, 154
Cataldo, Everett M., 355
Chaffee, Steven, 185
Charlesworth, James C., 270, 322, 325
Cheesen, Eli S., 127
Childs, Arvin L., 126

Childs, Harwood, 152
Christie, R., 127
Clark, R.A., 126
Claude, Inis L., Jr., 355
Cnudde, Charles F., 353
Cohen, A.R., 154, 322
Cohen, Morris, 40
Coleman, J.S., 182, 231, 298, 299, 324
Collins, Barry, 154
Connery, Robert H., 355
Connor, Walker, 324
Converse, Phillip E., 95, 127, 151, 152, 155, 354
Conway, M. Margaret, 125, 184, 185
Coombs, Clyde, 152
Cooper, Homer C., 230
Coser, Lewis A., 231, 232
Crew, Robert E., Jr., 353
Crotty, William J., 208, 232

Dahl, Robert A., 15, 16, 17, 41, 207, 230, 268, 269, 297, 354
Dahlgren, Harold E., 184
Davies, James C., 125
Davis, Otis, 353
Dawson, Richard, 183, 184, 332, 352, 353
Dean, John P., 96
Debnam, Geoffrey, 270
Dempster, M.A.H., 353
Denney, Reuel, 124
Dennis, Jack, 182, 185, 186, 187
Dentler, Robert, 127
Deutsch, Karl, 15, 155, 267, 322, 324, 325
Dexter, Lewis Anthony, 96
Dillehay, Ronald C., 127
Dogan, Mattei, 94
Dollard, John, 124, 125
Doob, Leonard W., 125, 324
Downs, Anthony, 268
Dunphy, Dexter C., 94
Dyson, James W., 126, 353

Easton, David, 15, 16, 182, 185, 186, 187, 231, 267, 268, 270, 279, 298, 299
Eckstein, Harry, 232
Edinger, Lewis J., 155, 182
Edwards, Allen L., 16
Ehrmann, Henry W., 182, 232
Eldersveld, Samuel J., 15, 94, 125, 128, 208
Ellsworth, John W., 93
Epstein, Leon, 353
Erikson, Erik, 124
Eulau, Heinz, 15, 128, 207, 355, 356
Eyestone, Robert, 356

Feagin, Joe R., 354
Feigert, Frank B., 93, 125, 267
Feldbaum, Eleanor, 185
Fenno, Richard, 94
Ferguson, George A., 96
Ferguson, Leroy C., 207
Ferman, Louis A., 125
Festinger, Leon, 153, 154
Fiore, Quentin, 323
Flavell, J.H., 183
Fleron, Frederick J., Jr., 184, 186
Francis, Wayne, 208
Frasure, William G., 230
Freeman, Linton C., 16
Frenkel-Brunswick, Else, 127, 155
Freud, Sigmund, 124, 127
Frey, Frederick W., 324
Fritschler, A. Lee, 230
Froman, Lewis A., 151, 182, 231, 238, 267, 323

Gallatin, Judith, 183
Garcia, F. Chris, 184, 186
Gaudet, Hazel, 323, 354
Geetz, Clifford, 182
George, Alexander L., 127, 128
George, Juliette L., 127, 128
Getz, Robert S., 93
Gibson, Quentin, 40
Ginzburg, Eugenia, 124
Gitlin, Todd, 269
Glad, Betty, 128

Glazer, Nathan, 124, 230
Goldman, Jerry, 230
Goldrich, Daniel, 263, 269
Golembiewski, Robert T., 232
Goode, William G., 41
Gottfried, Alex, 128
Graham, George J., Jr., 16
Greenberg, Edward S., 184, 186
Greenstein, Fred I., 16, 124, 125, 182,
  183, 185, 187
Grinker, Roy R., 298
Gross, Neal, 206, 207
Gurin, Gerald, 96, 125, 354
Gurr, Ted, 299

Hahn, Harlan, 354
Harary, Frank, 154
Hare, A. Paul, 154
Harsanyi, John, 207
Hatt, Paul K., 41
Hays, William, 16
Head, Kendra, 16, 126
Heard, Alexander, 15
Hedlund, Ronald D., 207
Heider, Fritz, 153, 154
Helmstadter, G.C., 95
Hempel, Carl G., 40, 41
Henkel, Ramon E., 96
Hennessy, Bernard, 152, 155
Hess, Robert, 16, 183, 184, 185, 186
Hill, Winifred F., 183
Hirsch, Herbert, 184, 185, 186
Hobbes, Thomas, 124
Hofferbert, Richard I., 353
Hollander, Neil, 185
Holsti, Ole, 16, 93
Holt, Robert T., 284
Homans, George C., 124, 231
Horney, Karen, 124
Hovland, Carl I., 151, 153, 154, 322,
  323
Hunter, Floyd, 268
Huntington, Samuel P., 15, 155, 299
Hursh, Gerald D., 64, 95
Hyman, Herbert H., 95, 182, 185
Hyneman, Charles S., 15

Inhelder, Barbel, 183
Insko, Chester A., 154
Irish, Marian D., 300

Jacob, Herbert, 186, 353
Jacob, Philip E., 299, 324
Jahoda, M., 127
Janis, I.C., 151, 153, 154, 322, 323
Janowitz, Morris, 15, 128
Jaros, Dean, 16, 183, 184, 186, 187
Jennings, M. Kent, 152, 153, 184,
  185, 187, 269, 323
Johnson, Richard M., 324, 355
Jung, C.G., 124

Kahn, Herman, 355
Kaplan, Abraham, 41
Kaplan, Harold, 298
Kaplan, Morton A., 300
Katz, Daniel, 151
Katz, Elihu, 323
Kaufman, Herbert, 269
Kelley, Harold H., 151, 153, 154, 322,
  323
Kellstedt, Lyman A., 269, 355
Kemeny, John, 17, 25, 40, 41
Kerlinger, Fred N., 40, 41, 96, 208
Key, V.O., Jr., 16, 152, 323, 354
Kiesler, Charles A., 154
Kiesler, Sara B., 154
Kirkpatrick, Samuel A., 153
Kirscht, John P., 127
Klapper, Joseph T., 185, 324
Knutson, Jeanne, 125, 128
Koffka, Kurt, 124
Kohler, Wolfgang, 124
Kolson, Kenneth L., 184
Komarovsky, Mira, 124
Kornberg, Allan, 207
Kramer, Michael S., 230
Kuhn, Alfred, 299
Kuhn, Thomas, 41
Kutner, B., 152

Lamare, James, 184, 186
Lamb, Karl A., 270

363

Lane, Robert F., 96, 125, 127, 154, 229
Langton, Kenneth P., 153, 183, 184, 185, 187, 208
Lasswell, Harold, 17, 41, 124, 125, 126, 231, 267
Laurence, Joan, 186
Lazarsfeld, Paul F., 323, 354
Lazarus, Richard S., 123, 124, 128
Leege, David, 285
Leiserson, Avery, 15
Lerner, Daniel, 155
Levin, Martin, 185, 187
Levine, Robert, 182, 183
Levinson, Daniel J., 127, 155
Levy, Mark R., 230
Liebschutz, Sarah F., 184, 186
Lin, Nan, 319, 325
Lind, Alden E., 187
Lindzey, Gardner, 126, 151, 206, 324
Linton, Ralph, 206
Lipset, Seymour Martin, 125, 231, 353
Lipskey, Michael, 299, 353
Litt, Edgar, 230
Liu, Alan P.L., 324
Lowell, E.L., 126
Lubell, Samuel, 354
Lynd, Helen M., 268
Lynd, Robert S., 268

McClelland, David C., 125, 126
McClosky, Herbert, 95, 184
McClure, Robert D., 323
Maccoby, Eleanor, 153, 184, 207
McConaughy, John B., 128
McCoy, Charles A., 269
McCrone, Donald J., 353
McCullough, Celeste, 16
McEachern, Alexander W., 206, 207
McGuire, William J., 151, 152, 153, 154, 155, 322
Machiavelli, Niccolo, 207
MacKean, Dayton D., 15
McLuhan, Marshall, 323
McPhee, William N., 354
Macridis, Roy, 16, 155

Madron, Thomas W., 94
Maier, Henry W., 183
Marsh, David, 187
Marvick, Dwaine, 186
Maslow, Abraham, 124
Mason, Ward S., 206, 207
Matthews, Donald R., 155, 207, 354
Matthews, Richard E., 153, 185
Mazlish, Bruce, 127
Mazo, Earl, 323
Meehan, Eugene J., 41, 299, 300, 325
Merelman, Richard, 183, 269, 270
Merriam, Charles, 17
Merritt, Richard L., 95, 155
Merton, Robert K., 17, 352
Michels, Robert, 270
Milbrath, Lester, 96, 125, 126, 231, 322, 354, 355
Miller, Arthur, 154
Miller, Delbert, 93
Miller, James G., 298
Miller, Neal E., 124, 125
Miller, Norman, 154
Miller, Warren E., 93, 96, 125, 127, 155, 354
Milnor, A.J., 300
Mitchell, William, 207, 285
Monsma, Stephen V., 300
Morrison, Denton E., 96
Morton, Anton S., 153, 184
Mosca, Gaetano, 17
Mosteller, Frederick, 93
Mowrer, O.H., 125
Moynihan, Daniel Patrick, 230
Murray, Henry, 123

Nagel, Ernest, 17, 40, 41
Nebergall, Roger E., 153
Newcomb, Theodore M., 151, 152, 153, 154
Niemi, Richard G., 184, 185, 186, 187, 323
Nixon, Charles, 186
North, Robert C., 16, 93, 322, 325

Odegard, Peter H., 232
Ogilvie, Daniel M., 94

Ordeshook, Peter C., 267, 268
Osgood, Charles E., 153, 154

Parenti, Michael, 230
Pareto, Vilfredo, 17
Parsons, Talcott, 206, 283, 298
Parten, Mildred, 95
Patterson, Samuel C., 95, 207
Patterson, Thomas F., 323
Peabody, Robert L., 230
Phillips, Kevin P., 230
Piaget, Jean, 183
Playford, John, 269
Polsby, Nelson, 41, 127, 268
Pomper, Gerald, 153, 354
Pool, Ithiel de Sola, 322, 324, 355
Popkin, Samuel L., 355
Post, K.W.J., 94
Powell, G. Bingham, Jr., 208, 299
Prewitt, Kenneth, 183, 184, 186, 355, 356
Prothro, James W., 155, 300, 354
Pye, Lucian, 152, 183, 185, 187

Ranney, Austin, 94
Reisman, David, 124
Renshon, Stanley, 125
Riker, William H., 267, 268
Robinson, James A., 155, 352, 353
Robinson, John P., 16, 126, 185, 332
Robinson, W.S., 94
Rogers, Everett M., 323
Rogow, Arnold A., 128
Rokeach, Milton, 127, 151, 152, 155
Rokkan, Stein, 94, 95, 353
Rose, Douglas D., 94
Rosenau, James N., 270
Rosenberg, Milton J., 153, 154
Rosenberg, Morris, 95
Rossiter, Clinton, 298
Rothman, Stanley, 232
Rudin, Stanley A., 125, 126
Rusk, Jerrold G., 16, 126
Russett, Bruce M., 355

St. Angelo, Douglas, 126, 353
Sanford, R. Nevitt, 127, 155

Sapin, Burton, 267
Sarbin, Theodore, 206
Sayre, Wallace S., 269
Schramm, Wilbur, 322
Schwartz, David C., 155, 187
Searing, Donald, 41, 187
Sears, David O., 154, 229, 355
Sears, Robert R., 125
Sebert, Suzanne Koprince, 187
Sharkansky, Ira, 353
Shepherd, Clovis R., 154
Sheppard, Harold L., 125
Shepsle, Kenneth A., 268
Sherif, Carolyn W., 153
Sherif, Muzafer, 153, 154
Shils, Edward A., 94, 206, 298
Siegel, Sidney, 16, 96
Sigel, Roberta, 185, 186, 187
Simon, Herbert A., 267, 270
Sklar, Richard L., 94
Skolnick, Jerome H., 231
Smelser, Neil J., 283
Smith, M. Brewster, 96, 128, 154
Smith, Marshall S., 94
Smith, Paul A., 127, 270
Snyder, Eloise, 229, 230
Snyder, Richard, 16, 267
Somit, Albert, 16
Sorokins, Pitirim, 124
Sorzano, J.S., 298
Steiner, Gary, 126, 152, 229
Stevens, A. Jay, 184
Stokes, Donald E., 93, 127, 155, 354
Stone, Phillip J., 94
Storing, Herbert J., 297
Stouffer, Samuel A., 323
Stratmann, William C., 268
Strouse, James C., 353
Sullivan, Denis, 153
Sundquist, James L., 354
Swanson, Bert E., 236, 269

Tannenhaus, Joseph, 16
Taube, Mortimer, 325
Tedin, Kent, 183
Tennenbaum, Percy, 153, 154
Terchek, Ronald J., 230, 299

Teune, Henry, 299
Thomas, Edwin J., 206
Tingsten, Herbert, 17
Tipton, Leonard P., 185
Tolley, Howard, 185
Torgeson, William S., 16
Torney, Judith, 16, 183, 184, 185, 186
Toscano, James V., 299, 324
Truman, David B., 15, 16, 42, 152, 230, 231, 297, 352
Tubbesing, Carl D., 355
Tugwell, Rexford, 298
Tullock, Gordon, 267
Turner, John E., 284
Turner, Ralph H., 151, 152

Ulmer, S. Sidney, 15, 153, 184

Van Atta, Loche, 16
Van Dyke, Vernon, 41, 99
Verba, Sidney, 126, 152, 154, 155, 182, 183, 185, 187, 208, 298
Vose, Clement A., 231

Wahlke, John C., 207
Wallace, David L., 93

Wallas, Graham, 17, 125
Walter, Benjamin, 208
Ward, L. Scott, 185
Weber, Max, 17
Weiner, Norbert, 297, 322, 324
Weiss, Walter, 324
Welsh, William A., 232
White, Robert W., 96, 154
Whyte, William Foote, 96
Wildavsky, Aaron, 269, 353
Wilkens, C., 152
Wilson, James Q., 229, 232
Winter-Berger, Robert N., 230
Wolfinger, Raymond E., 230
Wylie, Lawrence, 184

Yarrow, P.R., 152
Ynge, V.H., 325
Young, Oran R., 232, 325
Young, Roland, 16, 267

Zaninovich, M. George, 16, 93
Zavoina, William James, 267, 268
Zeigler, L. Harmon, 152, 153, 208
Zigler, Edward, 126
Zinnes, Dina, 16, 93
Zisk, Betty H., 355, 356

Subject Index

Adams, John, 114
Aggregate data analysis, 56–59
Aristotle, 103, 157
Arrow's Paradox, 247–48
Association. *See* Correlation
Attitude change, 137–47
  functions, 144–45
Attitudes
  definition, 357
  functions, 144–45
  objects of, 132–34
  in party systems, 338–46
  properties, 132–34
  in role theory, 203
Authoritarianism, 102, 115–19, 122,
  147

Beliefs, definition of, 357

Cermak, Anton, 120, 122
Change
  political, 3, 222–26, 290–92
  social, 204–05
Cognitive dissonance, 141–44
  definition, 357
Communications. *See also* Information
  flow
  in attitude change, 137–38
  concepts, 301–05
Community power
  combined approach, 258–61
  decisional/pluralist school, 254–58
  reputational/elite school, 252–54
  and researcher's values, 36–38
  time and ideology, 261–63
Computers. *See* Data management

Concepts
  characteristics, 26–28
  definition, 358
  types, 28–29
Conflict
  community, 221–26
  role, 193–96
  in systems analysis, 276–77
Content analysis, 9, 53–56, 108–12
Coolidge, Calvin, 114
Correlation, 80–84, 85
Cross-pressures
  definition, 358
  in group conflict, 224

Data management, 71–80
Decision, definitions of, 37
Decision making
  functions, 236
  rational basis for, 239–51
Deduction, 24
Dogmatism, 102, 118, 122

Education, as factor in political
  socialization, 168–70
Elites. *See* Community power
Ethics, in research, 52–53
Ethnicity, 215–16, 341
Explanation, 3, 32–33

Falsification, 24
Family, as factor in political
  socialization, 165–68
Feedback
  definition, 358

Feedback (*cont.*)
  in communications theory, 304–05
  in systems analysis, 277, 279–81, 342
Forrestal, James, 120–21, 122
Functions. *See also* Systems analysis
  of attitudes, 144–45
  in decision-making analysis, 236

Group maintenance, 223
Groups. *See also* Conflict; Interest groups; Peer groups
  definition, 211
  in communications theory, 306–08
  influence on beliefs and values, 146–47, 212–16
  in party systems, 338–46
  in systems analysis, 290–92
  types, 211–12

Hollerith, Herman, 72
Hypothesis, 4, 23–26, 29, 47
  definition, 358
  null, 25, 47, 86–88
  testing of, 24–26, 86–89

Induction, 23–24
Information flow, 236–37, 313–14, 315–17
Inputs. *See also* Systems analysis
  functions, 277–78
  in party systems, 342–46
Interaction process analysis, 61
Interest groups, 216–20, 226–28, 290–92, 350–52
Inter-University Consortium for Political Research, 13
Interviewing, in-depth, 68–71. *See also* Survey research

Johnson, Lyndon B., 114, 160, 190, 276–77

Kennedy, John F., 114, 308
King, Martin Luther, Jr., 291–92

Law, 29, 33. *See also* Theory

Literature, review of, 49–52
Lobbying, 218–20
Logical consequences, 24, 30, 31

Macro theory, 100, 328–29
Madison, James, 114
Mass media, 171, 307–12
Measurement, levels of, 84–86
Meta theory, 31
Micro theory, 99–100, 328–29
Motivation, 103–12
  definition, 358
  and personality, 101, 103–12
  types of, 104–11

Nationalism, 313–15
Nixon, Richard M., 43–44, 45, 115, 127, 219–20, 276–77, 320
Nondecisions, 257–58, 264–65, 269–70
Null hypothesis, 25, 47, 86–88

Observation of behavior, 59–63, 244, 245–47
Opinion, definition of, 358
Outputs. *See also* Systems analysis
  functions, 277–79
  in party systems, 342–46

Paradigm, 38–40
  definition of, 359
Party competition, 332–34
Party identification. *See* Political socialization
Pattern variables, 191, 282, 288–89
Peer groups, 146–47, 170
Perceptions
  in attitude change, 145
  in communications, 305–06
  in decision making, 237
  and saliency, 134–36
  in systems analysis, 275–77
Personality
  and attitudes, 147
  approaches to study of, 101–03
  competence and, 112
  consistency, 101

Personality (*cont.*)
   definition of, 359
Plato, 103, 157
Pluralism. *See* Community power
Political efficacy, 89–90, 105, 168,
      341, 347
Political science
   definitions, 8–11
   institutional origins, 12–14
   purpose, 3–4, 19, 20, 32
   utility, 346–52
Political socialization
   agents of, 165–71
   definition of, 359
   discontinuities in, 164–65
   in systems analysis, 288–89
   theories of, 159–64
Political violence, 7, 290–92
Power. *See also* Community power;
      Role
   definition, 359
   and role behavior, 198–99
Prediction, 33
Public opinion, 129–32
Public policy, 5, 331–38, 347–52

Questionnaires. *See* Interviewing;
      Survey research

Rationality, in decision making,
      239–51, 264, 266
Reliability, 89
   definition, 359
Research design, 43–49
Resocialization, 197–98
Role
   conflict, 193–96
   definition of, 359
   expectations, 190–91, 193–96, 205
   learning of, 165–72, 174, 288–89
   orientations, 201–04
   in political systems, 287
   socialization, 196–98
   systems, 191–93
Roosevelt, Franklin D., 114, 343
Roosevelt, Theodore, 114

Science, 19–22
Scientific method, 6, 19, 22–29
Significance
   analytical, 88
   statistical, 81–84, 85, 86–89, 360
Structural–functionalism, in study of
      party systems, 338–46. *See also*
      Systems analysis
Structures, in decision-making
      analysis, 236–39. *See also* Systems
      analysis
Survey research, 63–68
   and decision making, 247–49
   and personality, 111–12
System maintenance, 274, 277–79,
      282, 296–97
Systems analysis
   Almond's approach, 287–90
   applications, 338–46
   Easton's approach, 274–81, 342–46
   Parsonian structural–functionalism,
      281–87, 339
System stability, 279, 290–92,
      296–97

Theory, 29–34. *See also* Macro theory;
      Meta theory; Micro theory
   definition of, 360
   evaluating, 33–34
   types of, 4–6, 29–31
Thucydides, 103

Validity
   definition of, 360
   personality studies and, 123
   types of, 89–92
Values, 131–32
   definition of, 360
   in research, 34–38
   study of, 147–49
Value systems, 147–49
   definition of, 360
Verification, 24

Washington, George, 114
Wilson, Woodrow, 119–20, 122